LEARNING
INDEPENDENTLY

LEARNING INDEPENDENTLY

A Directory of Self-Instruction Resources,
Including Correspondence Courses, Programmed
Learning Products, Audio Cassettes, Multi-Media Kits,
and Conventional Learning Materials Such as
Books Intended for Non-Formal Education

Paul Wasserman
Managing Editor

James Sanders
and
Elizabeth Talbot Sanders
Associate Editors

Gale Research Company ● Book Tower ● Detroit, Michigan 48226 ● 1979

Effie Knight, *Editorial Staff Manager*

Marek Kaszubski, George Pirpiris, *Editorial Assistants*

Library of Congress Cataloging in Publication Data

Main entry under title:

Learning independently.

"A directory of self-instruction resources,
including correspondence courses, programmed learning
products, audio cassettes, multi-media kits, and
conventional learning materials such as books intended
for non-formal education."
    Includes indexes.
    1. Self-culture--Audio-visual aids--Catalogs.
2. Self-culture--Directories.   3. Correspondence
schools and courses--United States--Directories.
4. Programmed instruction--United States--Directories.
5. Non-formal education--United States--Directories.
I. Wasserman, Paul.   II. Sanders, James, 1951-
III. Sanders, Elizabeth Talbot.
LC32.L42   371.39'34   79-21025
ISBN 0-8103-0317-5

TABLE OF CONTENTS

CONTENTS

CONTENTS

CONTENTS

CONTENTS

CONTENTS

CONTENTS

CONTENTS

SECTION II
INDEXES

PREFACE

Adult education and continuous learning have become extremely widespread phenomena in this education-conscious age. But, for many, formal courses offered by educational and training institutions are not convenient because of time and location. One effective alternative is the self-teaching product designed for use by individuals at times and places of their own choosing for enhancing their knowledge and performance skills. LEARNING INDEPENDENTLY identifies such products and opportunities.

LEARNING INDEPENDENTLY contains 3,198 entries and offers a comprehensive directory of self-teaching materials, products, and services which adults may use to improve their understanding and enhance their professional or technical skills through independent study. Learning and training products which require an instructor working with a class or group interaction are excluded from the listings. However, some materials which are not designed specifically for individual use, but which can be effectively used in that manner are included on a selective basis.

This book comprehends every type of material which bears upon professional or work-related interests. Certain personal development-type learning materials have therefore been included in such substantive areas as career planning, time management, personal motivation, and like subjects. Generally excluded are those learning materials treating sports, hobby interests, religious insight, and other non-occupational pursuits.

The content of this work describes learning products available, with prices in effect, in late spring of 1979. Prices are, of course, subject to change.

The materials described in LEARNING INDEPENDENTLY include correspondence courses, programmed learning products, audio cassettes, multi-media kits, and conventional learning materials such as books intended for self-instruction. Selective coverage only is provided for video cassettes, films, games, and simulations since emphasis has been placed upon the more easily accessible and commonly used learning devices which individuals would be more inclined to make use of in their own homes or private offices.

The details for each listing are as complete as it was possible to make them after examination of the materials or working from the information provided by the producers or distributors of the learning aids. The following information is given for each entry: Title of the work; author or preparer; publisher or distributor's name and address; price of the material (when available); and date of publication or original preparation. When only the distributor could be identified, the distributor's address, rather than that of the publisher or original producer, has been provided. Brief annotations have been added when the title itself is not self-explanatory.

The process of compiling the work included the solicitation and review of catalogs and descriptive materials from producers and distributors of learning products and services, as well as examination of the actual products. Mail inquiries were addressed to hundreds of training organizations, trade and professional bodies, and colleges and universities, as well as to publishing companies and producers of learning media. The listings were prepared, typically, by drawing upon the descriptive information provided in the producers' own catalogs. Catalogs and descriptive materials, however, vary widely in the completeness of the information concerning the products available as well as in the terminology used to describe the learning format. The editors have sought to follow a standard terminology in describing the learning formats. While every attempt has been made to utilize appropriate subject headings in order to describe accurately the content of the material, the varying quality and limits of the detailed information provided through the source material, and the sheer quantity of entries, have increased the difficulty of the process. The comprehensive nature and the broad scope of the work has made it necessary to call forth the ideas and efforts of many individuals. Particular thanks are due to Lori Talbot Lazarek for her assistance in the preparation of the manuscript and to Linda Stemmy for its meticulous typing.

Readers are invited to send information, suggestions, and corrections which will be helpful in the preparation of future editions.

HOW TO USE THIS BOOK

LEARNING INDEPENDENTLY is arranged basically by subject with the specific learning materials listed under the appropriate subject according to the following categories of material:

Audio Cassettes/Tapes
Correspondence Courses
Films/Video/Filmstrips
Games/Simulations
Multimedia Kits
Printed Materials
Programmed Learning Materials

In order to facilitate an overall scanning of the content of the work, the entire list of subject headings and cross references used in the basic part of the volume are listed in the extended and detailed table of contents.

Access to the listings is also made possible through three indexes:

1. TITLE AND KEYWORD INDEX. This index provides an approach to the content by titles and keywords in context of each learning product.

2. AUTHOR INDEX. This index identifies the individual who is credited with the intellectual preparation of the work.

3. PRODUCERS AND DISTRIBUTORS INDEX. This index is an alphabetical listing of the producers and distributors of the learning materials with their addresses.

SECTION I

LEARNING INDEPENDENTLY

ACCOUNTABILITY

See also: Assessment; Performance
Appraisal

Audio Cassettes/Tapes

★ 1 ★
MEASURING ACCOUNTABILITY
Educational Century Programming
1201 East Johnson Street
Jonesboro, Arkansas 72401
Cassette. $6.00.

Films/Video/Filmstrips

★ 2 ★
ACCOUNTABILITY
Thompson-Mitchell and Associates
3384 Peachtree Road Northeast
Atlanta, Georgia 30326
Filmstrip 15 minutes. $24.95.

ACCOUNTING

See also: Accounting, Special Applications;
Certified Public Accounting (CPA); Cost
Accounting; Financial Analysis; Taxes

Audio Cassettes/Tapes

★ 3 ★
THE ACCOUNTING CYCLE
National Book Company
1019 Southwest Tenth Avenue
Portland, Oregon 97206
12 Cassettes. $172.20.

★ 4 ★
ACCOUNTING-ELEMENTARY/ACCOUNTING-
INTERMEDIATE
Educational Century Programming
1201 East Johnson Street
Jonesboro, Arkansas 72401
Cassette. $6.00.

★ 5 ★
ADVANCED ACCOUNTING - A SERIES
National Book Company
1019 Southwest Tenth Avenue
Portland, Oregon 97205
Cassette.

★ 6 ★
BASIC ACCOUNTING
Thompson-Mitchell and Associates
3384 Peachtree Road Northeast
Atlanta, Georgia 30326
Cassette. $9.98.

★ 7 ★
INTRODUCTORY ACCOUNTING
Charles F. Grant
Charles E. Merrill Publishing Company
1300 Alum Creek Drive
Box 508
Columbus, Ohio 43216
Text and cassettes. 1977. $10.95.

★ 8 ★
SPECIAL ACCOUNTING PROCEDURES
National Book Company
1019 Southwest Tenth Avenue
Portland, Oregon 97206
12 cassettes. $174.75.

Correspondence Courses

★ 9 ★
ACCOUNTING
International Correspondence School
Scranton, Pennsylvania 18515
Multi-module correspondence course.

★ 10 ★
ACCOUNTING
North American Correspondence School
4401 Birch Street
Newport Beach, California 92663
Correspondence course.

★ 11 ★
ACCOUNTING PRINCIPLES
University of North Carolina
Independent Study by Extension
121 Abernethy Hall 002A
Chapel Hill, North Carolina 27514
Correspondence course. $14.95.

★ 12 ★
ADVANCED ACCOUNTING
Dun and Bradstreet Incorporated
Business Education Division
Box 803
Church Street Station
New York, New York 10008

Instruction through self-study text and correspondence with instructor. $175.00.

★ 13 ★
ADVANCED ACCOUNTING
La Salle Extension University
417 South Dearborn Street
Chicago, Illinois 60605
Correspondence course.

★ 14 ★
FUNDAMENTALS OF ACCOUNTING
University of South Carolina
Department of Correspondence Study
Division of Continuing Education
Columbia, South Carolina 29208
Correspondence course. $69.00.

★ 15 ★
GENERAL ACCOUNTING
La Salle Extension University
417 South Dearborn Street
Chicago, Illinois 60605
Correspondence course.

★ 16 ★
INTRODUCTORY ACCOUNTING
Dun and Bradstreet Incorporated
Business Education Division
Box 803
Church Street Station
New York, New York 10008
Instruction through self-study text and correspondence with instructor. $175.00.

★ 17 ★
INTRODUCTORY ACCOUNTING
University of Nebraska
511 Nebraska Hall
Lincoln, Nebraska 68588
Correspondence course.

★ 18 ★
PRACTICAL ACCOUNTING
International Correspondence School
Scranton, Pennsylvania 18515
Multi-module correspondence course.

★ 19 ★
PRINCIPLES OF ACCOUNTING
University of Arkansas
Department of Independent Study
346 West Avenue
Fayetteville, Arkansas 72701
Correspondence course.

★ 20 ★
PRINCIPLES OF ACCOUNTING
University of Kentucky
Independent Study Program
Freeze Hall, Room 1
Lexington, Kentucky 40506
Correspondence course.

★ 21 ★
PRINCIPLES OF ACCOUNTING
Western Washington State College
Center for Continuing Education
Edens Hall South
Bellingham, Washington 98225
Correspondence course.

Films/Video/Filmstrips

★ 22 ★
ESSENTIALS OF ACCOUNTING
J. Dearden
Addison Wesley Publishing Company Incorporated
Jacob Way
Reading, Massachusetts 01867
Filmstrip and text.

Multimedia Kits

★ 23 ★
ACCOUNTING PRINCIPLES
Curry and Frame
Charles E. Merrill Publishing Company
1300 Alum Creek Drive
Box 508
Columbus, Ohio 43216
A multimedia unit of 30 modules: worktext, filmstrips, cassettes. $300.00.

Printed Materials

★ 24 ★
ACCOUNTANCY FOR MANAGERS
J. Batty
International Publications Service
114 East 32nd Street
New York, New York 10016.
Book. 1971. $15.00.

★ 25 ★
ACCOUNTING: A SELF INSTRUCTION GUIDE TO
PROCEDURES AND THEORY
Morton Bluestone
        MacMillan Publishing Company Incorporated
        Riverside, New Jersey 08075
Book. 1973. $2.95.

★ 26 ★
ACCOUNTING FOR BUSINESS
John Cerepak
        Charles E. Merrill Publishing Company
        1300 Alum Creek Drive
        Box 508
        Columbus, Ohio 43216
Text with exercises and examinations.

★ 27 ★
ACCOUNTING FOR BUSINESS COMBINATIONS
John Burton
        Financial Executives
        Research Foundation
        633 Third Avenue
        New York, New York 10017
Book. 1970. $5.00.

★ 28 ★
ACCOUNTING IN BUSINESS DECISIONS:
THEORY, METHOD AND USE
Homer Black
        Prentice-Hall Incorporated
        Englewood Cliffs, New Jersey 07632
Book. 1973. $13.95.

★ 29 ★
ADVANCED ACCOUNTING: AN ORGANIZATIONAL
APPROACH
        John Wiley and Sons Incorporated
        605 Third Avenue
        New York, New York 10016
Book. 1973. $15.95.

★ 30 ★
COMPUTERIZED ACCOUNTING
Henry J. Beck, Roy J. Parrish, Jr.
        Charles E. Merrill Publishing Company
        1300 Alum Creek Drive
        Box 508
        Columbus, Ohio 43216
Text with exercises. $5.95.

★ 31 ★
ELEMENTARY ACCOUNTING
Royal Bauer, Paul Darby
        Barnes and Noble Incorporated
        Keystone Industrial Park
        Scranton, Pennsylvania 18512
Book. 1971. $2.95.

★ 32 ★
ESSENTIALS OF ACCOUNTING
        Addison Wesley Publishing Company Incorporated
        Jacob Way
        Reading, Massachusetts 01867
Book and tests. 1976. $9.95.

★ 33 ★
FINANCIAL ACCOUNTING CONCEPTS
James Rossell, William Frasure
        Charles E. Merrill Publishing Company
        1300 Alum Creek Drive
        Box 508
        Columbus, Ohio 43216
Text. 1974. $15.95.

★ 34 ★
FUNDAMENTAL ACCOUNTING PRINCIPLES
William Pyle, John White
        Richard D. Irwin Incorporated
        1818 Ridge Road
        Homewood, Illinois 60430
Workbook and study guides. $12.50.

★ 35 ★
INTRODUCTION TO ACCOUNTING: ECONOMIC
MEASUREMENT FOR DECISIONS
        Addison Wesley Publishing Company Incorporated
        Jacob Way
        Reading, Massachusetts 01867
Book. 1971. $14.50.

★ 36 ★
UNACCOUNTABLE ACCOUNTING
Abraham Briloff
        Harper and Row Publishers Incorporated
        Scranton, Pennsylvania 18512
Book. 1972. $11.95.

★ 37 ★
USING ACCOUNTING INFORMATION
Paul Fentig
        Harcourt Brace Jovanovich Incorporated
        757 Third Avenue
        New York, New York 10017
Manuals and game available.

Programmed Learning Materials

★ 38 ★
ACCOUNTING: A PROGRAMMED TEXT
J. D. Edwards, R. H. Hermanson, R. F. Salmonson
    Richard D. Irwin Incorporated
    1818 Ridge Road
    Homewood, Illinois 60430
2 volume programmed text. $10.75 each.

★ 39 ★
THE ACCOUNTING PROCESS: A PROGRAM OF
SELF INSTRUCTION
Wentworth, Montgomery, Gowen, Harrell
    McGraw-Hill Book Company
    1221 Avenue of the Americas
    New York, New York 10019
Programmed text. $7.50.

★ 40 ★
ACCOUNTING SERIES
    American Book Company
    300 Pike Street
    Cincinnati, Ohio 45215
9 units. $1.25 each.

★ 41 ★
THE BASIC ACCOUNTING CYCLE
James Don Edwards
    Learning Systems Company
    1818 Ridge Road
    Homewood, Illinois 60430
Programmed learning aid. $5.95.

★ 42 ★
ELEMENTARY ACCOUNTING
William W. Pyle
    Learning Systems Corporation
    60 Connolly Parkway
    Hamden, Connecticut 06514
2 volumes programmed text. $2.95 each.

★ 43 ★
ESSENTIALS OF ACCOUNTING
Robert Anthony
    Addison Wesley Publishing Company Incorporated
    Jacob Way
    Reading, Massachusetts 01867
Programmed course. $5.75.

★ 44 ★
FINANCIAL ACCOUNTING
    Richard D. Irwin Incorporated
    1818 Ridge Road
    Homewood, Illinois 60430
Programmed text.

★ 45 ★
INTERMEDIATE ACCOUNTING
Glenn A. Welsch
    Learning Systems Corporation
    60 Connolly Parkway
    Hamden, Connecticut 06514
2 volumes programmed text. $2.95 each.

★ 46 ★
MCGRAW HILL 36 HOUR ACCOUNTING COURSE
    McGraw Hill Book Company
    582 Princeton Road
    Hightstown, New Jersey 08520
Programmed course. $21.95.

★ 47 ★
A ONE YEAR ACCOUNTING COURSE
Trevor Gambling
    Pergamon Press Incorporated
    Maxwell House
    Fairview Park
    Elmsford, New York 10523
Programmed text.   1969.

★ 48 ★
PRINCIPLES OF ACCOUNTING
    Educational Methods Incorporated
    500 North Dearborn Street
    Chicago, Illinois 60610
Programmed text. $4.95.

ACCOUNTING, MANAGERIAL
See: MANAGERIAL ACCOUNTING

ACCOUNTING, SPECIAL APPLICATIONS

See also: Accounting; Budgeting;
Financial Analysis; Taxes

Audio Cassettes/Tapes

★ 49 ★
ACCOUNTING - ADVANCED/THE PAYROLL
Educational Century Programming
1201 East Johnson Street
Jonesboro, Arkansas 72401
Cassette. $6.00.

★ 50 ★
INFLATION
BFA Educational Media
2211 Michigan Avenue
Santa Monica, California 90406
Cassette.

★ 51 ★
SPECIAL ACCOUNTING PROCEDURES
National Book Company
1019 Southwest Tenth Street
Portland, Oregon 97205
Cassettes.

★ 52 ★
SPECIAL JOURNALS, ADJUSTING AND CLOSING
National Book Company
1019 Southwest Tenth Avenue
Portland, Oregon 97205
15 cassettes. $213.75.

Correspondence Courses

★ 53 ★
ACCOUNTING FOR BUSINESS COMBINATIONS
University of Tennessee
Center for Extended Learning
447 Communications and Extension Building
Knoxville, Tennessee 37916
Correspondence course.

★ 54 ★
FUND AND GOVERNMENT ACCOUNTING
Western Washington State College
Center for Continuing Education
Edens Hall South
Bellingham, Washington 98225
Correspondence course.

Printed Materials

★ 55 ★
ACCOUNTING AND THE COMPUTER

Kenneth Goosen
General Learning Press
250 James Street
Morristown, New Jersey 07960
Book. 1974. $5.50.

★ 56 ★
ACCOUNTING WITH THE COMPUTER
Joseph W. Wilkinson
Richard D. Irwin Incorporated
1818 Ridge Road
Homewood, Illinois 60430
Book. 1975. $5.95.

★ 57 ★
BASIC PRINCIPLES: ACCOUNTING
Horace Brock
McGraw-Hill Book Company
1221 Avenue of the Americas
New York, New York 10036
Book. 1974. $10.65.

★ 58 ★
COLLEGE ACCOUNTING FOR SECRETARIES
Horace Brock, et al.
McGraw-Hill Book Company
1221 Avenue of the Americas
New York, New York 10019
Book. $14.25.

★ 59 ★
INFLATION ACCOUNTING: A GUIDE FOR NON
ACCOUNTANTS
P. R. Kirkman
Halsted Press
Division of John Wiley and Sons Incorporated
605 Third Avenue
New York, New York 10016
Book. 1975. $17.50.

★ 60 ★
PRACTICAL ACCOUNTING AND COST KEEPING
FOR CONTRACTORS
Frank Waiker
Funk and Wagnalls Company
666 Fifth Avenue
New York, New York 10019
Book. 1975. $12.95.

ACOUSTICS

Printed Materials

★ 61 ★
ACOUSTICS DESIGN AND NOISE CONTROL
Michael Rettinger
     International Publications Service
     114 East 32nd Street
     New York, New York 10016
Book. 1972. $22.50.

★ 62 ★
NOISE REDUCTION
Leo Beranek
     McGraw-Hill Book Company
     1221 Avenue of the Americas
     New York, New York 10019
Book. 1960. $26.00.

★ 63 ★
PHYSICAL ACOUSTICS
Bruce Lindsay
     International Publications Service
     114 East 32nd Street
     New York, New York 10016
Book. 1974. $24.00.

ADVERTISING

See also: Marketing

Audio Cassettes/Tapes

★ 64 ★
NEW TRENDS IN DIRECT RESPONSE PRINT
ADVERTISING
     Tape Rental Library Incorporated
     Post Office Box 2107
     2507 Edna Drive
     South Vineland, New Jersey 08360
Cassette. $12.00.

Correspondence Courses

★ 65 ★
ADVERTISING
     University of Washington
     Office of Independent Study
     222 Lewis Hall DW-30
     Seattle, Washington 98195
Correspondence course.

★ 66 ★
ELEMENTS OF ADVERTISING
     University of Florida
     Division of Continuing Education
     2012 West University Avenue
     Gainesville, Florida 32603
Correspondence course.

★ 67 ★
ELEMENTS OF ADVERTISING
     University of Kansas
     Division of Continuing Education
     Lawrence, Kansas 66045
Home study program.

Films/Video/Filmstrips

★ 68 ★
ADVERTISING GRAPHICS
     Scope Productions Incorporated
     Post Office Box 5515
     Fresno, California 93755
4 films (8 mm) and student guides. $84.00.

Multimedia Kits

★ 69 ★
PRINCIPLES OF ADVERTISING
     Lansford Publishing Company
     Post Office Box 8711
     San Jose, California 95155
Multimedia kit. $190.00.

★ 70 ★
PSYCHOLOGY OF ADVERTISING
     Lansford Publishing Company
     Post Office Box 8711
     San Jose, California 95155
Multimedia kit. $150.00.

Printed Materials

★ 71 ★
ADVERTISING
David S. Nicholl
     International Publications Service
     114 East 32nd Street
     New York, New York 10016
Book. 1974. $9.00.

★ 72 ★
ADVERTISING
E. McGregor
> David McKay Company Incorporated
> 750 Third Avenue
> New York, New York 10017

Book. 1973. $2.95.

★ 73 ★
ADVERTISING
Dorothy Cohen
> John Wiley and Sons Incorporated
> 605 Third Avenue
> New York, New York 10016

Book. 1972. $13.75.

★ 74 ★
ADVERTISING FOR MODERN RETAILERS
Shirley Milton
> Fairchild Publications Incorporated
> Seven East 12th Street
> New York, New York 10003

Book. 1974. $10.00.

★ 75 ★
ADVERTISING: PLANNING, IMPLEMENTATION
AND CONTROL
> South-Western Publishing Company
> 5101 Madison Road
> Cincinnati, Ohio 45227

Book. 1975. $12.95.

★ 76 ★
ADVERTISING PRACTICE: ANALYTIC AND
CREATIVE EXERCISES
Barbare Coe
> Prentice-Hall Incorporated
> Englewood Cliffs, New Jersey 07632

Book. $6.95.

★ 77 ★
HOW INDUSTRIAL ADVERTISING AND PROMOTION
CAN INCREASE MARKETING POWER
W. H. Gross
> American Media Incorporated
> 5907 Meredith Drive
> Des Moines, Iowa 50324

Book. 1973. $12.95.

★ 78 ★
HOW TO BECOME AN ADVERTISING MAN
James Young
> Crain Books
> 740 Rush Street
> Chicago, Illinois 60611

Book. $3.95.

★ 79 ★
HOW TO MAKE ADVERTISING WORK
Burton Durkee
> McGraw-Hill Book Company
> 1221 Avenue of the Americas
> New York, New York 10019

Book. $6.95.

★ 80 ★
MORE PROFITS THROUGH ADVERTISING
R. Cook
> Drake Publishers
> 801 Second Avenue
> New York, New York 10017

Book. 1974. $3.95.

★ 81 ★
RETAIL ADVERTISING
William Haight
> International Publications Service
> 114 East 32nd Street
> New York, New York 10016

Book. 1976. $11.95.

★ 82 ★
RETAIL ADVERTISING: A MANAGEMENT
APPROACH
> Chain Store Publishing Company
> 425 Park Avenue
> New York, New York 10022

Book. 1976. $14.95.

Programmed Learning Materials

★ 83 ★
THE FUNDAMENTALS OF ADVERTISING
> Penton/IPC Education Division
> 614 Superior Avenue, West
> Cleveland, Ohio 44113

Programmed text. $15.00.

AERONAUTICS
See: AVIATION

AFFIRMATIVE ACTION
See: EQUAL EMPLOYMENT OPPORTUNITY

AGRICULTURE

See also: Horticulture

Correspondence Courses

★ 84 ★
AGRICULTURAL ECONOMICS
  Texas Tech University
  Division of Continuing Education
  Post Office Box 4110
  Lubbock, Texas 79409
Correspondence course.

★ 85 ★
AGRICULTURAL FINANCE
  Texas Tech University
  Division of Continuing Education
  Post Office Box 4110
  Lubbock, Texas 79409
Correspondence course.

★ 86 ★
AGRICULTURAL PLANT SCIENCE
  University of Kentucky
  Independent Study Program
  Freeze Hall, Room 1
  Lexington, Kentucky 40506
Correspondence course.

★ 87 ★
AGRICULTURAL SOCIAL SCIENCE
  University of Kentucky
  Independent Study Program
  Freeze Hall, Room 1
  Lexington, Kentucky 40506
Correspondence course.

★ 88 ★
AGRICULTURE ECONOMICS
  University of Arkansas
  Department of Independent Study
  346 West Avenue
  Fayetteville, Arkansas 72701

Correspondence course.

★ 89 ★
PRINCIPLES OF MARKETING AGRICULTURAL
PRODUCTS
  Texas Tech University
  Division of Continuing Education
  Post Office Box 4110
  Lubbock, Texas 79409
Correspondence course.

Printed Materials

★ 90 ★
BASIC FARM MACHINERY
J. M. Shippen,   J. C. Turner
  Pergamon Press Incorporated
  Maxwell House
  Fairview Park
  Elmsford, New York 10523
Book. 1974. $8.50.

★ 91 ★
FARM PLANNING AND CONTROL
C. S. Barnard,   J. S. Nix
  Cambridge University Press
  510 North Avenue
  New Rochelle, New York 10801
Book. $27.50.

★ 92 ★
FARMING
James Merridew – Teach Yourself Series
  David McKay Company Incorporated
  750 Third Avenue
  New York, New York 10017
Book. 1975. $3.95.

★ 93 ★
FINANCIAL MANAGEMENT IN AGRICULTURE
John Hopkin
  Interstate Incorporated
  1927 North Jackson Street
  Danville, Illinois 61832
Book. 1973. $11.95.

★ 94 ★
FUNDAMENTALS OF MODERN AGRICULTURE
C. D. Blake
  International Scholarly Book Services Incorporated
  2130 Pacific Avenue
  Forest Grove, Oregon 97116
Book. 1974. $15.00.

★ 95 ★
HERE'S HOW: ON-JOB-TRAINING –
AGRICULTURAL MECHANICS
Paul Curtis
    Interstate Incorporated
    1927 North Jackson Street
    Danville, Illinois 61832
Book. 1972. $3.50.

★ 96 ★
HOW TO GROW FOOD ORGANICALLY
Gary Null
    Belmont-Tower Books Incorporated
    185 Madison Avenue
    New York, New York 10016
Book. $.95.

★ 97 ★
A PRACTICAL COURSE IN AGRICULTURAL
CHEMISTRY
    Pergamon Press Incorporated
    Maxwell House
    Fairview Park
    Elmsford, New York 10523
Book. $3.50.

★ 98 ★
SELF TEACHER IN FARM MECHANICS
L. I. Brakensiek, Lloyd Phipps
    Interstate Incorporated
    1927 North Jackson Street
    Danville, Illinois 61832
Book. $5.50.

★ 99 ★
SOIL CHEMISTRY
G. H. Bolt, M. G. Bruggenwert
    Elsevier Scientific Publishing Company
        Incorporated
    52 Vanderbilt Avenue
    New York, New York 10017
Book. 1976. $16.50.

AIR CONDITIONING AND REFRIGERATION

See also: Heating

Correspondence Courses

★ 100 ★
ADVANCED AIR CONDITIONING COURSE
    Technical Information Center
    64 Society Street
    Charleston, South Carolina 29401

Multimedia correspondence course. $65.00.

★ 101 ★
AIR CONDITIONING AND REFRIGERATION
    La Salle Extension University
    417 South Dearborn Street
    Chicago, Illinois 60605
Correspondence course.

★ 102 ★
AIR CONDITIONING AND REFRIGERATION
    NRI Schools
    3939 Wisconsin Avenue
    Washington, D.C. 20016
30 lesson home study program. $595.00.

★ 103 ★
AIR CONDITIONING, HEATING AND
REFRIGERATION
    International Correspondence School
    Scranton, Pennsylvania 18515
Multi-module correspondence course.

★ 104 ★
AIR CONDITIONING MAINTENANCE
    International Correspondence School
    Scranton, Pennsylvania 18515
Multi-module correspondence course.

★ 105 ★
AIR CONDITIONING, REFRIGERATION AND
HEATING
    Commercial Trades Institute
    6201 West Howard Street
    Chicago, Illinois 60648
Correspondence course. $895.00.

★ 106 ★
GENERAL AIR CONDITIONING COURSE
    Technical Information Center
    64 Society Street
    Charleston, South Carolina 29401
Multimedia correspondence course. $69.00.

★ 107 ★
INDUSTRIAL AIR CONDITIONING
    International Correspondence School
    Scranton, Pennsylvania 18515
Multi-module correspondence course.

★ 108 ★
MASTER COURSE IN AIR CONDITIONING,
REFRIGERATION AND HEATING
     NRI Schools
     3939 Wisconsin Avenue
     Washington, D.C. 20016
51 lesson home study program. $795.00.

Multimedia Kits

★ 109 ★
ELECTRIC SPACE CONDITIONING
     The Electrification Council
     90 Park Avenue
     New York, New York 10016
Slides and text. $200.00.

Printed Materials

★ 110 ★
AIR CONDITIONING ENGINEERING
W. P. Jones
     Crane, Russak and Company Incorporated
     347 Madison Avenue
     New York, New York 10017
Book. 1974. $22.75.

★ 111 ★
AIR CONDITIONING FOR BUILDING ENGINEERS
AND MANAGERS
Seymour Price
     International Publications Service
     114 East 32nd Street
     New York, New York 10016
Book. 1970. $17.50.

★ 112 ★
AIR CONDITIONING – REPAIR AND MAINTENANCE
Herbert Leavy
     Drake Publishers
     801 Second Avenue
     New York, New York 10017
Book. 1976.

★ 113 ★
CONTROL SYSTEMS FOR HEATING, VENTILATING,
AND AIR CONDITIONING
Roger Haines
     Van Nos Reinhold Company
     300 Pike Street
     Cincinnati, Ohio 45202
Book. $14.50.

★ 114 ★
MODERN REFRIGERATION AND AIR CONDITIONING
Andrew Althouse
     International Publications Service
     114 East 32nd Street
     New York, New York 10016
Book. 1975. $22.00.

★ 115 ★
PRINCIPLES OF AIR CONDITIONING
     Delmar Publications
     50 Wolf Road
     Albany, New York 12205
Book. 1972. $9.80.

Programmed Learning Materials

★ 116 ★
AIR CONDITIONING AND REFRIGERATION
COMPRESSORS
TPC Training Systems
     Technical Publishing Company
     1301 South Grove Avenue
     Barrington, Illinois 60010
Programmed text of 5 lessons. $16.75.

★ 117 ★
AIR CONDITIONING AND REFRIGERATION
EVAPORATORS
TPC Training Systems
     Technical Publishing Company
     1301 South Grove Avenue
     Barrington, Illinois 60010
Programmed text of 5 lessons. $16.75.

★ 118 ★
AIR CONDITIONING AND REFRIGERATION
PIPING
TPC Training Systems
     Technical Publishing Company
     1301 South Grove Avenue
     Barrington, Illinois 60010
Programmed text of 5 lessons. $16.75.

★ 119 ★
AIR HANDLING SYSTEMS FOR AIR CONDITIONING
TPC Training Systems
     Technical Publishing Company
     1301 South Grove Avenue
     Barrington, Illinois 60010
Programmed text of 5 lessons. $16.75.

★ 120 ★
CONDENSERS AND COOLING TOWERS
TPC Training Systems
        Technical Publishing Company
        1301 South Grove Avenue
        Barrington, Illinois 60010
Programmed text of 5 lessons. $16.75.

★ 121 ★
CONTROL SYSTEMS FOR AIR CONDITIONING AND
REFRIGERATION
TPC Training Systems
        Technical Publishing Company
        1301 South Grove Avenue
        Barrington, Illinois 60010
Programmed text of 5 lessons. $16.75.

★ 122 ★
INTRODUCTION TO AIR CONDITIONING AND
REFRIGERATION
TPC Training Systems
        Technical Publishing Company
        1301 South Grove Avenue
        Barrington, Illinois 60010
Programmed text of 5 lessons. $16.75.

★ 123 ★
REFRIGERANTS AND REFRIGERANT OILS
TPC Training Systems
        Technical Publishing Company
        1301 South Grove Avenue
        Barrington, Illinois 60010
Programmed text of 5 lessons. $16.75.

★ 124 ★
TROUBLESHOOTING AIR CONDITIONING SYSTEMS
TPC Training Systems
        Technical Publishing Company
        1301 South Grove Avenue
        Barrington, Illinois 60010
Programmed text of 5 lessons. $16.75.

★ 125 ★
TROUBLESHOOTING REFRIGERATION SYSTEMS
TPC Training Systems
        Technical Publishing Company
        1301 South Grove Avenue
        Barrington, Illinois 60010
Programmed text of 5 lessons. $16.75.

AIRCRAFT MAINTENANCE

See also: Aviation

Correspondence Courses

★ 126 ★
JET ENGINE COURSE
        American Jet School
        Darby, Montana 59829
Correspondence course. $450.00.

★ 127 ★
JET ENGINE/GAS TURBINE COURSE
        American Jet School
        Darby, Montana 59829
Correspondence course. $595.00.

★ 128 ★
GAS TURBINE COURSE
        American Jet School
        Darby, Montana 59829
Correspondence course. $195.00.

★ 129 ★
MISSILE AND ROCKET COURSE
        American Jet School
        Darby, Montana 59829
Correspondence course. $180.00.

AIRPORT MANAGEMENT

Printed Materials

★ 130 ★
AIRPORT MANAGEMENT AND OPERATIONS
George Campbell
        Claitors Publishing Division
        3165 South Acadian at Interstate 10
        Box 239
        Baton Rouge, Louisiana 70821
Book.   1972. $15.00.

ALGEBRA

See also: Mathematics

Audio Cassettes/Tapes

★ 131 ★
COLLEGE ALGEBRA
        Thompson-Mitchell and Associates
        3384 Peachtree Road Northeast
        Atlanta, Georgia 30326
Cassette. $9.98.

★ 132 ★
INTERMEDIATE ALGEBRA
        Thompson-Mitchell and Associates
        3384 Peachtree Road Northeast
        Atlanta, Georgia 30326
Cassette. $9.98.

Printed Materials

★ 133 ★
ALGEBRA
P. Abbot - Teach Yourself Series
        David McKay Company Incorporated
        750 Third Avenue
        New York, New York 10017
Book. 1974. $2.95.

★ 134 ★
CONTEMPORARY ALGEBRA
Butschun and Mueller
        International Publications Service
        114 East 32nd Street
        New York, New York 10016
Book. 1975. $11.95.

★ 135 ★
DISCOVERY METHOD ALGEBRA
E. Halsey, S. Partee
        International Publications Service
        114 East 32nd Street
        New York, New York 10016
Book. 1976. $8.95.

★ 136 ★
FIRST COURSE IN LINEAR ALGEBRA
Daniel Zelinsky
        Academic Press Incorporated
        111 Fifth Avenue
        New York, New York 10003
Book. 1973. $11.50.

★ 137 ★
MODERN ALGEBRA: AN INTRODUCTION
Tim Anderson
        Charles E. Merrill Company
        1300 Alum Creek Drive
        Columbus, Ohio 43216
Book. $11.95.

★ 138 ★
SELF TEACHING INTERMEDIATE ALGEBRA
Vernon Howes, Roy Dubisch
        John Wiley and Sons Incorporated
        605 Third Avenue
        New York, New York 10016
Book. 1970. $7.95.

Programmed Learning Materials

★ 139 ★
BASIC ALGEBRA
        General Learning Corporation
        250 James Street
        Morristown, New Jersey 07960
Programmed text. $12.00.

★ 140 ★
BASIC ALGEBRA
E. Wain Martin, Jr.
        Learning Systems Company
        1818 Ridge Road
        Homewood, Illinois 60430
Programmed learning aid. $4.50.

★ 141 ★
FUNDAMENTALS OF ALGEBRA
Wiles Keller
        International Publications Service
        114 East 32nd Street
        New York, New York 10016
Programmed. 1975. $7.95.

★ 142 ★
FUNDAMENTALS OF ALGEBRA
        McGraw-Hill Book Company
        1221 Avenue of the Americas
        New York, New York 10019
Programmed text. $3.95.

★ 143 ★
FUNDAMENTALS OF ELEMENTARY ALGEBRA
D. Eraut
    McGraw-Hill Book Company
    1221 Avenue of the Americas
    New York, New York 10019
Programmed text. 1970. $5.25.

★ 144 ★
SIMPLE ALGEBRA
    E. I. du Pont de Nemours and Company
    Applied Technology Division
    Room B 4204
    Wilmington, Delaware 19898
Programmed course of approximately 10 hours. $18.85.

ALGOL
See: COMPUTER LANGUAGES

AMHARIC

Multimedia Kits

★ 145 ★
AMHARIC - BASIC COURSE
    General Services Administration
    Foreign Service Institute Language Course
    National Audiovisual Center
    Order Section RR
    Washington, D.C. 20409
Audio tapes, cassettes and text available. Approximately $200.00.

ANATOMY
See: headings under HEALTH

ANIMAL HUSBANDRY

Correspondence Courses

★ 146 ★
AGRICULTURAL ANIMAL SCIENCE
    University of Kentucky
    Independent Study Program
    Freeze Hall, Room 1
    Lexington, Kentucky 40506
Correspondence course.

★ 147 ★
ANIMAL CARE
    North American Correspondence School
    4401 Birch Street
    Newport Beach, California 92663
Correspondence course.

★ 148 ★
ANIMAL SCIENCE
    Texas Tech University
    Division of Continuing Education
    Post Office Box 4110
    Lubbock, Texas 79409
Correspondence course.

Printed Materials

★ 149 ★
EARNING YOUR LIVING WITH ANIMALS
Jeremy Mallinson
    International Publications Service
    114 East 32nd Street
    New York, New York 10016
Book. 1975. $8.95.

★ 150 ★
INTRODUCTION TO FEEDING FARM LIVESTOCK
R. H. Nelson
    Pergamon Press Incorporated
    Maxwell House
    Fairview Park
    Elmsford, New York 10523
Book. $3.50.

APPLIANCE REPAIR
See also: Small Engine Repair

Correspondence Courses

★ 151 ★
APPLIANCE AND MOTOR SERVICING
    International Correspondence School
    Scranton, Pennsylvania 18515
Multi-module correspondence course.

★ 152 ★
APPLIANCE SERVICING COURSE
    NRI Schools
    3939 Wisconsin Avenue
    Washington, D.C. 20016
42 lesson home study program.

★ 153 ★
ELECTRICAL APPLIANCE SERVICING
        International Correspondence School
        Scranton, Pennsylvania 18515
Multi-module correspondence course.

Films/Video/Filmstrips

★ 154 ★
BASIC APPLIANCE REPAIR
Cliff Porter
        Hayden Book Company Incorporated
        50 Essex Street
        Rochelle Park, New Jersey   07662
Text and transparencies.   1971.

Printed Materials

★ 155 ★
HOW TO REPAIR ELECTRICAL APPLIANCES
Gershon Wheeler
        Reston Publishing Company
        Distributed by Prentice Hall
        Englewood Cliffs, New Jersey   07632
Book.   1972. $10.00.

ARABIC

Audio Cassettes/Tapes

★ 156 ★
BERLITZ COURSE IN ARABIC
        Berlitz Language Program
        Post Office Box 5109
        FDR Station
        New York, New York   10022
Cassette. $5.95.

★ 157 ★
LEARN ARABIC
        Arabic Teaching Center
        210 East 47th Street
        New York, New York   10017
Textbook and cassettes. $30.00.

Correspondence Courses

★ 158 ★
ARABIC
        University of Wisconsin-Extension
        Independent Study
        432 North Lake Street
        Madison, Wisconsin   53706
Various level courses available.

Multimedia Kits

★ 159 ★
ARABIC-LEVANTINE, INTRODUCTION TO
PRONUNCIATION
        General Services Administration
        Foreign Service Institute Language Course
        National Audiovisual Center
        Order Section RR
        Washington, D.C.   20409
Audio tapes, cassettes and text available.   Approximately $60.00.

★ 160 ★
ARABIC - MODERN WRITTEN
        General Services Administration
        Foreign Service Institute Language Course
        National Audiovisual Center
        Order Section RR
        Washington, D.C.   20409
Audio tapes, cassettes and texts available.   Approximately $150.00.

★ 161 ★
SAUDI ARABIC BASIC COURSE - URBAN HIJAZI
DIALECT
        General Services Administration
        Foreign Service Institute Language Course
        National Audiovisual Center
        Order Section RR
        Washington, D.C.   20409
Audio tapes, cassettes and text available.   Approximately $80.00.

Printed Materials

★ 162 ★
ARABIC IN A NUTSHELL
Dilaver Berberi
        International Publications Service
        114 East 32nd Street
        New York, New York   10016
Book.   1974. $2.95.

★ 163 ★
ARABIC LANGUAGE FOR SELF-STUDY
Peter Ashy
        Furman University Press
        Post Office Box 28638
        Greenville, South Carolina   29613
Book.   1973. $12.00.

★ 164 ★
A BASIC COURSE IN GULF ARABIC
Hamdi Qafisheh
    University of Arizona Press
    Post Office Box 3398
    Tucson, Arizona 85722
Book. $7.95.

★ 165 ★
COLLOQUIAL ARABIC: AN ORAL APPROACH
Raja Nasr
    Lawrence Verry Incorporated
    16 Holmes Street
    Mystic, Connecticut 06355
Book. 1972. $5.00.

★ 166 ★
EGYPTIAN-ARABIC MANUAL FOR SELF-STUDY
E. E. Elias, E. A. Elias
    International Publications Service
    114 East 32nd Street
    New York, New York 10016
Book. $4.50.

★ 167 ★
TEACH YOURSELF ARABIC
Arthur Tritton
    David McKay Company Incorporated
    750 Third Avenue
    New York, New York 10017
Book. $3.95.

ARBITRATION

See also: Collective Bargaining;
Conflict Resolution; Labor
Relations

Games/Simulations

★ 168 ★
SETTLE OR STRIKE (A contract negotiation involving real life tradeoffs on crucial union issues)
    ABT Publications
    55 Wheeler Street
    Cambridge, Massachusetts 02138
Game. $45.00.

Printed Materials

★ 169 ★
PRACTICE AND PROCEDURE IN LABOR ARBITRATION
Owen Fairweather
    Bureau of National Affairs
    1231 25th Street, Northwest
    Washington, D.C. 20037
Book. 1973. $25.00.

★ 170 ★
STRIKES: A STUDY OF CONFLICT AND HOW TO RESOLVE IT
Walter Baer
    American Management Associations
    135 West 50th Street
    New York, New York 10020
Book. 1975. $12.95.

ARCHITECTURE

See also: Building Construction

Correspondence Courses

★ 171 ★
ARCHITECTURAL DRAWING AND DESIGNING
    International Correspondence School
    Scranton, Pennsylvania 18515
Multi-module correspondence course.

★ 172 ★
ARCHITECTURE
    International Correspondence School
    Scranton, Pennsylvania 18515
Multi-module correspondence course.

★ 173 ★
HOUSE PLANNING AND INTERIOR DESIGN
    International Correspondence School
    Scranton, Pennsylvania 18515
Multi-module correspondence course.

ARSON INVESTIGATION

See also: Fire Fighting

Correspondence Courses

★ 174 ★
ARSON INVESTIGATION
    University of Nebraska
    511 Nebraska Hall
    Lincoln, Nebraska 68588
Correspondence course.

ART

Correspondence Courses

★ 175 ★
ART TRAINING COURSE
    La Salle Extension University
    417 South Dearborn Street
    Chicago, Illinois 60605
Correspondence course.

★ 176 ★
COMMERCIAL ART, ILLUSTRATION AND DESIGN
    Famous Schools
    Westport, Connecticut 06880
Correspondence course.

★ 177 ★
FINE ART PAINTING
    Famous Schools
    Westport, Connecticut 06880
Correspondence course.

Films/Video/Filmstrips

★ 178 ★
BATIK
    Scope Productions Incorporated
    Post Office Box 5515
    Fresno, California 93755
3 films (8 mm) and student guides. $63.00.

★ 179 ★
CONSTRUCTION - ART
    Scope Productions Incorporated
    Post Office Box 5515
    Fresno, California 93755
13 films (8 mm) and student guides. $273.00.

★ 180 ★
CONSTRUCTION - WHEEL; CLAY
    Scope Productions Incorporated
    Post Office Box 5515
    Fresno, California 93755
3 films (8 mm) and student guides. $63.00.

★ 181 ★
CONSTRUCTION - WOOD
    Scope Productions Incorporated
    Post Office Box 5515
    Fresno, California 93755
5 films (8 mm) and student guides. $105.00.

★ 182 ★
COSTUME DESIGN
    Scope Productions Incorporated
    Post Office Box 5515
    Fresno, California 93755
3 films (8 mm) and student guides. $63.00.

★ 183 ★
DRAWING
    Scope Productions Incorporated
    Post Office Box 5515
    Fresno, California 93755
15 films (8 mm) and student guides. $358.75.

★ 184 ★
JEWELRY DESIGN
    Scope Productions Incorporated
    Post Office Box 5515
    Fresno, California 93755
2 films (8 mm) and student guides. $42.00.

★ 185 ★
PAINTING
    Scope Productions Incorporated
    Post Office Box 5515
    Fresno, California 93755
9 films (8 mm) and student guides. $209.25.

★ 186 ★
SCULPTURE
    Scope Productions Incorporated
    Post Office Box 5515
    Fresno, California 93755
3 films (8 mm) and student guides. $63.00.

★ 187 ★
SILK SCREEN
    Scope Productions Incorporated
    Post Office Box 5515
    Fresno, California 93755
12 films (8 mm) and student guides. $252.00

Printed Materials

★ 188 ★
COMMERCIAL ART TECHNIQUES
Ralph Maurello
    Leon Amiel Publications
    225 Secaucus Road
    Secaucus, New Jersey 07094
Book. $5.95.

ASSERTIVENESS

Audio Cassettes/Tapes

★ 189 ★
ASSERTIVENESS FOR CAREER AND PERSONAL
SUCCESS
    AMACOM
    American Management Associations
    135 West 50th Street
    New York, New York 10020
6 cassettes and workbook. $100.00.

★ 190 ★
ASSERTIVENESS TRAINING
    Jaine Carter Personnel Development Incorporated
    112 West Garden Avenue
    Palatine, Illinois 60067
Cassette workbook program.

★ 191 ★
CONSTRUCTIVE AGGRESSION (HOW TO FIGHT
FAIR)
Dr. George Bach
    Tape Rental Library Incorporated
    Post Office Box 2107
    2507 Edna Drive
    South Vineland, New Jersey 08360
10 cassettes.

Films/Video/Filmstrips

★ 192 ★
ASSERTION SKILLS: TINTYPES
    Salenger Educational Media
    1635 12th Street
    Santa Monica, California 90404
Film, guide and worksheets. $425.00 (rental available).

Multimedia Kits

★ 193 ★
ASSERTION TRAINING
    Lansford Publishing Company
    Post Office Box 8711
    San Jose, California 95155
Multimedia kit. $40.00.

★ 194 ★
INCREASING ASSERTION - A METHOD OF
REDUCING APPREHENSION
    Lansford Publishing Company
    Post Office Box 8711
    San Jose, California 95155
Multimedia kit. $106.00.

Printed Materials

★ 195 ★
ASSERTING YOURSELF: A PRACTICAL GUIDE FOR
POSITIVE CHANGE
    Addison Wesley Publishing Company Incorporated
    Jacob Way
    Reading, Massachusetts 01867
Book. 1976. $8.95.

★ 196 ★
AN INTRODUCTION TO ASSERTIVE TRAINING
FOR WOMEN
    American Personnel and Guidance Association
    1607 New Hampshire Avenue, Northwest
    Washington, D.C. 20009
Book. 1973. $2.25.

★ 197 ★
TALKING STRAIGHT: ASSERTION WITHOUT
AGGRESSION
Ronald B. Adler
    Professional Book Distributors
    Post Office Box 4892
    Columbus, Ohio 43202
Training book. $10.95.

ASSESSMENT

See also: Accountability; Performance
Appraisal

Audio Cassettes/Tapes

★ 198 ★
THE APPRAISAL INTERVIEW
George Odiorne
      MBO Incorporated
      157 Pontoosic Road
      Westfield, Massachusetts 01085
Cassette and manual. $15.00.

Multimedia Kits

★ 199 ★
THE ASSESSMENT CENTER
      Resources for Education and Management
        Incorporated
      544 Medlock Road, Suite 210
      Decatur, Georgia 30030
Filmstrip with cassette. $60.00.

★ 200 ★
ASSESSMENT METHODS
      Resources for Education and Management
        Incorporated
      544 Medlock Road, Suite 210
      Decatur, Georgia 30030
Filmstrip with cassette. $60.00.

★ 201 ★
GENERAL PROBLEMS IN ASSESSING EMPLOYEES
      Resources for Education and Management
        Incorporated
      544 Medlock Road, Suite 210
      Decatur, Georgia 30030
Filmstrip with cassette. $60.00.

★ 202 ★
HOW AND WHEN TO APPRAISE
      Resources for Education and Management
        Incorporated
      544 Medlock Road, Suite 210
      Decatur, Georgia 30030
Filmstrip with cassette. $70.00.

★ 203 ★
ON THE JOB ASSESSMENT
      Resources for Education and Management
        Incorporated
      544 Medlock Road, Suite 210
      Decatur, Georgia 30030

Filmstrip with cassette. $60.00.

★ 204 ★
WHAT TO APPRAISE
      Resources for Education and Management
        Incorporated
      544 Medlock Road, Suite 210
      Decatur, Georgia 30030
Filmstrip with cassette. $70.00.

★ 205 ★
WHY APPRAISE?
      Resources for Education and Management
        Incorporated
      544 Medlock Road, Suite 210
      Decatur, Georgia 30030
Filmstrip with cassette. $70.00.

ASTRONOMY

Films/Video/Filmstrips

★ 206 ★
ASTRONOMY
William Protheroe, Eugene Capriotti, Gerald
Newsom
      Charles E. Merrill Publishing Company
      1300 Alum Creek Drive
      Box 508
      Columbus, Ohio 43216
Text and sound filmstrips. $600.00.

AUDITING

See also: Accounting

Printed Materials

★ 207 ★
BASIC AUDITING
Arthur Holmes
      Richard D. Irwin Incorporated
      1818 Ridge Road
      Homewood, Illinois 60430
Book. 1976. $12.95.

★ 208 ★
FUNDAMENTALS OF AUDITING
Robert Mautz
      John Wiley and Sons Incorporated
      605 Third Avenue
      New York, New York 10016
Book. $15.75.

★ 209 ★
MANAGEMENT CONTROL, AUDITING AND THE
COMPUTER
H. Washbrook
     Crane, Russak and Company, Incorporated
     347 Madison Avenue
     New York, New York 10017
Book. 1971. $9.50.

Programmed Learning Materials

★ 210 ★
AUDITING
Walter B. Meigs
     Learning Systems Company
     1818 Ridge Road
     Homewood, Illinois 60430
Programmed learning aid. $4.95.

AUTHORITY
See: headings under MANAGEMENT; headings under SUPERVISION

AUTOMOBILE MECHANICS

See also: Diesel Mechanics

Correspondence Courses

★ 211 ★
AUTOMOBILE CUSTOMIZING
     North American Correspondence School
     4401 Birch Street
     Newport Beach, California 92663
Correspondence course.

★ 212 ★
AUTOMOBILE TUNE-UP
     International Correspondence School
     Scranton, Pennsylvania 18515
Multi-module correspondence course.

★ 213 ★
AUTOMOTIVE AIR CONDITIONING COURSE
     NRI Schools
     3939 Wisconsin Avenue
     Washington, D.C. 20016
15 lesson home study program. $195.00.

★ 214 ★
AUTOMOTIVE BODY REBUILDING
     International Correspondence School
     Scranton, Pennsylvania 18515
Multi-module correspondence course.

★ 215 ★
AUTOMOTIVE MECHANIC
     International Correspondence School
     Scranton, Pennsylvania 18515
Multi-module correspondence course.

★ 216 ★
AUTOMOTIVE MECHANICS
     Commercial Trades Institute
     6201 West Howard Street
     Chicago, Illinois 60648
Correspondence course. $895.00.

★ 217 ★
GASOLINE ENGINE MECHANICS
     International Correspondence School
     Scranton, Pennsylvania 18515
Multi-module correspondence course.

Films/Video/Filmstrips

★ 218 ★
ALTERNATORS
     DCA Educational Products
     424 Valley Road
     Warrington, Pennsylvania 18976
2 film loops (8 mm). $27.00 each.

★ 219 ★
THE AUTO PAINT SHOP
     DCA Educational Products
     424 Valley Road
     Warrington, Pennsylvania 18976
4 film loops (8 mm). $27.00 each.

★ 220 ★
BATTERY STARTER TEST
     DCA Educational Products
     424 Valley Road
     Warrington, Pennsylvania 18976
3 film loops (8 mm). $27.00 each.

★ 221 ★
THE BRAKE LATHE
    DCA Educational Products
    424 Valley Road
    Warrington, Pennsylvania 18976
6 film loops (8 mm). $27.00 each.

★ 222 ★
CRANKCASE VENTILATION SYSTEMS
    DCA Educational Products
    424 Valley Road
    Warrington, Pennsylvania 18976
Film loop (8 mm). $27.00.

★ 223 ★
DIAGNOSTIC INSPECTION
    DCA Educational Products
    424 Valley Road
    Warrington, Pennsylvania 18976
8 film loops (8 mm). $27.00 each.

★ 224 ★
DISC BRAKE SYSTEM
    DCA Educational Products
    424 Valley Road
    Warrington, Pennsylvania 18976
6 film loops (8 mm). $27.00 each.

★ 225 ★
THE ELECTRICAL SYSTEM
    DCA Educational Products
    424 Valley Road
    Warrington, Pennsylvania 18976
Filmstrips and self-study text. $90.00.

★ 226 ★
THE FUEL SYSTEM
    DCA Educational Products
    424 Valley Road
    Warrington, Pennsylvania 18976
Filmstrips and self-study text. $110.00.

★ 227 ★
IGNITION SYSTEMS
    DCA Educational Products
    424 Valley Road
    Warrington, Pennsylvania 18976
2 film loops (8 mm). $27.00 each.

★ 228 ★
SELF-ADJUSTING BRAKE SYSTEM
    DCA Educational Products
    424 Valley Road
    Warrington, Pennsylvania 18976
3 film loops (8 mm). $27.00 each.

★ 229 ★
TIRE CHANGING
    DCA Educational Products
    424 Valley Road
    Warrington, Pennsylvania 18976
2 film loops (8 mm). $27.00 each.

★ 230 ★
WHEEL ALIGNMENT
    DCA Educational Products
    424 Valley Road
    Warrington, Pennsylvania 18976
9 film loops (8 mm). $27.00 each.

★ 231 ★
WHEEL BALANCING
    DCA Educational Products
    424 Valley Road
    Warrington, Pennsylvania 18976
3 film loops (8 mm). $27.00 each.

Multimedia Kits

★ 232 ★
ENGINE DISASSEMBLY AND INSPECTION
    Bobbs-Merrill Educational Publishing
    4300 West 62nd Street
    Indianapolis, Indiana 46206
Cassette and slide kit. $99.00.

★ 233 ★
ENGINE REASSEMBLY
    Bobbs-Merrill Educational Publishing
    4300 West 62nd Street
    Indianapolis, Indiana 46206
Cassette and slide kit. $99.00.

★ 234 ★
TUNE-UP
    Bobbs-Merrill Educational Publishing
    4300 West 62nd Street
    Indianapolis, Indiana 46206
Cassette and slide kit. $99.00.

Programmed Learning Materials

★ 235 ★
INTERNAL COMBUSTION ENGINES
  E. I. du Pont de Nemours and Company
  Applied Technology Division
  Room B-4204
  Wilmington, Delaware 19898
Programmed text. $4.25.

AUTOMOBILE SAFETY
See: SAFETY, AUTOMOBILE

AVIATION

See also: Aircraft Maintenance

Printed Materials

★ 236 ★
AVIATION MAINTENANCE LAW
Fred Biehler
  Aviation Book Company
  555 West Glenoaks Boulevard
  Box 4187
  Glendale, California 91202
Book. $10.95.

★ 237 ★
COMMERCIAL PILOT PROGRAMMED COURSE
  Aviation Book Company
  555 West Glenoaks Boulevard
  Box 4187
  Glendale, California   91202
Book.   1976. $17.98.

★ 238 ★
FROM THE GROUND UP: BASIC AERONAUTICS
FOR STUDENT PILOTS
Sandy MacDonald
  Aviation Book Company
  555 West Glenoaks Boulevard
  Box 4187
  Glendale, California   91202
Book.   1976. $7.50.

★ 239 ★
FUNDAMENTALS OF FLIGHT
  Aviation Book Company
  555 West Glenoaks Boulevard
  Box 4187
  Glendale, California   91202
Book. 1975. $.75.

★ 240 ★
INTRODUCTION TO AVIATION SCIENCE
Joseph Benkert
  Prentice-Hall Incorporated
  Englewood Cliffs, New Jersey 07632
Book.   1971. $16.75.

★ 241 ★
PRIVATE AND COMMERCIAL PILOT: COMPLETE
PROGRAMMED COURSE
  Aero Press Incorporated
  Department of Aviation Education
  Post Office Box 209
  Fall River, Massachusetts 02722
Book.   1975. $19.98.

★ 242 ★
PRIVATE PILOT STUDY GUIDE
Leroy Simonson
  Aviation Book Company
  555 West Glenoaks Boulevard
  Box 4187
  Glendale, California   91202
Book.   1974. $10.00.

BALUCHI

Multimedia Kits

★ 243 ★
BALUCHI - BASIC COURSE
  General Services Administration
  Foreign Service Institute Language Course
  National Audiovisual Center
  Order Section RR
  Washington, D.C. 20409
Audio tapes, cassettes and text available.   Approximately $100.00.

BANKING

Audio Cassettes/Tapes

★ 244 ★
REMINDER TRAINING FOR BANK PERSONNEL
    Thompson-Mitchell and Associates
    3384 Peachtree Road Northeast
    Atlanta, Georgia 30326
6 cassettes. $125.00.

Correspondence Courses

★ 245 ★
BANKING AND FINANCE
    La Salle Extension University
    417 South Dearborn Street
    Chicago, Illinois 60605
Correspondence course.

★ 246 ★
COMMERCIAL AND CENTRAL BANKING
    University of South Carolina
    Department of Correspondence Study
    Division of Continuing Education
    Columbia, South Carolina 29208
Correspondence course. $69.00.

★ 247 ★
COMMERCIAL BANK MANAGEMENT
Harold D. Fletcher
    Western Kentucky University
    Office of Special Programs
    Bowling Green, Kentucky 42101
Independent study course.

★ 248 ★
MONEY AND BANKING
    University of Missouri
    Center for Independent Study
    514 South Fifth Street
    Columbia, Missouri 65211
Correspondence course. $80.00.

Films/Video/Filmstrips

★ 249 ★
HOW TO SUCCEED IN BANKING
    Better Selling Bureau
    1150 West Olive Avenue
    Burbank, California 91506
Filmstrips. $395.00.

Multimedia Kits

★ 250 ★
MONEY AND BANKING
    Lansford Publishing Company
    Post Office Box 8711
    San Jose, California 95155
Multimedia kit. $150.00.

Printed Materials

★ 251 ★
MARKETING FOR THE BANK EXECUTIVE
L. Berry, L. Capaldini
    Petrocelli Books
    384 Fifth Avenue
    New York, New York 10018
Book.   1974. $14.95.

★ 252 ★
PRACTICAL BANKING FOR BEGINNERS
J. K. Gerrar
    Panther House Limited
    Post Office Box 3552
    New York, New York 10017
Book.   1972. $4.00.

★ 253 ★
PROBLEMS IN BANK MANAGEMENT: AN IN-
BASKET TRAINING EXERCISE
Cabot Jaffee
    Addison Wesley Publishing Company Incorporated
    Jacob Way
    Reading, Massachusetts 01867
Book. $8.95.

Programmed Learning Materials

★ 254 ★
CHECKS
    American Bankers Association
    1120 Connecticut Avenue, Northwest
    Washington, D.C. 20036
Programmed text and tests.   1976. $15.00.

★ 255 ★
LOSS PREVENTION - CHECKS
    American Bankers Association
    1120 Connecticut Avenue, Northwest
    Washington, D.C. 20036
Programmed text and tests. $15.00.

★ 256 ★
SECURED TRANSACTIONS
American Bankers Association
1120 Connecticut Avenue, Northwest
Washington, D.C. 20036
Programmed text of 4 lessons. $6.00.

★ 257 ★
SELLING BANK SERVICES
American Bankers Association
1120 Connecticut Avenue, Northwest
Washington, D.C. 20036
Programmed text. $22.00.

BASIC
See: COMPUTER LANGUAGES

BEEKEEPING

Printed Materials

★ 258 ★
BEE-KEEPING
A. N. Schonfield - Teach Yourself Series
David McKay Company Incorporated
750 Third Avenue
New York, New York 10017
Book. 1974. $2.95.

★ 259 ★
FIRST LESSONS IN BEEKEEPING
C. P. Dadant
Dadant and Sons Incorporated
51 South Second Street
Hamilton, Illinois 62341
Book. 1976. $1.00.

BEHAVIORAL ASPECTS OF MANAGEMENT
See: MANAGEMENT, BEHAVIORAL
ASPECTS

BIOCHEMISTRY

Printed Materials

★ 260 ★
AN INTRODUCTION TO BIOCHEMISTRY
A. J. McMillan

Pergamon Press Incorporated
Maxwell House
Fairview Park
Elmsford, New York 10523
Programmed text. $6.00.

BIOLOGY

Printed Materials

★ 261 ★
THE CARDIOVASCULAR SYSTEM
Robert J. Brady Company
Charles Press Publishers
Prentice-Hall Companies
Bowie, Maryland 20715
Book. $3.75.

★ 262 ★
THE CELL
Robert J. Brady Company
Charles Press Publishers
Prentice-Hall Companies
Bowie, Maryland 20715
Book. $3.75.

★ 263 ★
THE DIGESTIVE SYSTEM
Robert J. Brady Company
Charles Press Publishers
Prentice-Hall Companies
Bowie, Maryland 20715
Book. $4.75.

★ 264 ★
THE ENDOCRINE SYSTEM
Robert J. Brady Company
Charles Press Publishers
Prentice-Hall Companies
Bowie, Maryland 20715
Book. $3.75.

★ 265 ★
THE LYMPHATIC AND RETICUBENDOTHELIAL
SYSTEMS
Robert J. Brady Company
Charles Press Publishers
Prentice-Hall Companies
Bowie, Maryland 20715
Book. $3.75.

★ 266 ★
THE MUSCULAR SYSTEM
    Robert J. Brady Company
    Charles Press Publishers
    Prentice-Hall Companies
    Bowie, Maryland 20715
Book. $4.75.

★ 267 ★
THE NERVOUS SYSTEM
    Robert J. Brady Company
    Charles Press Publishers
    Prentice-Hall Companies
    Bowie, Maryland 20715
Book. $5.25.

★ 268 ★
REPRODUCTION IN HUMANS
    Robert J. Brady Company
    Charles Press Publishers
    Prentice-Hall Companies
    Bowie, Maryland 20715
Book. $4.75.

★ 269 ★
THE REPRODUCTIVE SYSTEM
    Robert J. Brady Company
    Charles Press Publishers
    Prentice-Hall Companies
    Bowie, Maryland 20715
Book. $4.75.

★ 270 ★
THE RESPIRATORY SYSTEM
    Robert J. Brady Company
    Charles Press Publishers
    Prentice-Hall Companies
    Bowie, Maryland 20715
Book. $3.75.

★ 271 ★
SKELETAL SYSTEM
    Robert J. Brady Company
    Charles Press Publishers
    Prentice-Hall Companies
    Bowie, Maryland 20715
Book. $3.75.

★ 272 ★
SKIN
    Robert J. Brady Company
    Charles Press Publishers
    Prentice-Hall Companies
    Bowie, Maryland 20715
Book. $3.75.

★ 273 ★
SPECIAL SENSES
    Robert J. Brady Company
    Charles Press Publishers
    Prentice-Hall Companies
    Bowie, Maryland 20715
Book. $4.75.

★ 274 ★
URINARY SYSTEM
    Robert J. Brady Company
    Charles Press Publishers
    Prentice-Hall Companies
    Bowie, Maryland 20715
Book. $4.75.

BIOMATHEMATICS

See also: Mathematics

Printed Materials

★ 275 ★
BIOSTATISTICAL ANALYSIS
Jerrold Zar
    Prentice-Hall Incorporated
    Englewood Cliffs, New Jersey 07632
Book. 1974. $17.95.

★ 276 ★
FUNDAMENTALS OF BIOMETRY
L. N. Balaam
    Halsted Press
    Division of John Wiley and Sons Incorporated
    605 Third Avenue
    New York, New York 10016
Book. 1972. $12.95.

★ 277 ★
FUNDAMENTALS OF BIOSTATISTICS
Edwin Vann
    D. C. Heath and Company
    2700 North Richardt Avenue
    Indianapolis, Indiana 46219
Book. 1972. $4.95.

★ 278 ★
INTRODUCTION TO MATHEMATICAL BIOLOGY
S. I. Rubinow
    John Wiley and Sons Incorporated
    605 Third Avenue
    New York, New York 10016
Book. 1975. $22.00.

★ 279 ★
MATHEMATICS FOR BIOLOGISTS
A. Crowe
    Academic Press Incorporated
    111 Fifth Avenue
    New York, New York 10003
Book. $10.50.

BLACKSMITHING

Printed Materials

★ 280 ★
DRAKE'S MODERN BLACKSMITHING
J. G. Holstrom
    Drake Publishers
    801 Second Avenue
    New York, New York 10017
Book. 1970. $6.95.

BLUEPRINT READING

See also: Building Design;
                Drafting

Correspondence Courses

★ 281 ★
READING ARCHITECT'S BLUEPRINTS
    International Correspondence School
    Scranton, Pennsylvania 18515
Multi-module correspondence course.

★ 282 ★
READING ELECTRICAL BLUEPRINTS
    International Correspondence School
    Scranton, Pennsylvania 18515
Multi-module correspondence course.

★ 283 ★
READING HIGHWAY BLUEPRINTS
    International Correspondence School
    Scranton, Pennsylvania 18515
Multi-module correspondence course.

★ 284 ★
READING STRUCTURAL BLUEPRINTS
    International Correspondence School
    Scranton, Pennsylvania 18515
Multi-module correspondence course.

Printed Materials

★ 285 ★
BLUEPRINT READING FOR MACHINISTS
    Delmar Publications
    50 Wolf Road
    Albany, New York 12205
Book. 1971. $6.00.

★ 286 ★
BLUEPRINT READING FOR WELDERS
Bennett and Sly
    Delmar Publications
    50 Wolf Road
    Albany, New York 12205
Book. 1973. $5.80.

★ 287 ★
BUILDING TRADES BLUEPRINT READING
    McGraw-Hill Book Company
    1221 Avenue of the Americas
    New York, New York 10019
Book. 1975. $7.72.

★ 288 ★
ELEMENTARY BLUEPRINT READING FOR BEGINNERS
IN MACHINE SHOP PRACTICE
    Delmar Publications
    50 Wolf Road
    Albany, New York 12205
Book. 1970. $2.60.

★ 289 ★
PRIMER OF BLUEPRINT READING
Thomas Diamond
    Bruce Books
    MacMillan Publishing Company
    Riverside, New Jersey 08075
Book. $1.48.

★ 290 ★
SHEET METAL BLUEPRINT READING FOR THE
BUILDING TRADES
Zinngrabe
    Delmar Publications
    50 Wolf Road
    Albany, New York 12205
Book. 1971. $8.00.

★ 291 ★
STARTER BLUEPRINT FOR PRE-JOB TRAINING
Joseph R. Todd
         National Tool, Die and Precision
            Machining Association
         9300 Livingston Road
         Washington, D.C. 20022
Workbook and project blueprints.

BOAT BUILDING

Printed Materials

★ 292 ★
BOATBUILDING METHODS
Peter Cook
         Beekman Publishers Incorporated
         38 Hicks Street
         Brooklyn Heights, New York 11201
Book. 1974. $8.95.

★ 293 ★
PRACTICAL FERRO-CEMENT BOATBUILDING
Jay Benford
         International Marine Publishing Company
         21 Elm Street
         Camden, Maine 04843
Book. 1972. $10.00.

★ 294 ★
SIMPLIFIED BOATBUILDING
Harry Sucher
         W. W. Norton and Company Incorporated
         500 Fifth Avenue
         New York, New York 10036
Book. 1973. $18.95.

BOAT MAINTENANCE

Printed Materials

★ 295 ★
BOAT MAINTENANCE
Charles Chapman
         Seven Seas Press
         Associated Booksellers
         147 McKinley Avenue
         Bridgeport, Connecticut 06606
Book. $8.00.

BOOK COLLECTING

Printed Materials

★ 296 ★
BOOK COLLECTING
Jack Matthews
         G. P. Putnam's Sons
         200 Madison Avenue
         New York, New York 10016
Book. 1977. $12.50.

BOOK REVIEWING

Printed Materials

★ 297 ★
GUIDE TO WRITING A CRITICAL REVIEW
Eliot Allen, Ethel Colbrunn
         Everett/Edwards Incorporated
         Post Office Box 1060
         DeLand, Florida 32720
Book. $1.50.

BOOK SELLING

Printed Materials

★ 298 ★
BEGINNING IN BOOK SELLING
         Academic Press Incorporated
         111 Fifth Avenue
         New York, New York 10003
Book. 1971. $2.50.

★ 299 ★
HOW TO BUY AND SELL OLD BOOKS
L. Freeman
         Century House Incorporated
         Old Irelandville
         Watkins Glen, New York 14891
Book. $5.00.

★ 300 ★
A MANUAL ON BOOK SELLING: HOW TO OPEN
AND RUN YOUR OWN BOOKSTORE
American Booksellers Association
         Harmony Press
         419 Park Avenue South
         New York, New York 10016
Book. 1974. $3.95.

BOOKBINDING

Printed Materials

★ 301 ★
BASIC BOOKBINDING
A. W. Lewis
　　　Peter Smith Publisher Incorporated
　　　Six Lexington Avenue
　　　Magnolia, Massachusetts　01930
Book.　$5.00.

★ 302 ★
SIMPLIFIED BOOKBINDING
Henry Gross
　　　Charles Scribner's Sons
　　　Vreeland Avenue
　　　Totowa, New Jersey　07512
Book.　$3.95.

BOOKKEEPING

See also:　Accounting;　Record Keeping

Audio Cassettes/Tapes

★ 303 ★
BOOKKEEPING
　　　Thompson-Mitchell and Associates
　　　3384 Peachtree Road Northeast
　　　Atlanta, Georgia　30326
Cassette.　$9.98.

Correspondence Courses

★ 304 ★
BOOKKEEPING AND GENERAL ACCOUNTING
　　　Commercial Trades Institute
　　　6201 West Howard Street
　　　Chicago, Illinois　60648
Correspondence course.　$595.00.

Printed Materials

★ 305 ★
BOOKKEEPING
D. Cousins - Teach Yourself Series
　　　David McKay Company Incorporated
　　　750 Third Avenue
　　　New York, New York　10017
Book.　1975.　$3.95.

★ 306 ★
BOOKKEEPING MADE EASY
Alexander Sheff
　　　Barnes and Noble Incorporated
　　　Keystone Industrial Park
　　　Scranton, Pennsylvania　18512
Book.　1971.　$2.50.

★ 307 ★
STEP BY STEP BOOKKEEPING
Robert Ragan
　　　Drake Publishers
　　　801 Second Avenue
　　　New York, New York　10017
Book.　1974.　$3.95.

BRAILLE

Correspondence Courses

★ 308 ★
BRAILLE
　　　University of Florida
　　　Division of Continuing Education
　　　2012 West University Avenue
　　　Gainesville, Florida　32603
Correspondence course.

BRICKLAYING
See: MASONRY

BROADCAST ENGINEERING

Correspondence Courses

★ 309 ★
BROADCAST ENGINEERING
　　　Cleveland Institute of Electronics
　　　1776 East 17th Street
　　　Cleveland, Ohio　44114
Correspondence course.

★ 310 ★
FCC LICENSE
　　　Cleveland Institute of Electronics
　　　1776 East 17th Street
　　　Cleveland, Ohio　44114
Correspondence course.

★ 311 ★
FCC LICENSE AND COMMUNICATION
    Cleveland Institute of Electronics
    1776 East 17th Street
    Cleveland, Ohio 44114
Correspondence course.

★ 312 ★
FCC LICENSE COURSE
    La Salle Extension University
    417 South Dearborn Street
    Chicago, Illinois 60605
Correspondence course.

BUDGETING

See also: Financial Planning; Zero-Base
                    Budgeting

Audio Cassettes/Tapes

★ 313 ★
BASIC BUDGETING
    Management Resources Incorporated
    757 Third Avenue
    New York, New York 10017
2 audio cassettes and workbook. $49.95.

★ 314 ★
FUNDAMENTALS OF BUDGETING
    Westinghouse Learning Press
    College Publications
    Post Office Box 10680
    Palo Alto, California 94303
Cassette with study guide. $60.00.

Printed Materials

★ 315 ★
THE BASIC ARTS OF BUDGETING
T. S. McAlpine
    Cahners Publishing Company Incorporated
    221 Columbus Avenue
    Boston, Massachusetts 02166
Book.   1976. $18.00.

★ 316 ★
BUDGET: PROFIT PLANNING AND CONTROL
Glenn Welsch
    Prentice-Hall Incorporated
    Englewood Cliffs, New Jersey 07632
Book.   1970. $14.95.

★ 317 ★
BUDGETING BASICS: A "HOW TO" GUIDE FOR
MANAGERS
    American Management Associations
    135 West 50th Street
    New York, New York 10020
Book.   1975. $8.00.

★ 318 ★
HOW TO PREPARE AN OPERATING BUDGET
J. H. Halsall
    Longman Incorporated
    19 West 44th Street, Suite 1012
    New York, New York 10036
Book.   1974. $5.00.

★ 319 ★
THE INTEGRATED COMPANY BUDGET
    American Management Associations
    135 West 50th Street
    New York, New York 10020
3 course set.   1972. $85.00.

★ 320 ★
A PRIMER ON BUSINESS FINANCE
Frank De Felice
    Mss Information Corporation
    655 Madison Avenue
    New York, New York 10021
Book. $11.00.

BUILDING CONSTRUCTION

Audio Cassettes/Tapes

★ 321 ★
HOUSING AND CONSTRUCTION IN THE 70'S
    Tape Rental Library Incorporated
    Post Office Box 2107
    2507 Edna Drive
    South Vineland, New Jersey 08360
Cassette.

Correspondence Courses

★ 322 ★
BUILDING CONSTRUCTION
    Commercial Trades Institute
    6201 West Howard Street
    Chicago, Illinois 60648
Correspondence course. $895.00.

★ 323 ★
BUILDING CONTRACTING
        International Correspondence School
        Scranton, Pennsylvania 18515
Multi-module correspondence course.

★ 324 ★
BUILDING ESTIMATING
        International Correspondence School
        Scranton, Pennsylvania 18515
Multi-module correspondence course.

Multimedia Kits

★ 325 ★
LIGHT CONSTRUCTION TECHNIQUES
        Bobbs-Merrill Educational Publishing
        4300 West 62nd Street
        Indianapolis, Indiana 46206
12 program multimedia course.

Printed Materials

★ 326 ★
BUILDING CONSTRUCTION AND DESIGN
        Theodore Audel Company
        Distributed by Bobbs-Merrill Company
            Incorporated
        4300 West 62nd Street
        Indianapolis, Indiana 46268
Book.   1970. $6.75.

★ 327 ★
BUILDING CONSTRUCTION CARPENTRY
A. B. Amary
        Drake Publishers
        801 Second Avenue
        New York, New York 10017
Book.   1970. $5.95.

★ 328 ★
CONSTRUCTION
Jack Landers
        Goodheart-Wilcox Company Incorporated
        123 West Taft Drive
        South Holland, Illinois 60473
Book.   1976. $6.96.

★ 329 ★
CONSTRUCTION OF BUILDINGS
R. Barry
        Beekman Publishers Incorporated
        38 Hicks Street
        Brooklyn Heights, New York 11201
4 volume spiral binding set.   1971. $30.00.

★ 330 ★
CONSTRUCTION MANAGEMENT PRACTICE
Peter Volpe
        John Wiley and Sons Incorporated
        605 Third Avenue
        New York, New York 10016
Book.   1972. $12.25.

★ 331 ★
CONSTRUCTION PLANNING, EQUIPMENT AND
METHODS
Robert Peurifoy
        McGraw-Hill Book Company
        1221 Avenue of the Americas
        New York, New York 10019
Book.   1970. $19.00.

★ 332 ★
CONSTRUCTION: PRINCIPLES MATERIALS AND
METHODS
John Schmidt
        Interstate Incorporated
        1927 North Jackson Street
        Danville, Illinois 61832
Book.   1975. $22.50.

★ 333 ★
CONSTRUCTION TECHNOLOGY
Roy Chudley
        Longman Incorporated
        19 West 44th Street, Suite 1012
        New York, New York 10036
Book.   1974. $6.50.

★ 334 ★
DEVELOPMENT BUILDING: THE TEAM APPROACH
C. W. Griffin
        American Institute of Architects
        1735 New York Avenue, Northwest
        Washington, D.C. 20006
Book.   1972. $15.00.

★ 335 ★
ELECTRICAL DESIGN FOR BUILDING CONSTRUCTION
John Traister
    McGraw-Hill Book Company
    1221 Avenue of the Americas
    New York; New York 10019
Book. 1976. $15.00.

★ 336 ★
PRINCIPLES OF STRUCTURAL STABILITY THEORY
Alexander Chajes
    Prentice-Hall Incorporated
    Englewood Cliffs, New Jersey 07632
Book. 1974. $18.75.

BUILDING DESIGN

See also: Architecture

Printed Materials

★ 337 ★
BUILDING DESIGN FOR MAINTAINABILITY
Edwin Feldman
    McGraw-Hill Book Company
    1221 Avenue of the Americas
    New York, New York 10019
Book. 1975. $12.50.

★ 338 ★
DESIGN FOR SECURITY
R. J. Healy
    John Wiley and Sons Incorporated
    605 Third Avenue
    New York, New York 10016
Book. $18.50.

★ 339 ★
SIMPLIFIED GUIDE TO CONSTRUCTION FOR
ARCHITECTS AND ENGINEERS
James Gorman
    Cahners Publishing Company Incorporated
    221 Columbus Avenue
    Boston, Massachusetts 02166
Book. 1976. $14.95.

BUILDING INSPECTION

Correspondence Courses

★ 340 ★
BUILDING INSPECTION
    International Correspondence School
    Scranton, Pennsylvania 18515
Multi-module correspondence course.

★ 341 ★
METHODS FOR INSPECTORS
    The Thomas Institute
    Box 22
    New Canaan, Connecticut 06840
Self-study course. $150.00.

Films/Video/Filmstrips

★ 342 ★
PLANS APPROVED (Explains importance of building
codes)
    American Plywood Association
    1119 A Street
    Tacoma, Washington 98401
Film.

BULGARIAN

Multimedia Kits

★ 343 ★
BULGARIAN - BASIC COURSE
    General Services Administration
    Foreign Service Institute Language Course
    National Audiovisual Center
    Order Section RR
    Washington, D.C. 20409
Audio tapes, cassettes and text available. Approxi-
mately $200.00.

BUSINESS LAW

Audio Cassettes/Tapes

★ 344 ★
BUSINESS LAW
    Thompson-Mitchell and Associates
    3384 Peachtree Road Northeast
    Atlanta, Georgia 30326
2 cassettes. $9.98 each.

★ 345 ★
BUSINESS LAW/PERSONAL DEVELOPMENT
    Educational Century Programming
    1201 East Johnson Street
    Jonesboro, Arkansas 72401
Cassette. $6.00.

★ 346 ★
BUSINESS LAW SERIES
    National Book Company
    1019 Southwest Tenth Avenue
    Portland, Oregon 97206
30 cassettes. $402.15.

Correspondence Courses

★ 347 ★
BUSINESS LAW
    University of Arkansas
    Department of Independent Study
    346 West Avenue
    Fayetteville, Arkansas 72701
Correspondence course.

★ 348 ★
BUSINESS LAW
    University of Florida
    Division of Continuing Education
    2012 West University Avenue
    Gainesville, Florida 32603
Correspondence course.

★ 349 ★
BUSINESS LAW
    University of Kentucky
    Independent Study Program
    Freeze Hall, Room 1
    Lexington, Kentucky 40506
Correspondence course.

★ 350 ★
BUSINESS LAW
    Pennsylvania State University
    Department of Independent Study by
        Correspondence
    Three Sheilds Building
    University Park, Pennsylvania 16802
Correspondence course.

★ 351 ★
BUSINESS LAW
    Texas Tech University
    Division of Continuing Education
    Post Office Box 4110
    Lubbock, Texas 79409
Correspondence course.

★ 352 ★
COMMERCIAL LAW
    University of South Carolina
    Department of Correspondence Study
    Division of Continuing Education
    Columbia, South Carolina 29208
Correspondence course. $69.00.

★ 353 ★
THE LEGAL ENVIRONMENT OF BUSINESS
    University of Kentucky
    Independent Study Program
    Freeze Hall, Room 1
    Lexington, Kentucky 40506
Correspondence course.

★ 354 ★
THE LEGAL ENVIRONMENT OF BUSINESS
    University of Southern Mississippi
    Department of Independent Study
    Southern Station Box 56
    Hattiesburg, Mississippi 39401
Correspondence course.

Printed Materials

★ 355 ★
BUSINESS AND THE LAW
Robert R. Rosenberg, William Ott
    McGraw-Hill Book Company
    1221 Avenue of the Americas
    New York, New York 10019
Book. 1975. $9.50.

★ 356 ★
FUNDAMENTALS OF BUSINESS LAW
Barbara George
    Prentice-Hall Incorporated
    Englewood Cliffs, New Jersey 07632
Book. 1974. $4.95.

★ 357 ★
INTRODUCTION TO BUSINESS LAW
R. Howell
    Holt Rinehart and Winston Incorporated
    383 Madison Avenue
    New York, New York 10017
Book. 1974. $12.95.

★ 358 ★
LAW FOR BUSINESS AND MANAGEMENT
Gail Beekman
    McGraw-Hill Book Company
    1221 Avenue of the Americas
    New York, New York 10036
Book. 1975. $8.95.

★ 359 ★
PRINCIPLES OF BUSINESS LAW
Robert Corley, William Robert
    Prentice-Hall Incorporated
    Englewood Cliffs, New Jersey 07632
Book with study guide. 1975. $21.00.

Programmed Learning Materials

★ 360 ★
BUSINESS LAW
James Barnes
    Learning Systems Company
    1818 Ridge Road
    Homewood, Illinois 60430
Programmed learning aid. $4.50.

BUSINESS LETTERS

See also: Business Writing; Communication, Written

Audio Cassettes/Tapes

★ 361 ★
LETTER WRITING FOR THE OFFICE
    National Book Company
    1019 Southwest Tenth Avenue
    Portland, Oregon 97206
12 cassette tapes. $165.85.

★ 362 ★
LETTER WRITING TIPS THAT CUT COSTS AND IMPROVE RESULTS
    Thompson-Mitchell and Associates
    3384 Peachtree Road Northeast
    Atlanta, Georgia 30326
Cassette. $15.00.

★ 363 ★
WRITING BETTER LETTERS IN BUSINESS
    Thompson-Mitchell and Associates
    3384 Peachtree Road Northeast
    Atlanta, Georgia 30326
10 cassettes. $99.00.

★ 364 ★
WRITING BUSINESS LETTERS
    Educational Century Programming
    1201 East Johnson Street
    Jonesboro, Arkansas 72401
Cassette. $6.00.

Films/Video/Filmstrips

★ 365 ★
LETTER WRITING AT WORK
    Roundtable Films
    113 North San Vincente Boulevard
    Beverly Hills, California 90211
Film.

Multimedia Kits

★ 366 ★
BETTER BUSINESS LETTER WRITING
John W. Lippert, Instructor
    Telstar Productions Incorporated
    366 North Prior Avenue
    Saint Paul, Minnesota 55104
6 video tapes, 6 audio tapes and workbook.
$2,400.00.

★ 367 ★
HOW TO WRITE CLEAR, CONCISE, EFFECTIVE BUSINESS LETTERS
    Dartnell Incorporated
    4660 Ravenswood Avenue
    Chicago, Illinois 60640
5 filmstrips with records. $250.00.

Printed Materials

★ 368 ★
COMMERCIAL CORRESPONDENCE
F. Addington-Symonds
    David McKay Company Incorporated
    750 Third Avenue
    New York, New York 10017
Self-study text. 1973. $2.95.

★ 369 ★
EXECUTIVE'S GUIDE TO EFFECTIVE LETTERS AND
REPORTS
William Parr
　　　Prentice-Hall Incorporated
　　　Englewood Cliffs, New Jersey　07632
Book.　1976.　$10.95.

★ 370 ★
WRITING LETTERS THAT SELL YOU, YOUR IDEAS,
PRODUCTS AND SERVICES
Patrick Monaghan
　　　Fairchild Publications Incorporated
　　　Seven East 12th Street
　　　New York, New York　10003
Book.　$6.95.

Programmed Learning Materials

★ 371 ★
BUSINESS COMMUNICATIONS
William C. Himstreet
　　　Learning Systems Company
　　　1818 Ridge Road
　　　Homewood, Illinois　60430
Programmed learning aid.　$4.95.

★ 372 ★
EFFECTIVE LETTERS:　A PROGRAM FOR SELF
INSTRUCTION
Robert Wendlinger,　James Reid
　　　McGraw-Hill Book Company
　　　1221 Avenue of the Americas
　　　New York, New York　10036
Programmed text.　1973.　$9.50.

BUSINESS MACHINES

See also:　Computers;　Dictation;　Typewriting

Audio Cassettes/Tapes

★ 373 ★
CARD PUNCH OPERATOR/THE ACCOUNTING
MACHINE
　　　Educational Century Programming
　　　1201 East Johnson Street
　　　Jonesboro, Arkansas　72401
Cassette.　$6.00.

★ 374 ★
ELECTRONIC CALCULATOR
　　　National Book Company
　　　1019 Southwest Tenth Avenue
　　　Portland, Oregon　97206
4 cassettes.　$56.35.

★ 375 ★
FULL KEY ADDING MACHINE
　　　National Book Company
　　　1019 Southwest Tenth Avenue
　　　Portland, Oregon　97206
9 cassettes.　$120.85.

★ 376 ★
PRINTING CALCULATOR
　　　National Book Company
　　　1019 Southwest Tenth Avenue
　　　Portland, Oregon　97206
3 cassettes.　$43.15.

★ 377 ★
ROTARY CALCULATOR
　　　National Book Company
　　　1019 Southwest Tenth Avenue
　　　Portland, Oregon　97206
7 cassettes.　$95.15.

★ 378 ★
TEN KEY ADDING MACHINES
　　　National Book Company
　　　1019 Southwest Tenth Avenue
　　　Portland, Oregon　97206
9 cassettes.　$120.95.

Printed Materials

★ 379 ★
CARD PUNCH MACHINE OPERATION
P. Pactor
　　　McGraw-Hill Book Company
　　　1221 Avenue of the Americas
　　　New York, New York　10036
Text and study guide.　1973.　$8.75.

BUSINESS MACHINES, REPAIR

Correspondence Courses

★ 380 ★
BUSINESS MACHINE REPAIR
　　　Technical Home Study School
　　　1500 Cardinal Drive
　　　Little Falls, New Jersey　07424
Correspondence course.

BUSINESS MATHEMATICS

See also: Mathematics

Audio Cassettes/Tapes

★ 381 ★
APPLIED MATHEMATICS FOR BUSINESS
        Educational Century Programming
        1201 East Johnson Street
        Jonesboro, Arkansas 72401
12 cassettes. $72.00.

★ 382 ★
COLLEGE BUSINESS MATHEMATICS (AN
AUDIO TUTORIAL APPROACH)
Stanleigh Ayres
        Charles E. Merrill Company
        1300 Alum Creek Drive
        Columbus, Ohio 43216
Audio and book. 1977. $10.95.

Printed Materials

★ 383 ★
MATHEMATICS FOR RETAIL BUYING
Bette Tepper, Newton Godnick
        Fairchild Publications Incorporated
        Seven East 12th Street
        New York, New York 10003
Book. 1973. $7.95.

Programmed Learning Materials

★ 384 ★
BUSINESS AND CONSUMER MATHEMATICS
        Learning Systems Company
        1818 Ridge Road
        Homewood, Illinois 60430
Programmed learning aid. $4.95.

★ 385 ★
PROGRAMMED BUSINESS MATHEMATICS
Harry Huffman, J. Schmidt
        McGraw-Hill Book Company
        1221 Avenue of the Americas
        New York, New York 10019
Programmed text. $6.35.

BUSINESS MEETINGS
See: MEETINGS

BUSINESS PRINCIPLES

Audio Cassettes/Tapes

★ 386 ★
BUSINESS PRINCIPLES
        National Book Company
        1019 Southwest Tenth Avenue
        Portland, Oregon 97206
15 cassettes. $204.50.

★ 387 ★
OFFICE CAREERS/BUSINESS
        Educational Century Programming
        1201 East Johnson Street
        Jonesboro, Arkansas 72401
Cassette. $6.00.

Correspondence Courses

★ 388 ★
INTRODUCTION TO BUSINESS
        University of Arkansas
        Department of Independent Study
        346 West Avenue
        Fayetteville, Arkansas 72701
Correspondence course.

Multimedia Kits

★ 389 ★
BIG GOVERNMENT AND PRIVATE ENTERPRISE IN
THE 70'S
        Thompson-Mitchell and Associates
        3384 Peachtree Road Northeast
        Atlanta, Georgia 30326
Filmstrip with cassette. $22.00.

Printed Materials

★ 390 ★
GENERAL BUSINESS FOR ECONOMIC UNDER-
STANDING
Debrum
        South-Western Publishing Company
        5101 Madison Road
        Cincinnati, Ohio 45227
Book. 1976. $7.88.

★ 391 ★
IMPROVING BUSINESS RESULTS
John Humble
    McGraw-Hill Book Company
    1221 Avenue of the Americas
    New York, New York 10019
Book. $8.50.

★ 392 ★
INTRODUCTION TO BUSINESS DYNAMICS
John Mallonee
    Holbrook Press Incorporated
    Rockleigh, New Jersey 07647
Book. 1976. $12.95.

★ 393 ★
INTRODUCTION TO BUSINESS: A MANAGEMENT
APPROACH
Arthur Weimer
    Richard D. Irwin Incorporated
    1818 Ridge Road
    Homewood, Illinois 60430
Book. 1974. $12.95.

Programmed Learning Materials

★ 394 ★
INTRODUCTION TO BUSINESS
Walter W. Perlick
    Learning Systems Company
    1818 Ridge Road
    Homewood, Illinois 60430
Programmed learning aid. $4.50.

★ 395 ★
INTRODUCTION TO BUSINESS: A PROGRAMMED
TEXT
C. J. Knapp, A. Blanchard
    Pergamon Press Incorporated
    Maxwell House
    Fairview Park
    Elmsford, New York 10523
Programmed text.

BUSINESS WRITING

See also: Business Letters

Correspondence Courses

★ 396 ★
EFFECTIVE BUSINESS WRITING

Dun and Bradstreet Incorporated
Business Education Division
Box 803
Church Street Station
New York, New York 10008
Instruction through self-study text and correspondence
with instructor. $125.00.

Multimedia Kits

★ 397 ★
CLEAR BUSINESS WRITING
    Resources for Education and Management
      Incorporated
    544 Medlock Road, Suite 210
    Decatur, Georgia 30030
Filmstrip with cassette. $60.00.

★ 398 ★
EFFECTIVE BUSINESS WRITING
    Resources for Education and Management
      Incorporated
    544 Medlock Road, Suite 210
    Decatur, Georgia 30030
Filmstrip with cassette. $60.00.

★ 399 ★
FRIENDLY BUSINESS WRITING
    Resources for Education and Management
      Incorporated
    544 Medlock Road, Suite 210
    Decatur, Georgia 30030
Filmstrip with cassette. $60.00.

★ 400 ★
GENERAL PRINCIPLES OF BUSINESS WRITING
    Resources for Education and Management
      Incorporated
    544 Medlock Road, Suite 210
    Decatur, Georgia 30030
Filmstrip with cassette. $60.00.

★ 401 ★
ORGANIZING BUSINESS WRITING
    Resources for Education and Management
      Incorporated
    544 Medlock Road, Suite 210
    Decatur, Georgia 30030
Filmstrip with cassette. $60.00.

Printed Materials

★ 402 ★
BUSINESS COMMUNICATIONS: PRINCIPLES AND
METHODS
William Himstreet, Wayne Baty
    Wadsworth Publishing Company Incorporated
    Ten Davis Drive
    Belmont, California 94002
Book. 1972. $13.95.

★ 403 ★
BUSINESS COMMUNICATIONS WITH WRITING
IMPROVEMENT EXERCISES
Phyllis Hemphill
    Prentice-Hall Incorporated
    Englewood Cliffs, New Jersey 07632
Book. 1975. $7.95.

★ 404 ★
HOW TO WRITE A REPORT YOUR BOSS WILL
READ AND REMEMBER
Raymond Lesikar
    Dow Jones Books
    Post Office Box 445
    Chicopee, Massachusetts 01021
Book. 1974. $9.95.

CALCULATORS
See: BUSINESS MACHINES

CALLIGRAPHY

Correspondence Courses

★ 405 ★
LETTERING
    Western Washington State College
    Center for Continuing Education
    Edens Hall South
    Bellingham, Washington 98225
Correspondence course.

Printed Materials

★ 406 ★
CALLIGRAPHIC LETTERING
Ralph Douglass
    Watson-Guptill Publications Incorporated
    2160 Patterson Street
    Cincinnati, Ohio 45214
Book. 1975. $7.95.

★ 407 ★
IRENE WELLINGTON COPY BOOK: A HOME
STUDY COURSE IN ITALIC HANDWRITING
    Pentalic
    132 West 22nd Street
    New York, New York 10011
Book. $3.95.

CAMBODIAN

Multimedia Kits

★ 408 ★
CAMBODIAN - BASIC COURSE
    General Services Administration
    Foreign Service Institute Language Course
    National Audiovisual Center
    Order Section RR
    Washington, D.C. 20409
Audio tapes, cassettes and text available. Approximately $250.00.

★ 409 ★
CONTEMPORARY CAMBODIAN - INTRODUCTION
    General Services Administration
    Foreign Service Institute Language Course
    National Audiovisual Center
    Order Section RR
    Washington, D.C. 20409
Audio tapes, cassettes and text available. Approximately $250.00.

CANTONESE

Multimedia Kits

★ 410 ★
CANTONESE - BASIC COURSE
    General Services Administration
    Foreign Service Institute Language Course
    National Audiovisual Center
    Order Section RR
    Washington, D.C. 20409
Audio tapes, cassettes and text available. Approximately $200.00.

CARD PUNCH
See: BUSINESS MACHINES

CAREER PLANNING

See also: Vocational Guidance

Audio Cassettes/Tapes

★ 411 ★
CAREER EDUCATION: IMPLICATIONS FOR TRAINING
     Development Digest Incorporated
     3347 Motor Avenue
     Los Angeles, California 90034
Cassette tape. $13.75.

★ 412 ★
CAREER PLANNING FOR MEN
     Jaine Carter Personnel Development Incorporated
     112 West Garden Avenue
     Palatine, Illinois 60067
Cassette workbook program.

★ 413 ★
CAREER PLANNING FOR WOMEN
     Jaine Carter Personnel Development Incorporated
     112 West Garden Avenue
     Palatine, Illinois 60067
Cassette workbook program.

★ 414 ★
GETTING A JOB
     Thompson-Mitchell and Associates
     3384 Peachtree Road Northeast
     Atlanta, Georgia 30326
12 cassettes. $131.00.

★ 415 ★
HOW TO LOCATE AND LAND A BETTER JOB
     Tape Rental Library Incorporated
     Post Office Box 2107
     2507 Edna Drive
     South Vineland, New Jersey 08360
Cassette. $9.98.

★ 416 ★
THE LANGUAGE OF WORK "CROSS-VOCATIONAL
SKILLS AND INFO"
     Thompson-Mitchell and Associates
     3384 Peachtree Road Northeast
     Atlanta, Georgia 30326
15 cassettes with workbooks. $175.00.

★ 417 ★
SUCCESSFUL RETIREMENT
Paul W. Schuette
     Tape Rental Library Incorporated
     Post Office Box 2107
     2507 Edna Drive
     South Vineland, New Jersey 08360
Cassette. $7.95.

Correspondence Courses

★ 418 ★
PREPARATION FOR RETIREMENT
     University of Kansas
     Division of Continuing Education
     Lawrence, Kansas 66045
Home study program.

Multimedia Kits

★ 419 ★
CAREER AWARENESS FOR WOMEN
     Instructional Dynamics Incorporated
     450 East Ohio Street
     Chicago, Illinois 60611
Multimedia training program. $79.50.

★ 420 ★
CAREER PLANNING FOR MANAGERS
     Lansford Publishing Company
     Post Office Box 8711
     San Jose, California 95155
Multimedia kit. $149.95.

Programmed Learning Materials

★ 421 ★
WRITING RESUMES, LOCATING JOBS AND
HANDLING JOB INTERVIEWS
Michael Freeman
     Learning Systems Company
     1818 Ridge Road
     Homewood, Illinois 60430
Programmed learning aid. $3.95.

CARPENTRY

See also: Wood Working

Correspondence Courses

★ 422 ★

CARPENTER BUILDER COURSE
        International Correspondence School
        Scranton, Pennsylvania 18515
Multi-module correspondence course.

★ 423 ★

CARPENTRY AND MILL WORK
        International Correspondence School
        Scranton, Pennsylvania 18515
Multi-module correspondence course.

CASHIERING

See also: Retailing

Audio Cassettes/Tapes

★ 424 ★

MODERN CASHIERING MADE EASY
        Thompson-Mitchell and Associates
        3384 Peachtree Road Northeast
        Atlanta, Georgia 30326
Cassette. $25.00.

Films/Video/Filmstrips

★ 425 ★

CASHIERING: MONEY TRANSACTIONS
        National Restaurant Association
        One IBM Plaza, Suite 2600
        Chicago, Illinois 60611
Film cartridge. $60.00.

★ 426 ★

HANDLING CHECKS
        National Restaurant Association
        One IBM Plaza, Suite 2600
        Chicago, Illinois 60611
8 mm, 16 mm or video cartridge, study guide.
$190.00.

★ 427 ★

HANDLING CREDIT CARDS
        National Restaurant Association
        One IBM Plaza, Suite 2600
        Chicago, Illinois 60611
8 mm, 16 mm or video cartridge, study guide.
$190.00.

★ 428 ★

HANDLING MONEY
        National Restaurant Association
        One IBM Plaza, Suite 2600
        Chicago, Illinois 60611
8 mm, 16 mm or video cartridge, study guide.
$190.00.

★ 429 ★

REGISTER TRAINING
        Thompson-Mitchell and Associates
        3384 Peachtree Road Northeast
        Atlanta, Georgia 30326
Filmstrip. $95.00.

CERAMICS

Films/Video/Filmstrips

★ 430 ★

CONSTRUCTING RAKU KILN
        Scope Productions Incorporated
        Post Office Box 5515
        Fresno, California 93755
3 films (8 mm) and student guides. $63.00.

★ 431 ★

CONSTRUCTING RAKU POTTERY
        Scope Productions Incorporated
        Post Office Box 5515
        Fresno, California 93755
6 films (8 mm) and student guides. $126.00.

CERTIFIED PUBLIC ACCOUNTING (CPA)

Audio Cassettes/Tapes

★ 432 ★

PASS THE CPA EXAM
        Total Tape
        Post Office Box 372
        Columbia, Maryland 21045
60 hours of cassettes, 1,005 pages of workbook.
$320.00.

★ 433 ★
STARTING A CPA PRACTICE
        American Institute of Certified Public
            Accountants
        1211 Avenue of the Americas
        New York, New York 10003
Cassette and workbook. $30.00.

Correspondence Courses

★ 434 ★
CPA REVIEW
        La Salle Extension University
        417 South Dearborn Street
        Chicago, Illinois 60605
Correspondence course.

Printed Materials

★ 435 ★
CPA BUSINESS LAW REVIEW
Edmund F. Ficek
        Charles E. Merrill Publishing Company
        1300 Alum Creek Drive
        Box 508
        Columbus, Ohio 43216
Text with exams and answers.   1977. $16.95.

★ 436 ★
CPA REVIEW MANUAL
Herbert Miller, George Mead
        Prentice-Hall Incorporated
        Englewood Cliffs, New Jersey 07632
Book. 1972. $21.95.

CHEMICAL OPERATIONS

Correspondence Courses

★ 437 ★
CHEMICAL ENGINEERING
        International Correspondence School
        Scranton, Pennsylvania 18515
Multi-module correspondence course.

★ 438 ★
CHEMICAL ENGINEERING TECHNOLOGY
        International Correspondence School
        Scranton, Pennsylvania 18515
Multi-module correspondence course.

★ 439 ★
CHEMICAL LABORATORY TECHNICIAN
        International Correspondence School
        Scranton, Pennsylvania 18515
Multi-module correspondence course.

Programmed Learning Materials

★ 440 ★
COLORIMETER OPERATION
        E. I. du Pont de Nemours and Company
        Applied Technology Division
        Room B 4204
        Wilmington, Delaware 19898
Programmed course of approximately 16 hours.
$28.00.

★ 441 ★
INORGANIC CHEMISTRY FOR PLANT OPERATORS
        E. I. du Pont de Nemours and Company
        Applied Technology Division
        Room B 4204
        Wilmington, Delaware 19898
Programmed course of approximately 10 hours.
$18.80.

★ 442 ★
INTRODUCTION TO CHOMATOGRAPHY
        E. I. du Pont de Nemours and Company
        Applied Technology Division
        Room B 4204
        Wilmington, Delaware 19898
Programmed course of approximately 16 hours.
$28.00.

★ 443 ★
PRACTICAL DISTILLATION
        E. I. du Pont de Nemours and Company
        Applied Technology Division
        Room B 4204
        Wilmington, Delaware 19898
Programmed course of approximately 8 hours.
$15.60.

★ 444 ★
PRINCIPLES OF DISTILLATION
        E. I. du Pont de Nemours and Company
        Applied Technology Division
        Room B 4204
        Wilmington, Delaware 19898
Programmed course of approximately 6 hours.
$12.70.

★ 445 ★
TITRATION AND ITS GLASSWARE
    E. I. du Pont de Nemours and Company
    Applied Technology Division
    Room B 4204
    Wilmington, Delaware 19898
Programmed course of approximately 3 hours. $7.40.

CHEMISTRY

Audio Cassettes/Tapes

★ 446 ★
CHEMICAL BITS IN THE LABORATORY
Wanda Sterner, Wendell Markham
    Charles E. Merrill Publishing Company
    1300 Alum Creek Drive
    Box 508
    Columbus, Ohio 43216
Lab manual and cassettes. $130.00.

★ 447 ★
CHEMISTRY
    Thompson-Mitchell and Associates
    3384 Peachtree Road Northeast
    Atlanta, Georgia 30326
Cassettes. $9.98.

★ 448 ★
CHEMISTRY: AN AUDIO-TUTORIAL APPROACH
W. W. Wendlandt, D. Barry, R. A. Geangel
    Charles E. Merrill Publishing Company
    1300 Alum Creek Drive
    Box 508
    Columbus, Ohio 43216
Workbooks and cassettes. $12.00.

Correspondence Courses

★ 449 ★
CHEMICAL SCIENCE
    University of Washington
    Office of Independent Study
    222 Lewis Hall DW-30
    Seattle, Washington 98195
Correspondence course.

★ 450 ★
GENERAL CHEMISTRY
    International Correspondence School
    Scranton, Pennsylvania 18515
Multi-module correspondence course.

★ 451 ★
GENERAL CHEMISTRY
    University of Washington
    Office of Independent Study
    222 Lewis Hall DW-30
    Seattle, Washington 98195
Correspondence course.

Programmed Learning Materials

★ 452 ★
NAMES AND STRUCTURES OF ORGANIC
COMPOUNDS
Otto Benfey
    John Wiley and Sons Incorporated
    605 Third Avenue
    New York, New York 10016
Programmed text. $6.25.

CHINESE

Audio Cassettes/Tapes

★ 453 ★
MODERN CHINESE: A BASIC COURSE
Peking University Faculty
    Dover Publications Incorporated
    180 Varick Street
    New York, New York 10014
Record and book. $12.50.

Printed Materials

★ 454 ★
MANDARIN MADE EASY
Chaing Ker Chiu
    S F Book Imports
    Post Office Box 526
    San Francisco, California 94101
Book. $7.50.

★ 455 ★
TEACH YOURSELF CHINESE
W. R. Williamson
    David McKay Company Incorporated
    750 Third Avenue
    New York, New York 10017
Book. $3.95.

CHINYANJA

Multimedia Kits

★ 456 ★
CHINYANJA - BASIC COURSE
General Services Administration
Foreign Service Institute Language Course
National Audiovisual Center
Order Section RR
Washington, D.C. 20409
Audio tapes, cassettes and text available. Approximately $100.00.

CINEMATOGRAPHY

Printed Materials

★ 457 ★
HOW TO MAKE A GOOD SOUND MOVIE
Eastman Kodak Company
343 State Street
Rochester, New York 14650
Book. 1973. $2.50.

★ 458 ★
PRINCIPLES OF CINEMATOGRAPHY
Leslie Wheeler
Morgan and Morgan Incorporated
145 Palisades Street
Dobbs Ferry, New York 10522
Book. $16.00.

CIVIL ENGINEERING

See also: Engineering

Correspondence Courses

★ 459 ★
CIVIL ENGINEERING
Pennsylvania State University
Department of Independent Study by
Correspondence
Three Sheilds Building
University Park, Pennsylvania 16802
Correspondence course.

★ 460 ★
CIVIL ENGINEERING TECHNOLOGY
International Correspondence School
Scranton, Pennsylvania 18515
Multi-module correspondence course.

Printed Materials

★ 461 ★
AMERICAN CIVIL ENGINEERING PRACTICE
R. W. Abbett
John Wiley and Sons Incorporated
605 Third Avenue
New York, New York 10016
3 volumes. $36.75.

★ 462 ★
CIVIL ENGINEERING LICENSE REVIEW
Donald Newnan
Engineering Press
Post Office Box 5
San Jose, California 95103
Self-study text. $12.50.

CLAIM ADJUSTMENT

Correspondence Course

★ 463 ★
INSURANCE INVESTIGATION AND CLAIM
ADJUSTING
Universal Schools
1500 Cardinal Drive
Little Falls, New Jersey 07424
Correspondence course.

Programmed Learning Materials

★ 464 ★
A PROGRAMMED INSTRUCTION COURSE IN CLAIM
ADJUSTMENT
The Bekins Company
1335 South Figueroa Street
Los Angeles, California 90015
Programmed text.

CLASSROOM INSTRUCTION

See also: Training Techniques

Films/Video/Filmstrips

★ 465 ★
FOR TEACHERS AND AIDES TOGETHER--
RESPONSIBILITIES OF THE TEACHERS AND OF
THE AIDE
    Thompson-Mitchell and Associates
    3384 Peachtree Road Northeast
    Atlanta, Georgia 30326
Filmstrip. $55.00.

★ 466 ★
FOR TEACHERS ONLY - HOW CAN THE AIDE
BE OF MOST HELP
    Thompson-Mitchell and Associates
    3384 Peachtree Road Northeast
    Atlanta, Georgia 30326
Filmstrip. $55.00.

★ 467 ★
STRICTLY FOR THE AIDES - AN INTRODUCTION
TO THE CLASSROOM
    Thompson-Mitchell and Associates
    3384 Peachtree Road Northeast
    Atlanta, Georgia 30326
Filmstrip. $55.00.

★ 468 ★
THE SUBSTITUTE TEACHER - AN IDEA EXCHANGE
    Thompson-Mitchell and Associates
    3384 Peachtree Road Northeast
    Atlanta, Georgia 30326
Filmstrip. $55.00.

Multimedia Kits

★ 469 ★
CLASSROOM ARRANGEMENTS
    Addison Wesley Publishing Company Incorporated
    Jacob Way
    Reading, Massachusetts 01867
Filmstrip with cassette. $60.00.

★ 470 ★
ELEMENTS OF EFFECTIVE TEACHING
    Addison Wesley Publishing Company Incorporated
    Jacob Way
    Reading, Massachusetts 01867
5 filmstrips with cassettes. $260.00.

★ 471 ★
HANDLING CLASSROOM PROBLEMS
    Addison Wesley Publishing Company Incorporated
    Jacob Way
    Reading, Massachusetts 01867
Filmstrip with cassette. $60.00.

★ 472 ★
HOW TO USE VISUAL AIDS
    Addison Wesley Publishing Company Incorporated
    Jacob Way
    Reading, Massachusetts 01867
Filmstrip with cassette. $60.00.

★ 473 ★
INDIVIDUALIZED INSTRUCTION (Describes the
role of teacher and student)
    Thompson-Mitchell and Associates
    3384 Peachtree Road Northeast
    Atlanta, Georgia 30326
Filmstrip with audio cassette. $24.95.

★ 474 ★
LEARNER CONTROLLED INSTRUCTION
    Addison Wesley Publishing Company Incorporated
    Jacob Way
    Reading, Massachusetts 01867
Filmstrip with cassette. $60.00.

★ 475 ★
MANAGING CLASSROOM TIME
    Addison Wesley Publishing Company Incorporated
    Jacob Way
    Reading, Massachusetts 01867
Filmstrip with cassette. $60.00.

★ 476 ★
USING TEACHING MATERIALS
    Addison Wesley Publishing Company Incorporated
    Jacob Way
    Reading, Massachusetts 01867
Filmstrip with cassette. $60.00.

CLIMATOLOGY

Audio Cassettes/Tapes

★ 477 ★
WEATHER AROUND US
Richard A. Anthes
        Charles E. Merrill Publishing Company
        1300 Alum Creek Drive
        Box 508
        Columbus, Ohio   43216
Workbook and cassette. $140.00.

Printed Materials

★ 478 ★
CLIMATE WORKBOOK
Melvin Kazeck
        Stipes Publishing Company
        Ten Chester Street
        Champaign, Illinois   61820
Workbook. $2.60.

★ 479 ★
CLIMATOLOGY: FUNDAMENTALS AND
APPLICATIONS
John Mather
        McGraw-Hill Book Company
        1221 Avenue of the Americas
        New York, New York   10036
Book. $13.95.

★ 480 ★
A SHORT COURSE IN CLOUD PHYSICS
R. R. Rogers, et al.
        Pergamon Press Incorporated
        Maxwell House
        Fairview Park
        Elmsford, New York   10523
Book.   1975. $14.50.

CLOCK AND WATCH REPAIR

Printed Materials

★ 481 ★
ADVANCED WATCH AND CLOCK REPAIR
H. G. Harris
        Emerson Books Incorporated
        Reynolds Lane
        Buchanan, New York   10511
Book.   1973. $7.95.

★ 482 ★
HOW TO BUILD CLOCKS AND WATCHES
Byron Wels
        Mason/Charter
        641 Lexington Avenue
        New York, New York   10022
Book. $5.95.

★ 483 ★
MODERN WATCH AND CLOCK REPAIRING
P. Buford Harris
        Nelson-Hall Publishers
        325 West Jackson Boulevard
        Chicago, Illinois   60606
Text. $10.95.

★ 484 ★
PRACTICAL CLOCK REPAIRING
Don DeCarle
        Wehman Brothers Incorporated
        Ridgedale Avenue
        Cedar Knolls, New Jersey   07927
Book. $9.95.

★ 485 ★
PRACTICAL WATCH ADJUSTING
Don DeCarle
        Wehman Brothers Incorporated
        Ridgedale Avenue
        Cedar Knolls, New Jersey   07927
Book. $5.95.

★ 486 ★
WATCH AND CLOCK: MAKING AND REPAIR
Gazeley
        Transatlantic Arts Incorporated
        North Village Green
        Levittown, New York   11756
Book.   1974. $18.00.

COACHING

Printed Materials

★ 487 ★
THE PRINCIPLES AND PROBLEMS OF COACHING
John Massengale
        Charles C. Thomas, Publishers
        301-327 East Lawrence Avenue
        Springfield, Illinois 62717
Book.   1975. $11.95.

★ 488 ★
SCIENTIFIC PRINCIPLES OF COACHING
John Bunn
　　　Prentice-Hall Incorporated
　　　Englewood Cliffs, New Jersey 07632
Book. 1972. $11.95.

COBOL
See: COMPUTER LANGUAGES

COLLECTIVE BARGAINING

See also: Arbitration; Labor Relations

Correspondence Courses

★ 489 ★
COLLECTIVE BARGAINING
　　　University of Florida
　　　Division of Continuing Education
　　　3012 West University Avenue
　　　Gainesville, Florida 32603
Correspondence course.

Printed Materials

★ 490 ★
PRACTICE OF COLLECTIVE BARGAINING
Edwin Beal
　　　Richard D. Irwin Incorporated
　　　1818 Ridge Road
　　　Homewood, Illinois 60430
Book. 1976. $14.95.

COMEDY WRITING
See: WRITING, COMEDY

COMMERCE

Printed Materials

★ 491 ★
COMMERCE
Ronald Warson
　　　David McKay Company Incorporated
　　　750 Third Avenue
　　　New York, New York 10017
Self-study text. 1975. $3.95.

★ 492 ★
PRACTICAL COMMERCE
J. B. King
　　　Pergamon Press Incorporated
　　　Maxwell House
　　　Fairview Park
　　　Elmsford, New York 10523
Book. 1970. $3.65.

COMMERCIAL ART
See: ART

COMMERCIAL LAW
See: BUSINESS LAW

COMMUNICATION

See also: Communication, Oral;
Communication, Written; Listening;
Non-Verbal Communication

Audio Cassettes/Tapes

★ 493 ★
THE ART AND SKILL OF TALKING WITH PEOPLE
Hugh P. Fellows
　　　Tape Rental Library Incorporated
　　　Post Office Box 2107
　　　2507 Edna Drive
　　　South Vineland, New Jersey 08360
Cassette.

★ 494 ★
BETTER COMMUNICATIONS
　　　Tape Rental Library Incorporated
　　　Post Office Box 2107
　　　2507 Edna Drive
　　　South Vineland, New Jersey 08360
Cassette.

★ 495 ★
COMMUNICATING BOTH WAYS
　　　American Management Associations
　　　135 West 50th Street
　　　New York, New York 10020
Cassette. $18.00.

★ 496 ★
COMMUNICATING FOR PROFIT
Management Resources Incorporated
757 Third Avenue
New York, New York 10017
2 audio cassettes and workbooks. $49.95.

★ 497 ★
EXECUTIVE WRITING, SPEAKING AND LISTENING SKILLS
American Management Associations
135 West 50th Street
New York, New York 10020
6 cassettes with workbook. $100.00.

★ 498 ★
GETTING BETTER RESULTS WITH BETTER TALKING SKILLS
Thompson-Mitchell and Associates
3384 Peachtree Road Northeast
Atlanta, Georgia 30326
Cassette. $15.00.

★ 499 ★
INTRODUCTION TO INTERPERSONAL COMMUNICATIONS
Training House Incorporated
Box 688
Binghamton, New York 13902
Cassette with workbook. $36.00.

★ 500 ★
MANAGERIAL COMMUNICATIONS
Dr. John R. Van De Water
Van De Water Associates
7914 Jason Avenue
Canoga Park, California 91304
Cassette with workbook. $23.50.

★ 501 ★
PRINCIPLES OF PERSONAL COMMUNICATION
Thompson-Mitchell and Associates
3384 Peachtree Road Northeast
Atlanta, Georgia 30326
Cassette. $9.95.

★ 502 ★
TERMINOLOGY AND THE COMMUNICATIONS PROBLEM
Tape Rental Library Incorporated
Post Office Box 2107
2507 Edna Drive
South Vineland, New Jersey 08360
Cassette.

★ 503 ★
WHAT'S NEW IN COMMUNICATIONS: A PERSONAL APPROACH TO SOME IMPERSONAL MEDIA
Development Digest Incorporated
3347 Motor Avenue
Los Angeles, California 90034
Cassette. $13.75.

Correspondence Courses

★ 504 ★
INTERPERSONAL COMMUNICATION
Ergonco Performance Source
Northwest O'Hare Office Park, Suite 119
2474 Dempster Street
Des Plains, Illinois 60016
Self-study program.

Films/Video/Filmstrips

★ 505 ★
COMMUNICATION (A program designed for health professionals)
Telstar Productions Incorporated
366 North Prior Avenue
Saint Paul, Minnesota 55104
24 video tape lessons. $250.00 each.

★ 506 ★
COMMUNICATION FEEDBACK
BNA Communications Incorporated
9401 Decoverly Hall Road
Rockville, Maryland 20850
Film.

★ 507 ★
COMMUNICATIONS AND LEARNING
Addison Wesley Publishing Company
    Incorporated
Jacob Way
Reading, Massachusetts 01867
Filmstrip. $55.00.

★ 508 ★
DESK TO DESK (Effective communication with peers)
Thompson-Mitchell and Associates
3384 Peachtree Road Northeast
Atlanta, Georgia 30326
Filmstrip (16 mm). $250.00.

★ 509 ★

WHAT DO YOU MEAN, WHAT DO I MEAN?
(Case studies in communication)
      Salenger Educational Media
      1635 12th Street
      Santa Monica, California 90404
Film, guide and worksheets. $365.00 (rental available.

Games/Simulations

★ 510 ★

COMMUNICATING FOR RESULTS
      Didactic Systems Incorporated
      Box 457
      Cranford, New Jersey 07016
Simulation game. $24.00.

★ 511 ★

THE COMMUNICATION GAME
      Training House Incorporated
      Box 688
      Binghamton, New York 13902
Simulation game. $60.00.

Multimedia Kits

★ 512 ★

BARRIERS TO COMMUNICATING
      Resources for Education and Management
        Incorporated
      544 Medlock Road, Suite 210
      Decatur, Georgia 30030
Filmstrip with cassette. $60.00.

★ 513 ★

CAPITALIZING ON GROUP DYNAMICS
      Resources for Education and Management
        Incorporated
      544 Medlock Road, Suite 210
      Decatur, Georgia 30030
Filmstrip with cassette. $70.00.

★ 514 ★

COMMUNICATION
      Lansford Publishing Company
      Post Office Box 8711
      San Jose, California 95155
Multimedia kit. $110.00.

★ 515 ★

EFFECTIVE GROUP COMMUNICATING
      Resources for Education and Management
        Incorporated
      544 Medlock Road, Suite 210
      Decatur, Georgia 30030
Filmstrip with cassette. $60.00.

★ 516 ★

GENERAL PRINCIPLES OF COMMUNICATING
      Resources for Education and Management
        Incorporated
      544 Medlock Road, Suite 210
      Decatur, Georgia 30030
Filmstrip with cassette. $60.00.

★ 517 ★

HOW TO DISAGREE AGREEABLY
      Resources for Education and Management
        Incorporated
      544 Medlock Road, Suite 210
      Decatur, Georgia 30030
Filmstrip with cassette. $60.00.

★ 518 ★

IMPROVING COMMUNICATION
      Thompson-Mitchell and Associates
      3384 Peachtree Road, Northeast
      Atlanta, Georgia 30326
Filmstrip with cassette. $75.00.

★ 519 ★

IMPROVING YOUR COMMUNICATION SKILLS
      Resources for Education and Management
        Incorporated
      544 Medlock Road, Suite 210
      Decatur, Georgia 30030
Filmstrip with cassette. $60.00.

★ 520 ★

INTERPERSONAL COMMUNICATIONS
      XICOM
      Sterling Forest
      Tuxedo, New York 10987
Multimedia learning program.

Printed Materials

★ 521 ★

EFFECTIVE COMMUNICATIONS
      Didactic System Incorporated
      Box 457
      Cranford, New Jersey 07016
Self-study text. $9.00.

★ 522 ★
FUNCTIONAL BUSINESS COMMUNICATION
Jessamon Dawe, William Lord
         Prentice-Hall Incorporated
         Englewood Cliffs, New Jersey 07632
Book. 1974. $12.95.

★ 523 ★
I SPEAK YOUR LANGUAGE
         Management Resources Incorporated
         757 Third Avenue
         New York, New York 10017
Survey and workbook. $13.95.

Programmed Learning Materials

★ 524 ★
HOW TO SAY WHAT YOU MEAN
         AMACOM
         American Management Associations
         135 West 50th Street
         New York, New York 10020
Programmed text. $15.00.

COMMUNICATION, ORAL

See also: Public Speaking

Audio Cassettes/Tapes

★ 525 ★
THE ART OF CONVERSATION
         Educational Century Programming
         1201 East Johnson Street
         Jonesboro, Arkansas 72401
Cassette. $6.00.

★ 526 ★
THE COMMUNICATING SKILLS SERIES
         Addison Wesley Publishing Company
             Incorporated
         Jacob Way
         Reading, Massachusetts 01867
6 cassettes with leaders guide. $65.00.

★ 527 ★
COMMUNICATION THROUGH HUMOR
Dave Yoho
         Tape Rental Library Incorporated
         Post Office Box 2107
         2507 Edna Drive
         South Vineland, New Jersey 08360
Cassette. $9.95.

★ 528 ★
EFFECTIVE SPEAKING FOR MANAGERS
Robert L. Montgomery
         American Management Associations
         135 West 50th Street
         New York, New York 10020
Cassette and guide. $80.00.

★ 529 ★
STORY IDEAS AROUND YOU
Art Fettig
         Tape Rental Library Incorporated
         Post Office Box 2107
         2507 Edna Drive
         South Vineland, New Jersey 08360
Cassette. $8.35.

Films/Video/Filmstrips

★ 530 ★
APPLAUSE! SEVEN STEPS TO EFFECTIVE SPEECH
         Cally Curtis Company
         1111 North Palmas
         Hollywood, California 90038
Film.

★ 531 ★
PERSON TO PERSON COMMUNICATION
         Roundtable Films
         113 North San Vincente Boulevard
         Beverly Hills, California 90211
Film and guidebook.

Multimedia Kits

★ 532 ★
IMPROVING PERSONAL COMMUNICATIONS
         Resources for Education and Management
             Incorporated
         544 Medlock Road, Suite 210
         Decatur, Georgia 30030
Filmstrip with cassette. $60.00.

★ 533 ★
SPEAKING FOR THE LISTENER
         Resources for Education and Management
             Incorporated
         544 Medlock Road, Suite 210
         Decatur, Georgia 30030
Filmstrip with cassette. $55.00.

Printed Materials

★ 534 ★
FACE TO FACE COMMUNCATION
Thomas Anastasi
> General Electric Company Training and
> Education Publications
> One River Road
> Box BP
> Schenectady, New York 12345
Book. 1974. $5.00.

★ 535 ★
HOW TO MANAGE YOUR SPEAKING
Thomas Anastasi
> General Electric Company Training and
> Education Publications
> One River Road
> Box BP
> Schenectady, New York 12345
Book. 1974. $5.00.

★ 536 ★
HOW TO SAY WHAT YOU MEAN
> American Management Associations
> 135 West 50th Street
> New York, New York 10020
Self-study workbook with tests. $20.00.

★ 537 ★
LEARNING TO SPEAK EFFECTIVELY
James Cox
> Baker Book House
> 1019 Wealthy Street Southeast
> Grand Rapids, Michigan 49506
Book. 1974. $.95.

★ 538 ★
A PROGRAM ON THE PROCESS OF
COMMUNICATION
Thomas King
> Charles E. Merrill Company
> 1300 Alum Creek Drive
> Columbus, Ohio 43216
Book. 1972. $2.50.

★ 539 ★
SKILLS FOR EFFECTIVE COMMUNICATION: A
GUIDE TO BUILDING RELATIONSHIPS
Raphael Becvar
> John Wiley and Sons Incorporated
> 605 Third Avenue
> New York, New York 10016
Self teaching text. 1974. $4.95.

COMMUNICATION, WRITTEN

See also: Business Letters; Business
Writing; Journalism

Audio Cassettes/Tapes

★ 540 ★
CORRESPONDENCE AND REPORTS/BETTER ENGLISH
AND CORRESPONDENCE
> Educational Century Programming
> 1201 East Johnson Street
> Jonesboro, Arkansas 72401
Cassette. $6.00.

★ 541 ★
DEVELOPING HUMAN RELATIONS/BETTER ENGLISH
AND CORRESPONDENCE
> Educational Century Programming
> 1201 East Johnson Street
> Jonesboro, Arkansas 72401
Cassette. $6.00.

★ 542 ★
HOW THEY WRITE COPY
> Tape Rental Library Incorporated
> Post Office Box 2107
> 2507 Edna Drive
> South Vineland, New Jersey 08360
Cassette. $32.00.

★ 543 ★
HOW TO WRITE EFFECTIVELY
> Tape Rental Library Incorporated
> Post Office Box 2107
> 2507 Edna Drive
> South Vineland, New Jersey 08360
Cassette. $9.98.

★ 544 ★
HOW TO WRITE WORKABLE PLANS AND
PROCEDURES
> Thompson-Mitchell and Associates
> 3384 Peachtree Road Northeast
> Atlanta, Georgia 30326
Cassette. $15.00.

★ 545 ★
IS WRITING FOR YOU
Art Fettig
> Tape Rental Library Incorporated
> Post Office Box 2107
> 2507 Edna Drive
> South Vineland, New Jersey 03360
Cassette. $8.35.

★ 546 ★
PUNCTUATION
  National Book Company
  1019 Southwest Tenth Avenue
  Portland, Oregon 97206
3 cassettes. $46.00.

★ 547 ★
THE WINNING WORDS OF WILBUR POE (How
to put more "Sell" into your letters)
  Close Productions
  2020 San Carlos Boulevard
  Fort Myers Beach, Florida 33931
6 cassettes. $34.50.

★ 548 ★
WRITING GUIDE
  Thompson-Mitchell and Associates
  3384 Peachtree Road Northeast
  Atlanta, Georgia 30326
Cassette. $9.98.

★ 549 ★
WRITING MORE EFFECTIVE LETTERS, MEMOS,
AND REPORTS
  Training House Incorporated
  Box 688
  Binghamton, New York 13902
Cassette and workbook. $36.00.

★ 550 ★
WRITING SKILLS
Virginia Underwood, Merriellyn Kett
  Charles E. Merrill Publishing Company
  1300 Alum Creek Drive
  Box 508
  Columbus, Ohio 43216
Text and cassettes. $130.00.

Correspondence Courses

★ 551 ★
IMPROVING YOUR WRITTEN COMMUNICATIONS
  Society of Manufacturing Engineers
  20501 Ford Road
  Post Office Box 930
  Dearborn, Michigan 48128
5 hours self instruction course. $10.00.

Films/Video/Filmstrips

★ 552 ★
EFFECTIVE WRITING
Harold J. Alford
  Telstar Productions Incorporated
  366 North Prior Avenue
  Saint Paul, Minnesota 55104
10 video tape lessons. $2,200.00.

★ 553 ★
LETTER WRITING AT WORK
  Roundtable Films
  113 North San Vincente Boulevard
  Beverly Hills, California 90211
Film and guidebook.

★ 554 ★
NOW THAT'S A REPORT
  Roundtable Films
  113 North San Vincente Boulevard
  Beverly Hills, California 90211
Film and guidebook.

★ 555 ★
WRITING LETTERS THAT GET RESULTS
  Roundtable Films
  113 North San Vincente Boulevard
  Beverly Hills, California 90211
Film and guidebook.

Games/Simulations

★ 556 ★
ACHIEVING RESULTS WITH WORDS
  Society of Manufacturing Engineers
  20501 Ford Road
  Post Office Box 930
  Dearborn, Michigan 48128
Simulation with correspondent feedback. $110.00.

Multimedia Kits

★ 557 ★
HOW TO WRITE EFFECTIVE REPORTS
  Resources for Education and Management
   Incorporated
  544 Medlock Road, Suite 210
  Decatur, Georgia 30030
Filmstrip with cassette. $55.00.

★ 558 ★
PUT IT IN WRITING
     Industrial Writing Institute
     Hanna Building
     Cleveland, Ohio 44115
Cassettes, slides and workbook.

★ 559 ★
WRITING EFFECTIVE LETTERS, MEMOS AND
REPORTS
     Ergonco Performance Source
     Northwest O'Hare Office Park, Suite 119
     2474 Dempster Street
     Des Plains, Illinois 60016
Multimedia self-study program.

Printed Materials

★ 560 ★
HOW TO MANAGE YOUR WRITING
Thomas Anastasi
     General Electric Company Training and
        Education Publications
     One River Road
     Box BP
     Schenectady, New York 12345
Book. 1974. $5.00.

★ 561 ★
HOW TO WRITE FOR THE WORLD OF WORK
Thomas Pearsall, Donald Cunningham
     Professional Book Distributors
     Post Office Box 4892
     Columbus, Ohio 43202
Training book. $12.75.

★ 562 ★
IMPROVING YOUR WRITTEN COMMUNICATION
     Preston Publishing Company
     151 East 50th Street
     New York, New York 10022
Book. $11.00.

★ 563 ★
LET'S COMMUNICATE: A SELF HELP PROGRAM
ON WRITING LETTERS AND MEMOS
George Martin
     Addison Wesley Publishing Company Incorporated
     Jacob Way
     Reading, Massachusetts 01867
Book. 1970. $5.95.

COMMUNITY HEALTH
See: HEALTH, COMMUNITY

COMPUTER LANGUAGES

Printed Materials

★ 564 ★
ALGOL 60 AND FORTRAN IV
     John Wiley and Sons Incorporated
     605 Third Avenue
     New York, New York 10016
Book. 1974. $4.95.

★ 565 ★
BASIC "BASIC" PROGRAMMING: SELF
INSTRUCTIONAL MANUAL AND TEXT
Anthony Peluso
     Addison Wesley Publishing Company Incorporated
     Jacob Way
     Reading, Massachusetts 01867
Book. 1971. $8.95.

★ 566 ★
BASIC IN CHEMISTRY: A SELF INSTRUCTIONAL
COMPUTING COURSE
G. Beech
     International Publications Service
     114 East 32nd Street
     New York, New York 10016
Book. 1976. $7.50.

★ 567 ★
FORTRAN IV
Jehosua Friedmann, Philip Greenberg, Alan
Hoffberg
     John Wiley and Sons
     605 Third Avenue
     New York, New York 10016
Book. $5.95.

★ 568 ★
INTRODUCTION TO ALGOL
F. L. Bauer
     Prentice-Hall Incorporated
     Englewood Cliffs, New Jersey 07632
Book. $10.75.

★ 569 ★
AN INTRODUCTION TO ALGOL
F. R. Watson
      Transatlantic Arts Incorporated
      North Village Green
      Levittown, New York 11756
Book. 1976. $7.50.

★ 570 ★
INTRODUCTION TO ALGOL PROGRAMMING
Torgil Ekman, Carl Froberg
      Oxford University Press
      16-00 Pollitt Drive
      Fair Lawn, New Jersey 07410
Book. $10.95.

★ 571 ★
INTRODUCTION TO ALGOL 60
Christian Andersen
      Addison Wesley Publishing Company Incorporated
      Jacob Way
      Reading, Massachusetts 01867
Book. $4.50.

★ 572 ★
INTRODUCTION TO COMPUTER PROGRAMMING
FOR BIOLOGICAL SCIENTISTS
Howard Orr
      Allyn and Bacon Incorporated
      Rockleigh, New Jersey 07647
Book. 1973. $8.95.

★ 573 ★
INTRODUCTION TO DATA PROCESSING AND
COBOL
T. M. Wendel, W. H. Williams
      McGraw-Hill Book Company
      1221 Avenue of the Americas
      New York, New York 10019
Text and guide. $18.00.

★ 574 ★
LEARNING BASIC FAST
Claude De Rossi
      Reston Publishing Company
      Distributed by Prentice Hall
      Englewood Cliffs, New Jersey 07632
Book. 1974. $8.95.

★ 575 ★
SIMULATION WITH GPSS AND GPSSR
P. A. Bobillier
      Prentice-Hall Incorporated
      Englewood Cliffs, New Jersey 07632
Book. 1976. $18.50.

Programmed Learning Materials

★ 576 ★
ANS COBOL
Ruth Ashley
      John Wiley and Sons
      605 Third Avenue
      New York, New York 10016
Programmed text. 242 pages. $4.95.

★ 577 ★
BASIC FOR PERSONAL COMPUTERS
Robert Albrecht, Le Roy Finkel, Jerald Brown
      John Wiley and Sons
      605 Third Avenue
      New York, New York 10016
Programmed text.

★ 578 ★
BASIC PROGRAMMING LANGUAGE
Allen H. Brady, James Richardson
      Learning Systems Company
      1818 Ridge Road
      Homewood, Illinois 60430
Programmed learning aid. $3.95.

★ 579 ★
COBOL: A FIRST COURSE
Richard Lott
      Learning Systems Company
      1818 Ridge Road
      Homewood, Illinois 60430
Programmed learning aid. $4.95.

★ 580 ★
FORTRAN: A BEGINNER'S APPROACH
Daniel Couger, Loren E. Shannon
      Learning Systems Company
      1818 Ridge Road
      Homewood, Illinois 60430
Programmed learning aid. $4.50.

★ 581 ★
FORTRAN FOUR: A PROGRAMMED APPROACH
Daniel Couger, Loren Shannon
        Richard D. Irwin Incorporated
        1818 Ridge Road
        Homewood, Illinois 60430
Programmed instruction. 1976. $8.50.

★ 582 ★
JOB CONTROL LANGUAGE
Ruth Ashley, Judi Fernandez
        John Wiley and Sons
        605 Third Avenue
        New York, New York 10016
Programmed text.

COMPUTERS

See also: Business Machines; Data
                Processing

Audio Cassettes/Tapes

★ 583 ★
BIT SLICE (Microprocessors)
        Sybex Incorporated
        2020 Milvia Street
        Berkeley, California 94704
Text and cassettes. $49.95.

★ 584 ★
COMPUTER FUNDAMENTALS FOR THE MANAGER
        American Management Associations
        135 West 50th Street
        New York, New York 10020
Cassettes and workbook. $100.00.

★ 585 ★
INDUSTRIAL MICROPROCESSOR SYSTEM
        Sybex Incorporated
        2020 Milvia Street
        Berkeley, California 94704
Text and cassettes. $49.95.

★ 586 ★
INTRODUCTION TO MICROPROCESSORS
        Sybex Incorporated
        2020 Milvia Street
        Berkeley, California 94704
Text and 2 cassettes. $29.95.

★ 587 ★
INTRODUCTION TO PERSONAL COMPUTING
        Sybex Incorporated
        2020 Milvia Street
        Berkeley, California 94704
Cassette and text. $14.95.

★ 588 ★
MICROPROCESSOR INTERFACING
        Sybex Incorporated
        2020 Milvia Street
        Berkeley, California 94704
Text and cassettes. $49.95.

★ 589 ★
MICROPROCESSORS
        Sybex Incorporated
        2020 Milvia Street
        Berkeley, California 94704
Text and cassettes. $59.95.

★ 590 ★
MILITARY (Severe Environment) MICROPROCESSOR
SYSTEMS
        Sybex Incorporated
        2020 Milvia Street
        Berkeley, California 94704
Text and cassettes. $49.95.

★ 591 ★
PROGRAMMING MICROPROCESSORS
        Sybex Incorporated
        2020 Milvia Street
        Berkeley, California 94704
Text and 2 cassettes. $29.95.

Correspondence Courses

★ 592 ★
COMPUTER TECHNOLOGY
        Electronics Technical Institute
        1500 Cardinal Drive
        Little Falls, New Jersey 07424
Correspondence course.

Films/Video/Filmstrips

★ 593 ★
MAKING IT COUNT (A course in hardware and soft-
ware fundamentals, computer language and programming logic)
        Boeing Computer Services Company
        Post Office Box 24346
        Seattle Washington 98124
Video tape lessons. $6,495.00 per set.

Games/Simulations

★ 594 ★
SYSTEMS AND INFORMATION MANAGEMENT
      Society of Manufacturing Engineers
      20501 Ford Road
      Post Office Box 930
      Dearborn, Michigan 48128
Simulation with correspondent feedback. $85.00.

Multimedia Kits

★ 595 ★
DATA PROCESSING AND COMPUTERS
R. A. Fleck Jr., C. Brian Honess
      Charles E. Merrill Publishing Company
      1300 Alum Creek Drive
      Box 508
      Columbus, Ohio 43216
Text with audio tapes and filmstrips. $11.95.

Printed Materials

★ 596 ★
COMPUTER ALGORITHMS AND FLOWCHARTING
G. Silver, J. Silver
      McGraw-Hill Book Company
      1221 Avenue of the Americas
      New York, New York 10019
Book. 1975. $7.65.

★ 597 ★
COMPUTING, ONE - A FOUNDATION COURSE
      Harper and Row Publishers Incorporated
      Scranton, Pennsylvania 18512
Book. $3.00.

★ 598 ★
INTRODUCTION TO COMPUTER APPLICATIONS
FOR NON-SCIENCE STUDENTS
W. R. Bennett
      Prentice-Hall Incorporated
      Englewood Cliffs, New Jersey 07632
Book. 1976. $13.95.

★ 599 ★
INTRODUCTION TO COMPUTER SCIENCE
Francis Scheid
      McGraw-Hill Book Company
      1221 Avenue of the Americas
      New York, New York 10036
Book. 1970. $4.95.

★ 600 ★
AN INTRODUCTION TO COMPUTING: PROBLEM-
SOLVING ALGORITHMS AND DATA STRUCTURES
Daniel U. Wilde
      Prentice-Hall Incorporated
      Englewood Cliffs, New Jersey 07632
Book. 1973. $14.50.

★ 601 ★
MICROPROCESSORS
Rodnay Zaks
      Sybex Incorporated
      2020 Milvia Street
      Berkeley, California 94704
Text. $9.95.

Programmed Learning Materials

★ 602 ★
ASSEMBLER CODING
      IBM (International Business Machines
         Corporation)
      Box 390
      Poughkeepsie, New York 12602
Programmed text. $10.40.

★ 603 ★
BASIC COMPUTERS AND DATA PROCESSING
Robert Albrecht, Le Roy Finkel, Jerald Brown
      John Wiley and Sons
      605 Third Avenue
      New York, New York 10016
Programmed text. 325 pages. $4.95.

★ 604 ★
BOOLEAN ALGEBRA: A SELF-INSTRUCTIONAL
PROGRAMMED MANUAL
Federal Electric Corporation
      Prentice-Hall Incorporated
      Englewood Cliffs, New Jersey 07632
Programmed. $15.95.

★ 605 ★
FLOWCHARTING: A TOOL FOR UNDERSTANDING
COMPUTER LOGIC
Nancy Stern
      John Wiley and Sons
      605 Third Avenue
      New York, New York 10016
Programmed text. 341 pages. $4.95.

★ 606 ★
FUNDAMENTALS OF PROGRAMMING
   IBM (International Business Machines
      Corporation)
   Box 390
   Poughkeepsie, New York   12602
Programmed text. $2.40.

★ 607 ★
LINEAR PROGRAMMING
E. Wain Martin
   Learning Systems Company
   1818 Ridge Road
   Homewood, Illinois   60430
Programmed learning aid. $4.95.

★ 608 ★
MICROCIRCUIT LEARNING COMPUTERS
I. Aleksander
   Crane, Russak and Company Incorporated
   347 Madison Avenue
   New York, New York   10017
Programmed.   1971. $5.50.

CONFERENCES

See also: Meetings

Audio Cassettes/Tapes

★ 609 ★
CONFERENCE PLANNING AND LEADERSHIP
   Development Digest Incorporated
   3347 Motor Avenue
   Los Angeles, California   90034
Cassette. $13.75.

Multimedia Kits

★ 610 ★
MAXIMIZING YOUR CONFERENCE RESOURCES
   Resources for Education and Management
      Incorporated
   544 Medlock Road, Suite 210
   Decatur, Georgia   30030
Filmstrip with cassette. $70.00.

★ 611 ★
PREPARING FOR THE CONFERENCE
   Resources for Education and Management
      Incorporated
   544 Medlock Road, Suite 210
   Decatur, Georgia   30030
Filmstrip with cassette. $70.00.

CONFLICT RESOLUTION

See also: Arbitration; Negotiation

Films/Video/Filmstrips

★ 612 ★
CONFLICT: CAUSES AND RESOLUTIONS
   Roundtable Films
   113 North San Vincente Boulevard
   Beverly Hills, California   90211
Film and guidebook.

★ 613 ★
HOW TO HANDLE CONFLICT AND COMPLAINTS
   Thompson-Mitchell and Associates
   3384 Peachtree Road Northeast
   Atlanta, Georgia   30326
Filmstrip. $125.00.

★ 614 ★
MANAGEMENT OF CONFLICT
   XICOM
   Sterling Forest
   Tuxedo, New York   10987
Films and workbooks.

Games/Simulations

★ 615 ★
HANDLING CONFLICT IN MANAGEMENT
SUPERIOR/SUBORDINATE - GROUP CONFLICT
   Didactic Systems Incorporated
   Box 457
   Cranford, New Jersey   07016
Simulation game. $24.00.

Multimedia Kits

★ 616 ★
REDUCING CONFLICTS IN THE ORGANIZATION
   Resources for Education and Management
      Incorporated
   544 Medlock Road, Suite 210
   Decatur, Georgia   30030
Filmstrip with cassette. $60.00.

★ 617 ★
RESOLVING INTERPERSONAL CONFLICTS WITH
THE DISADVANTAGED
   Resources for Education and Management
      Incorporated
   544 Medlock Road, Suite 210
   Decatur, Georgia   30030
Filmstrip with cassette. $60.00.

CONSERVATION

Correspondence Courses

★ 618 ★
CONSERVATION
North American Correspondence School
4401 Birch Street
Newport Beach, California 92663
Correspondence course.

CONSTRUCTION
See: BUILDING CONSTRUCTION

CONSULTING

See also: Freelancing

Audio Cassettes/Tapes

★ 619 ★
CONSULTING PRACTICE SEMINAR
H. L. Shenson, Lecturer
Howard L. Shenson Company
16400 Ventura Boulevard, Suite 215 C
Encino, California 91436
Cassette seminar with visuals. $49.00.

CONTROL VALVE INSTRUMENTATION

See also: Mechanical Maintenance

Audio Cassettes/Tapes

★ 620 ★
ACTUATORS AND ACCESSORIES
Jerry Lyons
Instrument Society of America
400 Stanwix Street
Pittsburgh, Pennsylvania 15222
Workbook and cassette. $12.00.

★ 621 ★
CONTROL VALVE MAINTENANCE
Instrument Society of America
400 Stanwix Street
Pittsburgh, Pennsylvania 15222
Workbook and cassette. $12.00.

★ 622 ★
CONTROL VALVE SIZING
L. R. Driscoll
Instrument Society of America
400 Stanwix Street
Pittsburgh, Pennsylvania 15222
Workbook and cassette. $12.00.

★ 623 ★
COST, CONNECTIONS AND GEOMETRY
CONSIDERATIONS
E. Ross Forman
Instrument Society of America
400 Stanwix Street
Pittsburgh, Pennsylvania 15222
Workbook and cassette. $12.00.

★ 624 ★
FLOW CHARACTERISTICS
R. L. Moore
Instrument Society of America
400 Stanwix Street
Pittsburgh, Pennsylvania 15222
Workbook and cassette.

★ 625 ★
FLOW CONTROL, RANGEABILITY, CHARACTERISTICS
AND LEAKAGE
Carl Askland
Instrument Society of America
400 Stanwix Street
Pittsburgh, Pennsylvania 15222
Workbook and cassette. $12.00.

★ 626 ★
GENERAL REVIEW OF FACTORS INFLUENCING
VALVE SELECTION
Herb Simon
Instrument Society of America
400 Stanwix Street
Pittsburgh, Pennsylvania 15222
Workbook and cassette. $12.00.

★ 627 ★
HIGH TEMPERATURE, PRESSURE AND MASS FLOW,
LOW FLOW CONTROL
Instrument Society of America
400 Stanwix Street
Pittsburgh, Pennsylvania 15222
Workbook and cassette. $12.00.

★ 628 ★
PRESSURE DROP, CAVITATION, NOISE AND
TWO-PHASE FLOW
        Instrument Society of America
        400 Stanwix Street
        Pittsburgh, Pennsylvania 15222
Workbook and cassette. $12.00.

★ 629 ★
SUSPENSION AND SLURRY SERVICE CONDITIONS
        Instrument Society of America
        400 Stanwix Street
        Pittsburgh, Pennsylvania 15222
Workbook and cassette. $12.00.

★ 630 ★
VALVE BODIES AND VALVE TRIM
Mathew Freeman
        Instrument Society of America
        400 Stanwix Street
        Pittsburgh, Pennsylvania 15222
Workbook and cassette. $12.00.

Films/Video/Filmstrips

★ 631 ★
FUNDAMENTALS OF CONTROL VALVES
        Instrument Society of America
        400 Stanwix Street
        Pittsburgh, Pennsylvania 15222
Film. $500.00.

★ 632 ★
FUNDAMENTALS OF CONTROL VALVES –
MAINTENANCE AND OVERHAUL PROCEDURES
        Instrument Society of America
        400 Stanwix Street
        Pittsburgh, Pennsylvania 15222
Film $220.00.   Videotape $200.00.   Workbook $4.00.

Programmed Learning Materials

★ 633 ★
INTRODUCTION TO VALVES
        E. I. du Pont de Nemours and Company
        Applied Technology Division
        Room B 4204
        Wilmington, Delaware 19898
Programmed course of approximately 1 hour. $5.35.

★ 634 ★
OPERATION AND MAINTENANCE OF VALVES
        E. I. du Pont de Nemours and Company
        Applied Technology Division
        Room B 4204
        Wilmington, Delaware 19898
Programmed course of approximately 12 hours.
$22.10.

CORPORATE PLANNING
See: PLANNING

COST ACCOUNTING

See also: Accounting;   Budgeting;
Financial Analysis

Correspondence Courses

★ 635 ★
COST ACCOUNTING
        University of Colorado
        Center for Lifelong Learning
        170 Aurora Avenue
        Boulder, Colorado 80302
Correspondence course.

★ 636 ★
COST ACCOUNTING
        University of Kentucky
        Independent Study Program
        Freeze Hall, Room 1
        Lexington, Kentucky 40506
Correspondence course.

★ 637 ★
COST ACCOUNTING
        University of South Carolina
        Department of Correspondence Study
        Division of Continuing Education
        Columbia, South Carolina 29208
Correspondence course. $69.00.

★ 638 ★
COST ACCOUNTING
        Western Washington State College
        Center for Continuing Education
        Edens Hall South
        Bellingham, Washington 98225
Correspondence course.

Printed Materials

★ 639 ★
BASICS OF COST ACCOUNTING
 American Management Associations
 135 West 50th Street
 New York, New York 10020
Self-study text. $65.00.

★ 640 ★
COST ACCOUNTING: PRINCIPLES AND
MANAGERIAL APPLICATIONS
 International Publications Service
 114 East 32nd Street
 New York, New York 10016
Book. 1974. $14.50.

Programmed Learning Materials

★ 641 ★
COST ACCOUNTING
Homer Black
 Learning Systems Company
 1818 Ridge Road
 Homewood, Illinois 60430
Programmed learning aid.

★ 642 ★
ESSENTIALS OF COST ACCOUNTING
J. Dearden
 Addison Wesley Publishing Company
  Incorporated
 Jacob Way
 Reading, Massachusetts 01867
Programmed text. $6.95.

COST CONTROL

Audio Cassettes/Tapes

★ 643 ★
FUNDAMENTALS OF COST CONTROL
 Westinghouse Learning Press
 College Publications
 Post Office Box 10680
 Palo Alto, California 94303
Cassette with manual. $60.00.

Printed Materials

★ 644 ★
COST REDUCTION FOR OPERATORS
 Howell Training
 2040 North Loop West, Suite 204
 Houston, Texas 77018
Workbooks and tests. $4.85.

Programmed Learning Materials

★ 645 ★
APPLICATION OF RELIABILITY TECHNIQUES
 Preston Publishing Company
 151 East 50th Street
 New York, New York 10022
Programmed text. $12.00.

★ 646 ★
READY WORK – FACTOR LINE STANDARDS
 WOFAC Company
 Fellowship Road
 Moorestown, New Jersey 08057
Programmed text. $10.00.

CPA (CERTIFIED PUBLIC ACCOUNTING)
See: CERTIFIED PUBLIC ACCOUNTING (CPA)

CPM
See: CRITICAL PATH METHOD (CPM)

CREATIVITY

See also: Inventing

Audio Cassettes/Tapes

★ 647 ★
CREATIVE THINKING – HOW TO WIN WITH IDEAS
Earl Nightingale, Dr. Whitt N. Schultz
 Tape Rental Library Incorporated
 Post Office Box 2107
 2507 Edna Drive
 South Vineland, New Jersey 08360
3 cassettes with workbook. $36.00.

★ 648 ★
EVERYDAY CREATIVITY: TWELVE STEPS TO
INNOVATIVE THINKING
    AMACOM
    American Management Associations
    135 West 50th Street
    New York, New York   10020
7 cassettes and workbook. $115.00.

★ 649 ★
HOW TO TAP YOUR CREATIVE POTENTIAL
    Tape Rental Library Incorporated
    Post Office Box 2107
    2507 Edna Drive
    South Vineland, New Jersey   08360
Cassette. $9.98.

★ 650 ★
MANAGERIAL CREATIVITY
    Van De Water Associates
    7914 Jason Avenue
    Canoga Park, California   91304
Cassette and workbook. $23.50.

★ 651 ★
THINKING CREATIVELY
    Educational Century Programming
    1201 East Johnson Street
    Jonesboro, Arkansas   72401
Cassette. $6.00.

Multimedia Kits

★ 652 ★
CREATIVITY AND IMAGINATION
    Lansford Publishing Company
    Post Office Box 8711
    San Jose, California   95155
Multimedia kit. $99.95.

CREDIT MANAGEMENT

Correspondence Courses

★ 653 ★
FUNDAMENTALS OF CREDIT FUNCTION
    Dun and Bradstreet Incorporated
    Business Education Division
    Box 803
    Church Street Station
    New York, New York   10008
Instruction through self-study text and correspondence
with instructor. $115.00.

Printed Materials

★ 654 ★
EVERYDAY CREDIT CHECKING
Sol Barzman
    National Association of Credit Management
    475 Park Avenue South
    New York, New York   10016
Book.   1973. $6.95.

★ 655 ★
HOW TO COLLECT WHAT OTHERS OWE YOU
Philip Fry
    National Council to Eliminate Death Taxes
        Incorporated
    Route 1
    New Concord, Ohio   43762
Book.   1976. $15.00.

CREDITS AND COLLECTIONS
See: CREDIT MANAGEMENT

CRITICAL PATH METHOD (CPM)

Films/Video/Filmstrips

★ 656 ★
CRITICAL PATH METHOD
    Roundtable Films
    113 North San Vincente Boulevard
    Beverly Hills, California   90211
Film and guidebook.

Printed Materials

★ 657 ★
CRITICAL PATH METHOD
Byron Radcliffe
    Cahners Publishing Company Incorporated
    221 Columbus Avenue
    Boston, Massachusetts   02166
Book. $8.95.

Programmed Learning Materials

★ 658 ★
CRITICAL PATH ANALYSIS
C. W. Lowe
    Petrocelli Books
    384 Fifth Avenue
    New York, New York   10018
Programmed text.

CROSS-CULTURAL TRAINING

Audio Cassettes/Tapes

★ 659 ★
A COMPARATIVE ANALYSIS OF ORGANIZATIONAL
AND COMMUNITY CHANGE METHODS AND THEIR
IMPLICATIONS FOR THE BLACK COMMUNITY
> Development Digest Incorporated
> 3347 Motor Avenue
> Los Angeles, California   90034

Cassette. $13.75.

★ 660 ★
THE TRANSITION TO INDUSTRIALIZATION;
CROSS-CULTURAL CONSIDERATIONS
> Development Digest Incorporated
> 3347 Motor Avenue
> Los Angeles, California   90034

Cassette. $13.75.

CUSTODIAL MAINTENANCE

See also: Electrical Maintenance

Correspondence Courses

★ 661 ★
BUILDING MAINTENANCE
> International Correspondence School
> Scranton, Pennsylvania   18515

Multi-module correspondence course.

Printed Materials

★ 662 ★
BUILDING MAINTENANCE
Jules Oravetz
> Theodore Audel Company
> Distributed by Bobbs Merrill Company Incorporated
> 4300 West 62nd Street
> Indianapolis, Indiana   46268

Book.   1966. $7.50.

CUSTOMER RELATIONS

Audio Cassettes/Tapes

★ 663 ★
IMPROVING CUSTOMER RELATIONS
> Universal Training Systems Company
> 3201 Old Glenview Road
> Wilmette, Illinois   60091

Cassette and workbook. $99.00.

Films/Video/Filmstrips

★ 664 ★
" THE CUSTOMER AND ME" (How to make our
business contacts more effective)
> Resource Incorporated
> 13902 North Dale Mabry Highway
> Tampa, Florida   33624

Video cartridge, workbook available. $100.00.

★ 665 ★
CUSTOMER RELATIONS
> Resource Incorporated
> 13902 North Dale Mabry Highway
> Tampa, Florida   33624

Video cartridge. $100.00.

★ 666 ★
"GOOD MORNING, CUSTOMER SERVICE"
(Telephone etiquette for business)
> Resource Incorporated
> 13902 North Dale Mabry Highway
> Tampa, Florida   33624

Video cartridge, workbook available. $100.00.

Multimedia Kits

★ 667 ★
SUCCESSFUL SERVICE SERIES
> Thompson-Mitchell and Associates
> 3384 Peachtree Road   Northeast
> Atlanta, Georgia   30326

3 filmstrips with cassette. $150.00.

Printed Materials

★ 668 ★
CUSTOMER SERVICES
L. M. Buckner
> McGraw-Hill Book Company
> 1221 Avenue of the Americas
> New York, New York   10036

Book.

CYBERNETICS

Audio Cassettes/Tapes

★ 669 ★
THOM NORMAN - ON CYBERNETICS
> General Cassette Corporation
> 1324 North 22nd Avenue
> Post Office Box 6940
> Phoenix, Arizona   85005

2 cassettes. $15.90.

DANISH

Audio Cassettes/Tapes

★ 670 ★
BERLITZ COURSE IN DANISH
    Berlitz Language Program
    Post Office Box 5109
    FDR Station
    New York, New York 10022
Cassette $5.95.   Also available on LP record.

Correspondence Courses

★ 671 ★
DANISH LANGUAGE STUDIES
    University of Washington
    Office of Independent Study
    222 Lewis Hall DW-30
    Seattle, Washington 98195
Correspondence course.

Printed Materials

★ 672 ★
LEARN DANISH: FOR ENGLISH SPEAKERS
    Saphrograph Company
    194 Elizabeth Street
    New York, New York 10012
Book. $5.00.

★ 673 ★
TEACH YOURSELF DANISH
H. A. Koefoed
    David McKay Company Incorporated
    750 Third Avenue
    New York, New York 10017
Book.

DATA PROCESSING

See also: Computers

Audio Cassettes/Tapes

★ 674 ★
BASIC PRINCIPLES OF DATA PROCESSING
James A. Saxan, Wesley A. Steyer
    Tape Rental Library Incorporated
    Post Office Box 2107
    2507 Edna Drive
    South Vineland, New Jersey 08360
Cassette.

★ 675 ★
COST ANALYSIS/DATA PROCESSING
    Educational Century Programming
    1201 East Johnson Street
    Jonesboro, Arkansas 72401
Cassette. $6.00.

★ 676 ★
DATA PROCESSING - CARD PUNCH/
DATA PROCESSING - ELECTRONIC
    Educational Century Programming
    1201 East Johnson Street
    Jonesboro, Arkansas 72401
Cassette. $6.00.

★ 677 ★
INFORMATION SYSTEMS DEVELOPMENT AND THE
NON EDP MANAGER
    QED Incorporated
    Box 1608
    Burbank, California 91507
6 cassettes and workbook. $195.00.

Printed Materials

★ 678 ★
BUSINESS DATA PROCESSING
S. Fink
    Prentice-Hall Incorporated
    Englewood Cliffs, New Jersey 07632
Text and study guide.   1974. $20 00.

★ 679 ★
COMPUTERIZED ACCOUNTING METHODS AND
CONTROL
Michael Tyran
    Prentice-Hall Incorporated
    Englewood Cliffs, New Jersey 07632
Book.   1972. $22.95.

★ 680 ★
DATA PROCESSING IN BIOLOGY AND GEOLOGY
J. L. Cutbill
    Academic Press Incorporated
    111 Fifth Avenue
    New York, New York 10003
Book.   1971. $17.25.

★ 681 ★
MANAGEMENT PLANNING FOR DATA
PROCESSING
Dick Brandon
        Petrocelli Books
        384 Fifth Avenue
        New York, New York   10018
Book.   1970. $14.95.

★ 682 ★
MODERN DATA PROCESSING
Robert Arnold
        John Wiley and Sons Incorporated
        605 Third Avenue
        New York, New York   10016
Text and workbook. $20.00.

Programmed Learning Materials

★ 683 ★
INTRODUCTION TO DATA PROCESSING
C. Orville Elliott
        Learning Systems Company
        1818 Ridge Road
        Homewood, Illinois   60430
Programmed learning aid. $4.50.

★ 684 ★
MACRO PROCESSORS
A. J. Cole
        Cambridge University Press
        510 North Avenue
        New Rochelle, New York   10801
Programmed text.   1976. $8.95.

DECISION MAKING

See also: Problem Solving

Audio cassettes/Tapes

★ 685 ★
CONQUERING DECISIONS
        Educational Century Programming
        1201 East Johnson Street
        Jonesboro, Arkansas   72401
Cassette. $6.00.

★ 686 ★
DECISION MAKING
George Odiorne
        MBO Incorporated
        157 Pontoosic Road
        Westfield, Massachusetts   01085
Cassette and manual.

★ 687 ★
DECISION MAKING IN THE SEVENTIES -
IMPLICATIONS FOR TRAINING
        Development Digest Incorporated
        3347 Motor Avenue
        Los Angeles, California   90034
Cassette. $13.75.

★ 688 ★
HOW TO APPLY THE TOUGH-MINDED DECISION
MAKING PROCESS
        Creative Media Films
        820 Keo Way
        Des Moines, Iowa   50309
Cassette. $7.95.

★ 689 ★
HOW TO MAKE DECISIONS
        Tape Rental Library Incorporated
        Post Office Box 2107
        2507 Edna Drive
        South Vineland, New Jersey   08360
Cassette. $9.98.

★ 690 ★
MAKING DECISIONS MANAGEMENT SKILLS
        Thompson-Mitchell and Associates
        3384 Peachtree Road Northeast
        Atlanta, Georgia   30326
Cassette. $6.00.

★ 691 ★
PRACTICAL DECISION MAKING
        Thompson-Mitchell and Associates
        3384 Peachtree Road Northeast
        Atlanta, Georgia   30326
Cassette. $9.95.

★ 692 ★
RATIONAL PROBLEM SOLVING AND DECISION
MAKING
        Van De Water Associates
        7914 Jason Avenue
        Canoga Park, California   91304
Cassette and workbook. $23.50.

Correspondence Courses

★ 693 ★
EFFECTIVE DECISION MAKING
 Society of Manufacturing Engineers
 20501 Ford Road
 Post Office Box 930
 Dearborn, Michigan 48128
4 hours self instruction course. $10.00.

★ 694 ★
GROUP DECISIONS IN INDUSTRY
 Society of Manufacturing Engineers
 20501 Ford Road
 Post Office Box 930
 Dearborn, Michigan 48128
6 two hour lessons self instruction course. $6.50.

★ 695 ★
METHODS FOR DECISION MAKING
 The Thomas Institute
 Box 22
 New Canaan, Connecticut 06840
Self-study course. $150.00.

Films/Video/Filmstrips

★ 696 ★
THE ABC'S OF DECISION MAKING
Featuring: Joe Batten
 Creative Media Films
 820 Keo Way
 Des Moines, Iowa 50309
Film or video cassettes and guide. $450.00 (rental available).

★ 697 ★
BREAK-EVEN POINT ANALYSIS
 Salenger Educational Media
 1635 12th Street
 Santa Monica, California 90404
Film and worksheets. $350.00.

Games/Simulations

★ 698 ★
DECISION MAKING GAME: AN INTEGRATED
OPERATIONS MANAGEMENT SIMULATION
Bill Darden, William Lucas
 Prentice-Hall Incorporated
 Englewood Cliffs, New Jersey 07632
Game.

Multimedia Kits

★ 699 ★
THE DECISION MAKING PROCESS
 Lansford Publishing Company
 Post Office Box 8711
 San Jose, California 95155
Multimedia kit. $99.95.

★ 700 ★
DECISION MAKING SKILLS
 Resources for Education and Management
  Incorporated
 544 Medlock Road, Suite 210
 Decatur, Georgia 30030
Filmstrip with cassette. $60.00.

★ 701 ★
A PROGRAM IN CREATIVE/INNOVATIVE PROBLEM
SOLVING AND DECISION MAKING
 Addison Wesley Publishing Company
  Incorporated
 Jacob Way
 Reading, Massachusetts 01867
5 modules and workbook. $500.00.

Printed Materials

★ 702 ★
ADMINISTRATIVE POLICY: CASES IN
MANAGERIAL DECISION MAKING
Earl D. Bennett, Floyd S. Brandt, Charles R.
Klasson
 Charles E. Merrill Publishing Company
 1300 Alum Creek Drive
 Box 508
 Columbus, Ohio 43216
Text with exercises. 1978. $16.95.

★ 703 ★
PARTICIPATIVE DECISION MAKING
 American Management Associations
 135 West 50th Street
 New York, New York 10020
Book. 1974. $6.00.

DELEGATION

See also: headings under Supervision

Audio Cassettes/Tapes

★ 704 ★
DIVISION OF AUTHORITY
Educational Century Programming
1201 East Johnson Street
Jonesboro, Arkansas   72401
Cassette. $6.00.

Correspondence Courses

★ 705 ★
HOW TO DELEGATE EFFECTIVELY
Society of Manufacturing Engineers
20501 Ford Road
Post Office Box 930
Dearborn, Michigan 48128
4 hour self instruction course. $10.00.

Films, Video, Filmstrips

★ 706 ★
DELEGATE - DON'T ABDICATE
National Restaurant Association
One IBM Plaza, Suite 2600
Chicago, Illinois 60611
Video cartridge or 8 mm, 16 mm, study guide.
$190.00.

★ 707 ★
NO-NONSENSE DELEGATION
Featuring Dale McConkey
Creative Media Films
820 Keo Way
Des Moines, Iowa 50309
Film or video cassette, guide and manual.
$450.00 (rental available).

Games/Simulations

★ 708 ★
ASSIGNING WORK
Didactic Systems Incorporated
Box 457
Cranford, New Jersey 07016
Simulation game. $24.00.

★ 709 ★
EFFECTIVE DELEGATION
Didactic Systems Incorporated
Box 457
Cranford, New Jersey 07016
Simulation game. $24.00.

Multimedia Kits

★ 710 ★
DIRECTING
Resources for Education and Management
Incorporated
544 Medlock Road, Suite 210
Decatur, Georgia 30030
Filmstrip with cassette. $60.00.

Printed Materials

★ 711 ★
EFFECTIVE DELEGATION
Didactic Systems Incorporated
Box 457
Cranford, New Jersey 07016
Self-study text. $9.00.

★ 712 ★
PLANNING AND ASSIGNING WORK
Didactic Systems Incorporated
Box 457
Cranford, New Jersey 07016
Self-study text. $9.00.

Programmed Learning Materials

★ 713 ★
HOW TO DELEGATE EFFECTIVELY
Preston Publishing Company
151 East 50th Street
New York, New York 10022
Programmed text. $10.00.

DENTAL INDUSTRY

Correspondence Courses

★ 714 ★
DENTAL OFFICE ASSISTANT COURSE
La Salle Extension University
417 South Dearborn Street
Chicago, Illinois 60605
Correspondence course.

Multimedia Kits

★ 715 ★

INTRODUCTION TO THE DENTAL INDUSTRY
    American Dental Trade Association
    1140 Connecticut Avenue
    Washington, D.C. 20036
Cassettes, slides and workbooks. $1,300.00.

DICTATION

See also: Office Practices; Secretarial
            Skills

Audio Cassettes/Tapes

★ 716 ★

THE ART OF DICTATION
    Addison Wesley Publishing Company
      Incorporated
    Jacob Way
    Reading, Massachusetts 01867
Cassette and workbook. $14.95.

Multimedia Kits

★ 717 ★

WRITING WITH A MICROPHONE: APPLIED
DICTATION SKILLS
    Ergonco Performance Source
    Northwest O'Hare Office Park, Suite 119
    2474 Dempster Street
    Des Plains, Illinois 60016
Multimedia self-study program.

DIEMAKING
See: TOOL AND DIEMAKING

DIESEL MECHANICS

See also: Automobile Mechanics

Correspondence Courses

★ 718 ★

BASIC DIESEL MECHANICS
    International Correspondence School
    Scranton, Pennsylvania 18515
Multi-module correspondence course.

★ 719 ★
BASIC TRUCK MECHANICS
    International Correspondence School
    Scranton, Pennsylvania 18515
Multi-module correspondence course.

★ 720 ★
DIESEL MECHANICS COURSE
    La Salle Extension University
    417 South Dearborn Street
    Chicago, Illinois 60605
Correspondence course.

★ 721 ★
FUEL INJECTION MECHANICS
    International Correspondence School
    Scranton, Pennsylvania 18515
Multi-module correspondence course.

★ 722 ★
HEAVY DUTY MECHANICS
    International Correspondence School
    Scranton, Pennsylvania 18515
Multi-module correspondence course.

★ 723 ★
TRUCK TECHNOLOGY FOR THE DRIVER
    International Correspondence School
    Scranton, Pennsylvania 18515
Multi-module correspondence course.

DIRECT MAIL

See also: Marketing

Audio Cassettes/Tapes

★ 724 ★
DIRECT MAIL AND MAIL ORDER
    Tape Rental Library Incorporated
    Post Office Box 2107
    2507 Edna Drive
    South Vineland, New Jersey 08360
Cassette. $12.00.

★ 725 ★
HOW TO ORGANIZE A PERSONALIZED DIRECT
MAIL PROGRAM
    General Cassette Corporation
    1324 North 22nd Avenue
    Post Office Box 6940
    Phoenix, Arizona 85005
4 cassettes. $49.00.

DISCIPLINE

See also: Personnel Management

Audio Cassettes/Tapes

★ 726 ★
CONSTRUCTIVE DISCIPLINE ON THE JOB
        American Management Associations
        135 West 50th Street
        New York, New York 10020
2 cassettes with workbook. $60.00.

★ 727 ★
DISCIPLINE
George Odiorne
        MBO Incorporated
        157 Pontoosic Road
        Westfield, Massachusetts 01085
Cassette and manual. $15.00.

Films / Video/Filmstrips

★ 728 ★
CONSTRUCTIVE DISCIPLINE
        Van De Water Associates
        7914 Jason Avenue
        Canoga Park, California 91304
Video tape. $495.00 (rental available).

★ 729 ★
DISCIPLINE - A MATTER OF JUDGMENT
        National Restaurant Association
        One IBM Plaza, Suite 2600
        Chicago, Illinois 60611
Video cartridge or 8mm, 16mm, study guide.
$190.00.

Programmed Learning Materials

★ 730 ★
CONSTRUCTIVE DISCIPLINE ON THE JOB
        American Management Associations
        135 West 50th Street
        New York, New York 10020
Programmed text. $25.00.

DISTRIBUTION

Correspondence Courses

★ 731 ★
PHYSICAL DISTRIBUTION
        Pennsylvania State University
        Department of Independent Study by
            Correspondence
        Three Sheilds Building
        University Park, Pennsylvania 16802
Correspondence course.

★ 732 ★
TRANSPORTATION SYSTEMS
        Pennsylvania State University
        Department of Independent Study by
            Correspondence
        Three Sheilds Building
        University Park, Pennsylvania 16802
Correspondence course.

Games/Simulations

★ 733 ★
PHYSICAL DISTRIBUTION MANAGEMENT
        Didactic Systems Incorporated
        Box 457
        Cranford, New Jersey 07016
Simulation game. $24.00.

DRAFTING

See also: Architecture; Blueprint Reading

Correspondence Courses

★ 734 ★
ARCHITECTURAL DRAFTING TECHNOLOGY
        International Correspondence School
        Scranton, Pennsylvania 18515
Multi-module correspondence course.

★ 735 ★
BASIC DRAFTING
        International Correspondence School
        Scranton, Pennsylvania 18515
Multi-module correspondence course.

★ 736 ★
DESIGN DRAFTING
        International Correspondence School
        Scranton, Pennsylvania 18515
Multi-module correspondence course.

★ 737 ★
DRAFTING
        Commercial Trades Institute
        6201 West Howard Street
        Chicago, Illinois 60648
Correspondence course.

★ 738 ★
DRAFTING
        Electronics Technical Institute
        1500 Cardinal Drive
        Little Falls, New Jersey 07424
Correspondence course.

★ 739 ★
DRAFTING COURSE
        La Salle Extension University
        417 South Dearborn Street
        Chicago, Illinois 60605
Correspondence course.

★ 740 ★
ENGINEERING DRAFTING
        Pennsylvania State University
        Department of Independent Study by
            Correspondence
        Three Sheilds Building
        University Park, Pennsylvania 16802
Correspondence course.

★ 741 ★
ENGINEERING DRAWING
        University of Southern Mississippi
        Department of Independent Study
        Southern Station, Box 56
        Hattiesburg, Mississippi 39401
Correspondence course.

★ 742 ★
GENERAL DRAFTING COURSE
        North American Correspondence School
        4401 Birch Street
        Newport Beach, California 92663
Correspondence course.

★ 743 ★
MECHANICAL DRAFTING
        International Correspondence School
        Scranton, Pennsylvania 18515
Multi-module correspondence course.

Films/Video/Filmstrips

★ 744 ★
CASTINGS
        Robert J. Brady Company
        Charles Press Publishers
        Prentice-Hall Companies
        Bowie, Maryland 20715
Filmstrip $60.00.   Slide $90.00.

★ 745 ★
DESCRIPTIVE GEOMETRY
        Robert J. Brady Company
        Charles Press Publishers
        Prentice-Hall Companies
        Bowie, Maryland 20715
Filmstrip $60.00.   Slide $90.00.

★ 746 ★
DIMENSIONING AND MACHINE SHOP
        Robert J. Brady Company
        Charles Press Publishers
        Prentice-Hall Companies
        Bowie, Maryland 20715
Filmstrip $60.00.   Slide $90.00.

★ 747 ★
DIMENSIONING RULES
        Robert J. Brady Company
        Charles Press Publishers
        Prentice-Hall Companies
        Bowie, Maryland 20715
Filmstrip $60.00.   Slide $90.00.

★ 748 ★
INTRODUCTION TO DRAFTING
        Robert J. Brady Company
        Charles Press Publishers
        Prentice-Hall Companies
        Bowie, Maryland 20715
Filmstrip $19.95.   Slide $29.95.

★ 749 ★
LETTERING FOR DRAFTING
        Robert J. Brady Company
        Charles Press Publishers
        Prentice-Hall Companies
        Bowie, Maryland 20715
Filmstrip $60.00.   Slide $90.00.

★ 750 ★
MULTIVIEW DRAWING
        Robert J. Brady Company
        Charles Press Publishers
        Prentice-Hall Companies
        Bowie, Maryland 20715
Filmstrip $60.00.   Slide $90.00.

★ 751 ★
SECTIONAL VIEWS
        Robert J. Brady Company
        Charles Press Publishers
        Prentice-Hall Companies
        Bowie, Maryland 20715
Filmstrip $60.00.   Slide $90.00.

Printed Materials

★ 752 ★
AUXILIARY VIEWS/DESCRIPTIVE GEOMETRY
        Robert J. Brady Company
        Charles Press Publishers
        Prentice-Hall Companies
        Bowie, Maryland 20715
Work text. $6.95.

★ 753 ★
BASIC DRAFTING SKILLS
        Robert J. Brady Company
        Charles Press Publishers
        Prentice-Hall Companies
        Bowie, Maryland 20715
Work text. $6.95.

★ 754 ★
DIMENSIONING
        Robert J. Brady Company
        Charles Press Publishers
        Prentice-Hall Companies
        Bowie, Maryland 20715
Work text. $6.95.

★ 755 ★
INTRODUCTION TO CONSTRUCTION DRAFTING
Lee Hooper
        Prentice-Hall Incorporated
        Englewood Cliffs, New Jersey 07632
Book.   1970. $14.95.

★ 756 ★
MULTIVIEW DRAWING
        Robert J. Brady Company
        Charles Press Publishers
        Prentice-Hall Companies
        Bowie, Maryland 20715
Work text. $7.95.

DRAWING
See: ART

DRIVING

See also: Safety, Automobile

Audio Cassettes/Tapes

★ 757 ★
ALCOHOL AND DRIVING - DON'T MIX
        Close Productions
        2020 San Carlos Boulevard
        Fort Myers Beach, Florida 33931
Cassette. $8.00.

★ 758 ★
AVOID HEAD-ON-COLLISIONS - AT ANY COST!
        Close Productions
        2020 San Carlos Boulevard
        Fort Myers Beach, Florida 33931
Cassette. $8.00.

★ 759 ★
DEFENSIVE DRIVING MEANS YOU
        Close Productions
        2020 San Carlos Boulevard
        Fort Myers Beach, Florida 33931
Cassette. $8.00.

★ 760 ★
DRIVING PSYCHOLOGY - AND YOUR
RESPONSIBILITIES
Close Productions
2020 San Carlos Boulevard
Fort Myers Beach, Florida   33931
Cassette. $8.00.

★ 761 ★
DRIVING PSYCHOLOGY - THE OTHER GUY
Close Productions
2020 San Carlos Boulevard
Fort Myers Beach, Florida   33931
Cassette. $8.00.

★ 762 ★
DRIVING PSYCHOLOGY - UNDERSTANDING
OURSELVES
Close Productions
2020 San Carlos Boulevard
Fort Myers Beach, Florida   33931
Cassette. $8.00.

★ 763 ★
DRIVING WITH MINOR ILLNESS, MEDICINE,
DRUGS, CARBON MONOXIDE - THE QUIET
KILLER
Close Productions
2020 San Carlos Boulevard
Fort Myers Beach, Florida   33931
Cassette. $8.00.

★ 764 ★
EXPECT THE UNEXPECTED - THE ODDS ARE
AGAINST YOU
Close Productions
2020 San Carlos Boulevard
Fort Myers Beach, Florida   33931
Cassette. $8.00.

★ 765 ★
HIGHWAY WARNING SIGNS CAN SAVE YOUR
LIFE
Close Productions
2020 San Carlos Boulevard
Fort Myers Beach, Florida   33931
Cassette. $8.00.

★ 766 ★
HOW TO REACT: WHEN YOU MUST STOP ON
A BUSY HIGHWAY; WHEN YOU HAVE A BLOW-
OUT AT HIGH SPEED
Close Productions
2020 San Carlos Boulevard
Fort Myers Beach, Florida   33931
Cassette. $8.00.

★ 767 ★
HOW TO REACT WHEN YOUR ACCELERATOR PEDAL
STICKS
Close Productions
2020 San Carlos Boulevard
Fort Myers Beach, Florida   33931
Cassette. $8.00.

★ 768 ★
HOW TO REACT WHEN YOUR BRAKES FAIL
Close Productions
2020 San Carlos Boulevard
Fort Myers Beach, Florida   33931
Cassette. $8.00.

★ 769 ★
HOW TO REACT: WHEN YOUR HEADLIGHTS GO
OUT; WHEN YOUR CAR CATCHES FIRE
Close Productions
2020 San Carlos Boulevard
Fort Myers Beach, Florida   33931
Cassette. $8.00.

★ 770 ★
HOW TO REACT: WHEN YOUR RIGHT WHEEL
DROPS OFF THE PAVEMENT; WHEN YOUR HOOD
FLIES OPEN
Close Productions
2020 San Carlos Boulevard
Fort Myers Beach, Florida   33931
Cassette. $8.00.

★ 771 ★
HOW TO STAY ALIVE ON THE HIGHWAY
Tape Rental Library Incorporated
Post Office Box 2107
2507 Edna Drive
South Vineland, New Jersey 08360
Cassette. $16.95.

★ 772 ★
HOW TO USE YOUR EYES TO BECOME A BETTER
DRIVER
Close Productions
2020 San Carlos Boulevard
Fort Myers Beach, Florida   33931
Cassette. $8.00.

★ 773 ★
RAILROAD CROSSING EMERGENCIES: BUCKLE
UP FOR THE ODDS SAKE
    Close Productions
    2020 San Carlos Boulevard
    Fort Myers Beach, Florida 33931
Cassette. $8.00.

★ 774 ★
RIGHT OF WAY ISN'T ALWAYS RIGHT - TRAFFIC
CONTROL
    Close Productions
    2020 San Carlos Boulevard
    Fort Myers Beach, Florida 33931
Cassette. $8.00.

★ 775 ★
RULES OF THE ROAD - RIGHT OF WAY ISN'T
ALWAYS RIGHT
    Close Productions
    2020 San Carlos Boulevard
    Fort Myers Beach, Florida 33931
Cassette. $8.00.

★ 776 ★
SKIDS - AND HOW TO HANDLE THEM
    Close Productions
    2020 San Carlos Boulevard
    Fort Myers Beach, Florida 33931
Cassette. $8.00.

★ 777 ★
THE UNSEEN DANGERS OF DRIVING AT NIGHT
    Close Productions
    2020 San Carlos Boulevard
    Fort Myers Beach, Florida 33931
Cassette. $8.00.

★ 778 ★
WHAT TO DO AFTER AN ACCIDENT
    Close Productions
    2020 San Carlos Boulevard
    Fort Myers Beach, Florida 33931
Cassette. $8.00.

★ 779 ★
YOUR PHYSICAL FITNESS FOR DRIVING: HOW TO
PREVENT FATIGUE
    Close Productions
    2020 San Carlos Boulevard
    Fort Myers Beach, Florida 33931
Cassette. $8.00.

Films/Video/Filmstrips

★ 780 ★
ADVERSE WEATHER DRIVING
    Resource Incorporated
    13902 North Dale Mabry Highway
    Tampa, Florida 33624
Video cartridge. $75.00.

★ 781 ★
BE YOUR OWN TRAFFIC JUDGE (Definition of
preventable accidents)
    Resource Incorporated
    13902 North Dale Mabry Highway
    Tampa, Florida 33624
Video cartridge. $75.00.

★ 782 ★
BETTER BACKING (Backing techniques for truck
drivers)
    Resource Incorporated
    13902 North Dale Mabry Highway
    Tampa, Florida 33624
Video cartridge. $75.00.

★ 783 ★
CAR CARE
    Gamco-Siboney
    Box 1911
    Big Spring, Texas 79720
4 transparencies, manual. $29.40.

★ 784 ★
CITY DRIVING
    Resource Incorporated
    13902 North Dale Mabry Highway
    Tampa, Florida 33624
Video cartridge. $75.00.

★ 785 ★
GET 'EM OUT SAFELY (Evacuation techniques)
    Resource Incorporated
    13902 North Dale Mabry Highway
    Tampa, Florida 33624
Video cartridge. $75.00.

★ 786 ★
HOW TO DRIVE
    Gamco-Siboney
    Box 1911
    Big Spring, Texas 79720
7 transparencies, manual. $51.40.

★ 787 ★
PARKING
    Gamco-Siboney
    Box 1911
    Big Spring, Texas   79720
4 transparencies, manual. $29.40.

★ 788 ★
ROAD PROBLEMS – CITY
    Gamco-Siboney
    Box 1911
    Big Spring, Texas   79720
6 transparencies, manual. $44.10.

★ 789 ★
ROAD PROBLEMS – HIGHWAY
    Gamco-Siboney
    Box 1911
    Big Spring, Texas   79720
7 transparencies, manual. $51.45.

★ 790 ★
SEE-THINK-DO   (Prompt and correct decisions in defensive driving)
    Resource Incorporated
    13902 North Dale Mabry Highway
    Tampa, Florida   33624
Video cartridge. $75.00.

★ 791 ★
SIGNS
    Gamco-Siboney
    Box 1911
    Big Spring, Texas   79720
6 transparencies, manual. $44.10.

★ 792 ★
VEHICLE MANEUVERS
    Resource Incorporated
    13902 North Dale Mabry Highway
    Tampa, Florida   33624
Video cartridge. $75.00.

★ 793 ★
VISION AND REACTION
    Gamco-Siboney
    Box 1911
    Big Spring, Texas   79720
5 transparencies, manual. $36.75.

★ 794 ★
WINTER HAZARDS
    Resource Incorporated
    13902 North Dale Mabry Highway
    Tampa, Florida   33624
Video cartridge. $75.00.

Programmed Learning Materials

★ 795 ★
CITY
    Research Media Company
    96 Mount Auburn Street
    Cambridge, Massachusetts   02138
Programmed booklet. $1.50.

★ 796 ★
HIGHWAY
    Research Media Company
    96 Mount Auburn Street
    Cambridge, Massachusetts   02138
Programmed booklet. $1.50.

★ 797 ★
TROUBLE SHOOTING
    Research Media Company
    96 Mount Auburn Street
    Cambridge, Massachusetts   02138
Programmed booklet. $1.50.

DUTCH

Audio Cassettes/Tapes

★ 798 ★
BERLITZ COURSE IN DUTCH
    Berlitz Language Program
    Post Office Box 5109
    FDR Station
    New York, New York   10022
Cassette $5.95.   Also available on LP record.

★ 799 ★
SPOKEN DUTCH
Leonard Bloomfield
    Spoken Language Services Incorporated
    Post Office Box 783
    Ithaca, New York   14850
Coursebook and cassettes.

Printed Materials

★ 800 ★
DUTCH IN THREE MONTHS
David McKay Company Incorporated
750 Third Avenue
New York, New York 10017
Book. $3.95.

★ 801 ★
INTRODUCTION TO DUTCH
William S. Heinman Incorporated
1966 Broadway
New York, New York 10023
Book. 1975. $8.50.

★ 802 ★
TEACH YOURSELF DUTCH
H. Koolhoven
David McKay Company Incorporated
750 Third Avenue
New York, New York 10017
Book. $2.95.

EARTH SCIENCE

Films/Video/Filmstrips

★ 803 ★
THE EARTH: MAN'S GEOLOGIC ENVIRONMENT
George Brown, George Ladd
Charles E. Merrill Publishing Company
1300 Alum Creek Drive
Box 508
Columbus, Ohio 43216
Text and 7 sound filmstrips.

★ 804 ★
THE UNIVERSE
John C. Brandt
Charles E. Merrill Publishing Company
1300 Alum Creek Drive
Box 508
Columbus, Ohio 43216
Text and 5 sound filmstrips.

Printed Materials

★ 805 ★
DYNAMIC EARTH: AN INTRODUCTION TO EARTH
SCIENCE
H. Lepp

McGraw-Hill Book Company
1221 Avenue of the Americas
New York, New York 10036
Book. 1973. $13.95.

ECONOMICS

Audio Cassettes/Tapes

★ 806 ★
ECHOES THE GROWTH OF THE NATION AND
IT'S ECONOMY
Thompson-Mitchell and Associates
3384 Peachtree Road Northeast
Atlanta, Georgia 30326
9 cassettes. $75.00.

★ 807 ★
ECONOMICS
National Book Company
1019 Southwest Tenth Avenue
Portland, Oregon 97206
14 cassettes. $191.55.

★ 808 ★
ECONOMICS
Thompson-Mitchell and Associates
3384 Peachtree Road Northeast
Atlanta, Georgia 30326
2 cassettes. $9.98 each.

★ 809 ★
GENERAL ECONOMICS/CONSUMER ECONOMICS
Educational Century Programming
1201 East Johnson Street
Jonesboro, Arkansas 72401
Cassette. $6.00.

★ 810 ★
INTRODUCTION TO ECONOMICS
Tape Rental Library Incorporated
Post Office Box 2107
2507 Edna Drive
South Vineland, New Jersey 08360
Cassette. $6.95.

★ 811 ★
MISTY MONEY IN THE WORLD OF WORK
Gamco-Siboney
Box 1911
Big Spring, Texas 79720
Cassette. $12.50.

★ 812 ★
SOUND OF THE ECONOMY
     Citibank
     399 Park Avenue
     New York, New York 10022
Monthly cassette and transcript. $96.00 annually.

Correspondence Courses

★ 813 ★
BASIC ECONOMICS
     University of Florida
     Division of Continuing Education
     2012 West University Avenue
     Gainesville, Florida 32603
Correspondence course.

★ 814 ★
ECONOMICS
     University of Arkansas
     Department of Independent Study
     346 West Avenue
     Fayetteville, Arkansas 72701
Correspondence course.

★ 815 ★
PRINCIPLES OF ECONOMICS
     University of Kentucky
     Independent Study Program
     Freeze Hall, Room 1
     Lexington, Kentucky 40506
Correspondence course.

★ 816 ★
PRINCIPLES OF ECONOMICS
     University of Nebraska
     511 Nebraska Hall
     Lincoln, Nebraska 68588
Correspondence course.

★ 817 ★
PRINCIPLES OF ECONOMICS
     University of South Carolina
     Department of Correspondence Study
     Division of Continuing Education
     Columbia, South Carolina 29208
Correspondence course. $69.00.

Films/Video/Filmstrips

★ 818 ★
ECONOMIC HISTORY
     Gamco-Siboney
     Box 1911
     Big Spring, Texas 79720
11 transparencies and manual. $77.00.

★ 819 ★
ECONOMICS IN ACTION
     Gamco-Siboney
     Box 1911
     Big Spring, Texas 79720
17 transparencies and manual. $119.00.

★ 820 ★
THE MODERN ECONOMY IN ACTION: AN
ANALYTICAL APPROACH
     United Transparencies
     Box 688
     Binghamton, New York 13902
32 transparencies and manual. $62.70.

★ 821 ★
POLITICAL ECONOMY AND PHILOSOPHY
     Gamco-Siboney
     Box 1911
     Big Spring, Texas 79720
7 transparencies and manual. $49.00.

★ 822 ★
PRINCIPLES OF BUSINESS AND ECONOMICS
     United Transparencies
     Box 688
     Binghamton, New York 13902
80 transparencies and manual. $139.70.

Multimedia Kits

★ 823 ★
THE DOLLAR IN TODAY'S WORLD (WHAT YOUR
DOLLAR BUYS AT HOME AND ABROAD)
     Thompson-Mitchell and Associates
     3384 Peachtree Road Northeast
     Atlanta, Georgia 30326
Filmstrip with cassette. $22.00.

Programmed Learning Materials

★ 824 ★
PRINCIPLES OF ECONOMICS: MACRO
Lloyd Reynolds
    Learning Systems Company
    1818 Ridge Road
    Homewood, Illinois 60430
Programmed learning aid. $4.50.

★ 825 ★
PRINCIPLES OF ECONOMICS: MICRO
Lloyd Reynolds
    Learning Systems Company
    1818 Ridge Road
    Homewood, Illinois 60430
Programmed learning kit. $4.50.

EDITING

See also: Communication, Written;
          Journalism

Printed Materials

★ 826 ★
TECHNICAL EDITING
Benjamin Will
    Greenwood Press Incorporated
    51 Riverside Avenue
    Westport, Connecticut 06880
Book. 1975. $14.50.

★ 827 ★
TECHNICAL EDITING: PRINCIPLES AND
PRACTICES
    Society for Technical Communication
    1010 Vermont Avenue, Northwest
    Washington, D.C. 20005
Book. 1975. $9.00.

EDUCATIONAL PLANNING

See also: Classroom Instruction

Audio Cassettes/Tapes

★ 828 ★
MEASUREMENT AND EVALUATION IN THE
CLASSROOM
John R. Hills
    Charles E. Merrill Publishing Company
    1300 Alum Creek Drive
    Box 508
    Columbus, Ohio 43216
Text workbook and audio tapes. $135.00.

Films/Video/Filmstrips

★ 829 ★
CONTINGENCY MANAGEMENT
Anne Langstaff, Cara Volkmor
    Charles E. Merrill Publishing Company
    1300 Alum Creek Drive
    Box 508
    Columbus, Ohio 43216
4 filmstrips and guidebook.

★ 830 ★
INSTRUCTIONAL SUPERVISION
Norman J. Boyan, Willis D. Copeland
    Charles E. Merrill Publishing Company
    1300 Alum Creek Drive
    Box 508
    Columbus, Ohio 43216
Text and audiovisual materials.

★ 831 ★
STRUCTURING THE CLASSROOM FOR SUCCESS
Cara Volkmor, Anne Langstaff, Marilyn Higgins
    Charles E. Merrill Publishing Company
    1300 Alum Creek Drive
    Box 508
    Columbus, Ohio 43216
6 sound filmstrips and guidebooks. $130.00.

★ 832 ★
VALUES IN THE CLASSROOM
Cara Volkmore, Anne Langstaff,
Louis Raths
    Charles E. Merrill Publishing Company
    1300 Alum Creek Drive
    Box 508
    Columbus, Ohio 43216
Workbook and 6 sound filmstrips. $130.00.

Multimedia Kits

★ 833 ★
CRITERION TEST ITEMS
    Education Systems for the Future
    10451 Twin Rivers Road
    Columbia, Maryland 21044
Cassettes and slides. $45.00.

★ 834 ★

DEVELOPING INSTRUCTIONAL MATERIAL
        Education Systems for the Future
        10451 Twin Rivers Road
        Columbia, Maryland 21044
Cassettes and slides. $45.00.

★ 835 ★

LEARNING HIERARCHY CONSTRUCTION
        Education Systems for the Future
        10451 Twin Rivers Road
        Columbia, Maryland 21044
Cassettes and slides. $45.00.

★ 836 ★

OVERVIEW AND TASK ANALYSIS
        Education Systems for the Future
        10451 Twin Rivers Road
        Columbia, Maryland 21044
Cassettes and slides. $45.00.

★ 837 ★

PRODUCTION TECHNIQUES FOR INSTRUCTIONAL
GRAPHIC MATERIAL
C. Y. Oh, R. Christie, C. Nishimura
        Charles E. Merrill Publishing Company
        1300 Alum Creek Drive
        Box 508
        Columbus, Ohio 43216
Manual, sound filmstrips and cassettes.

★ 838 ★

QUESTIONING AND SENSITIVE LISTENING
TECHNIQUES
Arthur A. Carin
        Charles E. Merrill Publishing Company
        1300 Alum Creek Drive
        Box 508
        Columbus, Ohio 43216
Text with filmstrips and cassettes. $185.00.

★ 839 ★

SELECTING STRATEGIES, MEDIA AND MATERIALS
        Education Systems for the Future
        10451 Twin Rivers Road
        Columbia, Maryland 21044
Cassettes and slides. $45.00.

★ 840 ★

VALIDATING INSTRUCTIONAL MATERIALS
        Education Systems for the Future
        10451 Twin Rivers Road
        Columbia, Maryland 21044
Cassettes and slides. $45.00.

Printed Materials

★ 841 ★

BEHAVIOR TASK ANALYSIS
        Education Systems for the Future
        10451 Twin Rivers Road
        Columbia, Maryland 21044
Self instructional workbook. $4.50.

★ 842 ★

CRITERION TEST ITEMS
        Education Systems for the Future
        10451 Twin Rivers Road
        Columbia, Maryland 21044
Self instructional workbook. $4.50.

★ 843 ★

DEVELOPING INSTRUCTIONAL MATERIAL
        Education Systems for the Future
        10451 Twin Rivers Road
        Columbia, Maryland 21044
Self instructional workbook. $3.98.

★ 844 ★

LEARNING HIERARCHIES AND MODULES
        Education Systems for the Future
        10451 Twin Rivers Road
        Columbia, Maryland 21044
Self instructional workbook. $3.98.

★ 845 ★

SELECTING INSTRUCTIONAL STRATEGIES
        Education Systems for the Future
        10451 Twin Rivers Road
        Columbia, Maryland 21044
Self instructional workbook. $3.98.

★ 846 ★

SELECTING MEDIA AND MATERIALS
        Education Systems for the Future
        10451 Twin Rivers Road
        Columbia, Maryland 21044
Self instructional workbook. $3.98.

★ 847 ★

VALIDATING INSTRUCTIONAL MATERIALS
        Education Systems for the Future
        10451 Twin Rivers Road
        Columbia, Maryland 21044
Self instructional workbook. $3.98.

ELECTRICAL MAINTENANCE

Correspondence Courses

★ 848 ★
ELECTRICAL CIRCUITS
University of Arkansas
Department of Independent Study
346 West Avenue
Fayetteville, Arkansas   72701
Correspondence course.

★ 849 ★
ELECTRICAL CONTRACTOR
International Correspondence School
Scranton, Pennsylvania 18515
Multi-module correspondence course.

★ 850 ★
ELECTRICIAN COURSE
International Correspondence School
Scranton, Pennsylvania 18515
Multi-module correspondence course.

★ 851 ★
INDUSTRIAL ELECTRICAL TECHNICIAN
International Correspondence School
Scranton, Pennsylvania 18515
Multi-module correspondence course.

★ 852 ★
INDUSTRIAL ELECTRICIAN
International Correspondence School
Scranton, Pennsylvania 18515
Multi-module correspondence course.

★ 853 ★
INDUSTRIAL MAINTENANCE ELECTRICIAN COURSE
International Correspondence School
Scranton, Pennsylvania 18515
Multi-module correspondence course.

Films/Video/Filmstrips

★ 854 ★
HOUSE WIRING
DCA Educational Products
424 Valley Road
Warrington, Pennsylvania 18976
Sound filmstrips of 3 units. $45.00 each.

Programmed Learning Materials

★ 855 ★
SINGLE-PHASE MOTORS
TPC Training Services
Technical Publishing Company
1301 South Grove Avenue
Barrington, Illinois 60010
Programmed text of 10 lessons. $22.50.

★ 856 ★
THREE-PHASE SYSTEMS
TPC Training Systems
Technical Publishing Company
1301 South Grove Avenue
Barrington, Illinois 60010
Programmed text of 10 lessons. $22.50.

ELECTRONICS

Audio Cassettes/Tapes

★ 857 ★
BASIC ELECTRONICS LABORATORY
Donald Beaty
Charles E. Merrill Publishing Company
1300 Alum Creek Drive
Box 508
Columbus, Ohio 43216
Workbooks and cassettes. $275.00.

Correspondence Courses

★ 858 ★
AUTOMATION ELECTRONICS
Commercial Trades Institute
6201 West Howard Street
Chicago, Illinois 60648
Correspondence course. $895.00.

★ 859 ★
ELECTRICAL ENGINEERING
Engineering Registration Studies
Post Office Box 24550
Los Angeles, California 90024
Home study course. $65.00.

★ 860 ★
ELECTRONICS ENGINEERING
Cleveland Institute of Electronics
1776 East 17th Street
Cleveland, Ohio 44114
Correspondence course.

★ 861 ★

ELECTRONICS TECHNOLOGY
    Cleveland Institute of Electronics
    1776 East 17th Street
    Cleveland, Ohio 44114
Correspondence course.

★ 862 ★

ELECTRONICS TECHNOLOGY
    International Correspondence School
    Scranton, Pennsylvania 18515
Multi-module correspondence course.

★ 863 ★

ELECTRONICS TECHNOLOGY AND ENGINEERING
WITH LABORATORY
    Cleveland Institute of Electronics
    1776 East 17th Street
    Cleveland, Ohio 44114
Correspondence course.

★ 864 ★

FUNDAMENTAL ELECTRONICS
    Electronics Technical Institute
    1500 Cardinal Drive
    Little Falls, New Jersey 07424
Correspondence course.

★ 865 ★

FUNDAMENTALS OF ELECTRICITY
    University of Nebraska
    511 Nebraska Hall
    Lincoln, Nebraska 68588
Correspondence course.

★ 866 ★

INDUSTRIAL ELECTRONICS
    Cleveland Institute of Electronics
    1776 East 17th Street
    Cleveland, Ohio 44114
Correspondence course.

Films/Video/Filmstrips

★ 867 ★

A C REACTANCE
    Resource Incorporated
    13902 North Dale Mabry Highway
    Tampa, Florida 33624
Video cartridge with workbook. $100.00.

★ 868 ★

ATOM AND ELECTRON FLOW
    Resource Incorporated
    13902 North Dale Mabry Highway
    Tampa, Florida 33624
Video cartridge with workbook. $100.00.

★ 869 ★

D.C. AND A.C. CIRCUITS
    Resource Incorporated
    13902 North Dale Mabry Highway
    Tampa, Florida 33624
Video cartridge with workbook. $100.00.

★ 870 ★

ELECTRIC UTILITY DOLLAR (Basic economies of
utility operation)
    Resource Incorporated
    13902 North Dale Mabry Highway
    Tampa, Florida 33624
Video cartridge. $100.00.

★ 871 ★

ELECTRICAL CONCEPTS AND TERMS
    Resource Incorporated
    13902 North Dale Mabry Highway
    Tampa, Florida 33624
Video cartridge. $100.00.

★ 872 ★

ELECTRICAL CONCEPTS AND TERMS, PARTS
1, 2, and 3
    Resource Incorporated
    13902 North Dale Mabry Highway
    Tampa, Florida 33624
Video cartridge with workbook. $100.00 each.

★ 873 ★

A HERITAGE OF SERVICE (History of the electric
utility industry)
    Resource Incorporated
    13902 North Dale Mabry Highway
    Tampa, Florida 33624
Video cartridge. $100.00.

★ 874 ★

HOW TO GENERATE AND DISTRIBUTE ELECTRICITY
    Resource Incorporated
    13902 North Dale Mabry Highway
    Tampa, Florida 33624
Video cartridge. $100.00.

★ 875 ★
MAGNETISM AND POWER
Resource Incorporated
13902 North Dale Mabry Highway
Tampa, Florida 33624
Video cartridge with workbook. $100.00.

★ 876 ★
PRINCIPLES OF FREQUENCY RESPONSE
Instrument Society of America
400 Stanwix Street
Pittsburgh, Pennsylvania 15222
Film with study guide.

Printed Materials

★ 877 ★
INTRODUCTORY CIRCUIT ANALYSIS
Robert Boylestad
Charles E. Merrill Publishing Company
1300 Alum Creek Drive
Box 508
Columbus, Ohio 43216
Text with examinations. $16.95.

★ 878 ★
UNDERSTANDING I C OPERATIONAL AMPLIFIERS
Roger Melen, Harry Garland
Howard W. Sams and Company
4300 West 62nd Street
Indianapolis, Indiana 46268
Book. 1971. $3.95.

Programmed Learning Materials

★ 879 ★
A-C CONTROL EQUIPMENT
TPC Training Systems
Technical Publishing Company
1301 South Grove Avenue
Barrington, Illinois 60010
Programmed text of 10 lessons. $22.50.

★ 880 ★
BATTERIES AND D C CIRCUITS
TPC Training Systems
Technical Publishing Company
1301 South Grove Avenue
Barrington, Illinois 60010
Programmed text of 10 lessons. $22.50.

★ 881 ★
CONTROL OF STATIC ELECTRICITY
E. I. du Pont de Nemours and Company
Applied Technology Division
Room B 4204
Wilmington, Delaware 19898
Programmed course of approximately 4 hours. $8.60.

★ 882 ★
D-C EQUIPMENT AND CONTROLS
TPC Training Systems
Technical Publishing Company
1301 South Grove Avenue
Barrington, Illinois 60010
Programmed text of 10 lessons. $22.50.

★ 883 ★
ELECTRICAL MEASURING INSTRUMENTS
TPC Training Systems
Technical Publishing Company
1301 South Grove Avenue
Barrington, Illinois 60010
Programmed text of 10 lessons. $22.50.

★ 884 ★
ELECTRICAL PROTECTIVE DEVICES
TPC Training Services
Technical Publishing Company
1301 South Grove Avenue
Barrington, Illinois 60010
Programmed text of 10 lessons. $22.50.

★ 885 ★
ELECTRICAL SCIENCE
Norman Balabanian, Wilbur Le Page
McGraw-Hill Book Company
1221 Avenue of the Americas
New York, New York 10036
Programmed instruction. 1973. $10.00.

★ 886 ★
ELECTRICAL TROUBLESHOOTING
TPC Training Systems
Technical Publishing Company
1301 South Grove Avenue
Barrington, Illinois 60010
Programmed text of 10 lessons. $22.50.

★ 887 ★
INTRODUCTION TO ELECTRICITY AND
ELECTRONICS
TPC Training Systems
    Technical Publishing Company
    1301 South Grove Avenue
    Barrington, Illinois 60010
Programmed text of 10 lessons. $22.50.

★ 888 ★
RECOGNIZING CIRCUIT SYMBOLS, ELECTRONICS
EDITION
M. McGaulley
    University of Alabama
    Post Office Box 2847
    University, Alabama 35486
Programmed text. $2.00.

★ 889 ★
TRANSFORMERS AND A-C CIRCUITS
TPC Training Systems
    Technical Publishing Company
    1301 South Grove Avenue
    Barrington, Illinois 60010
Programmed text of 10 lessons. $22.50.

EMPLOYEE BENEFITS

See also: Profit Sharing

Audio Cassettes/Tapes

★ 890 ★
DEFERRED COMPENSATION/SALARY CONTINUATION
Charles H. Houseman
    Tape Rental Library Incorporated
    Post Office Box 2107
    2507 Edna Drive
    South Vineland, New Jersey 08360
Cassette.

★ 891 ★
EXPLAINING PAY POLICY
    American Management Associations
    135 West 50th Street
    New York, New York 10020
Cassette. $18.00.

EMPLOYEE HEALTH
See: HEALTH, EMPLOYEE

EMPLOYEE RELATIONS
See: PERSONNEL MANAGEMENT

EMPLOYEE TRAINING

See also: Organizational Development;
    Training Techniques

Audio Cassettes/Tapes

★ 892 ★
THE BOSS
Earl Nightingale
    Tape Rental Library Incorporated
    Post Office Box 2107
    2507 Edna Drive
    South Vineland, New Jersey 08360
Cassette. $9.00.

★ 893 ★
EVALUATING WORKABLE IDEAS – WORKING WITH
SUPERVISORS
    Thompson-Mitchell and Associates
    3384 Peachtree Road Northeast
    Atlanta, Georgia 30326
Cassette. $6.00.

★ 894 ★
ON THE JOB – NEW EMPLOYEE TRAINING
    Thompson-Mitchell and Associates
    3384 Peachtree Road Northeast
    Atlanta, Georgia 30326
20 cassettes. $230.00.

★ 895 ★
TEACHING A NEW EMPLOYEE HIS JOB
    Thompson-Mitchell and Associates
    3384 Peachtree Road Northeast
    Atlanta, Georgia 30326
Cassette. $15.00.

Films/Video/Filmstrips

★ 896 ★
BOSS/SECRETARY: MASTER KEY TO SUCCESS –
COMBINATION FOR RESULTS
Thompson–Mitchell and Associates
3384 Peachtree Road Northeast
Atlanta, Georgia 30326
Filmstrip (16 mm). $250.00.

★ 897 ★
BOSS/SECRETARY: MASTER KEY TO SUCCESS –
OPENING THE DOOR
Thompson–Mitchell and Associates
3384 Peachtree Road Northeast
Atlanta, Georgia 30326
Filmstrip (16 mm). $250.00.

★ 898 ★
ORIENTATION FOR NEW EMPLOYEES
Resource Incorporated
13902 North Dale Mabry Highway
Tampa, Florida 33624
Video cartridge. $100.00.

★ 899 ★
SOMETHING EXTRA (Effective Communication
with the Boss)
Thompson–Mitchell and Associates
3384 Peachtree Road Northeast
Atlanta, Georgia 30326
Filmstrip (16 mm). $250.00.

★ 900 ★
SUGGESTIONS FOR NEW EMPLOYEES
United Transparencies
Box 688
Binghamton, New York 13902
5 transparencies and manual. $9.74.

★ 901 ★
WELCOME ABOARD
Roundtable Films
113 North San Vincente Boulevard
Beverly Hills, California 90211
Film and guidebook.

Multimedia Kits

★ 902 ★
GETTING IT DONE RIGHT WITH PERSONAL JOB
ORIENTATION
Thompson–Mitchell and Associates
3384 Peachtree Road Northeast
Atlanta, Georgia 30326
Filmstrip with cassette. $55.00.

★ 903 ★
GETTING IT DONE RIGHT WITH PROPER JOB
INSTRUCTION
Thompson–Mitchell and Associates
3384 Peachtree Road Northeast
Atlanta, Georgia 30326
Filmstrip with cassette. $55.00.

★ 904 ★
MAKING THE BOSS LOOK GOOD
Resources for Education and Management
Incorporated
544 Medlock Road, Suite 210
Decatur, Georgia 30030
Filmstrip with cassette. $60.00.

Printed Materials

★ 905 ★
EFFECTIVE JOB TRAINING
General Motors Education and Training Division
1700 West Third Avenue
Flint, Michigan 48502
Self instruction workbook. $6.50.

Programmed Learning Materials

★ 906 ★
HOW TO TRAIN ON THE JOB
American Management Associations
135 West 50th Street
New York, New York 10020
Programmed text. $7.00.

★ 907 ★
ON THE JOB TRAINING
American Management Associations
135 West 50th Street
New York, New York 10020
Programmed text. $25.00.

ENGINEERING

See also: Civil Engineering

Correspondence Courses

★ 908 ★
BASIC ENGINEERING GRAPHICS
University of Kentucky
Independent Study Program
Freeze Hall, Room 1
Lexington, Kentucky 40506
Correspondence course.

★ 909 ★
CIVIL ENGINEERING
Engineering Registration Studies
Post Office Box 24550
Los Angeles, California 90024
Home study course. $65.00.

★ 910 ★
ENGINEERING ECONOMY
University of Florida
Division of Continuing Education
2012 West University Avenue
Gainesville, Florida 32603
Correspondence course.

★ 911 ★
ENGINEERING MECHANICS
University of Missouri
Center for Independent Study
514 South Fifth Street
Columbia, Missouri 65211
Correspondence course. $80.00.

★ 912 ★
FUNDAMENTALS OF ENGINEERING
Engineering Registration Studies
Post Office Box 24550
Los Angeles, California 90024
Home study course. $65.00.

★ 913 ★
HIGHWAY ENGINEERING TECHNOLOGY
International Correspondence School
Scranton, Pennsylvania 18515
Multi-module correspondence course.

★ 914 ★
STRUCTURAL ENGINEERING
International Correspondence School
Scranton, Pennsylvania 18515
Multi-module correspondence course.

★ 915 ★
SURVEY AND MAPPING
International Correspondence School
Scranton, Pennsylvania 18515
Multi-module correspondence course.

Programmed Learning Materials

★ 916 ★
READING ENGINEERING DRAWINGS
E. I. du Pont de Nemours and Company
Applied Technology Division
Room B 4204
Wilmington, Delaware 19898
Programmed course of approximately 12 hours.
$22.10.

ENGINEERING, BROADCAST
See: BROADCAST ENGINEERING

ENVIRONMENT
See: POLLUTION CONTROL

EQUAL EMPLOYMENT OPPORTUNITY

See also: Personnel Management;
Women in Business

Audio Cassettes/Tapes

★ 917 ★
DO YOU DISCRIMINATE?
Tape Rental Library Incorporated
Post Office Box 2107
2507 Edna Drive
South Vineland, New Jersey 08360
Cassette.

★ 918 ★
UNDER INVESTIGATION: AGE DISCRIMINATION
    AMACOM
    American Management Associations
    135 West 50th Street
    New York, New York 10020
Cassette with manual. $25.00.

919 ★
UNDER INVESTIGATION: EQUAL PAY
    AMACOM
    American Management Associations
    135 West 50th Street
    New York, New York 10020
Cassette with manual. $25.00.

Correspondence Courses

★ 920 ★
CURRENT ISSUES IN PERSONNEL/AFFIRMATIVE
ACTION POLICY
    Western Washington State College
    Center for Continuing Education
    Edens Hall South
    Bellingham, Washington 98225
Correspondence course.

Films/Video/Filmstrips

★ 921 ★
EQUAL OPPORTUNITY
    Salenger Educational Media
    1635 12th Street
    Santa Monica, California 90404
Film with guide and work sheets.   (Rental available).

★ 922 ★
MANAGEMENT MOTIVATION AND THE NEW
MINORITY WORKER
    Roundtable Films
    113 North San Vincente Boulevard
    Beverly Hills, California 90211
Film and guidebook.

Multimedia Kits

★ 923 ★
AFFIRMATIVE ACTION AND EQUAL EMPLOYMENT
OPPORTUNITY
    Lansford Publishing Company
    Post Office Box 8711
    San Jose, California 95155
Multimedia kit. $229.00.

★ 924 ★
CAREER-ORIENTED PROGRAMS FOR WOMEN AND
MINORITIES
    Ergonco Performance Source
    Northwest O'Hare Office Park, Suite 119
    2474 Dempster Street
    Des Plains, Illinois 60016
Multimedia self-study program.

★ 925 ★
EQUAL EMPLOYMENT OPPORTUNITY COMPLIANCE:
A PRACTICAL COURSE FOR MANAGERS
    American Management Associations
    135 West 50th Street
    New York, New York 10020
Cassettes, slides and workbooks. $189.00.

★ 926 ★
MANAGEMENT AND PREJUDICE: A PLAN FOR
AFFIRMATIVE ACTION
    Ergonco Performance Source
    Northwest O'Hare Office Park, Suite 119
    2474 Dempster Street
    Des Plains, Illinois 60016
Multimedia self-study program.

★ 927 ★
SEX FAIRNESS IN CAREER GUIDANCE
    ABT Publications
    55 Wheeler Street
    Cambridge, Massachusetts 02138
Learning kit.

★ 928 ★
TREEO TRAINING IN EQUAL EMPLOYMENT
OPPORTUNITY
    Saint Pierre Associates
    1237 Seventh Street
    Santa Monica, California 90410
160 page training manual, slides and cassette.
$475.00.

Printed Materials

★ 929 ★
FEDERAL WAGE HOUR EQUAL PAY AND EQUAL
OPPORTUNITY LAWS
    The Institute for Management
    IFM Building
    Old Saybrook, Connecticut 06475
Book. $29.95.

ESPERANTO

Printed Materials

★ 930 ★
LEARN ESPERANTO: FOR ENGLISH SPEAKERS
    Saphrograph Company
    194 Elizabeth Street
    New York, New York 10012
Book. $5.00.

★ 931 ★
TEACH YOURSELF ESPERANTO
John Cresswell, John Hartley
    David McKay Company Incorporated
    750 Third Avenue
    New York, New York 10017
Self-study text. $2.95.

ESTATE PLANNING

See also: Financial Planning

Audio Cassettes/Tapes

★ 932 ★
ESTATE PLANNING COURSE
    American Institute of Certified Public
       Accountants
    1211 Avenue of the Americas
    New York, New York 10003
4 cassettes, workbook and tests. $55.00.

★ 933 ★
ESTATE PLANNING FOR THE BUSINESS OWNER
L. D. Box
    Tape Rental Library Incorporated
    Post Office Box 2107
    2507 Edna Drive
    South Vineland, New Jersey 08360
Cassette.

★ 934 ★
ESTATE PLANNING ROUTES TO MULTI-MILLION
DOLLAR PRODUCTION
W. Lawrence Mackle
    Tape Rental Library Incorporated
    Post Office Box 2107
    2507 Edna Drive
    South Vineland, New Jersey 08360
Cassette.

★ 935 ★
YOUR WIFE: THE SURVIVING CAPTAIN OF YOUR
ESTATE PLANNING TEAM
Max B. Lewis
    Tape Rental Library Incorporated
    Post Office Box 2107
    2507 Edna Drive
    South Vineland, New Jersey 08360
Cassette.

Printed Materials

★ 936 ★
THE ESTATE PLANNER'S COMPLETE GUIDE AND
WORKBOOK
    Panel Publications
    14 Plaza Road
    Greenvale, New York 11548
Workbook. 1976. $75.00.

★ 937 ★
HOW TO SAVE TAXES THROUGH ESTATE
PLANNING
    Dow Jones Books
    Post Office Box 445
    Chicopee, Massachusetts 01021
Book. 1976. $6.95.

EVALUATION
See: PERFORMANCE APPRAISAL

EXECUTIVE COMPENSATION

See also: Employee Benefits;
           Personnel Management

Audio Cassettes/Tapes

★ 938 ★
A STRATEGY FOR COMPENSATION OF MANAGERS
    Thompson-Mitchell and Associates
    3384 Peachtree Road Northeast
    Atlanta, Georgia 30326
Cassette. $19.95.

EXECUTIVE SKILLS

See also: headings under Management;
headings under Supervision

Audio Cassettes/Tapes

★ 939 ★
THE DORMANT EXECUTIVE - SETTING EXAMPLES
Thompson-Mitchell and Associates
3384 Peachtree Road Northeast
Atlanta, Georgia 30326
Cassette. $6.00.

★ 940 ★
THE EFFECTIVE EXECUTIVE
Thompson-Mitchell and Associates
3384 Peachtree Road Northeast
Atlanta, Georgia 30326
Cassette. $6.00.

★ 941 ★
THE EXECUTIVE (Personal Motivation Course)
Tape Rental Library Incorporated
Post Office Box 2107
2507 Edna Drive
South Vineland, New Jersey 08360
14 cassettes. $95.00.

★ 942 ★
EXECUTIVE LECTURE SERIES
National Book Company
1019 Southwest Tenth Avenue
Portland, Oregon 97206
7 cassettes. $77.10.

★ 943 ★
EXECUTIVE SKILLS
George Odiorne
MBO Incorporated
157 Pontoosic Road
Westfield, Massachusetts 01085
12 cassettes and manual. $150.00.

★ 944 ★
WHAT ARE EXECUTIVE SKILLS
George Odiorne
MBO Incorporated
157 Pontoosic Road
Westfield, Massachusetts 01035
Cassette and manual. $15.00.

FARM MANAGEMENT
See: AGRICULTURE

FASHION

See also: Art

Films/Video/Filmstrips

★ 945 ★
FASHION RENDERING
Scope Productions Incorporated
Post Office Box 5515
Fresno, California 93755
2 films (8 mm) and student guides. $42.00.

FIBERGLASS REPAIR

Correspondence Courses

★ 946 ★
FIBERGLASS REPAIR
Fibertex Industries
412 South Lyon Street
Santa Ana, California 92701
Home study course.

FINANCIAL ANALYSIS

See also: Accounting

Audio Cassettes/Tapes

★ 947 ★
CAPITAL NEEDS ANALYSIS
Thomas J. Wolff
Tape Rental Library Incorporated
Post Office Box 2107
2507 Edna Drive
South Vineland, New Jersey 08360
Cassette.

★ 948 ★
PROFESSIONAL CORPORATIONS
Marshall Wolper, Bill Huey
Tape Rental Library Incorporated
Post Office Box 2107
2507 Edna Drive
South Vineland, New Jersey 08360
Cassette.

Correspondence Courses

★ 949 ★
ADVANCED CREDIT AND FINANCIAL ANALYSIS
 Dun and Bradstreet Incorporated
 Business Education Division
 Box 803
 Church Street Station
 New York, New York 10008
Instruction through self-study text and correspondence with instructor. $135.00.

★ 950 ★
CORPORATE ANALYSIS
 The Thomas Institute
 Box 22
 New Canaan, Connecticut 06840
Self-study course. $150.00.

★ 951 ★
CREDIT AND FINANCIAL ANALYSIS
 Dun and Bradstreet Incorporated
 Business Education Division
 Box 803
 Church Street Station
 New York, New York 10008
Instruction through self-study text and correspondence with instructor. $125.00.

★ 952 ★
PRINCIPLES OF FINANCE
 University of Missouri
 Center for Independent Study
 514 South Fifth Street
 Columbia, Missouri 65211
Correspondence course. $80.00.

Games/Simulations

★ 953 ★
FINANCIAL ANALYSIS
Erwin Rausch
 Didactic Systems Incorporated
 Box 457
 Cranford, New Jersey 07016
Simulation Game. $24.00.

Printed Materials

★ 954 ★
HOW TO ASSESS THE STRENGTHS AND WEAKNESSES OF A BUSINESS ENTERPRISE

 Scientific Methods Incorporated
 Box 195
 Austin, Texas 78767
6 workbooks. · $30.00.

FINANCIAL MANAGEMENT

 See also: Accounting; headings under Management; Managerial Accounting

Audio Cassettes/Tapes

★ 955 ★
ACQUIRING, MERGING, AND SELLING COMPANIES
 Tape Rental Library Incorporated
 Post Office Box 2107
 2507 Edna Drive
 South Vineland, New Jersey 08360
12 cassettes with workbook. $295.00.

★ 956 ★
FINANCE AND ACCOUNTING FOR NON-FINANCIAL MANAGERS
 American Management Associations
 135 West 50th Street
 New York, New York 10020
6 cassettes with workbook. $100.00.

★ 957 ★
MANAGERIAL FINANCE FOR NON-FINANCIAL MANAGERS
 Management Resources Incorporated
 757 Third Avenue
 New York, New York 10017
8 unit cassette with tests and feedback service. $225.00.

★ 958 ★
MANAGING THE CLOSELY HELD CORPORATION
 Tape Rental Library Incorporated
 Post Office Box 2107
 2507 Edna Drive
 South Vineland, New Jersey 08360
17 cassettes with workbooks. $295.00.

Correspondence Courses

★ 959 ★
BUSINESS MANAGEMENT
 International Correspondence School
 Scranton, Pennsylvania 18515
Multi-module correspondence course.

★ 960 ★
CORPORATE FINANCE
        University of Kentucky
        Independent Study Program
        Freeze Hall, Room 1
        Lexington, Kentucky   40506
Correspondence course.

★ 961 ★
CORPORATION FINANCE
        Pennsylvania State University
        Department of Independent Study by
            Correspondence
        Three Sheilds Building
        University Park, Pennsylvania   16802
Correspondence course.

★ 962 ★
PERSONAL FINANCIAL MANAGEMENT
        Indiana State University
        Independent Study Office
        Terre Haute, Indiana   47809
Independent study course.

Film/Video/Filmstrips

★ 963 ★
FINANCIAL MANAGEMENT
Frame and Curry
        Charles E. Merrill Publishing Company
        1300 Alum Creek Drive
        Box 508
        Columbus, Ohio   43216
Sound filmstrips with text. $420.00.

Games/Simulations

★ 964 ★
ACHIEVING RESULTS THROUGH FINANCIAL
MANAGEMENT
        Society of Manufacturing Engineers
        20501 Ford Road
        Post Office Box 930
        Dearborn, Michigan   48128
Simulation with correspondent feedback. $85.00.

★ 965 ★
FINANCIAL MANAGEMENT DECISION GAME
Leroy Brooks
        Richard D. Irwin Incorporated
        1818 Ridge Road
        Homewood, Illinois   60430
Game.   1975. $5.95.

Printed Materials

★ 966 ★
BUSINESS FINANCE: THE MANAGEMENT
APPROACH
Richard S. Osborn
        Irvington Publishers
        551 Fifth Avenue
        New York, New York   10017
Text and manual. $9.95.

★ 967 ★
FINANCIAL ACCOUNTING: A GENERAL
MANAGEMENT APPROACH
Almand Coleman
        John Wiley and Sons Incorporated
        605 Third Avenue
        New York, New York   10016
Book.   1970. $17.25.

★ 968 ★
FINANCIAL MANAGEMENT
        Scientific Methods Incorporated
        Box 195
        Austin, Texas   78767
Workbook. $6.00.

★ 969 ★
FINANCIALLY SPEAKING
        General Motors Education and Training
            Division
        1700 West Third Avenue
        Flint, Michigan   48502
Self instruction workbook. $6.50.

★ 970 ★
FUNDAMENTALS OF FINANCIAL MANAGEMENT
J. Van Horne
        Prentice-Hall Incorporated
        Englewood Cliffs, New Jersey   07632
Book.   1975. $15.95.

★ 971 ★
PRINCIPLES OF MANAGERIAL FINANCE
Lawrence Gitman
        Harper and Row Publishers Incorporated
        Scranton, Pennsylvania   18512
Text and study guide. $5.95.

Programmed Learning Materials

★ 972 ★
FINANCIAL MANAGEMENT
Fred Weston
        Learning Systems Company
        1818 Ridge Road
        Homewood, Illinois 60430
Programmed learning aid. $4.95.

FINANCIAL PLANNING

See also: Budgeting

Audio cassettes/Tapes

★ 973 ★
HOW TO BECOME FINANCIALLY INDEPENDENT
Paul J. Meyer
        Success Motivation Institute
        5000 Lakewood Drive
        Waco, Texas 76710
Cassette and booklet. $9.95.

★ 974 ★
HOW TO HAVE MORE MONEY AND END YOUR
FINANCIAL WORRIES
        Tape Rental Library Incorporated
        Post Office Box 2107
        2507 Edna Drive
        South Vineland, New Jersey 08360
Cassette. $9.98.

★ 975 ★
HOW TO SOLVE MONEY PROBLEMS
        Thompson-Mitchell and Associates
        3384 Peachtree Road Northeast
        Atlanta, Georgia 30326
Cassette. $9.95.

★ 976 ★
MANAGEMENT OF MONEY
        Educational Century Programming
        1201 East Johnson Street
        Jonesboro, Arkansas 72401
Cassette. $6.00.

★ 977 ★
PLAN A BUDGET/SAVE MONEY
        Educational Century Programming
        1201 East Johnson Street
        Jonesboro, Arkansas 72401
Cassette. $6.00.

Correspondence Courses

★ 978 ★
PERSONAL FINANCE
        Pennsylvania State University
        Department of Independent Study by
            Correspondence
        Three Sheilds Building
        University Park, Pennsylvania 16802
Correspondence course.

★ 979 ★
PERSONAL FINANCE
        University of South Carolina
        Department of Correspondence Study
        Division of Continuing Education
        Columbia, South Carolina 29208
Correspondence course. $69.00.

★ 980 ★
PERSONAL FINANCE
        Texas Tech University
        Division of Continuing Education
        Post Office Box 4110
        Lubbock, Texas 79409
Correspondence course.

Printed Materials

★ 981 ★
PERSONAL ECONOMICS
Fred Bartok, Edward Lee
        Holbrook Press Incorporated
        Rockleigh, New Jersey 07647
Book. 1977. $13.95.

★ 982 ★
PERSONAL FINANCIAL PLANNING
John Lyons
        American Management Associations
        135 West 50th Street
        New York, New York 10020
Book. 1970. $12.95.

Programmed Learning Materials

★ 983 ★
PERSONAL FINANCE
Jerome B. Cohen
        Learning Systems Company
        1818 Ridge Road
        Homewood, Illinois 60430
Programmed learning aid. $4.95.

FINNISH

Audio Cassettes/Tapes

★ 984 ★
BERLITZ COURSE IN FINNISH
        Berlitz Language Program
        Post Office Box 5109
        FDR Station
        New York, New York   10022
Cassette $5.95.   Also available on LP record.

★ 985 ★
SPOKEN FINNISH
Thomas Sebeok
        Spoken Language Services Incorporated
        Post Office Box 783
        Ithaca, New York   14850
Cassettes, records and coursebook.   1974.

Correspondence courses

★ 986 ★
FINNISH LANGUAGE STUDIES
        University of Washington
        Office of Independent Study
        222 Lewis Hall DW-30
        Seattle, Washington   98195
Correspondence course.

Multimedia Kits

★ 987 ★
FINNISH - BASIC COURSE
        General Services Administration
        Foreign Service Institute Language Course
        National Audiovisual Center
        Order Section RR
        Washington, D.C.   20409
Audio tapes, cassettes and text also available.
Approximately $200.00.

★ 988 ★
FINNISH - GRADED READER
        General Services Administration
        Foreign Service Institute Language Course
        National Audiovisual Center
        Order Section RR
        Washington, D.C.   20409
Audio tapes, cassettes and text also available.
Approximately $100.00.

Printed Materials

★ 989 ★
LEARN FINNISH FOR ENGLISH SPEAKERS
        Saphrograph Company
        194 Elizabeth Street
        New York, New York   10012
Book. $5.00.

★ 990 ★
TEACH YOURSELF FINNISH
A. H. Whitney
        David McKay Company Incorporated
        750 Third Avenue
        New York, New York   10017
Self-study text. $2.95.

FIRE FIGHTING

See also: Safety, Fire

Films/Video/Filmstrips

★ 991 ★
HOW TO FIGHT FIRES
        Resource Incorporated
        13902 North Dale Mabry Highway
        Tampa, Florida   33624
Video cartridge. $75.00.

Printed Materials

★ 992 ★
FIRE FIGHTING
        Howell Training
        2040 North Loop West,   Suite 204
        Houston, Texas   77018
Workbook and tests. $26.35.

FIRE SAFETY
See: SAFETY, FIRE

FIRST AID

Film /Video/Filmstrips

★ 993 ★
THINK FIRST AID (First aid tips on common types
of emergencies)
>Tape Rental Library Incorporated
>Post Office Box 2107
>2507 Edna Drive
>South Vineland, New Jersey 08360
Video cartridge. $75.00.

FLUIDICS

See also: Mechanical Maintenance;
Process Control

Audio Cassettes/Tapes

★ 994 ★
FUNDAMENTALS OF FLUIDICS
Charles K. Taft
>Instrument Society of America
>400 Stanwix Street
>Pittsburgh, Pennsylvania 15222
Workbook and cassette. $10.00.

Programmed Learning Materials

★ 995 ★
FLUID AND ELECTROLYTE BALANCE: A
PROGRAMMED TEXT
Margaret Dickens
>F. A. Davis Company
>1915 Arch Street
>Philadelphia, Pennsylvania 19103
Programmed text. 1974. $6.95.

★ 996 ★
FLUID FUNDAMENTALS AND FLUIDICS
>Society of Manufacturing Engineers
>20501 Ford Road
>Post Office Box 930
>Dearborn, Michigan 48128
Programmed learning course. $78.75.

FOOD PROCESSING

Audio Cassettes/Tapes

★ 997 ★
ABC'S OF CANNING

Classroom World Productions
Post Office Box 2090
22 Glenwood Avenue
Raleigh, North Carolina 27602
Cassette.

Film/Video/Filmstrips

★ 998 ★
BRAISING AND STEWING
>National Restaurant Association
>One IBM Plaza, Suite 2600
>Chicago, Illinois 60611
Video cartridge or 8mm, 16 mm, and study guide.
$190.00.

★ 999 ★
BROILING
>National Restaurant Association
>One IBM Plaza, Suite 2600
>Chicago, Illinois 60611
Video cartridge or 8 mm, 16 mm, and study guide.
$190.00.

★ 1000 ★
CARVING THE RIB ROAST
>National Restaurant Association
>One IBM Plaza, Suite 2600
>Chicago, Illinois 60611
Video cartridge or 8 mm, 16 mm, and study guide.
$190.00.

★ 1001 ★
A COOL HEAD FOR SALADS
>National Restaurant Association
>One IBM Plaza, Suite 2600
>Chicago, Illinois 60611
Video cartridge or 8 mm, 16 mm, and study guide.
$190.00.

★ 1002 ★
DEEP FAT FRYING
>National Restaurant Association
>One IBM Plaza, Suite 2600
>Chicago, Illinois 60611
Video cartridge or 8 mm, 16 mm, and study guide.
$190.00.

★ 1003 ★
FAST SANDWICH MAKING
        National Restaurant Association
        One IBM Plaza, Suite 2600
        Chicago, Illinois 60611
Video cartridge or 8 mm, 16 mm, and study guide.
$190.00.

★ 1004 ★
THE HAMBURGER SANDWICH
        National Restaurant Association
        One IBM Plaza, Suite 2600
        Chicago, Illinois 60611
Video cartridge or 8 mm, 16 mm, and study guide.
$190.00.

★ 1005 ★
ROASTING
        National Restaurant Association
        One IBM Plaza, Suite 2600
        Chicago, Illinois 60611
Video cartridge or 8 mm, 16 mm, and study guide.
$190.00.

★ 1006 ★
SANDWICH PREPARATION AND PRESENTATION
        National Restaurant Association
        One IBM Plaza, Suite 2600
        Chicago, Illinois 60611
Video cartridge or 8 mm, 16 mm, and study guide.
$190.00.

★ 1007 ★
SIMMERING AND POACHING
        National Restaurant Association
        One IBM Plaza, Suite 2600
        Chicago, Illinois 60611
Video cartridge or 8 mm, 16 mm, and study guide.
$190.00.

★ 1008 ★
VEGETABLE PREPARATION
        National Restaurant Association
        One IBM Plaza, Suite 2600
        Chicago, Illinois 60611
Video cartridge or 8 mm, 16 mm, and study guide.
$190.00.

Printed Materials

★ 1009 ★
BAKERY TECHNOLOGY AND ENGINEERING
Samuel Matz

Avi Publishing Company Incorporated
Post Office Box 831
Westport, Connecticut 06880
Book. 1972. $30.00.

★ 1010 ★
BREAD SCIENCE AND TECHNOLOGY
Y. Pomeranz, J. Shellenberger
        Avi Publishing Company Incorporated
        Post Office Box 831
        Westport, Connecticut 06880
Book. 1971. $19.00.

★ 1011 ★
FOOD PREPARATION: STUDY COURSE
Louise Dennier
        Iowa State University Press
        South State Avenue
        Ames, Iowa 50010
Book. $5.95.

★ 1012 ★
UNDERSTANDING BAKING
Joseph Amendola, Dr. Donald E. Lundberg
        National Restaurant Association
        One IBM Plaza, Suite 2600
        Chicago, Illinois 60611
Text. $7.95.

FOOD SERVICE

See also: Safety, Food Service

Audio Cassettes/Tapes

★ 1013 ★
THE SURE CURE FOR THE LUNCHEONETTE SERVICE
BLUES
        Thompson-Mitchell and Associates
        3384 Peachtree Road Northeast
        Atlanta, Georgia 30326
Cassette. $15.00.

Films/Video/Filmstrips

★ 1014 ★
BUSSING
        National Restaurant Association
        One IBM Plaza, Suite 2600
        Chicago, Illinois 60611
Video cartridge or 8 mm, 16 mm, and study guide.
$190.00.

★ 1015 ★
CAFETERIA SERVICE
National Restaurant Association
One IBM Plaza, Suite 2600
Chicago, Illinois 60611
Video cartridge or 8 mm, 16 mm, and study guide.
$190.00.

★ 1016 ★
COURTESY: FOOD SERVICE IS PEOPLE SERVICE
National Restaurant Association
One IBM Plaza, Suite 2600
Chicago, Illinois 60611
Video cartridge or 8 mm, 16 mm, and study guide.
$190.00.

★ 1017 ★
COURTESY: THE INSIDE STORY
National Restaurant Association
One IBM Plaza, Suite 2600
Chicago, Illinois 60611
Video cartridge or 8 mm, 16 mm, and study guide.
$190.00.

★ 1018 ★
DINING ROOM SANITATION
National Restaurant Association
One IBM Plaza, Suite 2600
Chicago, Illinois 60611
Video cartridge or 8 mm, 16 mm, and study guide.
$190.00.

★ 1019 ★
DISH MACHINE OPERATOR
National Restaurant Association
One IBM Plaza, Suite 2600
Chicago, Illinois 60611
Video cartridge or 8 mm, 16 mm, and study guide.
$190.00.

★ 1020 ★
ECONOMY AND EFFICIENCY: EVERYTHING
COUNTS
National Restaurant Association
One IBM Plaza, Suite 2600
Chicago, Illinois 60611
Sound filmstrip. $25.00.

★ 1021 ★
FOOD PURCHASING I: GENERAL PRINCIPLES
National Restaurant Association
One IBM Plaza, Suite 2600
Chicago, Illinois 60611

Video cartridge or 8 mm, 16 mm, and study guide.
$190.00.

★ 1022 ★
FOOD PURCHASING II: LET THE BUYER BEWARE
National Restaurant Association
One IBM Plaza, Suite 2600
Chicago, Illinois 60611
Video cartridge or 8 mm, 16 mm, and study guide.
$190.00.

★ 1023 ★
FOOD SERVICE: MEALS FOR MILLIONS
National Restaurant Association
One IBM Plaza, Suite 2600
Chicago, Illinois 60611
Sound filmstrip. $25.00.

★ 1024 ★
MACHINE DISHWASHING
National Restaurant Association
One IBM Plaza, Suite 2600
Chicago, Illinois 60611
Film cartridge. $60.00.

★ 1025 ★
THE MICROWAVE OVEN
National Restaurant Association
One IBM Plaza, Suite 2600
Chicago, Illinois 60611
Video cartridge or 8 mm, 16 mm, and study guide.
$190.00.

★ 1026 ★
PRESENTATION OF FOOD AND BEVERAGE
National Restaurant Association
One IBM Plaza, Suite 2600
Chicago, Illinois 60611
Video cartridge or 8 mm, 16 mm, and study guide.
$190.00.

★ 1027 ★
PREVENTING WASTE
National Restaurant Association
One IBM Plaza, Suite 2600
Chicago, Illinois 60611
Video cartridge or 8 mm, 16 mm, and study guide.
$190.00.

★ 1028 ★
RECEIVING AND STORING
National Restaurant Association
One IBM Plaza, Suite 2600
Chicago, Illinois 60611
Video cartridge or 8 mm, 16 mm, and study guide.
$190.00.

★ 1029 ★
RUSH HOUR SERVICE
National Restaurant Association
One IBM Plaza, Suite 2600
Chicago, Illinois 60611
Video cartridge or 8 mm, 16 mm, and study guide.
$190.00.

★ 1030 ★
SHORT ORDER COOKERY
National Restaurant Association
One IBM Plaza, Suite 2600
Chicago, Illinois 60611
Video cartridge or 8 mm, 16 mm, and study guide.
$190.00.

★ 1031 ★
THE SMART WAITRESS (Employee training)
National Restaurant Association
One IBM Plaza, Suite 2600
Chicago, Illinois 60611
4 sound filmstrips. $59.50.

★ 1032 ★
TABLE SETTING
National Restaurant Association
One IBM Plaza, Suite 2600
Chicago, Illinois 60611
Video cartridge or 8 mm, 16 mm, and study guide.
$190.00.

★ 1033 ★
TAKING THE ORDER (Food service)
National Restaurant Association
One IBM Plaza, Suite 2600
Chicago, Illinois 60611
Video cartridge or 8 mm, 16 mm, and study guide.
$190.00.

★ 1034 ★
TIPS FOR THE PROFESSIONAL
National Restaurant Association
One IBM Plaza, Suite 2600
Chicago, Illinois 60611
Film cartridge. $60.00.

★ 1035 ★
THE UNWANTED FOUR (food service safety)
National Restaurant Association
One IBM Plaza, Suite 2600
Chicago, Illinois 60611
Sound filmstrip. $14.95.

★ 1036 ★
USING STANDARDIZED RECIPES
National Restaurant Association
One IBM Plaza, Suite 2600
Chicago, Illinois 60611
Video cartridge or 8 mm, 16 mm, and study guide.
$190.00.

Printed Materials

★ 1037 ★
BEING A FOOD SERVICE WORKER
Robert J. Brady Company
Charles Press Publishers
Prentice-Hall Companies
Bowie, Maryland 20715
Book. $6.00.

★ 1038 ★
FOOD PREPARATION FOR HOTELS, RESTAURANTS,
AND CAFETERIAS
Robert G. Haines
National Restaurant Association
One IBM Plaza, Suite 2600
Chicago, Illinois 60611
Text. $11.25.

★ 1039 ★
FOOD PURCHASING: STUDY COURSE
National Restaurant Association
One IBM Plaza, Suite 2600
Chicago, Illinois 60611
Text. $4.95.

★ 1040 ★
FOOD SANITATION: STUDY COURSE
Anna Katherine Sernigan
National Restaurant Association
One IBM Plaza, Suite 2600
Chicago, Illinois 60611
Text. $4.95.

★ 1041 ★
TODAY'S BUSBOY
> National Restaurant Association
> One IBM Plaza, Suite 2600
> Chicago, Illinois 60611

Text. $2.50.

★ 1042 ★
TODAY'S COCKTAIL WAITRESS
> National Restaurant Association
> One IBM Plaza, Suite 2600
> Chicago, Illinois 60611

Text. $2.50.

★ 1043 ★
TODAY'S DISHWASHING MACHINE OPERATOR
> National Restaurant Association
> One IBM Plaza, Suite 2600
> Chicago, Illinois 60611

Text. $2.50.

★ 1044 ★
TODAY'S WAITRESS
> National Restaurant Association
> One IBM Plaza, Suite 2600
> Chicago, Illinois 60611

Text. $2.50.

★ 1045 ★
TOTAL WAITER-WAITRESS TRAINING
Ron Wilkinson
> National Restaurant Association
> One IBM Plaza, Suite 2600
> Chicago, Illinois 60611

Text. $12.50.

★ 1046 ★
WORK SIMPLIFICATION IN FOOD SERVICE
Lynne Ross
> National Restaurant Association
> One IBM Plaza, Suite 2600
> Chicago, Illinois 60611

Text. $4.95.

FOREIGN DIPLOMACY

Games/Simulations

★ 1047 ★
GRAND STRATEGY (Foreign diplomacy and international relations for grades 9 through college)

> ABT Publications
> 55 Wheeler Street
> Cambridge, Massachusetts 02138

Game. $32.00.

FOREIGN LANGUAGE INSTRUCTION
See: specific foreign language

FORESTRY

Correspondence Courses

★ 1048 ★
ELEMENTS OF FORESTRY
> University of Kentucky
> Independent Study Program
> Freeze Hall, Room 1
> Lexington, Kentucky 40506

Correspondence course.

FORTRAN
See: COMPUTER LANGUAGES

FREE-LANCING

See also: Consulting; Self Employment

Audio Cassettes/Tapes

★ 1049 ★
FREE-LANCING
Art Fettig
> Tape Rental Library Incorporated
> Post Office Box 2107
> 2507 Edna Drive
> South Vineland, New Jersey 08360

Cassette. $8.35.

FRENCH

Audio Cassettes/Tapes

★ 1050 ★
BASIC FRENCH: A PROGRAMMED COURSE
> Irvington Publishers
> 551 Fifth Avenue
> New York, New York 10017.

Audio tapes and workbooks. $129.00.

★ 1051 ★
BERLITZ COMPREHENSIVE COURSE IN FRENCH
    Berlitz Language Program
    Post Office Box 5109
    FDR Station
    New York, New York 10022
6 cassettes with workbook. $85.00.

★ 1052 ★
BERLITZ COURSE IN FRENCH
    Berlitz Language Program
    Post Office Box 5109
    FDR Station
    New York, New York 10022
Cassette $5.95.   Also available on 8 track and
LP record.

★ 1053 ★
FRENCH
    Thompson-Mitchell and Associates
    3384 Peachtree Road Northeast
    Atlanta, Georgia 30326
Cassette. $9.98.

Correspondence Courses

★ 1054 ★
BEGINNING FRENCH
    University of Nebraska
    511 Nebraska Hall
    Lincoln, Nebraska 68588
Correspondence course.

★ 1055 ★
FRENCH
    University of Arkansas
    Department of Independent Study
    346 West Avenue
    Fayetteville, Arkansas 72701
Correspondence course.

★ 1056 ★
FRENCH
    University of Wisconsin - Extension
    Independent Study
    432 North Lake Street
    Madison, Wisconsin 53706
Various level courses available.

Multimedia Kits

★ 1057 ★
FRENCH - BASIC COURSE

    General Services Administration
    Foreign Service Institute Language Course
    National Audiovisual Center
    Order Section RR
    Washington, D.C. 20409
Audio tapes, cassettes and text also available.
Approximately $300.00.

★ 1058 ★
INTRODUCTION TO FRENCH PHONOLOGY
    General Services Administration
    Foreign Service Institute Language Course
    National Audiovisual Center
    Order Section RR
    Washington, D.C. 20409
Audio tapes, cassettes and text also available.
Approximately $60.00.

Programmed Learning Materials

★ 1059 ★
AN INTRODUCTORY FRENCH PROGRAM
    Loyola University Press
    3441 North Ashland Avenue
    Chicago, Illinois 60657
Programmed text. $11.00.

FULA

Multimedia Kits

★ 1060 ★
FULA - BASIC COURSE
    General Services Administration
    Foreign Service Institute Language Course
    National Audiovisual Center
    Order Section RR
    Washington, D.C. 20409
Audio tapes, cassettes and text also available.
$100.00.

FUND RAISING

Audio Cassettes/Tapes

★ 1061 ★
HOW TO SUCCESSFULLY CONDUCT A FUND
RAISING CAMPAIGN
George M. Rudolphy
    Tape Rental Library Incorporated
    Post Office Box 2107
    2507 Edna Drive
    South Vineland, New Jersey 08360
Cassette. $5.95.

Printed Materials

★ 1062 ★
HOW TO BE SUCCESSFUL IN GROUP FUND
RAISING TODAY
Helen Knowles
    Bond, Wheelwright Company
    Porters Landing
    Freeport, Maine 04032
Book. 1975. $6.95.

★ 1063 ★
RAISE CASH - HAVE FUN
Christine Fagg
    Technical Impex Corporation
    Five South Union Street
    Lawrence, Massachusetts 01843
Book. 1969. $5.95.

★ 1064 ★
TECHNIQUES OF FUND RAISING
Daniel Conrad
    Lyle Stuart Incorporated
    120 Enterprise Avenue
    Secaucus, New Jersey 07094
Book. 1974. $25.00.

FURNACE THEORY

See also: Heating

Film/Video/Filmstrips

★ 1065 ★
FURNACE THEORY - COAL
    Resource Incorporated
    13902 North Dale Mabry Highway
    Tampa, Florida 33624
Video cartridge with workbook. $100.00.

★ 1066 ★
FURNACE THEORY - GAS
    Resource Incorporated
    13902 North Dale Mabry Highway
    Tampa, Florida 33624
Video cartridge with workbook. $100.00.

★ 1067 ★
FURNACE THEORY - OIL
    Resource Incorporated
    13902 North Dale Mabry Highway
    Tampa, Florida 33624
Video cartridge with workbook. $100.00.

Printed Materials

★ 1068 ★
FURNACE OPERATION
    Howell Training
    2040 North Loop West, Suite 204
    Houston, Texas 77018
Workbook and tests. $11.80.

GAELIC

Printed Materials

★ 1069 ★
GAELIC SELF-TAUGHT
J. Maclaren
    S F Book Imports
    Post Office Box 526
    San Francisco, California 94101
Book. $5.00.

★ 1070 ★
TEACH YOURSELF GAELIC
Roderick Mackinnon
    David McKay Company Incorporated
    750 Third Avenue
    New York, New York 10017
Book. 1972. $3.95.

GERMAN

Audio Cassettes/Tapes

★ 1071 ★
BERLITZ COMPREHENSIVE COURSE IN GERMAN
    Berlitz Language Program
    Post Office Box 5109
    FDR Station
    New York, New York 10022
6 cassettes with workbook. $85.00.

★ 1072 ★
BERLITZ COURSE IN GERMAN
    Berlitz Language Program
    Post Office Box 5109
    FDR Station
    New York, New York 10022
Cassette $5.95.   Also available on 8 track and
LP record.

★ 1073 ★
GERMAN
      Thompson-Mitchell and Associates
      3384 Peachtree Road Northeast
      Atlanta, Georgia 30326
Cassette. $9.98.

Correspondence Courses

★ 1074 ★
BEGINNING GERMAN
      University of Southern Mississippi
      Department of Independent Study
      Southern Station, Box 56
      Hattiesburg, Mississippi 39401
Correspondence course.

★ 1075 ★
GERMAN
      University of Arkansas
      Department of Independent Study
      346 West Avenue
      Fayetteville, Arkansas 72701
Correspondence course.

★ 1076 ★
GERMAN
      University of Florida
      Division of Continuing Education
      2012 West University Avenue
      Gainesville, Florida 32603
Correspondence course.

★ 1077 ★
GERMAN
      University of Wisconsin – Extension
      Independent Study
      432 North Lake Street
      Madison, Wisconsin 53706
Various level courses available.

★ 1078 ★
GERMAN LANGUAGE STUDIES
      University of Washington
      Office of Independent Study
      222 Lewis Hall DW-30
      Seattle, Washington 98195
Correspondence course.

Films/Video/Filmstrips

★ 1079 ★
CONVERSATIONAL GERMAN
Hedi Oplesch

      Telstar Productions Incorporated
      366 North Prior Avenue
      St. Paul, Minnesota 55104
10 video tape lessons. $2,200.00.

Multimedia Kits

★ 1080 ★
GERMAN - BASIC COURSE
      General Services Administration
      Foreign Service Institute Language Course
      National Audiovisual Center
      Order Section RR
      Washington, D.C. 20409
Audio tapes, cassettes and text also available.
Approximately $300.00.

★ 1081 ★
GERMAN - A PROGRAMMED INTRODUCTION
      General Services Administration
      Foreign Service Institute Language Course
      National Audiovisual Center
      Order Section RR
      Washington, D.C. 20409
Audio tapes, cassettes and text also available.
Approximately $90.00.

Printed Materials

★ 1082 ★
INDIVIDUALIZED INSTRUCTION PROGRAM IN
GERMAN
Klaus Mueller, Gerhard Clausing
      Random House Incorporated
      457 Hahn Road
      Westminister, Maryland 21157
Self instruction text. $4.95.

★ 1083 ★
SELF-TEACHER: GERMAN
Berlitz Schools of Languages
      Grosset and Dunlap Incorporated
      51 Madison Avenue
      New York, New York 10010
Self instruction book. $6.95.

★ 1084 ★
TEACH YOURSELF GERMAN
P. G. Wilson
      David McKay Company Incorporated
      750 Third Avenue
      New York, New York 10017
Self-study text. $2.95.

Programmed Learning Materials

★ 1085 ★
BASIC GERMAN: A PROGRAMMED COURSE
Ferdinand Ruplin
     Irvington Publishers
     551 Fifth Avenue
     New York, New York 10017
Programmed text. $4.00.

★ 1086 ★
A COURSE IN SCIENTIFIC GERMAN
Hans Meinel
     Irvington Publishers
     551 Fifth Avenue
     New York, New York 10017
Programmed course. 1972. $12.00.

GOAL SETTING

See also: Planning

Audio Cassettes/Tapes

★ 1087 ★
GOAL SETTING FOR PROFESSIONALS
     Development Digest Incorporated
     3347 Motor Avenue
     Los Angeles, California 90034
Cassette. $13.75.

★ 1088 ★
THE GOAL SETTING SESSION
     American Management Associations
     135 West 50th Street
     New York, New York 10020
Cassette. $18.00.

★ 1089 ★
HOW TO USE GOAL SETTING TO INCREASE
PRODUCTIVITY
     Development Digest Incorporated
     3347 Motor Avenue
     Los Angeles, California 90034
Cassette. $13.75.

★ 1090 ★
SETTING CLEAR GOALS
George Odiorne
     MBO Incorporated
     157 Pontoosic Road
     Westfield, Massachusetts 01085
Cassette and manual.

Films/Video/Filmstrips

★ 1091 ★
GOAL SETTING
     Resources for Education and Management
       Incorporated
     544 Medlock Road, Suite 210
     Decatur, Georgia 30030
Filmstrip with cassette. $70.00.

Games/Simulations

★ 1092 ★
THE GOAL SETTING GAME
     Training House Incorporated
     Box 688
     Binghamton, New York 13902
Simulation game. $60.00.

GRAPHIC DESIGN

Films/Video/Filmstrips

★ 1093 ★
PHOTO MECHANICAL GRAPHICS
     Scope Productions Incorporated
     Post Office Box 5515
     Fresno, California 93755
10 films (8 mm) and student guides. $210.00.

Printed Materials

★ 1094 ★
GRAPHIC DESIGN: PROBLEMS, METHODS,
SOLUTIONS
Jerzy Karo
     Van Nos Reinhold Company
     300 Pike Street
     Cincinnati, Ohio 45202
Book. 1975. $9.95.

GRAPHS AND TABLES

Printed Materials

★ 1095 ★
INTERPRETING GRAPHS AND TABLES
Peter Selby
     John Wiley and Sons Incorporated
     605 Third Avenue
     New York, New York 10016
Book. 1976. $4.95.

Programmed Learning Materials

★ 1096 ★
READING AND PREPARING SIMPLE GRAPHS
    E. I. du Pont de Nemours and Company
    Applied Technology Division
    Room B, 4204
    Wilmington, Delaware 19898
Programmed course of approximately 14 hours.
$25.30.

GREEK

Audio Cassettes/Tapes

★ 1097 ★
BERLITZ COURSE IN GREEK
    Berlitz Language Program
    Post Office Box 5109
    FDR Station
    New York, New York 10022
Cassette $5.95. Also available on LP record.

★ 1098 ★
LEARN MODERN GREEK IN RECORD TIME
    Doubleday and Company Incorporated
    501 Franklin Avenue
    Garden City, New York 11530
Book and records. $9.98.

Correspondence Courses

★ 1099 ★
GREEK
    University of Wisconsin - Extension
    Independent Study
    432 North Lake Street
    Madison, Wisconsin 53706
Various level courses available.

Multimedia Kits

★ 1100 ★
GREEK - BASIC COURSE
    General Services Administration
    Foreign Service Institute Language Course
    National Audiovisual Center
    Order Section RR
    Washington, D.C. 20409
Audio tapes, cassettes and text also available.
Approximately $250.00.

Printed Materials

★ 1101 ★
LEARN GREEK FOR ENGLISH SPEAKERS
    Saphrograph Company
    194 Elizabeth Street
    New York, New York 10012
Book. $5.00.

★ 1102 ★
MODERN GREEK IN 20 LESSONS
Cortina Method Language Series
    Doubleday and Company Incorporated
    501 Franklin Avenue
    Garden City, New York 11530
Book. $4.95.

★ 1103 ★
TEACH YOURSELF GREEK
F. K. Smith, T. W. Melluish
    David McKay Company Incorporated
    750 Third Avenue
    New York, New York 10017
Self instruction text. $3.95.

GROUP DEVELOPMENT

See also: Organizational Development

Audio Cassettes/Tapes

★ 1104 ★
PERSONAL, BALANCED GOAL DEVELOPMENT
    Van De Water Associates
    7914 Jason Avenue
    Canoga Park, California 91304
Cassette and workbook. $23.50.

★ 1105 ★
SMALL GROUPS AT WORK
George Odiorne
    MBO Incorporated
    157 Pontoosic Road
    Westfield, Massachusetts 01085
Cassette and manual. $15.00.

★ 1106 ★
TEAM BUILDING: A COMPREHENSIVE APPROACH
    Development Digest Incorporated
    3347 Motor Avenue
    Los Angeles, California 90034
Cassette. $13.75.

★ 1107 ★
TEAM BUILDING: CONFLICT AND NEGOTIATION
    Development Digest Incorporated
    3347 Motor Avenue
    Los Angeles, California 90034
Cassette. $13.75.

Films/Video/Filmstrips

★ 1108 ★
GROUP DYNAMICS: "GROUPTHINK"
    CRM McGraw Hill Films
    110 15th Street
    Del Mar, California· 92014
Film or video cassette.

★ 1109 ★
TEAM BUILDING
    BNA Communications Incorporated
    9401 Decoverly Hall Road
    Rockville, Maryland 20850
Film.

Multimedia Kits

★ 1110 ★
COMPONENTS OF SMALL GROUP INTERACTION
    Lansford Publishing Company
    Post Office Box 8711
    San Jose, California 95155
Multimedia kit. $146.95.

★ 1111 ★
GROUP CREATIVITY
    Lansford Publishing Company
    Post Office Box 8711
    San Jose, California 95155
Multimedia kit. $99.95.

★ 1112 ★
GROUP DYNAMICS
    Lansford Publishing Company
    Post Office Box 8711
    San Jose, California 95155
Multimedia kit. $149.95.

HAUSA

Multimedia Kits

★ 1113 ★
HAUSA - BASIC COURSE

    General Services Administration
    Foreign Service Institute Language Course
    National Audiovisual Center
    Order Section RR
    Washington, D.C. 20409
Audio tapes, cassettes and text also available.
Approximately $80.00.

HEALTH AND MEDICAL CARE

Audio Cassettes/Tapes

★ 1114 ★
CLINICAL PHARMACY
Robert M. Cunningham
    Thompson-Mitchell and Associates
    3384 Peachtree Road Northeast
    Atlanta, Georgia 30326
Cassette. $10.00.

★ 1115 ★
HEALTH EDUCATION
Robert M. Cunningham
    Thompson-Mitchell and Associates
    3384 Peachtree Road Northeast
    Atlanta, Georgia 30326
Cassette. $10.00.

★ 1116 ★
MEDICAL EDUCATION
Robert M. Cunningham
    Thompson-Mitchell and Associates
    3384 Peachtree Road Northeast
    Atlanta, Georgia 30326
Cassette. $10.00.

Correspondence Courses

★ 1117 ★
HEALTH ASSISTANT COURSE
The Barton School
    North American Correspondence School
    4401 Birch Street
    Newport Beach, California 92663
Correspondence course.

Films/Video/Filmstrips

★ 1118 ★
AMBULATION WITH I.V. IN PLACE
    Research Media Company
    96 Mount Auburn Street
    Cambridge, Massachusetts 02138
Film (8 mm). $22.00.

★ 1119 ★
ANATOMY AND PHYSIOLOGY
    Telstar Productions Incorporated
    366 North Prior Avenue
    Saint Paul, Minnesota 55104
60 videotape lessons. $250.00 each.

★ 1120 ★
APPLYING AN ELASTIC BANDAGE
    Research Media Company
    96 Mount Auburn Street
    Cambridge, Massachusetts 02138
Film (8 mm). $22.00.

★ 1121 ★
APPLYING THE SCULTETUS BINDER
    Research Media Company
    96 Mount Auburn Street
    Cambridge, Massachusetts 02138
Film (8 mm). $22.00.

★ 1122 ★
BODY FLUIDS
    Telstar Productions Incorporated
    366 North Prior Avenue
    Saint Paul, Minnesota 55104
4 video tapes. $250.00 each.

★ 1123 ★
ISOLATION TECHNIQUE
    Research Media Company
    96 Mount Auburn Street
    Cambridge, Massachusetts 02138
28 slides. $29.00.

★ 1124 ★
LIPID METABOLISM
    Research Media Company
    96 Mount Auburn Street
    Cambridge, Massachusetts 02138
26 slides. $27.00.

★ 1125 ★
MATH FOR MEDICATION (A program designed for
health professionals)
    Telstar Productions Incorporated
    366 North Prior Avenue
    Saint Paul, Minnesota 55104
7 video tapes. $250.00 each.

★ 1126 ★
THE NUTS AND BOLTS OF HEALTH CARE
MANAGEMENT COMMUNICATION
    Creative Media Films
    820 Keo Way
    Des Moines, Iowa 50309
Film.   Rental available.

★ 1127 ★
PASSIVE EXERCISE OF INACTIVE LIMBS
    Research Media Company
    96 Mount Auburn Street
    Cambridge, Massachusetts 02138
Film (8 mm). $22.00.

★ 1128 ★
PHARMACOLOGY
    Telstar Productions Incorporated
    366 North Prior Avenue
    Saint Paul, Minnesota 55104
26 video tape lessons. $250.00 each.

★ 1129 ★
PREVENTING DECUBITUS OF THE HEEL
    Research Media Company
    96 Mount Auburn Street
    Cambridge, Massachusetts 02138
Film (8 mm). $22.00.

★ 1130 ★
PREVENTING ROTATION OF THE LEG
    Research Media Company
    96 Mount Auburn Street
    Cambridge, Massachusetts 02138
Film (8 mm). $22.00.

★ 1131 ★
PREVENTING SHOULDER CURVATURE
    Research Media Company
    96 Mount Auburn Street
    Cambridge, Massachusetts 02138
Film (8 mm). $22.00.

★ 1132 ★
PROTECTING BONY PROMINENCES
    Research Media Company
    96 Mount Auburn Street
    Cambridge, Massachusetts 02138
Film (8 mm). $22.00.

★ 1133 ★
RADIOGRAPHIC PRODUCTION
 Research Media Company
 96 Mount Auburn Street
 Cambridge, Massachusetts 02138
25 slides. $27.00.

★ 1134 ★
RADIOLOGIC PHYSICS
 Research Media Company
 96 Mount Auburn Street
 Cambridge, Massachusetts 02138
50 slides. $38.00.

★ 1135 ★
SECURING A FINGER SPLINT
 Research Media Company
 96 Mount Auburn Street
 Cambridge, Massachusetts 02138
Film (8 mm). $22.00.

★ 1136 ★
SOCIAL SCIENCE (A program designed for health
professionals)
 Telstar Productions Incorporated
 366 North Prior Avenue
 Saint Paul, Minnesota 55104
36 video tape lessons. $250.00 each.

★ 1137 ★
TAKING THE BLOOD PRESSURE
 Research Media Company
 96 Mount Auburn Street
 Cambridge, Massachusetts 02138
Film (8 mm). $22.00.

★ 1138 ★
TOMOGRAPHY
 Research Media Company
 96 Mount Auburn Street
 Cambridge, Massachusetts 02138
28 slides. $29.00.

Multimedia Kits

★ 1139 ★
ADMINISTRATION OF ENEMAS
 Robert J. Brady Company
 Charles Press Publishers
 Prentice-Hall Companies
 Bowie, Maryland 20715
Filmstrip with cassette. $30.00.

★ 1140 ★
ADMINISTRATION OF MEDICATIONS –
GENERAL CONSIDERATIONS
 Robert J. Brady Company
 Charles Press Publishers
 Prentice-Hall Companies
 Bowie, Maryland 20715
Filmstrip with cassette. $30.00.

★ 1141 ★
ADMINISTRATION OF MEDICATIONS –
INTRAVENOUS FLUID THERAPY
 Robert J. Brady Company
 Charles Press Publishers
 Prentice-Hall Companies
 Bowie, Maryland 20715
Filmstrip with cassette. $30.00.

★ 1142 ★
ADMINISTRATION OF MEDICATIONS – ROUTES,
PROCEDURES, AND TECHNIQUES
 Robert J. Brady Company
 Charles Press Publishers
 Prentice-Hall Companies
 Bowie, Maryland 20715
Filmstrip with cassette. $30.00.

★ 1143 ★
ANATOMY AND PHYSIOLOGY
 Research Media Company
 96 Mount Auburn Street
 Cambridge, Massachusetts 02138
40 slides with cassette. $48.00.

★ 1144 ★
CARE OF PATIENT WITH MULTIPLE INJURIES
 Robert J. Brady Company
 Charles Press Publishers
 Prentice-Hall Companies
 Bowie, Maryland 20715
Filmstrip with cassette. $50.00.

★ 1145 ★
CARE OF PATIENTS WITH FRACTURES
 Robert J. Brady Company
 Charles Press Publishers
 Prentice-Hall Companies
 Bowie, Maryland 20715
Filmstrip with cassette. $50.00.

★ 1146 ★
CARE OF PATIENTS WITH NEUROLOGICAL
INJURIES
    Robert J. Brady Company
    Charles Press Publishers
    Prentice-Hall Companies
    Bowie, Maryland 20715
Filmstrip with cassette. $50.00.

★ 1147 ★
CARE OF SEVERELY BURNED PATIENT
    Robert J. Brady Company
    Charles Press Publishers
    Prentice-Hall Companies
    Bowie, Maryland 20715
Filmstrip with cassette. $50.00.

★ 1148 ★
CARE OF THE GERIATRIC PATIENT
    Thompson-Mitchell and Associates
    3384 Peachtree Road Northeast
    Atlanta, Georgia 30326
Filmstrip with cassette. $55.00.

★ 1149 ★
CARE OF THE TERMINALLY ILL
    Thompson-Mitchell and Associates
    3384 Peachtree Road Northeast
    Atlanta, Georgia 30326
Filmstrip with cassette. $55.00.

★ 1150 ★
CENTRAL MEDICAL AND SURGICAL SUPPLY
SERVICE OPERATIONS
    Robert J. Brady Company
    Charles Press Publishers
    Prentice-Hall Companies
    Bowie, Maryland 20715
10 filmstrips with cassettes. $250.00.

★ 1151 ★
COMMUNICABLE DISEASE TECHNIQUES
    Robert J. Brady Company
    Charles Press Publishers
    Prentice-Hall Companies
    Bowie, Maryland 20715
Filmstrip with cassette. $30.00.

★ 1152 ★
ENDOTRACHEAL INTUBATION AND
TRACHEOSTOMY CARE
    Thompson-Mitchell and Associates
    3384 Peachtree Road Northeast
    Atlanta, Georgia 30326
Filmstrip with cassette. $55.00.

★ 1153 ★
EQUIPMENT AND SUPPLIES FOR EMERGENCIES
    Robert J. Brady Company
    Charles Press Publishers
    Prentice-Hall Companies
    Bowie, Maryland 20715
Filmstrip with cassette. $50.00.

★ 1154 ★
HEALTH AND SAFETY: MAINTAINING A CLEAN
ENVIRONMENT
    Thompson-Mitchell and Associates
    3384 Peachtree Road Northeast
    Atlanta, Georgia 30326
Filmstrip with cassette. $55.00.

★ 1155 ★
INTRADERMAL INJECTION TECHNIQUES
    Robert J. Brady Company
    Charles Press Publishers
    Prentice-Hall Companies
    Bowie, Maryland 20715
Filmstrip with cassette. $30.00.

★ 1156 ★
INTRAMUSCULAR INJECTION TECHNIQUE
    Robert J. Brady Company
    Charles Press Publishers
    Prentice-Hall Companies
    Bowie, Maryland 20715
Filmstrip with cassette. $30.00.

★ 1157 ★
INTRAMUSCULAR INJECTIONS
    Thompson-Mitchell and Associates
    3384 Peachtree Road Northeast
    Atlanta, Georgia 30326
Filmstrip with cassette. $55.00.

★ 1158 ★
INTRAVENOUS INJECTION TECHNIQUE
    Robert J. Brady Company
    Charles Press Publishers
    Prentice-Hall Companies
    Bowie, Maryland 20715
Filmstrip with cassette. $30.00.

★ 1159 ★
INTRODUCTION TO SHOCK MANAGEMENT
    Thompson-Mitchell and Associates
    3384 Peachtree Road Northeast
    Atlanta, Georgia 30326
Filmstrip with cassette. $55.00.

★ 1160 ★
THE ISOLATED PATIENT
Thompson-Mitchell and Associates
3384 Peachtree Road Northeast
Atlanta, Georgia 30326
Filmstrip with cassette. $55.00.

★ 1161 ★
LABORATORY FIRE SERIES
Robert J. Brady Company
Charles Press Publishers
Prentice-Hall Companies
Bowie, Maryland 20715
3 filmstrips with cassette. $120.00.

★ 1162 ★
MEDICAL AND SURGICAL ASEPSIS
Robert J. Brady Company
Charles Press Publishers
Prentice-Hall Companies
Bowie, Maryland 20715
Filmstrip with cassette. $30.00.

★ 1163 ★
OBSERVING THE PATIENT
Thompson-Mitchell and Associates
3384 Peachtree Road Northeast
Atlanta, Georgia 30326
Filmstrip (35 mm) with cassette. $55.00.

★ 1164 ★
OPERATING ROOM FIRE SERIES
Robert J. Brady Company
Charles Press Publishers
Prentice-Hall Companies
Bowie, Maryland 20715
2 filmstrips with cassette. $80.00.

★ 1165 ★
PARENTERAL DRUG ADMINISTRATION
Robert J. Brady Company
Charles Press Publishers
Prentice-Hall Companies
Bowie, Maryland 20715
Filmstrip with cassette. $30.00.

★ 1166 ★
PATIENT ADJUSTMENT
Thompson-Mitchell and Associates
3384 Peachtree Road Northeast
Atlanta, Georgia 30326
Filmstrip with cassette. $55.00.

★ 1167 ★
PATIENT AREA FIRE SERIES
Robert J. Brady Company
Charles Press Publishers
Prentice-Hall Companies
Bowie, Maryland 20715
4 filmstrips with cassette. $160.00.

★ 1168 ★
PATIENT FLOW
Robert J. Brady Company
Charles Press Publishers
Prentice-Hall Companies
Bowie, Maryland 20715
Filmstrip with cassette. $50.00.

★ 1169 ★
PHYSICAL FACILITIES FOR EMERGENCIES
Robert J. Brady Company
Charles Press Publishers
Prentice-Hall Companies
Bowie, Maryland 20715
Filmstrip with cassette. $50.00.

★ 1170 ★
PHYSIOLOGY OF THE CENTRAL NERVOUS
SYSTEM
Research Media Company
96 Mount Auburn Street
Cambridge, Massachusetts 02138
44 slides with cassette. $52.00.

★ 1171 ★
PHYSIOLOGY OF THE HEART
Research Media Company
96 Mount Auburn Street
Cambridge, Massachusetts 02138
42 slides with cassette. $50.00.

★ 1172 ★
POSTURAL DRAINAGE: DIFFUSE LUNG
INFECTIONS
Thompson-Mitchell and Associates
3384 Peachtree Road Northeast
Atlanta, Georgia 30326
Filmstrip with cassette. $55.00.

★ 1173 ★
POSTURAL DRAINAGE: LOCALIZED LUNG
INFECTIONS
Thompson-Mitchell and Associates
3384 Peachtree Road Northeast
Atlanta, Georgia 30326
Filmstrip with cassette. $55.00.

★ 1174 ★
PREGNANCY AND CHILDBIRTH
            Research Media Company
            96 Mount Auburn Street
            Cambridge, Massachusetts 02138
31 slides with cassette. $38.00.

★ 1175 ★
THE PROBLEM ORIENTED MEDICAL RECORD
            Thompson-Mitchell and Associates
            3384 Peachtree Road Northeast
            Atlanta, Georgia 30326
Filmstrip with cassette. $39.95.

★ 1176 ★
RESPIRATORY EMERGENCIES
            Thompson-Mitchell and Associates
            3384 Peachtree Road Northeast
            Atlanta, Georgia 30326
Filmstrip with cassette. $55.00.

★ 1177 ★
SAFETY IN MEDICAL FACILITIES
            Robert J. Brady Company
            Charles Press Publishers
            Prentice-Hall Companies
            Bowie, Maryland 20715
Filmstrip with cassette. $30.00.

★ 1178 ★
SIPHONAGE ENEMA, COLONIC IRRIGATION
AND PLACEMENT OF RECTAL TUBES
            Robert J. Brady Company
            Charles Press Publishers
            Prentice-Hall Companies
            Bowie, Maryland 20715
Filmstrip with cassette. $30.00.

★ 1179 ★
SUBCUTANEOUS INJECTION TECHNIQUES
            Robert J. Brady Company
            Charles Press Publishers
            Prentice-Hall Companies
            Bowie, Maryland 20715
Filmstrip with cassette. $30.00.

★ 1180 ★
THEORY AND PRACTICE OF IMMUNODIFFUSION
AND COUNTERELECTROPHORESIS
            Telstar Productions Incorporated
            366 North Prior Avenue
            Saint Paul, Minnesota 55104
Slides and audio cassettes. $75.00.

★ 1181 ★
UNDERSTANDING THE DIFFICULT PATIENT
            Thompson-Mitchell and Associates
            3384 Peachtree Road Northeast
            Atlanta, Georgia 30326
Filmstrip with cassette. $55.00.

★ 1182 ★
THE USE OF TURNING FRAMES
            Robert J. Brady Company
            Charles Press Publishers
            Prentice-Hall Companies
            Bowie, Maryland 20715
Filmstrip with cassette. $30.00.

Printed Materials

★ 1183 ★
BEGINNER'S GUIDE TO INTENSIVE CORONARY
CARE
            Robert J. Brady Company
            Charles Press Publishers
            Prentice-Hall Companies
            Bowie, Maryland 20715
Book. $5.95.

★ 1184 ★
BRADY'S PROGRAMMED INTRODUCTION TO
RESPIRATORY THERAPY
            Robert J. Brady Company
            Charles Press Publishers
            Prentice-Hall Companies
            Bowie, Maryland 20715
Book. $8.50.

★ 1185 ★
BRADY'S PROGRAMMED ORIENTATION TO MEDICAL
TERMINOLOGY
            Robert J. Brady Company
            Charles Press Publishers
            Prentice-Hall Companies
            Bowie, Maryland 20715
Book. $5.95.

★ 1186 ★
EMERGENCY CARDIAC CARE
Robert J. Huszar, M.D.
            Robert J. Brady Company
            Charles Press Publishers
            Prentice-Hall Companies
            Bowie, Maryland 20715
Book. $9.95.

★ 1187 ★
EMERGENCY TREATMENT OF ACUTE RESPIRATORY
DISEASES
Llewellyn W. Stringer Jr., M.D.
  Robert J. Brady Company
  Charles Press Publishers
  Prentice-Hall Companies
  Bowie, Maryland 20715
Book. $4.50.

★ 1188 ★
FUNDAMENTALS OF ANESTHESIA CARE
Betty Smith
  C. V. Mosby Company
  11830 Westline Industrial Drive
  Saint Louis, Missouri 63141
Book. 1972. $6.25.

★ 1189 ★
INTRODUCTION TO THE NATURE AND MANAGE-
MENT OF HYPERTENSION
Edward D. Freis, M.D.
  Robert J. Brady Company
  Charles Press Publishers
  Prentice-Hall Companies
  Bowie, Maryland 20715
Book. $10.95.

★ 1190 ★
NUTRITION, METABOLISM, FLUID AND
ELECTROLYTE BALANCE
  Robert J. Brady Company
  Charles Press Publishers
  Prentice-Hall Companies
  Bowie, Maryland 20715
Book. $4.75.

★ 1191 ★
OXYGEN TRANSPORT, HYPOXIA, AND CYANOSIS
  Robert J. Brady Company
  Charles Press Publishers
  Prentice-Hall Companies
  Bowie, Maryland 20715
Book. $6.50.

★ 1192 ★
PRACTICAL BLOOD TRANSFUSION
Douglas Huestis
  Little, Brown and Company
  200 West Street
  Waltham, Massachusetts 02154
Book. 1976. $18.50.

★ 1193 ★
SELF-INSTRUCTIONAL WORKBOOK FOR EMERGENCY
CARE
J. David Bergeron
  Robert J. Brady Company
  Charles Press Publishers
  Prentice-Hall Companies
  Bowie, Maryland 20715
Book. $5.95.

★ 1194 ★
VEHICLE RESCUE - A SYSTEM OF OPERATIONS
Harvey Grant
  Robert J. Brady Company
  Charles Press Publishers
  Prentice-Hall Companies
  Bowie, Maryland 20715
Book. $13.95.

HEALTH, COMMUNITY

Correspondence Courses

★ 1195 ★
COMMUNITY HEALTH
  University of Southern Mississippi
  Department of Independent Study
  Southern Station, Box 56
  Hattiesburg, Mississippi 39401
Correspondence course.

★ 1196 ★
INTRODUCTION TO COMMUNITY HEALTH ECOLOGY
  University of Kentucky
  Independent Study Program
  Freeze Hall, Room 1
  Lexington, Kentucky 40506
Correspondence course.

HEALTH, EMPLOYEE

Films/Video/Filmstrips

★ 1197 ★
EMPLOYEE HEALTH (Ways to reduce employee sickness)
  Tape Rental Library Incorporated
  Post Office Box 2107
  2507 Edna Drive
  South Vineland, New Jersey 08360
Video cartridge. $75.00.

HEALTH INSURANCE
See: INSURANCE

HEALTH, NURSING

<u>See also:</u> Health and Medical Care

<u>Films/Video/Filmstrips</u>

★ 1198 ★
NURSING IN SOCIETY
    Telstar Productions Incorporated
    366 North Prior Avenue
    Saint Paul, Minnesota 55104
12 video tape lessons. $250.00.

<u>Multimedia Kits</u>

★ 1199 ★
EMERGENCY DEPARTMENT NURSING DURING
DISASTER
    Robert J. Brady Company
    Charles Press Publishers
    Prentice-Hall Companies
    Bowie, Maryland 20715
Filmstrip with cassette. $50.00.

★ 1200 ★
EMERGENCY DEPARTMENT NURSING DURING
MEDICAL EMERGENCIES
    Robert J. Brady Company
    Charles Press Publishers
    Prentice-Hall Companies
    Bowie, Maryland 20715
Filmstrip with cassette. $50.00.

★ 1201 ★
ETHICS FOR THE NURSING ASSISTANT
    Thompson-Mitchell and Associates
    3384 Peachtree Road Northeast
    Atlanta, Georgia 30326
Filmstrip with cassette. $55.00.

★ 1202 ★
INTERPERSONAL RELATIONS IN EMERGENCY
DEPARTMENT NURSING
    Robert J. Brady Company
    Charles Press Publishers
    Prentice-Hall Companies
    Bowie, Maryland 20715
Filmstrip with cassette. $50.00.

★ 1203 ★
NURSING CARE OF THE ORTHOPEDIC PATIENT -
CAST CARE

    Robert J. Brady Company
    Charles Press Publishers
    Prentice-Hall Companies
    Bowie, Maryland 20715
Filmstrip with cassette. $30.00.

★ 1204 ★
NURSING CARE OF THE ORTHOPEDIC PATIENT -
TRACTION
    Robert J. Brady Company
    Charles Press Publishers
    Prentice-Hall Companies
    Bowie, Maryland 20715
Filmstrip with cassette. $30.00.

★ 1205 ★
NURSING PROCEDURES FOR CARDIAC CARE
UNITS
    Robert J. Brady Company
    Charles Press Publishers
    Prentice-Hall Companies
    Bowie, Maryland 20715
Filmstrip with cassette. $30.00.

★ 1206 ★
NURSING PROCEDURES FOR THE RECOVERY ROOM
    Robert J. Brady Company
    Charles Press Publishers
    Prentice-Hall Companies
    Bowie, Maryland 20715
Filmstrip with cassette. $30.00.

★ 1207 ★
NURSING STAFF ORAL COMMUNICATIONS
    Thompson-Mitchell and Associates
    3384 Peachtree Road Northeast
    Atlanta, Georgia 30326
Filmstrip with cassette. $55.00.

★ 1208 ★
THE NURSING TEAM AND THE LAW
    Thompson-Mitchell and Associates
    3384 Peachtree Road Northeast
    Atlanta, Georgia 30326
Filmstrip with cassette. $55.00.

★ 1209 ★
PLANNING NURSING CARE
    Thompson-Mitchell and Associates
    3384 Peachtree Road Northeast
    Atlanta, Georgia 30326
Filmstrip with cassette. $55.00.

Printed Materials

★ 1210 ★
ADVANCED CARDIAC NURSING
    Robert J. Brady Company
    Charles Press Publishers
    Prentice-Hall Companies
    Bowie, Maryland 20715
Book. $5.00.

★ 1211 ★
NURSING MANAGEMENT
    W. L. Ganong Company
    Post Office Box 2727
    Chapel Hill, North Carolina 27514
Book. $15.00.

HEALTH, PERSONAL

Audio Cassettes/Tapes

★ 1212 ★
HEALING - GOOD HEALTH
Paul W. Schuette
    Tape Rental Library Incorporated
    Post Office Box 2107
    2507 Edna Drive
    South Vineland, New Jersey 08360
Cassette. $7.95.

★ 1213 ★
LISTEN AND LOSE (Weight control)
Robert Parrish
    Cassette House
    530 West Northwest Highway
    Mount Prospect, Illinois 60056
Cassette. $9.95.

★ 1214 ★
WALK FOR YOUR LIFE
Harry J. Johnson, M.D.
    Tape Rental Library Incorporated
    Post Office Box 2107
    2507 Edna Drive
    South Vineland, New Jersey 08360
Cassette. $9.98.

Correspondence Courses

★ 1215 ★
PERSONAL HEALTH
    University of Southern Mississippi
    Department of Independent Study
    Southern Station, Box 56
    Hattiesburg, Mississippi 39401

Correspondence course.

HEATING

See also: Air Conditioning and Refrigeration;
          Furnace Theory

Correspondence Courses

★ 1216 ★
DOMESTIC HEATING WITH OIL AND GAS
    International Correspondence School
    Scranton, Pennsylvania 18515
Multi-module correspondence course.

Film/Video/Filmstrips

★ 1217 ★
TEMPERATURE AND HEAT
    Resource Incorporated
    13902 North Dale Mabry Highway
    Tampa, Florida 33624
Video cartridge with workbook. $100.00.

Printed Materials

★ 1218 ★
THE NATURE OF HEAT
    Howell Training
    2040 North Loop West, Suite 204
    Houston, Texas 77018
Workbook and tests. $19.50.

Programmed Learning Materials

★ 1219 ★
DOWTHERM HEATING
    E. I. du Pont de Nemours and Company
    Applied Technology Division
    Room B 4204
    Wilmington, Delaware 19898
Programmed course of approximately 4 hours. $9.15.

HEBREW

Audio Cassettes/Tapes

★ 1220 ★
BERLITZ COURSE IN HEBREW
    Berlitz Language Program
    Post Office Box 5109, FDR Station
    New York, New York 10022
Cassette $5.95. Also available on 8 track and LP record.

Correspondence Courses

★ 1221 ★
HEBREW
      University of Wisconsin – Extension
      Independent Study
      432 North Lane Street
      Madison, Wisconsin 53706
Various level courses available.

Multimedia Kits

★ 1222 ★
HEBREW – BASIC COURSE
      General Services Administration
      Foreign Service Institute Language Course
      National Audiovisual Center
      Order Section RR
      Washington, D.C. 20409
Audio tapes, cassettes and text also available.
Approximately $200.00.

Printed Materials

★ 1223 ★
BASIC HEBREW: A TEXTBOOK OF
CONTEMPORARY
Marnin Feinstein
      Bloch Publishing Company
      915 Broadway
      New York, New York   10010
Book. 1973. $5.95.

★ 1224 ★
LEARN HEBREW FOR ENGLISH SPEAKERS
      Saphrograph Company
      194 Elizabeth Street
      New York, New York 10012
Book. $5.00.

★ 1225 ★
SAY IT IN MODERN HEBREW
Aleeza Cerf
      Dover Publications Incorporated
      180 Varick Street
      New York, New York 10014
Book. $1.25

★ 1226 ★
SELF TEACHER: HEBREW
Berlitz Schools of Languages
      Grosset and Dunlap Incorporated
      51 Madison Avenue
      New York, New York 10010
Self instructional text. $6.95.

★ 1227 ★
TEACH YOURSELF HEBREW
Roland Harrison
      David McKay Company Incorporated
      750 Third Avenue
      New York, New York 10017
Self instructional text. $3.95.

Programmed Learning Materials

★ 1228 ★
PROGRAMMED HEBREW
David Bridger
      Behrman House Incorporated
      1261 Broadway
      New York, New York 10001
Programmed instruction. 1971.

★ 1229 ★
PROGRAMMED HEBREW
Palmer Robertson
      Presbyterian and Reformed Publishing Company
      Box 185
      Nutley, New Jersey 07110
Programmed instruction. 1975. $7.50.

HINDI

Printed Materials

★ 1230 ★
HINDI – AN ACTIVE INTRODUCTION
      General Services Administration
      Foreign Service Institute Language Course
      National Audiovisual Center
      Order Section RR
      Washington, D.C. 20409
Text. $2.10.

★ 1231 ★
HINDI SELF TAUGHT
Ashutosh Ojha
      Inter Culture Associates
      Quaddick Road
      Post Office Box 277
      Thompson, Connecticut 06277
Book. 1973. $3.50.

★ 1232 ★
LEARN HINDI FOR ENGLISH SPEAKERS
      Saphrograph Company
      194 Elizabeth Street
      New York, New York 10012
Book. $5.00.

★ 1233 ★
UNIVERSAL SELF HINDI TEACHER
G. K. Ojha
>   S F Book Imports
>   Post Office Box 526
>   San Francisco, California 94101
Book. $3.75.

HORTICULTURE

Printed Materials

★ 1234 ★
HERE'S HOW: ON-JOB-TRAINING -
ORNAMENTAL HORTICULTURE
Paul Curtis
>   Interstate Incorporated
>   1927 North Jackson Street
>   Danville, Illinois 61832
Book. 1972. $3.50.

HOSPITAL ADMINISTRATION

Audio Cassettes/Tapes

★ 1235 ★
ALTERNATIVE ORGANIZATION TO
COMPREHENSIVE PREPAID HEALTH CARE
Richard Rand
>   Thompson-Mitchell and Associates
>   3384 Peachtree Road Northeast
>   Atlanta, Georgia 30326
Cassette . $12.00.

★ 1236 ★
ASSURING YOUR HOSPITAL'S FUTURE
Jerald Panas
>   Thompson-Mitchell and Associates
>   3384 Peachtree Road Northeast
>   Atlanta, Georgia 30326
Cassette. $12.00.

★ 1237 ★
COMMUNITY: BRIDGE TO HEALTH SERVICES
Donald Cook
>   Thompson-Mitchell and Associates
>   3384 Peachtree Road Northeast
>   Atlanta, Georgia 30326
Cassette. $12.00.

★ 1238 ★
COMPREHENSIVE HEALTH PLANNING
Robert M. Cunningham
>   Thompson-Mitchell and Associates
>   3384 Peachtree Road Northeast
>   Atlanta, Georgia 30326
Cassette. $10.00.

★ 1239 ★
THE COMPUTER, MEDICAL CARE, AND THE
MODERN HOSPITAL
Dr. Michael Jenkin
>   Thompson-Mitchell and Associates
>   3384 Peachtree Road Northeast
>   Atlanta, Georgia 30326
Cassette. $12.00.

★ 1240 ★
CONFLICT, CONFRONTATION, AND CONTROL
Dr. Montaque Brown
>   Thompson-Mitchell and Associates
>   3384 Peachtree Road Northeast
>   Atlanta, Georgia 30326
Cassette. $12.00.

★ 1241 ★
CONSTRUCTION MANAGEMENT FOR HOSPITAL
ADMINISTRATORS
William Eaves
>   Thompson-Mitchell and Associates
>   3384 Peachtree Road Northeast
>   Atlanta, Georgia 30326
Cassette. $12.00.

★ 1242 ★
DEBUNKING CHERISHED MANAGEMENT MYTHS
Frank Hoffman
>   Thompson-Mitchell and Associates
>   3384 Peachtree Road Northeast
>   Atlanta, Georgia 30326
Cassette. $12.00.

★ 1243 ★
DECISION MAKING AND THE ADMINISTRATOR
Dr. Stuart Wesbury
>   Thompson-Mitchell and Associates
>   3384 Peachtree Road Northeast
>   Atlanta, Georgia 30326
Cassette. $12.00.

★ 1244 ★

DEVELOPING THE HOSPITAL MANAGEMENT TEAM

Maxwell Canterbury

Thompson-Mitchell and Associates
3384 Peachtree Road Northeast
Atlanta, Georgia 30326

Cassette. $12.00.

★ 1245 ★

THE DILEMMA OF HOSPITALS - IS PUBLIC
UTILITY STATUS THE ANSWER?

Fred Morrissey

Thompson-Mitchell and Associates
3384 Peachtree Road Northeast
Atlanta, Georgia 30326

Cassette. $12.00.

★ 1246 ★

EMERGENCY MEDICAL SERVICES: NEW
DIRECTIONS AND OPPORTUNITIES

Dr. William Gemma

Thompson-Mitchell and Associates
3384 Peachtree Road Northeast
Atlanta, Georgia 30326

Cassette. $12.00.

★ 1247 ★

FINANCIAL MANAGEMENT FOR HOSPITAL
ADMINISTRATORS

Peter Laubach

Thompson-Mitchell and Associates
3384 Peachtree Road Northeast
Atlanta, Georgia 30326

Cassette. $12.00.

★ 1248 ★

FINANCIAL PROSPECTS AND COMPETITION
FOR CAPITOL AND COOPERATIVE SOLUTIONS
TO HEALTH CARE PROBLEMS

Thompson-Mitchell and Associates
3384 Peachtree Road Northeast
Atlanta, Georgia 30326

Cassette. $12.00.

★ 1249 ★

GOVERNING THE HOSPITAL - THE ADMINISTRA-
TOR'S EVOLVING ROLE

Ray E. Brown

Thompson-Mitchell and Associates
3384 Peachtree Road Northeast
Atlanta, Georgia 30326

Cassette. $12.00.

★ 1250 ★

HEALTH AND HOSPITALS IN 1975

Robert M. Cunningham

Thompson-Mitchell and Associates
3384 Peachtree Road Northeast
Atlanta, Georgia 30326

Cassette. $10.00.

★ 1251 ★

HMD'S - AN OPPORTUNITY FOR HOSPITALS

Dr. Milton Roemer

Thompson-Mitchell and Associates
3384 Peachtree Road Northeast
Atlanta, Georgia 30326

Cassette. $12.00.

★ 1252 ★

HOSPITAL MANAGEMENT AND GOVERNANCE

Robert M. Cunningham

Thompson-Mitchell and Associates
3384 Peachtree Road Northeast
Atlanta Georgia 30326

Cassette. $10.00.

★ 1253 ★

HOSPITAL MERGERS AND SHARED SERVICES

Richard L. Johnson

Thompson-Mitchell and Associates
3384 Peachtree Road Northeast
Atlanta, Georgia 30326

Cassette. $12.00.

★ 1254 ★

HOSPITAL TRAINING PROGRAMS

Robert M. Cunningham

Thompson-Mitchell and Associates
3384 Peachtree Road Northeast
Atlanta, Georgia 30326

Cassette. $10.00.

★ 1255 ★

HOW TO DEAL WITH "PROBLEM" EMPLOYEES

Ed Wessling

Thompson-Mitchell and Associates
3384 Peachtree Road Northeast
Atlanta, Georgia 30326

Cassette. $12.00.

★ 1256 ★

INVOLVING THE MEDICAL STAFF IN MANAGE-
MENT RESPONSIBILITIES
Dr. K. J. Williams
    Thompson-Mitchell and Associates
    3384 Peachtree Road Northeast
    Atlanta, Georgia 30326
Cassette. $12.00.

★ 1257 ★

LAY GOVERNING BOARDS: ASSET OR
LIABILITY
Dr. John Zwingle
    Thompson-Mitchell and Associates
    3384 Peachtree Road Northeast
    Atlanta, Georgia 30326
Cassette. $12.00.

★ 1258 ★

THE LEGAL BASE FOR ADMINISTRATIVE
EFFECTIVENESS
John Horty
    Thompson-Mitchell and Associates
    3384 Peachtree Road Northeast
    Atlanta, Georgia 30326
Cassette. $12.00.

★ 1259 ★

THE MANAGEMENT SPECIALIST IN A SERVICE
INDUSTRY
Daniel Carroll
    Thompson-Mitchell and Associates
    3384 Peachtree Road Northeast
    Atlanta, Georgia 30326
Cassette. $12.00.

★ 1260 ★

MANAGING BY OBJECTIVES OR DELUSIONS?
Edward Green
    Thompson-Mitchell and Associates
    3384 Peachtree Road Northeast
    Atlanta, Georgia 30326
Cassette. $12.00.

★ 1261 ★

A MODEL OF ORGANIZATIONAL DEVELOPMENT
John H. Farley
    Thompson-Mitchell and Associates
    3384 Peachtree Road Northeast
    Atlanta, Georgia 30326
Cassette. $12.00.

★ 1262 ★

ORGANIZATION GROWTH AND MANAGEMENT
OF CONFLICT
Dr. Leon Megginson
    Thompson-Mitchell and Associates
    3384 Peachtree Road Northeast
    Atlanta, Georgia 30326
Cassette. $12.00.

★ 1263 ★

PATHS FOR EMPLOYEE PROGRESS - PATH TO THE
TOP
Major Howard Lee
    Thompson-Mitchell and Associates
    3384 Peachtree Road Northeast
    Atlanta, Georgia 30326
Cassette. $12.00.

★ 1264 ★

PEOPLE CROSSING: STOP! LOOK! LISTEN!
Richard Underhill
    Thompson-Mitchell and Associates
    3384 Peachtree Road Northeast
    Atlanta, Georgia 30326
Cassette. $12.00.

★ 1265 ★

POSITIVE ACTION MANAGEMENT
Richard O. Evans
    Thompson-Mitchell and Associates
    3384 Peachtree Road Northeast
    Atlanta, Georgia 30326
Cassette. $12.00.

★ 1266 ★

PRESCRIPTION FOR MANAGING CHANGE
Dr. Thomas Calero
    Thompson-Mitchell and Associates
    3384 Peachtree Road Northeast
    Atlanta, Georgia 30326
Cassette. $12.00.

★ 1267 ★

PROBLEMS OF HEALTH SERVICES DELIVERY
IN RURAL AREAS
Harry Malm
    Thompson-Mitchell and Associates
    3384 Peachtree Road Northeast
    Atlanta, Georgia 30326
Cassette. $12.00.

★ 1268 ★
PROBLEMS OF HEALTH SERVICES DELIVERY
IN THE INNER CITY
Robert Cathcart
Thompson-Mitchell and Associates
3384 Peachtree Road Northeast
Atlanta, Georgia 30326
Cassette. $12.00.

★ 1269 ★
THE PROS AND CONS OF EMPLOYEE
INCENTIVES
Dr. Stanley Block
Thompson-Mitchell and Associates
3384 Peachtree Road Northeast
Atlanta, Georgia 30326
Cassette. $12.00.

★ 1270 ★
PROSPECTS FOR THE FUTURE OF THE HEALTH
SERVICES DELIVERY SYSTEM
Dr. Odin Anderson
Thompson-Mitchell and Associates
3384 Peachtree Road Northeast
Atlanta, Georgia 30326
Cassette. $12.00.

★ 1271 ★
RECRUITING PHYSICIANS
John Witt
Thompson-Mitchell and Associates
3384 Peachtree Road Northeast
Atlanta, Georgia 30326
Cassette. $12.00.

★ 1272 ★
THE RIGHTS OF THE INSTITUTION
Dr. F. W. Terrien
Thompson-Mitchell and Associates
3384 Peachtree Road Northeast
Atlanta, Georgia 30326
Cassette. $12.00.

★ 1273 ★
SELF PERCEPTION AND THE HOSPITAL
ADMINISTRATOR
Dr. William Henry
Thompson-Mitchell and Associates
3384 Peachtree Road Northeast
Atlanta, Georgia 30326
Cassette. $12.00.

★ 1274 ★
SKILLED MANAGEMENT IS A PEOPLE BUSINESS
Dr. A. R. Gornitzka
Thompson-Mitchell and Associates
3384 Peachtree Road Northeast
Atlanta, Georgia 30326
Cassette. $12.00.

★ 1275 ★
THREE WAYS TO MANAGE PEOPLE
Dr. Mungo Miller
Thompson-Mitchell and Associates
3384 Peachtree Road Northeast
Atlanta, Georgia 30326
Cassette. $12.00.

★ 1276 ★
VESTED INTERESTS IN HOSPITAL OPERATIONS
Dr. Frederick Elliot
Thompson-Mitchell and Associates
3384 Peachtree Road Northeast
Atlanta, Georgia 30326
Cassette. $12.00.

★ 1277 ★
WHO MANAGES THE MANAGEMENT ENGINEER?
Joseph R. Ryan
Thompson-Mitchell and Associates
3384 Peachtree Road Northeast
Atlanta, Georgia 30326
Cassette. $12.00.

★ 1278 ★
WHO'S RUNNING OUR HOSPITALS NOW?
Robert M. Cunningham
Thompson-Mitchell and Associates
3384 Peachtree Road Northeast
Atlanta, Georgia 30326
Cassette. $10.00.

HOTEL AND RESTAURANT MANAGEMENT

Correspondence Courses

★ 1279 ★
HOTEL AND RESTAURANT ADMINISTRATION
La Salle Extension University
417 South Dearborn Street
Chicago, Illinois 60605
Correspondence course.

★ 1280 ★
HOTEL, MOTEL OPERATIONS
    La Salle Extension University
    417 South Dearborn Street
    Chicago, Illinois 60605
Correspondence course.

★ 1281 ★
MOTEL/RESTAURANT MANAGEMENT
    International Correspondence School
    Scranton, Pennsylvania 18515
Multi-module correspondence course.

Films/Video/Filmstrips

★ 1282 ★
THE BELLMAN
    National Restaurant Association
    One IBM Plaza, Suite 2600
    Chicago, Illinois 60611
Video cartridge or 8 mm, 16 mm, and study guide.
$190.00.

★ 1283 ★
CLEANING THE BATHROOM (Hotel management)
    National Restaurant Association
    One IBM Plaza, Suite 2600
    Chicago, Illinois 60611
Video cartridge or 8 mm, 16 mm, and study guide.
$190.00.

★ 1284 ★
COURTESY IS THE ANSWER (Hotel management)
    National Restaurant Association
    One IBM Plaza, Suite 2600
    Chicago, Illinois 60611
Video cartridge or 8 mm, 16 mm, and study guide.
$190.00.

★ 1285 ★
THE FRONT DESK
    National Restaurant Association
    One IBM Plaza, Suite 2600
    Chicago, Illinois 60611
Video cartridge or 8 mm, 16 mm, and study guide.
$190.00.

★ 1286 ★
HOUSEKEEPING: BATHROOM CLEANING
    National Restaurant Association
    One IBM Plaza, Suite 2600
    Chicago, Illinois 60611
Film cartridge. $75.00.

★ 1287 ★
MAKING UP THE ROOM
    National Restaurant Association
    One IBM Plaza, Suite 2600
    Chicago, Illinois 60611
Video cartridge or 8 mm, 16 mm, and study guide.
$190.00.

★ 1288 ★
ROOM SERVICE
    National Restaurant Association
    One IBM Plaza, Suite 2600
    Chicago, Illinois 60611
Video cartridge or 8 mm, 16 mm, and study guide.
$190.00.

HOUSING CONSTRUCTION
See: BUILDING CONSTRUCTION

HUMAN RELATIONS

See also: Communication; Group Develop-
    ment; Personal Development; Personnel
    Management

Audio Cassettes/Tapes

★ 1289 ★
HOW TO USE TACT AND SKILL IN HANDLING
PEOPLE
Dr. Paul Parker
    Cassette House
    530 West Northwest Highway
    Mount Prospect, Illinois 60056
Cassette. $9.95.

★ 1290 ★
RELATIONS WITH OTHERS
    Educational Century Programming
    1201 East Johnson Street
    Jonesboro, Arkansas 72401
Cassette. $6.00.

★ 1291 ★
RELATIONS WITH SUPERVISORS
    Educational Century Programming
    1201 East Johnson Street
    Jonesboro, Arkansas 72401
Cassette. $6.00.

★ 1292 ★
RUMOR CONTROL
    Tape Rental Library Incorporated
    Post Office Box 2107
    2507 Edna Drive
    South Vineland, New Jersey   08360
Cassette.

★ 1293 ★
UNDERSTANDING OTHER PEOPLE
George Odiorne
    MBO Incorporated
    157 Pontoosic Road
    Westfield, Massachusetts   01085
Cassette and manual. $15.00.

Correspondence Courses

★ 1294 ★
MANAGING HUMAN RELATIONS
    Society of Manufacturing Engineers
    20501 Ford Road
    Post Office Box 930
5 hour self instruction course. $10.00.

Films/Video/Filmstrips

★ 1295 ★
INTERPERSONAL COMPETENCE
    Telstar Productions Incorporated
    366 North Prior Avenue
    Saint Paul, Minnesota   55104
47 video tape lessons and student manual.
$9,400.00.

★ 1296 ★
SUPERVISORS TRAINING IN HUMAN RELATIONS
    Better Selling Bureau
    1150 West Olive Avenue
    Burbank, California   91506
8 filmstrips, guide and manual. $795.00.

★ 1297 ★
UNDERSTANDING YOUR RELATIONSHIPS WITH
OTHERS
    Thompson-Mitchell and Associates
    3384 Peachtree Road Northeast
    Atlanta, Georgia   30326
Filmstrip. $125.00.

Games/Simulations

★ 1298 ★
SENSITIVITY BUSINESS GAMES FOR MANAGERS
(Game analyses supervisory situations)
    Educational Research
    Post Office Box 4205
    Warren, New Jersey   07060
For individual or group use. $6.95.

Multimedia Kits

★ 1299 ★
COACHING
    Resources for Education and Management
        Incorporated
    544 Medlock Road, Suite 210
    Decatur, Georgia   30030
Filmstrip, cassette and guide. $65.00.

★ 1300 ★
GENERAL PROBLEMS OF INTERPERSONAL CONFLICT
    Resources for Education and Management
        Incorporated
    544 Medlock Road, Suite 210
    Decatur, Georgia   30030
Filmstrip with cassette. $60.00.

★ 1301 ★
HOW TO BUILD LOYALTY
    Resources for Education and Management
        Incorporated
    544 Medlock Road, Suite 210
    Decatur, Georgia   30030
Filmstrip with cassette. $60.00.

★ 1302 ★
IMPROVING ATTITUDES TOWARD SUBORDINATES
    Resources for Education and Management
        Incorporated
    544 Medlock Road, Suite 210
    Decatur, Georgia   30030
Filmstrip with cassette. $60.00.

★ 1303 ★
IMPROVING ATTITUDES TOWARD SUPERVISORS
    Resources for Education and Management
        Incorporated
    544 Medlock Road, Suite 210
    Decatur, Georgia   30030
Filmstrip with cassette. $60.00.

★ 1304 ★
IMPROVING MANAGERIAL PERCEPTION
    Resources for Education and Management
      Incorporated
    544 Medlock Road,   Suite 210
    Decatur, Georgia   30030
Filmstrip with cassette. $60.00.

★ 1305 ★
IMPROVING RELATIONS BETWEEN PEERS
    Resources for Education and Management
      Incorporated
    544 Medlock Road, .Suite 210
    Decatur, Georgia   30030
Filmstrip with cassette. $60.00.

★ 1306 ★
INTERACTING WITH OTHERS IN FACE-TO-FACE
SITUATIONS
    Thompson-Mitchell and Associates
    3384 Peachtree Road Northeast
    Atlanta, Georgia   30326
Cassette with workbook. $36.00.

★ 1307 ★
MANAGING FOR RESULTS
    Resources for Education and Management
      Incorporated
    544 Medlock Road,   Suite 210
    Decatur, Georgia   30030
Filmstrip, cassette and guide. $65.00.

★ 1308 ★
A NEW ATTITUDE
    Resources for Education and Management
      Incorporated
    544 Medlock Road,   Suite 210
    Decatur, Georgia   30030
Filmstrip with cassette. $60.00.

★ 1309 ★
PERCEPTION
    Resources for Education and Management
      Incorporated
    544 Medlock Road,   Suite 210
    Decatur, Georgia   30030
Filmstrip with cassette. $60.00.

★ 1310 ★
SEEING THE ESSENTIALS - PERCEPTION
    Resources for Education and Management
      Incorporated
    544 Medlock Road,   Suite 210
    Decatur, Georgia   30030

Filmstrip with cassette. $60.00.

★ 1311 ★
WHATS BEHIND BEHAVIOR?
    Resources for Education and Management
      Incorporated
    544 Medlock Road,   Suite 210
    Decatur, Georgia   30030
Filmstrips, cassette and guide. $65.00.

★ 1312 ★
WORKING MORE EFFECTIVELY WITH PEOPLE
    Resources for Education and Management
      Incorporated
    544 Medlock Road,   Suite 210
    Decatur, Georgia   30030
Filmstrips, cassette and guide. $65.00.

Printed Materials

★ 1313 ★
COUNSELING TECHNIQUES FOR NON-
PERSONNEL EXECUTIVE
John D. Drake
    Management Resources Incorporated
    757 Third Avenue
    New York, New York 10017
Book and worksheets. $3.95.

Programmed Learning Materials

★ 1314 ★
MANAGING HUMAN RELATIONS
    Preston Publishing Company
    151 East 50th Street
    New York, New York   10022
Programmed text. $10.00.

HUNGARIAN

Audio Cassettes/Tapes

★ 1315 ★
SPOKEN HUNGARIAN
Thomas Sebeok
    Spoken Language Services Incorporated
    Post Office Box 783
    Ithaca, New York   14850
Text and cassettes. $55.00.

Multimedia Kits

★ 1316 ★
HUNGARIAN - BASIC COURSE
General Services Administration
Foreign Service Institute Language Course
National Audiovisual Center
Order Section RR
Washington, D.C. 20409
Audio tapes, cassettes and text also available.
Approximately $200.00.

ICELANDIC

Printed Materials

★ 1317 ★
TEACH YOURSELF ICELANDIC
P. J. Glendening
David McKay Company Incorporated
750 Third Avenue
New York, New York 10017
Book. $2.95.

IGBO

Multimedia Kits

★ 1318 ★
IGBO - BASIC COURSE
General Services Administration
Foreign Service Institute Language Course
National Audiovisual Center
Order Section RR
Washington, D.C. 20409
Audio tapes, cassettes and text also available.
Approximately $100.00.

INCOME TAX
See: TAXES

INDONESIAN

Printed Materials

★ 1319 ★
TEACH YOURSELF INDONESIAN
John B. Kwee
David McKay Company Incorporated
750 Third Avenue
New York, New York 10017
Book. $2.95.

INDUSTRIAL DESIGN

Films/Video/Filmstrips

★ 1320 ★
ARCHITECTURAL DESIGN
Scope Productions Incorporated
Post Office Box 5515
Fresno, California 93755
8 films (8 mm) and student guides. $168.00.

★ 1321 ★
BASIC INDUSTRIAL DESIGN
Scope Productions Incorporated
Post Office Box 5515
Fresno, California 93755
3 films (8 mm) and student guides. $63.00.

★ 1322 ★
MOLD MAKING
Scope Productions Incorporated
Post Office Box 5515
Fresno, California 93755
4 films (8 mm) and student guides. $84.00.

INDUSTRIAL SAFETY
See: SAFETY, INDUSTRIAL

INNOVATION
See: CREATIVITY

INSTALLATION

Programmed Learning Materials

★ 1323 ★
EQUIPMENT INSTALLATION
TPC Training Systems
Technical Publishing Company
1301 South Grove Avenue
Barrington, Illinois 60010
Programmed text of 5 lessons. $16.75.

★ 1324 ★
RIGGING
TPC Training Systems
    Technical Publishing Company
    1301 South Grove Avenue
    Barrington, Illinois 60010
Programmed text of 5 lessons. $16.75.

INSTRUCTIONAL DEVELOPMENT

See also: Classroom Instruction;   Training
                Techniques

Multimedia Kits

★ 1325 ★
CRITERION TESTS IN INSTRUCTIONAL TECHNOLOGY
    Thompson-Mitchell and Associates
    3384 Peachtree Road Northeast
    Atlanta, Georgia 30326
Filmstrip with cassettes and workbooks. $250.00.

★ 1326 ★
DESIGNING EFFECTIVE INSTRUCTION
    Thompson-Mitchell and Associates
    3384 Peachtree Road Northeast
    Atlanta, Georgia 30326
A workshop containing 15 audio cassettes, 12 film-
strips, 10 workbooks and 1 monitors manual. $725.00.

★ 1327 ★
INSTRUCTIONAL DEVELOPMENT LEARNING SYSTEM
    Thompson-Mitchell and Associates
    3384 Peachtree Road Northeast
    Atlanta, Georgia 30326
6 cassettes, slides and workbooks. $275.00.

★ 1328 ★
INSTRUCTIONAL MEDIA
    Thompson-Mitchell and Associates
    3384 Peachtree Road Northeast
    Atlanta, Georgia 30326
Filmstrip with cassettes and workbooks. $250.00.

★ 1329 ★
INSTRUCTIONAL METHODS
    Thompson-Mitchell and Associates
    3384 Peachtree Road Northeast
    Atlanta, Georgia 30326
Filmstrip with cassettes and workbooks. $600.00.

★ 1330 ★
INSTRUCTIONAL TECHNOLOGY WORKSHOP
    Thompson-Mitchell and Associates
    3384 Peachtree Road Northeast
    Atlanta, Georgia 30326
8 unit course with filmstrips, cassettes and workbook.
$2,700.00.

★ 1331 ★
INTRODUCTION TO INSTRUCTIONAL TECHNOLOGY
    Thompson-Mitchell and Associates
    3384 Peachtree Road Northeast
    Atlanta, Georgia 30326
Filmstrip with audio cassette. $24.95.

★ 1332 ★
OBJECTIVES IN INSTRUCTIONAL TECHNOLOGY
    Thompson-Mitchell and Associates
    3384 Peachtree Road Northeast
    Atlanta, Georgia 30326
Filmstrip with cassettes and workbooks. $360.00.

★ 1333 ★
OVERVIEW OF INSTRUCTIONAL TECHNOLOGY
    Thompson-Mitchell and Associates
    3384 Peachtree Road Northeast
    Atlanta, Georgia 30326
Filmstrip with cassettes and workbooks. $270.00.

★ 1334 ★
PRODUCING BETTER LEARNING
    Resources for Education and Management
        Incorporated
    544 Medlock Road, Suite 210
    Decatur, Georgia 30030
3 part series - filmstrips with cassettes and leaders
guide. $99.00.

★ 1335 ★
TASK ANALYSIS IN INSTRUCTIONAL TECHNOLOGY
    Thompson-Mitchell and Associates
    3384 Peachtree Road Northeast
    Atlanta, Georgia 30326
Filmstrips with cassettes and workbooks. $750.00.

★ 1336 ★
TRAINING REQUIREMENTS IN INSTRUCTIONAL
TECHNOLOGY
    Thompson-Mitchell and Associates
    3384 Peachtree Road Northeast
    Atlanta, Georgia 30326
Filmstrip with cassettes and workbooks. $485.00.

★ 1337 ★
VALIDATION IN INSTRUCTIONAL TECHNOLOGY
　　Thompson-Mitchell and Associates
　　3384 Peachtree Road Northeast
　　Atlanta, Georgia 30326
Filmstrip with cassettes and workbooks. $195.00.

INSTRUCTIONAL TECHNIQUES
See: TRAINING TECHNIQUES

INSTRUMENTATION

Audio Cassettes/Tapes

★ 1338 ★
FEEDFORWARD - NEW TECHNOLOGIES
　　Instrument Society of America
　　400 Stanwix Street
　　Pittsburgh, Pennsylvania 15222
Workbook and cassette. $7.00.

★ 1339 ★
MEASUREMENT OF ELECTRICAL QUANTITIES
Edward W. Ernst
　　Instrument Society of America
　　400 Stanwix Street
　　Pittsburgh, Pennsylvania 15222
Workbook and cassette.

★ 1340 ★
PROCESS ELECTROCHEMICAL INSTRUMENTATION
Thomas J. Kehoe
　　Instrument Society of America
　　400 Stanwix Street
　　Pittsburgh, Pennsylvania 15222
Workbook and cassette. $10.00.

Films/Video/Filmstrips

★ 1341 ★
BASIC INSPECTION INSTRUMENT AND METHODS
　　National Tool, Die and Precision Machining
　　　Association
　　9300 Livingston Road
　　Washington, D.C. 20022
Sound film, test and review.

Printed Materials

★ 1342 ★
INSTRUMENTATION FOR OPERATORS
　　Howell Training
　　2040 North Loop West, Suite 204
　　Houston, Texas 77018
Workbooks and tests. $37.05.

Programmed Learning Materials

★ 1343 ★
BASIC PRINCIPLES OF FLOW MEASUREMENT
　　E. I. du Pont de Nemours and Company
　　Applied Technology Division
　　Room B 4204
　　Wilmington, Delaware 19898
Programmed course of approximately 3 hours.
$15.60.

★ 1344 ★
CALIBRATION ADJUSTMENTS - ZERO SPAN AND
LINEARITY
　　E. I. du Pont de Nemours and Company
　　Applied Technology Division
　　Room B 4204
　　Wilmington, Delaware 19898
Programmed course of approximately 9 hours.
$17.10.

★ 1345 ★
HAND REAMERS
　　E. I. du Pont de Nemours and Company
　　Applied Technology Division
　　Room B 4204
　　Wilmington, Delaware 19898
3 unit programmed course.   Approximately $10.00
each unit.

★ 1346 ★
INSTRUMENTATION FOR OPERATORS
J. Victor
　　Resources Development Corporation
　　2040 North Loop West, Suite 204
　　Houston, Texas 77018
Programmed text. $29.00.

★ 1347 ★
INTEGRATION IN FLOW MEASUREMENT
　　E. I. du Pont de Nemours and Company
　　Applied Technology Division
　　Room B 4204
　　Wilmington, Delaware 19898
Programmed course of approximately 2 hours. $7.40.

★ 1348 ★
MEASURING ELEMENTS IN FLOW MEASUREMENT
E. I. du Pont de Nemours and Company
Applied Technology Division
Room B 4204
Wilmington, Delaware 19898
Programmed course of approximately 3 hours. $7.40.

★ 1349 ★
MODES OF INSTRUMENT CONTROL
E. I. du Pont de Nemours and Company
Applied Technology Division
Room B 4204
Wilmington, Delaware 19898
Programmed course of approximately 11 hours.
$20.30.

★ 1350 ★
PEDESTAL AND BENCH GRINDERS
E. I. du Pont de Nemours and Company
Applied Technology Division
Room B 4204
Wilmington, Delaware 19898
Programmed course of approximately 5 hours.
$10.90.

★ 1351 ★
PRIMARY ELEMENTS OF FLOW MEASUREMENT
E. I. du Pont de Nemours and Company
Applied Technology Division
Room B 4204
Wilmington, Delaware 19898
Programmed course of approximately 3 hours.
$7.40.

★ 1352 ★
READING A MICROMETER
Society of Manufacturing Engineers
20501 Ford Road
Post Office Box 930
Dearborn, Michigan 48128
Programmed learning course. $2.65.

★ 1353 ★
USING A PITOT TUBE
E. I. du Pont de Nemours and Company
Applied Technology Division
Room B 4204
Wilmington, Delaware 19898
Programmed course of approximately 2 hours.
$5.90.

INSULATION

Programmed Learning Materials

★ 1354 ★
THERMAL INSULATION
E. I. du Pont de Nemours and Company
Applied Technology Division
Room B 4204
Wilmington, Delaware 19898
2 unit programmed course of 25 hours. $32.00
each.

INSURANCE

Audio Cassettes/Tapes

★ 1355 ★
BUSINESS INSURANCE
Tape Rental Library Incorporated
Post Office Box 2107
2507 Edna Drive
South Vineland, New Jersey 03360
Cassette.

★ 1356 ★
BUY INSURANCE/BORROW MONEY
Educational Century Programming
1201 East Johnson Street
Jonesboro, Arkansas 72401
Cassette. $6.00.

★ 1357 ★
HEALTH INSURANCE UPDATE
Robert M. Cunningham
Thompson-Mitchell and Associates
3384 Peachtree Road Northeast
Atlanta, Georgia 30326
Cassette. $10.00.

★ 1358 ★
HOW SCARY IS THE FINE PRINT
Bernard Corak
Tape Rental Library Incorporated
Post Office Box 2107
2507 Edna Drive
South Vineland, New Jersey 08360
Cassette. $8.50.

Correspondence Courses

★ 1359 ★
CONSUMER PERSPECTIVES IN LIFE INSURANCE
          University of South Carolina
          Department of Correspondence Study
          Division of Continuing Education
          Columbia, South Carolina 29208
Correspondence course. $50.00.

★ 1360 ★
PRINCIPLES OF RISK AND INSURANCE
          University of South Carolina
          Department of Correspondence Study
          Division of Continuing Education
          Columbia, South Carolina 29208
Correspondence course. $69.00.

★ 1361 ★
RISK AND INSURANCE
          Indiana State University
          Independent Study Office
          Terre Haute, Indiana 47809
Independent study course.

Programmed Learning Materials

★ 1362 ★
PRINCIPLES OF INSURANCE
Robert Mehr
          Learning Systems Company
          1818 Ridge Road
          Homewood, Illinois 60430
Programmed learning aid. $4.50.

INSURANCE SALES

See also: Salesmanship

Audio Cassettes/Tapes

★ 1363 ★
THE AGENT/CLIENT RELATIONSHIP (Insurance)
          Thompson-Mitchell and Associates
          3384 Peachtree Road Northeast
          Atlanta, Georgia 30326
Cassette. $9.95.

★ 1364 ★
HOW I SOLD 40,000,000 OF LIFE INSURANCE
IN TWO YEARS WITH 1,212 PAID CASES
Joe Gandolfo

          Tape Rental Library Incorporated
          Post Office Box 2107
          2507 Edna Drive
          South Vineland, New Jersey 08360
Cassette. $11.95.

★ 1365 ★
HOW TO SELL $3,000,000 OF LIFE INSURANCE
TO THE TOWN AND COUNTRY MARKET EVERY
YEAR...A VAST AND UNTAPPED SOURCE OF
PROSPECTS
James C. Bradford
          Tape Rental Library Incorporated
          Post Office Box 2107
          2507 Edna Drive
          South Vineland, New Jersey 08360
Cassette. $11.95.

★ 1366 ★
HOW TO USE DIRECT MAIL TO SELL 1,500,000
OF LIFE INSURANCE EVERY YEAR...AND END
YOUR PROSPECTING PROBLEMS FOREVER
Jack Hartman
          Tape Rental Library Incorporated
          Post Office Box 2107
          2507 Edna Drive
          South Vineland, New Jersey 08360
Cassette. $11.95.

★ 1367 ★
SUCCESS IN LIFE INSURANCE
          Educational Century Programming
          1201 East Johnson Street
          Jonesboro, Arkansas 72401
6 cassettes. $40.00.

Films/Video/Filmstrips

★ 1368 ★
THE BETTER THINGS IN LIFE (Mutual funds)
          Better Selling Bureau
          1150 West Olive Avenue
          Burbank, California 91506
Filmstrip. $90.00.

★ 1369 ★
CAN YOU DECIDE? (Sole proprietor)
          Better Selling Bureau
          1150 West Olive Avenue
          Burbank, California 91506
Filmstrip. $90.00.

★ 1370 ★
THE CHOICE IS YOURS (Disability income)
    Better Selling Bureau
    1150 West Olive Avenue
    Burbank, California 91506
Filmstrip. $90.00.

★ 1371 ★
LET ME COUNT THE WAYS (Disability income insurance)
    Thompson-Mitchell and Associates
    3384 Peachtree Road Northeast
    Atlanta, Georgia 30326
Filmstrip. $60.00.

★ 1372 ★
THE QUESTION IS BUSINESS INSURANCE
    Better Selling Bureau
    1150 West Olive Avenue
    Burbank, California 91506
Filmstrip. $90.00.

★ 1373 ★
WHICH DO YOU WANT? (Retirement savings)
    Better Selling Bureau
    1150 West Olive Avenue
    Burbank, California 91506
Filmstrip. $90.00.

★ 1374 ★
WHICH WAY (Estate planning)
    Better Selling Bureau
    1150 West Olive Avenue
    Burbank, California 91506
Filmstrip. $90.00.

★ 1375 ★
WHICH WILL IT BE? (Mortgage cancelation)
    Better Selling Bureau
    1150 West Olive Avenue
    Burbank, California 91506
Filmstrip. $90.00.

Multimedia Kits

★ 1376 ★
HOW TO SELL AUTO INSURANCE
    Better Selling Bureau
    1150 West Olive Avenue
    Burbank, California 91506
6 filmstrips with cassette. $495.00.

★ 1377 ★
HOW TO SELL BUSINESS INSURANCE
    Better Selling Bureau
    1150 West Olive Avenue
    Burbank, California 91506
5 filmstrips with cassette. $395.00.

★ 1378 ★
HOW TO SELL CASUALTY AND FIRE INSURANCE
    Better Selling Bureau
    1150 West Olive Avenue
    Burbank, California 91506
6 filmstrips with cassettes. $495.00.

★ 1379 ★
HOW TO SELL LIFE INSURANCE SUCCESSFULLY
    Better Selling Bureau
    1150 West Olive Avenue
    Burbank, California 91506
6 filmstrips with cassette. $492.00.

★ 1380 ★
HUMAN NEEDS FOR LIFE INSURANCE
    Better Selling Bureau
    1150 West Olive Avenue
    Burbank, California 91506
7 filmstrips with records. $350.00.

★ 1381 ★
RECRUITING PROGRAM
    Better Selling Bureau
    1150 West Olive Avenue
    Burbank, California 91506
2 filmstrips with cassettes. $200.00.

★ 1382 ★
SELLING INSURANCE WITH FILMSTRIPS
    Better Selling Bureau
    1150 West Olive Avenue
    Burbank, California 91506
2 filmstrips with cassette. $200.00.

INTERIOR DECORATING

Correspondence Courses

★ 1383 ★
CUSTOM DECORATING
    Custom Decorating Institute
    412 South Lyon Street
    Santa Ana, California 92701
Home study course with consultation.

★ 1384 ★
INTERIOR DECORATING
        La Salle Extension University
        417 South Dearborn Street
        Chicago, Illinois 60605
Correspondence course.

★ 1385 ★
INTERIOR DECORATION
        University of Colorado
        170 Aurora Avenue
        Boulder, Colorado 80302
Correspondence course.

INTERNATIONAL MARKETING

See also: Marketing

Audio Cassettes/Tapes

★ 1386 ★
THE INTERNATIONAL MARKETPLACE
John A. Bowden
        Tape Rental Library Incorporated
        Post Office Box 2107
        2507 Edna Drive
        South Vineland, New Jersey 08360
Cassette.

Printed Materials

★ 1387 ★
EXPORTING
D. F. Taylor, E. A. Rutland
        David McKay Company Incorporated
        750 Third Avenue
        New York, New York 10017
Self-study text. 1974. $2.95.

INTERVIEWING

See also: Communication; Personnel
Selection; headings under Supervision

Audio Cassettes/Tapes

★ 1388 ★
ACQUIRE AN INTERVIEW/DRESS FOR AN INTERVIEW
        Educational Century Programming
        1201 East Johnson Street
        Jonesboro, Arkansas 72401
Cassette. $6.00.

★ 1389 ★
APPRAISAL AND CAREER-COUNSELING INTERVIEWS
        American Management Associations
        135 West 50th Street
        New York, New York 10020
Cassette with manual. $25.00.

★ 1390 ★
THE ART OF INTERVIEWING
        The Center for Cassette Studies Incorporated
        8010 Webb Avenue
        North Hollywood, California 91605
Cassette. $9.95.

★ 1391 ★
THE DISCIPLINARY INTERVIEW
        American Management Associations
        135 West 50th Street
        New York, New York 10020
Cassette. $18.00.

★ 1392 ★
THE EXIT INTERVIEW
        American Management Associations
        135 West 50th Street
        New York, New York 10020
Cassette with manual. $25.00.

★ 1393 ★
INTERVIEWING AND HIRING STORE PERSONNEL
        Thompson-Mitchell and Associates
        3384 Peachtree Road Northeast
        Atlanta, Georgia 30326
Cassette. $25.00.

★ 1394 ★
THE INTERVIEWING SKILLS SERIES
        Addison Wesley Publishing Company Incorporated
        Jacob Way
        Reading, Massachusetts 01867
6 cassettes. $65.00.

★ 1395 ★
THE PROBLEM EMPLOYEE INTERVIEW
        American Management Associations
        135 West 50th Street
        New York, New York 10020
Cassette with manual. $25.00.

★ 1396 ★

THE SELECTION INTERVIEW
American Management Associations
135 West 50th Street
New York, New York 10020
Cassette with manual. $25.00.

★ 1397 ★

SELECTION INTERVIEWING
The Drake Hypothesis Method
Management Resources Incorporated
757 Third Avenue
New York, New York 10017
6 cassettes and workbooks. $295.00.

Films/Video/Filmstrips

★ 1398 ★

THE CAMPUS INTERVIEW.
Management Resources Incorporated
757 Third Avenue
New York, New York 10017
Booklet and video cassette. $425.00 (rental available).

★ 1399 ★

THE FACE TO FACE PAYOFF: DYNAMICS OF THE INTERVIEW
Joe Batten
Creative Media Films
820 Keo Way
Des Moines, Iowa 50309
2 films or video cassettes and guides. $545.00 (rental available).

Games/Simulations

★ 1400 ★

ABELSON-BAKER INTERVIEW (Concepts and skills of interpersonal communication)
Training House Incorporated
Box 688
Binghamton, New York 13902
Simulation games. $60.00.

Multimedia Kits

★ 1401 ★

THE APPRAISAL INTERVIEW
Resources for Education and Management
Incorporated
544 Medlock Road, Suite 210
Decatur, Georgia 30030
Filmstrip (35 mm) with cassette. $55.00.

★ 1402 ★

THE COUNSELING INTERVIEW
Resources for Education and Management
Incorporated
544 Medlock Road, Suite 210
Decatur, Georgia 30030
Filmstrip (35 mm) with cassette. $55.00.

★ 1403 ★

THE DISCIPLINARY INTERVIEW
Resources for Education and Management
Incorporated
544 Medlock Road, Suite 210
Decatur, Georgia 30030
Filmstrip (35 mm) with cassette. $55.00.

★ 1404 ★

EFFECTIVE INTERVIEWING
Ergonco Performance Source
Northwest O'Hare Office Park, Suite 119
2474 Dempster Street
Des Plains, Illinois 60016
Multimedia self-study program.

★ 1405 ★

THE EMPLOYMENT INTERVIEW
Resources for Education and Management
Incorporated
544 Medlock Road, Suite 210
Decatur, Georgia 30030
Filmstrip (35 mm) with cassette. $55.00.

★ 1406 ★

THE EXIT INTERVIEW
Resources for Education and Management
Incorporated
544 Medlock Road, Suite 210
Decatur, Georgia 30030
Filmstrip (35 mm) with cassette. $55.00.

★ 1407 ★

GENERAL PRINCIPLES OF INTERVIEWING
Resources for Education and Management
Incorporated
544 Medlock Road, Suite 210
Decatur, Georgia 30030
Filmstrip (35 mm) with cassette. $55.00.

★ 1408 ★
THE GRIEVANCE INTERVIEW
       Resources for Education and Management
          Incorporated
       544 Medlock Road, Suite 210
       Decatur, Georgia 30030
Filmstrip with cassette. $75.00.

★ 1409 ★
INTERACTIVE QUESTIONING
       Ergonco Performance Source
       Northwest O'Hare Office Park, Suite 119
       2474 Dempster Street
       Des Plains, Illinois 60016
Multimedia self-study program.

★ 1410 ★
TECHNIQUES OF INTERVIEWING
       Resources for Education and Management
          Incorporated
       544 Medlock Road, Suite 210
       Decatur, Georgia 30030
Filmstrip with cassette. $75.00.

Programmed Learning Materials

★ 1411 ★
ILYIN ORAL INTERVIEW
       Newbury House Publishers
       68 Middle Road
       Rowley, Massachusetts 01969
Programmed instruction.   1971.

INVENTING

See also: Creativity

Printed Materials

★ 1412 ★
COMPLETE GUIDE TO MAKING MONEY WITH
YOUR IDEAS AND INVENTIONS
Richard Paige
       Barnes and Noble Incorporated
       Keystone Industrial Park
       Scranton, Pennsylvania 18512
Book.   1976. $2.95.

★ 1413 ★
HOW TO BE A SUCCESSFUL INVENTOR:
PATENTING, PROTECTING, MARKETING AND
SELLING YOUR INVENTIONS
Clarence Taylor

       Exposition Press Incorporated
       900 South Oyster Bay Road
       Hicksville, New York 11801
Book.   1972. $6.50.

★ 1414 ★
HOW TO INVENT
Forrest Gilmore
       Gulf Publishing Company
       3301 Allen Parkway
       Houston, Texas 77001
Book. $5.50.

INVENTORY CONTROL

Correspondence Courses

★ 1415 ★
INVENTORY CONTROL
       The Thomas Institute
       Box 22
       New Canaan, Connecticut 06840
Self-study course. $110.00.

Multimedia Kits

★ 1416 ★
INVENTORY CONTROL
       Lansford Publishing Company
       Post Office Box 8711
       San Jose, California 95155
Multimedia kit. $149.95.

Programmed Learning Materials

★ 1417 ★
INVENTORY MANAGEMENT
R. Mennell
       Entelek Incorporated
       42 Pleasant Street
       Newburyport, Massachusetts 01950
Programmed text. $38.00.

INVESTMENT

See also: Estate Planning; Financial
               Planning; Real Estate

Audio Cassettes/Tapes

★ 1418 ★
THE BATTLE FOR INVESTMENT SURVIVAL
Gerald M. Loeb

Tape Rental Library Incorporated
Post Office Box 2107
2507 Edna Drive
South Vineland, New Jersey 08360
Cassette.

★ 1419 ★
HOW TO BORROW TWICE THE MONEY
Somers H. White
Tape Rental Library Incorporated
Post Office Box 2107
2507 Edna Drive
South Vineland, New Jersey 08360
Cassette. $39.50.

★ 1420 ★
INVEST MONEY/SELECT A BANK
Educational Century Programming
1201 East Johnson Street
Jonesboro, Arkansas 72401
Cassette. $6.00.

★ 1421 ★
RATE OF RETURN ON INVESTMENTS
Tape Rental Library Incorporated
Post Office Box 2107
2507 Edna Drive
South Vineland, New Jersey 08360
12 cassettes with workbook. $295.00.

Correspondence Courses

★ 1422 ★
BROKERAGE OPERATIONS
DEPARTMENT PROCEDURES
New York Institute of Finance
70 Pine Street
New York, New York 10005
8 lesson correspondence course. $50.00.

★ 1423 ★
INVESTMENT ANALYSIS
New York Institute of Finance
70 Pine Street
New York, New York 10005
20 lesson correspondence course. $135.00.

★ 1424 ★
INVESTMENTS
University of Kentucky
Independent Study Program
Freeze Hall, Room 1
Lexington, Kentucky 40506
Correspondence course.

★ 1425 ★
INVESTMENTS
University of Missouri
514 South Fifth Street
Columbia, Missouri 65211
Correspondence course. $80.00.

★ 1426 ★
LISTED OPTIONS MARKET
New York Institute of Finance
70 Pine Street
New York, New York 10005
10 lesson correspondence course. $85.00.

★ 1427 ★
TRADING IN COMMODITY FUTURES
New York Institute of Finance
70 Pine Street
New York, New York 10005
Correspondence course. $85.00.

Printed Materials

★ 1428 ★
DEVELOPING SALES FOR SECURITIES FINANCIAL
SERVICES
M. Appleman
Prentice-Hall Incorporated
Englewood Cliffs, New Jersey 07632
Book. 1973. $5.95.

★ 1429 ★
FUNDAMENTALS OF INVESTING
Ben Branch
John Wiley and Sons Incorporated
605 Third Avenue
New York, New York 10016
Book. 1976. $12.95.

★ 1430 ★
HOW TO INVEST IN BONDS
Hugh Sherwood
Walker and Company
720 Fifth Avenue
New York, New York 10019
Book. 1974. $7.95.

★ 1431 ★
INVESTING MONEY: THE FACTS ABOUT STOCKS
AND BONDS
Ruth Brindze
Harcourt Brace Jovanovich Incorporated
757 Third Avenue
New York, New York 10017

Book. $5.50.

★ 1432 ★
RETURN ON INVESTMENT
        American Management Associations
        135 West 50th Street
        New York, New York   10020
Self-study text. $65.00.

Programmed Learning Materials

★ 1433 ★
HOW TO READ FINANCIAL STATEMENTS FOR
BETTER STOCK MARKET PERFORMANCE
C. M. Flumidni
        American Classical College Press
        Post Office Box 4526
        Albuquerque, New Mexico 87106
Programmed instruction.   1975. $29.50.

★ 1434 ★
PRINCIPLES OF INVESTMENTS
Fred Amling
        Learning Systems Company
        1818 Ridge Road
        Homewood, Illinois   60430
Programmed learning aid. $4.95.

ITALIAN

Audio Cassettes/Tapes

★ 1435 ★
BERLITZ COMPREHENSIVE COURSE IN ITALIAN
        Berlitz Language Program
        Post Office Box 5109
        FDR Station
        New York, New York   10022
6 cassettes with workbook. $85.00.

★ 1436 ★
BERLITZ COURSE IN ITALIAN
        Berlitz Language Program
        Post Office Box 5109
        FDR Station
        New York, New York   10022
Cassette $5.95.   Also available on 8 track and LP
record.

★ 1437 ★
ITALIAN
        Thompson-Mitchell and Associates
        3384 Peachtree Road Northeast
        Atlanta, Georgia 30326
Cassette. $9.98.

★ 1438 ★
ITALIAN WITHOUT TOIL
Albert Cherel
        French and European Publications Incorporated
        Rockerfeller Center Promenade
        610 Fifth Avenue
        New York, New York 10020
Book with cassettes or records.

Correspondence Courses

★ 1439 ★
ITALIAN
        University of Wisconsin - Extension
        Independent Study
        432 North Lake Street
        Madison, Wisconsin 53706
Various leval courses available.

★ 1440 ★
ITALIAN LANGUAGE STUDIES
        University of Washington
        Office of Independent Study
        222 Lewis Hall DW-30
        Seattle, Washington 98195
Correspondence course.

Multimedia Kits

★ 1441 ★
ITALIAN - PROGRAMMATIC
        General Services Administration
        Foreign Service Institute Language Course
        National Audiovisual Center
        Order Section RR
        Washington, D.C. 20409
Audio tapes, cassettes and text also available.
Approximately $100.00.

Printed Materials

★ 1442 ★
TEACH YOURSELF ITALIAN
K. Speight
        David McKay Company Incorporated
        750 Third Avenue
        New York, New York 10017
Book. $2.95.

JAPANESE

Audio Cassettes/Tapes

★ 1443 ★
BERLITZ COURSE IN JAPANESE
      Berlitz Language Program
      Post Office Box 5109
      FDR Station
      New York, New York 10022
Cassette $5.95.   Also available on LP record.

★ 1444 ★
LEARN JAPANESE IN RECORD TIME
      Doubleday and Company Incorporated
      501 Franklin Avenue
      Garden City, New York 11530
Text and records. $9.98.

Multimedia Kits

★ 1445 ★
BEGINNING JAPANESE
      General Services Administration
      Foreign Service Institute Language Course
      National Audiovisual Center
      Order Section RR
      Washington, D.C. 20409
Audio tapes, cassettes and text also available.
Approximately $200.00.

Printed Materials

★ 1446 ★
JAPANESE IN THIRTY HOURS
Elichi Kiyooka
      Japan Publications Trading Center Incorporated
      200 Clearbrook Road
      Elmsford, New York 10523
Book. $4.95.

JEWELRY MAKING

See also: Art

Correspondence Courses

★ 1447 ★
JEWELRY MAKING
      North American Correspondence School
      4401 Birch Street
      Newport Beach, California 92663
Correspondence course.

Printed Materials

★ 1448 ★
LAPIDARY
Del Fairfield
      David McKay Company Incorporated
      750 Third Avenue
      New York, New York 10017
Self-study text.   1975. $3.95.

JOB ENRICHMENT

Audio Cassettes/Tapes

★ 1449 ★
HOW TO GET MORE OUT OF THE JOB YOU
HAVE
      Innovative Systems Limited
      2301 Rockwell Road
      Wilmington, Delaware 19810
Cassettes and notebook. $22.90.

Films/Video/Filmstrips

★ 1450 ★
ANALYZING THE JOB
      Addison Wesley Publishing Company Incorporated
      Jacob Way
      Reading, Massachusetts 01867
Filmstrip. $55.00.

★ 1451 ★
JOB ENRICHMENT IN ACTION
      BNA Communications Incorporated
      9401 Decoverly Hall Road
      Rockville, Maryland 20850
Film.

★ 1452 ★
JOB ENRICHMENT: MANAGERIAL MILESTONE
OR MYTH
      Salenger Educational Media
      1635 12th Street
      Santa Monica, California 90404
Film.

Games/Simulations

★ 1453 ★
JOB ENRICHMENT - REDESIGNING JOB FOR
MOTIVATION
      Didactic Systems Incorporated
      Box 457
      Cranford, New Jersey 07016

Simulation games. $24.00.

Multimedia Kits

★ 1454 ★
HOW MAN'S WORK HAS CHANGED
 Resources for Education and Management
  Incorporated
 544 Medlock Road,   Suite 210
 Decatur, Georgia   30030
Filmstrip with cassette. $65.00.

★ 1455 ★
INSTALLING JOB ENRICHMENT
 Resources for Education and Management
  Incorporated
 544 Medlock Road,   Suite 210
 Decatur, Georgia   30030
Filmstrip with cassette. $65.00.

★ 1456 ★
JOB ANALYSIS
 Lansford Publishing Company
 Post Office Box 8711
 San Jose, California 95155
Multimedia kit. $100.00.

★ 1457 ★
JOB ENRICHMENT MULTIMEDIA PROGRAM
 Didactic System Incorporated
 Box 457
 Cranford, New Jersey 07016
Multimedia program. $75.00.

★ 1458 ★
JOB EVALUATION
 Lansford Publishing Company
 Post Office Box 8711
 San Jose, California 95155
Multimedia kit. $190.00.

★ 1459 ★
PROBLEMS IN JOB ENRICHMENT
 Resources for Education and Management
  Incorporated
 544 Medlock Road, Suite 210
 Decatur, Georgia   30030
Filmstrip with cassette. $65.00.

JOURNALISM

See also: Communication, Written

Correspondence Courses

★ 1460 ★
FEATURE WRITING
 University of Southern Mississippi
 Department of Independent Study
 Southern Station, Box 56
 Hattiesburg, Mississippi   39401
Correspondence course.

★ 1461 ★
FICTION WRITING
 La Salle Extension University
 417 South Dearborn Street
 Chicago, Illinois 60605
Correspondence course.

★ 1462 ★
THE MAGAZINE ARTICLE
 University of Nebraska
 511 Nebraska Hall
 Lincoln, Nebraska 68588
Correspondence course.

★ 1463 ★
NEWS WRITING
 University of Washington
 Office of Independent Study
 222 Lewis Hall DW-30
 Seattle, Washington 98195
Correspondence course.

★ 1464 ★
NEWS WRITING AND REPORTING
 University of Nebraska
 511 Nebraska Hall
 Lincoln, Nebraska 68588
Correspondence course.

★ 1465 ★
NON-FICTION WRITING
 La Salle Extension University
 417 South Dearborn Street
 Chicago, Illinois 60605
Correspondence course.

★ 1466 ★
PRINCIPLES OF NEWS WRITING
    University of Kentucky
    Independent Study Program
    Freeze Hall, Room 1
    Lexington, Kentucky   40506
Correspondence course.

★ 1467 ★
REPORTING
    University of Kansas
    Division of Continuing Education
    Lawrence, Kansas   66045
Home study program.

★ 1468 ★
WRITERS
    Famous Schools
    Westport, Connecticut   06880
Correspondence course.

Printed Materials

★ 1469 ★
WRITING BOOK REVIEWS
John Drewry
    Greenwood Press Incorporated
    51 Riverside Avenue
    Westport, Connecticut   06880
Book.   1974. $12.75.

KIRUNDI

Multimedia Kits

★ 1470 ★
KIRUNDI - BASIC COURSE
    General Services Administration
    Foreign Service Institute Language Course
    National Audiovisual Center
    Order Section RR
    Washington, D.C.   20409
Audio tapes, cassettes and text also available.
Approximately $100.00.

KITUBA

Multimedia Kits

★ 1471 ★
KITUBA - BASIC COURSE

    General Services Administration
    Foreign Service Institute Language Course
    National Audiovisual Center
    Order Section RR
    Washington, D.C.   20409
Audio tapes, cassettes and text also available.
Approximately $90.00.

KOREAN

Audio Cassettes/Tapes

★ 1472 ★
SPOKEN KOREAN
Fred Lukoff
    Spoken Language Services Incorporated
    Post Office Box 783
    Ithaca, New York   14850
Text and cassettes.   1974. $55.00.

Multimedia Kits

★ 1473 ★
KOREAN - BASIC COURSE
    General Services Administration
    Foreign Service Institute Language Course
    National Audiovisual Center
    Order Section RR
    Washington, D.C.   20409
Audio tapes, cassettes and text also available.
Approximately $200.00.

Printed Materials

★ 1474 ★
KOREAN IN A HURRY
Samuel Martin
    C. E. Tuttle Company
    28 South Main Street
    Rutland, Vermont   05701
Book. $2.95.

LABOR RELATIONS

See also: Arbitration

Audio Cassettes/Tapes

★ 1475 ★
LABOR RELATIONS AND THE SUPERVISOR
    American Management Associations
    135 West 50th Street
    New York, New York   10020
2 cassettes with workbook. $60.00.

★ 1476 ★

LABOR RELATIONS FOR SUPERVISORS
Management Resources Incorporated
757 Third Avenue
New York, New York 10017
2 cassettes and workbooks. $49.95.

★ 1477 ★

MANAGEMENT STRATEGY IN RESPONSE TO
UNION ORGANIZING CAMPAIGNS
Van De Water Associates
7914 Jason Avenue
Canoga Park, California 91304
Cassette and workbook. $23.50.

★ 1478 ★

MANAGING LABOR RELATIONS
AMACOM
American Management Associations
135 West 50th Street
New York, New York 10020
6 cassettes with workbook. $100.00.

★ 1479 ★

PROFESSIONAL MANAGEMENT PROGRAMS
(Dealing with labor unions)
Dr. John R. Van De Water
Tape Rental Library Incorporated
Post Office Box 2107
2507 Edna Drive
South Vineland, New Jersey 08360
Cassette. $23.50.

Correspondence Courses

★ 1480 ★

INDUSTRIAL RELATIONS
University of Kentucky
Independent Study Program
Freeze Hall, Room 1
Lexington, Kentucky 40506
Correspondence course.

Films/Video/Filmstrips

★ 1481 ★

AVOIDING UNIONIZATION
Van De Water Associates
7914 Jason Avenue
Canoga Park, California 91304
Video tape. $495.00 (rental available).

★ 1482 ★

THE EMPLOYER, THE UNION AND THE LAW
Van De Water Associates
7914 Jason Avenue
Canoga Park, California 91304
Video tape. $495.00 (rental available).

★ 1483 ★

NON-UNION CAMPAIGNING
Van De Water Associates
7914 Jason Avenue
Canoga Park, California 91304
Video tape. $495.00 (rental available).

★ 1484 ★

UNIONISM, A MANAGER'S VIEWPOINT
Van De Water Associates
7914 Jason Avenue
Canoga Park, California 91304
Video tape. $495.00 (rental available).

Printed Materials

★ 1485 ★

IMPROVING LABOR RELATIONS
Didactic System Incorporated
Box 457
Cranford, New Jersey 07016
Self-study text. $9.00.

LANGUAGE INSTRUCTION
See: specific foreign language

LAO

Multimedia Kits

★ 1486 ★

LAO - A PROGRAMMED INTRODUCTION
General Services Administration
Foreign Service Institute Language Course
National Audiovisual Center
Order Section RR
Washington, D.C. 20409
Audio tapes, cassettes and text also available.
Approximately $200.00.

LAW, BUSINESS
See: BUSINESS LAW

LAW ENFORCEMENT
See: POLICE SCIENCE

LEADERSHIP

Audio Cassettes/Tapes

★ 1487 ★
GROUP LEADERSHIP
    Lansford Publishing Company
    Post Office Box 8711
    San Jose, California 95155
4 cassettes and guide. $85.95.

★ 1488 ★
THE INTERPERSONAL RELATIONS SERIES
    Resources for Education and Management
        Incorporated
    544 Medlock Road, Suite 210
    Decatur, Georgia 30030
6 cassettes with workbook. $65.00.

★ 1489 ★
LEADERSHIP
    Educational Century Programming
    1201 East Johnson Street
    Jonesboro, Arkansas 72401
Cassette. $6.00.

★ 1490 ★
LEADERSHIP
George Odiorne
    MBO Incorporated
    157 Pontoosic Road
    Westfield, Massachusetts 01085
Cassette and manual. $15.00.

★ 1491 ★
WARREN BENNIS ON LEADERS
    American Management Associations
    135 West 50th Street
    New York, New York 10020
5 cassettes and 2 booklets. $125.00.

★ 1492 ★
WINNING WITH LEADERSHIP SKILLS
    American Management Associations
    135 West 50th Street
    New York, New York 10020
6 cassettes with workbook. $100.00.

Correspondence Courses

★ 1493 ★
HOW TO MANAGE THROUGH LEADERSHIP
    Society of Manufacturing Engineers
    20501 Ford Road
    Post Office Box 930
    Dearborn, Michigan 48128
4 hours self instruction course. $10.00.

★ 1494 ★
LEADERSHIP DEVELOPMENT (Religious)
    Southern Baptist Convention
    Seminary Extension Department
    460 James Robertson Parkway
    Nashville, Tennessee 37219
Home study course. $22.95.

Films/Video/Filmstrips

★ 1495 ★
LEADERSHIP: STYLE OR CIRCUMSTANCE
    CRM McGraw Hill Films
    110 15th Street
    Del Mar, California 92014
Film or video cassette.

★ 1496 ★
STYLES OF LEADERSHIP
    Roundtable Films
    113 North San Vincente Boulevard
    Beverly Hills, California 90211
Film and guidebook.

Multimedia Kits

★ 1497 ★
APPLIED LEADERSHIP
    Resources for Education and Management
        Incorporated
    544 Medlock Road, Suite 210
    Decatur, Georgia 30030
Filmstrip with cassette. $70.00.

★ 1498 ★
DOCTOR, LAWYER, MERCHANT, CHIEF (Case
studies in leadership)
      Salenger Educational Media
      1635 12th Street
      Santa Monica, California 90404
Film, guide and worksheets. $365.00 (rental
available).

★ 1499 ★
4-DIMENSION LEADERSHIP (Teaching techniques
in human behavior)
      Learning Dynamics Institute
      1401 Wilson Boulevard, #101
      Arlington, Virginia 22209
12 cassettes, albums, workbooks. $250.00.

★ 1500 ★
LEADER BEHAVIOR AND GROUP GUIDANCE
      Lansford Publishing Company
      Post Office Box 8711
      San Jose, California 95155
Multimedia kit. $149.95.

★ 1501 ★
LEADERSHIP
      Lansford Publishing Company
      Post Office Box 8711
      San Jose, California 95155
Multimedia kit. $199.95.

★ 1502 ★
LEADERSHIP OF COMPLEX ORGANIZATIONS
      Lansford Publishing Company
      Post Office Box 8711
      San Jose, California 95155
Multimedia kit. $199.95.

★ 1503 ★
LEADING PEOPLE
      Resources for Education and Management
        Incorporated
      544 Medlock Road, Suite 210
      Decatur, Georgia 30030
Filmstrip with cassette. $60.00.

★ 1504 ★
THE NATURE OF LEADERSHIP
      Resources for Education and Management
        Incorporated
      544 Medlock Road, Suite 210
      Decatur, Georgia 30030
Filmstrip with cassette. $70.00.

★ 1505 ★
STYLES OF LEADERSHIP
      Resources for Education and Management
        Incorporated
      544 Medlock Road, Suite 210
      Decatur, Georgia 30030
Filmstrip with cassette. $70.00.

Printed Materials

★ 1506 ★
CORPORATE LEADERSHIP
      Scientific Methods Incorporated
      Box 195
      Austin, Texas 78767
Workbook. $6.00.

★ 1507 ★
IMPROVING LEADERSHIP EFFECTIVENESS: THE
LEADER MATCH CONCEPT
Fred Fiedler, Martin Chemers
      John Wiley and Sons
      605 Third Avenue
      New York, New York 10016
Book, 229 pages. $6.95.

★ 1508 ★
LEADER EFFECTIVENESS TRAINING
Dr. Thomas Gordon
      Wyden Books
      747 Third Avenue
      New York, New York 10017
Book. $10.95.

LETTERING
See: CALLIGRAPHY

LETTERS
See: BUSINESS LETTERS

LIBRARY SCIENCE
Correspondence Courses

★ 1509 ★
BOOK SELECTION
      Loyola University of Chicago
      Correspondence Study Division
      820 North Michigan Avenue
      Chicago, Illinois 60611
Correspondence course. $75.00.

★ 1510 ★
CATALOGING AND CLASSIFICATION
Utah State University
Independent Study Division
UMC 50
Logan, Utah 84322
Correspondence course. $42.00.

★ 1511 ★
CATALOGING AND CLASSIFICATION OF
SPECIAL MATERIALS
University of Utah
Correspondence Study Department
Annex 1152
Salt Lake City, Utah 84112
Correspondence course.

★ 1512 ★
FUNDAMENTALS OF LIBRARY SCIENCE
University of New Mexico
Division of Continuing Education
805 Yale Boulevard Northeast
Albuquerque, New Mexico 87131
Correspondence course. $60.00.

★ 1513 ★
LIBRARY WORK WITH CHILDREN
University of Idaho Campus
Correspondence Study Office
Moscow, Idaho 83843
Correspondence course. $82.50.

★ 1514 ★
REFERENCE WORK
Loyola University of Chicago
Correspondence Study Division
820 North Michigan Avenue
Chicago, Illinois 60611
Correspondence course.

★ 1515 ★
SELECTION OF INSTRUCTIONAL MATERIALS
University of Utah
Division of Continuing Education
Annex 1152
Salt Lake City, Utah 84112
Correspondence course. $48.00.

LIFE INSURANCE
See: INSURANCE

LIFT TRUCKS

Programmed Learning Materials

★ 1516 ★
ADMINISTRATORS GUIDE
E. I. du Pont de Nemours and Company
Applied Technology Division
Room B 4204
Wilmington, Delaware 19898
Programmed course. $8.00.

★ 1517 ★
OPERATOR TRAINING
E. I. du Pont de Nemours and Company
Applied Technology Division
Room B 4204
Wilmington, Delaware 19898
Programmed course of approximately 7 hours.
$16.50.

LINEMAN TRAINING

Correspondence Courses

★ 1518 ★
UTILITY LINEMAN
International Correspondence School
Scranton, Pennsylvania 18515
Multi-module correspondence course.

Films/Video/Filmstrips

★ 1519 ★
CARE AND USE OF LINE PROTECTIVE DEVICES
Resource Incorporated
13902 North Dale Mabry Highway
Tampa, Florida 33624
Video cartridge and worksheets available. $120.00.

★ 1520 ★
CONDUCTOR FUNDAMENTALS
Resource Incorporated
13902 North Dale Mabry Highway
Tampa, Florida 33624
Video cartridge and worksheets available. $120.00.

★ 1521 ★
DISTRIBUTION TRANSFORMERS - THE PRIMARY
SYSTEM
Resource Incorporated
13902 North Dale Mabry Highway
Tampa, Florida 33624
Video cartridge and worksheets available. $120.00.

★ 1522 ★
GENERATOR OPERATIONS
    Resource Incorporated
    13902 North Dale Mabry Highway
    Tampa, Florida 33624
2 video cartridges with workbook. $200.00.

★ 1523 ★
INSTALLING AND REMOVING DE-ENERGIZED
LINES AND EQUIPMENT
    Resource Incorporated
    13902 North Dale Mabry Highway
    Tampa, Florida 33624
Video cartridge and worksheet available. $120.00.

★ 1524 ★
INSTALLING SINGLE-PHASE POLEMOUNTED
TRANSFORMERS
    Resource Incorporated
    13902 North Dale Mabry Highway
    Tampa, Florida 33624
Video cartridge and worksheets available. $120.00.

★ 1525 ★
INSTALLING TENSION SPLICES
    Resource Incorporated
    13902 North Dale Mabry Highway
    Tampa, Florida 33624
Video cartridge and worksheets available. $120.00.

★ 1526 ★
INSTALLING THREE-PHASE AND MULTIPLE
TRANSFORMERS
    Resource Incorporated
    13902 North Dale Mabry Highway
    Tampa, Florida 33624
Video cartridge and worksheets available. $120.00.

★ 1527 ★
INTRODUCTION TO DISTRIBUTION TRANSFORMERS
    Resource Incorporated
    13902 North Dale Mabry Highway
    Tampa, Florida 33624
Video cartridge and worksheets available. $120.00.

★ 1528 ★
INTRODUCTION TO POWER CAPACITORS
    Resource Incorporated
    13902 North Dale Mabry Highway
    Tampa, Florida 33624
Video cartridge and worksheets available. $120.00.

★ 1529 ★
MAKING SPLICES AND CONNECTIONS ON
OVERHEAD DISTRIBUTION LINES
    Resource Incorporated
    13902 North Dale Mabry Highway
    Tampa, Florida 33624
Video cartridge and worksheets available. $120.00.

★ 1530 ★
PAD-MOUNTED AND UNDERGROUND
TRANSFORMERS
    Resource Incorporated
    13902 North Dale Mabry Highway
    Tampa, Florida 33624
Video cartridge and worksheets available. $120.00.

★ 1531 ★
POLE TOP AND BUCKET RESCUE
    Resource Incorporated
    13902 North Dale Mabry Highway
    Tampa, Florida 33624
Video cartridge and worksheets available. $120.00.

★ 1532 ★
POWER CAPACITOR APPLICATION
    Resource Incorporated
    13902 North Dale Mabry Highway
    Tampa, Florida 33624
Video cartridge and worksheets available. $120.00.

★ 1533 ★
TRANSFORMER PROTECTION AND CSP UNITS
    Resource Incorporated
    13902 North Dale Mabry Highway
    Tampa, Florida 33624
Video cartridge and worksheets available. $120.00.

LISTENING

See also: Communication

Audio Cassettes/Tapes

★ 1534 ★
ART OF LISTENING
    Tape Rental Library Incorporated
    Post Office Box 2107
    2507 Edna Drive
    South Vineland, New Jersey 08360
Cassette. $9.00.

★ 1535 ★
THE ART OF LISTENING BUSINESS
COMMUNICATIONS
 Thompson-Mitchell and Associates
 3384 Peachtree Road Northeast
 Atlanta, Georgia 30326
Cassette. $6.00.

★ 1536 ★
IT PAYS TO LISTEN
 Tape Rental Library Incorporated
 Post Office Box 2107
 2507 Edna Drive
 South Vineland, New Jersey 08360
Cassette.

★ 1537 ★
LEARN TO LISTEN
 Educational Century Programming
 1201 East Johnson Street
 Jonesboro, Arkansas 72401
Cassette. $6.00.

★ 1538 ★
LEARNING POWER THROUGH EFFECTIVE
LISTENING
 Tape Rental Library Incorporated
 Post Office Box 2107
 2507 Edna Drive
 South Vineland, New Jersey 08360
Cassette. $9.98.

★ 1539 ★
LISTENING ON THE JOB
 Addison Wesley Publishing Company Incorporated
 Jacob Way
 Reading, Massachusetts 01867
3 cassette tapes and workbooks. $225.00.

★ 1540 ★
LISTENING/PROSPECTING
 Tape Rental Library Incorporated
 Post Office Box 2107
 2507 Edna Drive
 South Vineland, New Jersey 08360
Cassette. $9.00.

★ 1541 ★
RALPH G. NICHOL'S COMPLETE COURSE IN
LISTENING
 Dun and Bradstreet Incorporated
 Business Education Division
 Box 803
 Church Street Station
 New York, New York 10008
6 cassette tapes, workbooks and textbooks. $350.00.

★ 1542 ★
TUNE IN AND LISTEN
 Thompson-Mitchell and Associates
 3384 Peachtree Road Northeast
 Atlanta, Georgia 30326
3 cassettes. $59.50.

Films/Video/Filmstrips

★ 1543 ★
LISTEN, PLEASE
 BNA Communications Incorporated
 9401 Decoverly Hall Road
 Rockville, Maryland 20850
Film.

★ 1544 ★
LISTENING
 Roundtable Films
 113 North San Vincente Boulevard
 Beverly Hills, California 90211
Film and guidebook.

★ 1545 ★
THE POWER OF LISTENING
 CRM McGraw Hill Films
 110 15th Street
 Del Mar, California 92014
Film or video cassette.

Multimedia Kits

★ 1546 ★
EFFECTIVE LISTENING
 Lansford Publishing Company
 Post Office Box 8711
 San Jose, California 95155
Multimedia kit. $120.00.

★ 1547 ★
INTERACTIVE LISTENING
    Ergonco Performance Source
    Northwest O'Hare Office Park, Suite 119
    2474 Dempster Street
    Des Plains, Illinois 60016
Multimedia self-study program.

LOCKSMITHING

Correspondence Courses

★ 1548 ★
LOCKSMITHING
    Belsaw Institute
    315 Westport Road
    Kansas City, Missouri 64111
Home study program. $399.00.

★ 1549 ★
LOCKSMITHING
    Locksmithing Institute
    1500 Cardinal Drive
    Little Falls, New Jersey 07424
Correspondence course.

Printed Materials

★ 1550 ★
COMPLETE COURSE IN PROFESSIONAL
LOCKSMITHING
Robert Robinson
    Nelson-Hall Publishers
    325 West Jackson Boulevard
    Chicago, Illinois 60606
Text. $34.95.

★ 1551 ★
PRACTICAL COURSE IN MODERN LOCKSMITHING
Whitcomb Crichton
    Nelson-Hall Publishers
    325 West Jackson Boulevard
    Chicago, Illinois 60606
Text. $10.95.

LOSS PREVENTION

See also: Retailing

Audio Cassettes/Tapes

★ 1552 ★
GET ON THE BALL, STOP SHRINKAGE
    Thompson-Mitchell and Associates
    3384 Peachtree Road Northeast
    Atlanta, Georgia 30326
Cassette. $15.00.

★ 1553 ★
PAPER SHRINKAGE: SPOT IT AND STOP IT
    Thompson-Mitchell and Associates
    3384 Peachtree Road Northeast
    Atlanta, Georgia 30326
Cassette. $25.00.

★ 1554 ★
SHOPLIFTING THE PLOT AGAINST YOU
    Thompson-Mitchell and Associates
    3384 Peachtree Road Northeast
    Atlanta, Georgia 30326
Cassette. $15.00.

★ 1555 ★
STOP THE SHOP LIFTER/STOP THE SHORT CHANGE
ARTIST
    Close Productions
    2020 San Carlos Boulevard
    Fort Myers Beach, Florida 33931
6 cassettes. $35.00.

Films/Video/Filmstrips

★ 1556 ★
PREVENTING EMPLOYEE THEFT
    National Restaurant Association
    One IBM Plaza, Suite 2600
    Chicago, Illinois 60611
Video cartridge or 8 mm, 16 mm, and study guide.
$190.00.

★ 1557 ★
STOP THE SHORT CHANGE ARTIST
    Close Productions
    2020 San Carlos Boulevard
    Fort Myers Beach, Florida 33931
Filmstrip. $45.00.

Multimedia Kits

★ 1558 ★
CHECK AND DOUBLE CHECK (Loss prevention)
    Thompson-Mitchell and Associates
    3384 Peachtree Road Northeast
    Atlanta, Georgia 30326
Filmstrip with cassette. $75.00.

★ 1559 ★
GREEDY HANDS (Loss prevention)
    Thompson-Mitchell and Associates
    3384 Peachtree Road Northeast
    Atlanta, Georgia 30326
Filmstrip with cassette. $75.00.

★ 1560 ★
PAPER SHRINKAGE - SPOT IT AND STOP IT
    Merchandiser Film Productions
    Drawer J
    Huntington, New York 11743
Filmstrip with cassette. $45.00.

★ 1561 ★
SHOPLIFTING - THE PLOT AGAINST YOU
    Merchandiser Film Productions
    Drawer J
    Huntington, New York 11743
Filmstrip with cassette. $15.00.

LUNGALA

Multimedia Kits

★ 1562 ★
LUNGALA - BASIC COURSE
    General Services Administration
    Foreign Service Institute Language Course
    National Audiovisual Center
    Order Section RR
    Washington, D.C. 20409
Audio tapes, cassettes and text also available.
Approximately $70.00.

MACHINE OPERATIONS

Correspondence Courses

★ 1563 ★
MACHINE SHOP PRACTICE
    International Correspondence School
    Scranton, Pennsylvania 18515
Multi-module correspondence course.

Films/Video/Filmstrips

★ 1564 ★
BAND SAW
    DCA Educational Products
    424 Valley Road
    Warrington, Pennsylvania 18976

5 film loops (8 mm). $27.00 each.

★ 1565 ★
BAND SAW
    DCA Educational Products
    424 Valley Road
    Warrington, Pennsylvania 18976
Film (16 mm). $150.00.

★ 1566 ★
BELT AND DISC SANDER
    DCA Educational Products
    424 Valley Road
    Warrington, Pennsylvania 18976
Film (16 mm). $150.00.

★ 1567 ★
BELT SANDER
    DCA Educational Products
    424 Valley Road
    Warrington, Pennsylvania 18976
3 film loops (8 mm). $27.00 each.

★ 1568 ★
CIRCULAR SAW
    DCA Educational Products
    424 Valley Road
    Warrington, Pennsylvania 18976
6 film loops (8 mm). $27.00 each.

★ 1569 ★
CIRCULAR SAW
    DCA Educational Products
    424 Valley Road
    Warrington, Pennsylvania 18976
Film (16 mm). $150.00.

★ 1570 ★
DISC SANDER
    DCA Educational Products
    424 Valley Road
    Warrington, Pennsylvania 18976
3 film loops (8 mm). $27.00 each.

★ 1571 ★
DRILL PRESS
    DCA Educational Products
    424 Valley Road
    Warrington, Pennsylvania 18976
5 film loops (8 mm). $27.00 each.

★ 1572 ★
GRINDER (Machinery)
    DCA Educational Products
    424 Valley Road
    Warrington, Pennsylvania 18976
4 film loops (8 mm). $27.00 each.

★ 1573 ★
JOINTER
    DCA Educational Products
    424 Valley Road
    Warrington, Pennsylvania 18976
Film (16 mm). $150.00.

★ 1574 ★
JOINTER (Machinery)
    DCA Educational Products
    424 Valley Road
    Warrington, Pennsylvania 18976
4 film loops (8 mm). $27.00 each.

★ 1575 ★
METALWORKING LATHE
    DCA Educational Products
    424 Valley Road
    Warrington, Pennsylvania 18976
21 film loops (8 mm). $27.00 each.

★ 1576 ★
MILLING MACHINE
    DCA Educational Products
    424 Valley Road
    Warrington, Pennsylvania 18976
4 film loops (8 mm). $27.00 each.

★ 1577 ★
MILLING MACHINE
    DCA Educational Products
    424 Valley Road
    Warrington, Pennsylvania 18976
Film (16 mm). $150.00.

★ 1578 ★
OVERARM ROUTER
    DCA Educational Products
    424 Valley Road
    Warrington, Pennsylvania 18976
4 film loops (8 mm). $27.00 each.

★ 1579 ★
OVERARM ROUTER
    DCA Educational Products
    424 Valley Road
    Warrington, Pennsylvania 18976
Film (16 mm). $150.00.

★ 1580 ★
PLANER
    DCA Educational Products
    424 Valley Road
    Warrington, Pennsylvania 18976
5 film loops (8 mm). $27.00 each.

★ 1581 ★
RADIAL ARM SAW
    DCA Educational Products
    424 Valley Road
    Warrington, Pennsylvania 18976
5 film loops (8 mm). $27.00 each.

★ 1582 ★
RADIAL ARM SAW
    DCA Educational Products
    424 Valley Road
    Warrington, Pennsylvania 18976
Film (16 mm). $150.00.

★ 1583 ★
SCROLL SAW
    DCA Educational Products
    424 Valley Road
    Warrington, Pennsylvania 18976
4 film loops (8 mm). $27.00 each.

★ 1584 ★
SCROLL SAW
    DCA Educational Products
    424 Valley Road
    Warrington, Pennsylvania 18976
Film (16 mm). $150.00.

★ 1585 ★
SHAPER
    DCA Educational Products
    424 Valley Road
    Warrington, Pennsylvania 18976
6 film loops (8 mm). $27.00 each.

★ 1586 ★
TOOL GRINDER
　　　DCA Educational Products
　　　424 Valley Road
　　　Warrington, Pennsylvania 18976
7 film loops (8 mm). $27.00 each.

★ 1587 ★
UNIPLANE
　　　DCA Educational Products
　　　424 Valley Road
　　　Warrington, Pennsylvania 18976
4 film loops (8 mm). $27.00 each.

★ 1588 ★
UNIPLANE
　　　DCA Educational Products
　　　424 Valley Road
　　　Warrington, Pennsylvania 18976
Film (16 mm).

★ 1589 ★
WOOD TURNING LATHE
　　　DCA Educational Products
　　　424 Valley Road
　　　Warrington, Pennsylvania 18976
4 film loops (8 mm). $27.00 each.

★ 1590 ★
WOOD TURNING LATHE
　　　DCA Educational Products
　　　424 Valley Road
　　　Warrington, Pennsylvania 18976
Film (16 mm). $150.00.

Programmed Learning Materials

★ 1591 ★
BEARINGS
　　　E. I. du Pont de Nemours and Company
　　　Applied Technology Division
　　　Room B 4204
　　　Wilmington, Delaware 19898
Programmed course of approximately 8 hours.
$15.60.

★ 1592 ★
BEARINGS - ANTI FRICTION
　　　E. I. du Pont de Nemours and Company
　　　Applied Technology Division
　　　Room B 4204
　　　Wilmington, Delaware 19898
Programmed course of approximately 10 hours. $18.85.

★ 1593 ★
CHAINS AND SPROCKETS - ROLLER CHAINS
　　　E. I. du Pont de Nemours and Company
　　　Applied Technology Division
　　　Room B 4204
　　　Wilmington, Delaware 19898
Programmed course of approximately 7 hours. $13.80.

★ 1594 ★
CHAINS AND SPROCKETS - SPROCKETS AND
DRIVES
　　　E. I. du Pont de Nemours and Company
　　　Applied Technology Division
　　　Room B 4204
　　　Wilmington, Delaware 19898
Programmed course of approximately 12 hours.
$22.10.

★ 1595 ★
COUPLING ALIGNMENT (Shafts)
　　　E. I. du Pont de Nemours and Company
　　　Applied Technology Division
　　　Room B 4204
　　　Wilmington, Delaware 19898
Programmed course of approximately 14 hours. $25.30.

★ 1596 ★
EDGINGS, NOTCHINGS AND SEAMS
　　　E. I. du Pont de Nemours and Company
　　　Applied Technology Division
　　　Room B 4204
　　　Wilmington, Delaware 19898
Programmed course of approximately 12 1/2 hours.
$23.90.

★ 1597 ★
FIELD SKETCHING
　　　E. I. du Pont de Nemours and Company
　　　Applied Technology Division
　　　Room B 4204
　　　Wilmington, Delaware 19898
Programmed course of approximately 16 hours.
$28.00.

★ 1598 ★
GEARS AND GEARING
　　　E. I. du Pont de Nemours and Company
　　　Applied Technology Division
　　　Room B 4204
　　　Wilmington, Delaware 19898
6 unit programmed course. Approximately $12.00
per unit.

★ 1599 ★
MECHANICAL SEALS
E. I. du Pont de Nemours and Company
Applied Technology Division
Room B 4204
Wilmington, Delaware 19898
Programmed course of approximately 14 hours.
$25.30.

★ 1600 ★
SIMPLE SLIDE RULE
E. I. du Pont de Nemours and Company
Applied Technology Division
Room B 4204
Wilmington, Delaware 19898
Programmed course of approximately 5 hours.
$10.90.

MACHINE SHOP MATHEMATICS

Audio Cassettes/Tapes

★ 1601 ★
APPLIED MATHEMATICS FOR TECHNICAL PROGRAMS
Robert G. Moon
Charles E. Merrill Publishing Company
1300 Alum Creek Drive
Box 508
Columbus, Ohio 43216
51 units, 3 texts and cassettes.

Correspondence Courses

★ 1602 ★
SHOP MATHEMATICS
Thomas Institute
Box 22
New Canaan, Connecticut 06840
Self-study course. $110.00.

Films/Video/Filmstrips

★ 1603 ★
MATHEMATICS FOR MACHINISTS
National Tool, Die and Precision Machining
Association
9300 Livingston Road
Washington, D.C. 20022
Sound film, test and review.

Printed Materials

★ 1604 ★
PRACTICAL MATHEMATICS FOR METALWORKING
TRAINEES
National Tool, Die and Precision Machining
Association
9300 Livingston Road
Washington, D.C. 20022
Workbook.

★ 1605 ★
STARTER MATH FOR PRE JOB TRAINING
Joseph R. Todd
National Tool, Die and Precision Machining
Association
9300 Livingston Road
Washington, D.C. 20022
Workbook.

Programmed Learning Materials

★ 1606 ★
BASIC SHOP MATH
TPC Training Systems
Technical Publishing Company
1301 South Grove Avenue
Barrington, Illinois 60010
Programmed text of 10 lessons. $20.50.

★ 1607 ★
ELECTRICAL MATHEMATICS AT WORK
General Learning Corporation
250 James Street
•Morristown, New Jersey 07960
Programmed text. $4.20.

MACHINE SHOP PRACTICES

Programmed Learning Materials

★ 1608 ★
MACHINE SHOP PRACTICE
TPC Training Systems
Technical Publishing Company
1301 South Grove Avenue
Barrington, Illinois 60010
Programmed text of 6 lessons. $16.75.

★ 1609 ★
MACHINE SHOP SHAPING OPERATIONS
TPC Training Systems
Technical Publishing Company
1301 South Grove Avenue
Barrington, Illinois 60010
Programmed text of 5 lessons. $16.75.

★ 1610 ★
MACHINE SHOP TURNING OPERATIONS
TPC Training Systems
Technical Publishing Company
1301 South Grove Avenue
Barrington, Illinois 60010
Programmed text of 5 lessons. $16.75.

MAINTENANCE
See: CUSTODIAL MAINTENANCE

MALAY

Audio Cassettes/Tapes

★ 1611 ★
SPOKEN MALAY
Isidore Dyen
Spoken Language Services Incorporated
Post Office Box 783
Ithaca, New York 14850
Texts and cassettes.   1974. $60.00.

Printed Materials

★ 1612 ★
TEACH YOURSELF MALAY
M. B. Lewis
David McKay Company Incorporated
750 Third Avenue
New York, New York 10017
Book. $3.95.

MANAGEMENT, BEHAVIORAL ASPECTS

Audio Cassettes/Tapes

★ 1613 ★
BEHAVIOR CHANGE - TEMPORARY OR PERMANENT?
Development Digest Incorporated
3347 Motor Avenue
Los Angeles, California 90034
Cassette. $13.75.

★ 1614 ★
BEHAVIOR MANAGEMENT
Thompson-Mitchell and Associates
3384 Peachtree Road Northeast
Atlanta, Georgia 30326
12 cassettes with workbook. $149.50.

★ 1615 ★
BEHAVIORAL SCIENCES
George Odiorne
MBO Incorporated
157 Pontoosic Road
Westfield, Massachusetts 01085
12 cassettes and manual. $125.00.

★ 1616 ★
FUTURE AND APPLIED BEHAVIORAL SCIENCE
Development Digest Incorporated
3347 Motor Avenue
Los Angeles, California 90034
Cassette. $19.75.

★ 1617 ★
RELATING LEARNING THEORY TO BEHAVIOR
CHANGE IN ORGANIZATIONS
Development Digest Incorporated
3347 Motor Avenue
Los Angeles, California 90034
Cassette. $13.75.

Correspondence Courses

★ 1618 ★
HUMAN BEHAVIOR IN ORGANIZATIONS
University of Nebraska
511 Nebraska Hall
Lincoln, Nebraska 68588
Correspondence course.

Films/Video/Filmstrips

★ 1619 ★
BEYOND THEORY Y: THE CONTINGENCY
APPROACH TO MANAGEMENT
Salenger Educational Media
1635 12th Street
Santa Monica, California 90404
Film and worksheets. $340.00 (rental available).

★ 1620 ★
POWER OF POSITIVE REINFORCEMENT
    CRM McGraw Hill Films
    110 15th Street
    Del Mar, California 92014
Film or video cassette.

★ 1621 ★
THEORY X AND THEORY Y: TWO SETS OF
ASSUMPTIONS IN MANAGEMENT
    Salenger Educational Media
    1635 12th Street
    Santa Monica, California 90404
Film with worksheets. $300.00 (rental available).

Multimedia Kits

★ 1622 ★
APPLICATION OF BEHAVIOR MODIFICATION TO
BUSINESS
    Lansford Publishing Company
    Post Office Box 8711
    San Jose, California 95155
Multimedia kit. $200.00.

★ 1623 ★
BEHAVIORAL ASPECTS OF MANAGEMENT COURSE
    Lansford Publishing Company
    Post Office Box 8711
    San Jose, California 95155
25 to 50 hour multimedia course. $1,195.00.

★ 1624 ★
PARTICIPATIVE MANAGEMENT
    Lansford Publishing Company
    Post Office Box 8711
    San Jose, California 95155
Multimedia kit. $97.95.

Programmed Learning Materials

★ 1625 ★
BEHAVIOR MODIFICATION
Alan Kazdin
    Learning Systems Company
    1818 Ridge Road
    Homewood, Illinois 60430
Programmed learning aid. $1.75.

★ 1626 ★
HUMAN BEHAVIOR IN THE ORGANIZATION
    American Management Associations
    135 West 50th Street
    New York, New York 10020
Programmed text. $50.00.

MANAGEMENT BY OBJECTIVES

Audio Cassettes/Tapes

★ 1627 ★
THE ACTIVITY TRAP
George Odiorne
    MBO Incorporated
    157 Pontoosic Road
    Westfield, Massachusetts 01085
Cassette and manual. $15.00.

★ 1628 ★
ANALYSIS - USING YOUR HEAD TO SAVE YOUR
ENERGY
George Odiorne
    MBO Incorporated
    157 Pontoosic Road
    Westfield, Massachusetts 01085
Cassette and workbook. $15.00.

★ 1629 ★
AVOIDING THE DEADLY ACTIVITY TRAP
George Odiorne
    MBO Incorporated
    157 Pontoosic Road
    Westfield, Massachusetts 01085
Cassette and workbook. $15.00.

★ 1630 ★
DEVISING MANAGERIAL STRATEGY
George Odiorne
    MBO Incorporated
    157 Pontoosic Road
    Westfield, Massachusetts 01085
Cassette and manual. $15.00.

★ 1631 ★
GOAL SETTING
    Tape Rental Library Incorporated
    Post Office Box 2107
    2507 Edna Drive
    South Vineland, New Jersey 08360
Cassette.

★ 1632 ★
THE GOAL SETTING SESSION
    AMACOM
    American Management Associations
    135 West 50th Street
    New York, New York 10020
Cassette. $18.00.

★ 1633 ★
GOALS - THE DEFINITION OF SUCCESS
George Odiorne
    MBO Incorporated
    157 Pontoosic Road
    Westfield, Massachusetts   01085
Cassette and workbook. $15.00.

★ 1634 ★
HOW TO AVOID BEING A BUREAUCRAT
George Odiorne
    MBO Incorporated
    157 Pontoosic Road
    Westfield, Massachusetts   01085
Cassette and workbook. $15.00.

★ 1635 ★
HOW TO SET NEXT YEAR'S GOALS
George Odiorne
    MBO Incorporated
    157 Pontoosic Road
    Westfield, Massachusetts   01085
Cassette and manual. $15.00.

★ 1636 ★
INDICATORS - THE SYMBOLS MANAGERS LIVE BY
George Odiorne
    MBO Incorporated
    157 Pontoosic Road
    Westfield, Massachusetts   01085
Cassette and manual. $15.00.

★ 1637 ★
INNOVATION - HOW MANAGERS MAKE THINGS
HAPPEN
George Odiorne
    MBO Incorporated
    157 Pontoosic Road
    Westfield, Massachusetts   01085
Cassette and manual. $15.00.

★ 1638 ★
INTEGRATING MBO INTO YOUR MANAGEMENT
DEVELOPMENT PROGRAM
    Development Digest Incorporated
    3347 Motor Avenue
    Los Angeles, California   90034
Cassette. $13.75.

★ 1639 ★
IS MAN A MACHINE
George Odiorne
    MBO Incorporated
    157 Pontoosic Road
    Westfield, Massachusetts   01085
Cassette and manual. $15.00.

★ 1640 ★
IS THERE A MANAGEMENT ESTABLISHMENT
George Odiorne
    MBO Incorporated
    157 Pontoosic Road
    Westfield, Massachusetts   01085
Cassette and manual. $15.00.

★ 1641 ★
MANAGEMENT BY OBJECTIVES
    Lansford Publishing Company
    Post Office Box 8711
    San Jose, California   95155
3 cassettes and guide. $62.00.

★ 1642 ★
MANAGEMENT BY OBJECTIVES
    Penton/IPC Education Division
    614 Superior Avenue West
    Cleveland, Ohio   44113
On audio tape $60.00.   In print $15.00.

★ 1643 ★
MANAGEMENT BY OBJECTIVES AND RESULTS
    General Cassette Corporation
    1324 North 22nd Avenue
    Phoenix, Arizona   85009
6 cassettes and workbook. $59.50.

★ 1644 ★
MANAGEMENT BY OBJECTIVES AND RESULTS
OVERVIEW
George L. Morrisey
    Tape Rental Library Incorporated
    Post Office Box 2107
    2507 Edna Drive
    South Vineland, New Jersey   08360
Cassette. $15.00.

★ 1645 ★
MANAGEMENT DECISIONS BY OBJECTIVES
George S. Odiorne
    Tape Rental Library Incorporated
    Post Office Box 2107
    2507 Edna Drive
    South Vineland, New Jersey   08360
Cassette.

★ 1646 ★
MANAGING BY GOALS AND RESULTS
Van De Water Associates
7914 Jason Avenue
Canoga Park, California 91304
Cassette and workbook. $23.50.

★ 1647 ★
MANAGING BY OBJECTIVES
American Management Associations
135 West 50th Street
New York, New York 10020
6 cassettes and workbook. $100.00.

★ 1648 ★
MANAGING HIGH-TALENT MANPOWER
George Odiorne
MBO Incorporated
157 Pontoosic Road
Westfield, Massachusetts 01085
Cassette and manual. $15.00.

★ 1649 ★
OBJECTIVE - FOCUSED MANAGEMENT
AMACOM
American Management Associations
135 West 50th Street
New York, New York 10020
6 cassettes. $115.00.

★ 1650 ★
PARTICIPATIVE MANAGEMENT
George Odiorne
MBO Incorporated
157 Pontoosic Road
Westfield, Massachusetts 01085
Cassette and manual. $15.00.

★ 1651 ★
PERSONNEL ADMINISTRATION BY OBJECTIVES
Thompson-Mitchell and Associates
3384 Peachtree Road Northeast
Atlanta, Georgia 30326
6 cassettes. $100.00.

★ 1652 ★
PRODUCING OBJECTIVES MOTIVATION
George Odiorne
MBO Incorporated
157 Pontoosic Road
Westfield, Massachusetts 01085
Cassette and workbook. $15.00.

★ 1653 ★
SUPERVISING BY OBJECTIVES
Addison Wesley Publishing Company Incorporated
Jacob Way
Reading, Massachusetts 01867
12 cassettes and workbooks. $1,000.00.

★ 1654 ★
WHY MANAGEMENT PROBLEMS DON'T GET
SOLVED
George Odiorne
MBO Incorporated
157 Pontoosic Road
Westfield, Massachusetts 01085
Cassette and manual. $15.00.

Correspondence Courses

★ 1655 ★
HOW TO SET OBJECTIVES
Society of Manufacturing Engineers
20501 Ford Road
Post Office Box 930
Dearborn, Michigan 48128
3 hour self instruction course. $10.00.

Films/Video/Filmstrips

★ 1656 ★
PREPARING OBJECTIVES
Addison Wesley Publishing Company Incorporated
Jacob Way
Reading, Massachusetts 01867
Filmstrip. $55.00.

★ 1657 ★
A RECIPE FOR RESULTS: MAKING MANAGEMENT
BY OBJECTIVES WORK
Joe Batten
Creative Media Films
820 Keo Way
Des Moines, Iowa 50309
Film, or video cassette, guide and manual.
$450.00 (rental available).

Games/Simulations

★ 1658 ★
MANAGEMENT BY OBJECTIVES
Didactic Systems Incorporated
Box 457
Cranford, New Jersey 07016
Simulation game. $24.00.

Multimedia Kits

★ 1659 ★
INSTALLING "MANAGEMENT BY OBJECTIVES"
 Resources for Education and Management
  Incorporated
 544 Medlock Road, Suite 210
 Decatur, Georgia 30030
Filmstrip with cassette. $70.00.

★ 1660 ★
MANAGEMENT BY OBJECTIVES
 Lansford Publishing Company
 Post Office Box 8711
 San Jose, California 95155
Multimedia kit. $240.00.

★ 1661 ★
MANAGEMENT BY OBJECTIVES - AN OVERVIEW
 Resources for Education and Management
  Incorporated
 544 Medlock Road, Suite 210
 Decatur, Georgia 30030
Filmstrip with cassette. $70.00.

★ 1662 ★
PREPLANNING AND OBJECTIVES
 Resources for Education and Management
  Incorporated
 544 Medlock Road, Suite 210
 Decatur, Georgia 30030
Filmstrip with cassette. $55.00.

Printed Materials

★ 1663 ★
GETTING RESULTS THROUGH MBO
 American Management Associations
 135 West 50th Street
 New York, New York 10020
Self-study text. $65.00.

★ 1664 ★
MANAGEMENT BY OBJECTIVES FOR STAFF MANAGERS
Dale McConkey
 Vantage Press Incorporated
 516 West 34th Street
 New York, New York 10001
Book. $9.00.

MANAGEMENT CONSULTING
See: CONSULTING

MANAGEMENT DEVELOPMENT

Audio Cassettes/Tapes

★ 1665 ★
EXECUTAPE'S ALBUM ON MANAGEMENT
DEVELOPMENT
 Thompson-Mitchell and Associates
 3384 Peachtree Road Northeast
 Atlanta, Georgia 30326
5 cassettes. $75.00.

★ 1666 ★
THE MATURE EXECUTIVE
James L. Hayes
 American Management Associations
 135 West 50th Street
 New York, New York 10020
Cassettes and manual. $80.00.

★ 1667 ★
THE ROLE OF MANAGEMENT EDUCATION IN
MANAGEMENT DEVELOPMENT
 Development Digest Incorporated
 3347 Motor Avenue
 Los Angeles, California 90034
Cassette. $13.75.

Games/Simulations

★ 1668 ★
THE ACHIEVEMENT GAME
 Training House Incorporated
 Box 688
 Binghamton, New York 13902
Simulation game. $60.00.

★ 1669 ★
THE ASSUMPTION GAME
 Training House Incorporated
 Box 688
 Binghamton, New York 13902
Simulation game. $60.00.

★ 1670 ★
THE CONSTRUCTION GAME
 Training House Incorporated
 Box 688
 Binghamton, New York 13902
Simulation game. $60.00.

★ 1671 ★
THE 5:01 DEADLINE
        Training House Incorporated
        Box 688
        Binghamton, New York 13902
Simulation game. $60.00.

★ 1672 ★
THE INSTRUCTION GAME
        Training House Incorporated
        Box 688
        Binghamton, New York 13902
Simulation game. $60.00.

★ 1673 ★
NO CAUSE FOR ALARM
        Training House Incorporated
        Box 688
        Binghamton, New York 13902
Simulation game. $60.00.

Multimedia Kits

★ 1674 ★
DEVELOPING EFFECTIVE MANAGEMENT
        Resources for Education and Management
            Incorporated
        544 Medlock Road, Suite 210
        Decatur, Georgia 30030
Filmstrip with cassette. $60.00.

Printed Materials

★ 1675 ★
CONCEPTS
        John Wiley and Sons Incorporated
        605 Third Avenue
        New York, New York 10016
Printed material. $59.95.

★ 1676 ★
CORPORATE GROWTH THROUGH INTERNAL
MANAGEMENT DEVELOPMENT
        Dartnell
        4660 Ravenswood Avenue
        Chicago, Illinois 60640
204 pages, binder. $43.50.

MANAGEMENT ENGINEERING

Correspondence Courses

★ 1677 ★
INDUSTRIAL ENGINEERING TECHNOLOGY
        International Correspondence School
        Scranton, Pennsylvania 18515
Multi-module correspondence course.

Games/Simulations

★ 1678 ★
ACHIEVING RESULTS THROUGH ENGINEERING
MANAGEMENT
        Society of Manufacturing Engineers
        20501 Ford Road
        Post Office Box 930
        Dearborn, Michigan 48128
Simulation with correspondent feedback. $125.00.

MANAGEMENT (GENERAL)

        See also: Leadership; headings under
        Supervision; Volunteer Management

Audio Cassettes/Tapes

★ 1679 ★
APPLEY IN ACTION
        American Management Associations
        135 West 50th Street
        New York, New York 10020
3 cassettes. $49.95.

★ 1680 ★
THE EXECUTIVE EFFECTIVENESS PROGRAM
        American Management Associations
        135 West 50th Street
        New York, New York 10020
6 cassettes with workbook. $100.00.

★ 1681 ★
FOUR ESSENTIAL MANAGERIAL SKILLS (Planning,
Budgeting, Scheduling, Monitoring Progress)
        Management Resources Incorporated
        757 Third Avenue
        New York, New York 10017
4 unit cassette course with test and feedback service.
$225.00.

★ 1682 ★
MANAGERIAL SKILLS FOR NEW AND
PROSPECTIVE MANAGERS
        American Management Associations
        135 West 50th Street
        New York, New York 10020
Cassettes and workbook. $110.00.

★ 1683 ★
MANAGERIAL SKILLS PROGRAM
        Addison Wesley Publishing Company Incorporated
        Jacob Way
        Reading, Massachusetts 01867
5 cassettes and guide. $55.00.

★ 1684 ★
MANAGING THE NEW GENERATION
        Development Digest Incorporated
        3347 Motor Avenue
        Los Angeles, California 90034
Cassette. $13.75.

★ 1685 ★
SKILLFUL BUSINESS SERIES
        Thompson-Mitchell and Associates
        3384 Peachtree Road Northeast
        Atlanta, Georgia 30326
20 cassettes. $120.00.

Films/Video/Filmstrips

★ 1686 ★
OVERMANAGEMENT: OR HOW AN EXCITING
IDEA CAN BECOME A DULL PROJECT
        Salenger Educational Media
        1635 12th Street
        Santa Monica, California 90404
Film with worksheets. $350.00.

Multimedia Kits

★ 1687 ★
DETERMINING PAYOFF AREAS
        Resources for Education and Management
            Incorporated
        544 Medlock Road, Suite 210
        Decatur, Georgia 30030
Filmstrip with cassette. $70.00.

★ 1688 ★
EFFECTIVE MANAGEMENT SKILLS
        Resources for Education and Management
            Incorporated
        544 Medlock Road, Suite 210
        Decatur, Georgia 30030
Filmstrip with cassette. $60.00.

★ 1689 ★
THE MANAGEMENT CYCLE: PLANNING,
ORGANIZING, ACTIVATING AND CONTROLLING
THE WORK
        Ergonco Performance Source
        Northwest O'Hare Office Park, Suite 119
        2474 Dempster Street
        Des Plains, Illinois 60016
Multimedia self-study program.

★ 1690 ★
THE MESSAGE IS YOURS - DON'T LOSE IT
        Resources for Education and Management
            Incorporated
        544 Medlock Road, Suite 210
        Decatur, Georgia 30030
Filmstrip with cassette. $60.00.

★ 1691 ★
STYLES OF MANAGEMENT
        Ergonco Performance Source
        Northwest O'Hare Office Park, Suite 119
        2474 Dempster Street
        Des Plains, Illinois 60016
Multimedia self-study program.

Printed Materials

★ 1692 ★
MANAGEMENT SYSTEMS AND PROGRAMMING
        International Publications Service
        114 East 32nd Street
        New York, New York 10016
Book. $17.50.

Programmed Learning Materials

★ 1693 ★
EFFECTIVE DIRECTOR IN ACTION
Louden J. Keith
        American Management Associations
        135 West 50th Street
        New York, New York 10020
Programmed instruction.   1975. $14.50.

★ 1694 ★
HOW TO MASTER JOB DESCRIPTIONS
American Management Associations
135 West 50th Street
New York, New York   10020
Programmed text with separate tests. $35.00.

MANAGEMENT GRID

See also: Organizational Development

Audio Cassettes/Tapes

★ 1695 ★
CONFLICT SOLVING
Dr. Blake, Dr. Mouton
Scientific Methods Incorporated
Box 195
Austin, Texas   78767
Cassette. $10.00.

★ 1696 ★
MOTIVATION
Dr. Blake, Dr. Mouton
Scientific Methods Incorporated
Box 195
Austin, Texas   78767
Cassette. $10.00.

★ 1697 ★
STRESS
Dr. Blake, Dr. Mouton
Scientific Methods Incorporated
Box 195
Austin, Texas   78767
Cassette. $10.00.

Films/Video/Filmstrips

★ 1698 ★
THE GRID APPROACH TO PROBLEM SOLVING
BNA Communications Incorporated
9401 Decoverly Hall Road
Rockville, Maryland   20850
Film with participant booklets.

★ 1699 ★
THE GRID FOR SUPERVISORY EFFECTIVENESS
BNA Communications Incorporated
9401 Decoverly Hall Road
Rockville, Maryland   20850
Film with participant booklets.

★ 1700 ★
THE MANAGERIAL GRID IN ACTION
BNA Communications Incorporated
9401 Decoverly Hall Road
Rockville, Maryland   20850
Film with participant booklets.

Printed Materials

★ 1701 ★
GRID FEEDBACK FROM A SUBORDINATE TO A
BOSS
Scientific Methods Incorporated
Box 195
Austin, Texas   78767
Workbook. $5.00.

★ 1702 ★
GRID RECOGNITION
Scientific Methods Incorporated
Box 195
Austin, Texas   78767
Workbook. $3.00.

★ 1703 ★
THE MARKETING GRID
Scientific Methods Incorporated
Box 195
Austin, Texas   78767
Workbook. $20.00.

★ 1704 ★
MCDONALD'S FARM (A grid case study)
Scientific Methods Incorporated
• Box 195
Austin, Texas   78767
Workbook. $3.00.

★ 1705 ★
A SELF-EXAMINATION OF MANAGERIAL
GRID STYLES
Scientific Methods Incorporated
Box 195
Austin, Texas   78767
Workbook. $5.00.

★ 1706 ★
STEVE HUNT (A grid case study)
Scientific Methods Incorporated
Box 195
Austin, Texas   78767
Workbook. $7.50.

MANAGEMENT, JOB DESCRIPTION

Audio Cassettes/Tapes

★ 1707 ★
OVERLAPPING RESPONSIBILITY - MEASURING
MANAGEMENT FUNCTIONS
>Thompson-Mitchell and Associates
>3384 Peachtree Road Northeast
>Atlanta, Georgia   30326
Cassette. $6.00.

★ 1708 ★
A PERSPECTIVE FOR THE MANAGER: MAN IN
THE MIDDLE
>Training House Incorporated
>Box 688
>Binghamton, New York   13902
Cassette with workbook. $36.00.

Films/Video/Filmstrips

★ 1709 ★
DEFINING THE MANAGERS JOB
>BNA Communications Incorporated
>9401 Decoverly Hall Road
>Rockville, Maryland   20850
Film.

★ 1710 ★
PROFILE OF A MANAGER
>National Restaurant Association
>One IBM Plaza, Suite 2600
>Chicago, Illinois   60611
Video cartridge or 8 mm, 16 mm, and study guide.
$190.00.

Multimedia Kits

★ 1711 ★
THE MAJOR DIFFERENCE BETWEEN MANAGERS
>Resources for Education and Management
> Incorporated
>544 Medlock Road, Suite 210
>Decatur, Georgia   30030
Filmstrip with cassette. $60.00.

★ 1712 ★
THE SUCCESSFUL MANAGER
>Resources for Education and Management
> Incorporated
>544 Medlock Road, Suite 210
>Decatur, Georgia   30030
Filmstrip with cassette. $60.00.

MANAGEMENT, PERSONNEL
See: PERSONNEL MANAGEMENT

MANAGEMENT PRINCIPLES

Audio Cassettes/Tapes

★ 1713 ★
THE ART, SCIENCE AND PROFESSION OF
MANAGEMENT
Dr. John R. Van De Water
>Van De Water Associates
>7914 Jason Avenue
>Canoga Park, California   91304
Cassette with workbook. $23.50.

★ 1714 ★
BUSINESS MANAGEMENT
>Tape Rental Library Incorporated
>Post Office Box 2107
>2507 Edna Drive
>South Vineland, New Jersey   08360
Cassette. $6.95.

★ 1715 ★
DRUCKER ON MANAGEMENT
Peter F. Drucker
>American Management Associations
>135 West 50th Street
>New York, New York   10020
8 cassettes and guide. $200.00.

★ 1716 ★
FACE TO FACE MANAGEMENT
>Creative Media Films
>820 Keo Way
>Des Moines, Iowa   50309
4 cassettes. $45.00.

★ 1717 ★
HOW SUCCESSFUL MANAGERS MANAGE
>Management Resources Incorporated
>757 Third Avenue
>New York, New York   10017
6 unit cassette course with test and feedback service.
$225.00.

★ 1718 ★
THE "HOW TO" DRUCKER
Peter F. Drucker
American Management Associations
135 West 50th Street
New York, New York 10020
Cassette and manual. $120.00.

★ 1719 ★
JOE BATTEN ON MANAGEMENT
Creative Media Films
820 Keo Way
Des Moines, Iowa 50309
6 one hour cassettes. $49.95.

★ 1720 ★
MANAGEMENT BY EXCEPTION
Penton/IPC Education Division
614 Superior Avenue West
Cleveland, Ohio 44113
On audio tape $60.00.   In print $15.00.

★ 1721 ★
PROTECTING A COMPANY'S MOST VALUABLE
ASSET - IT'S KEY MAN
A. M. Hunter Jr.
Tape Rental Library Incorporated
Post Office Box 2107
2507 Edna Drive
South Vineland, New Jersey 08360
Cassette.

Correspondence Courses

★ 1722 ★
BASIC MANAGEMENT SKILLS
Development Consultants Incorporated
2060 East 54th Street
Indianapolis, Indiana 46220
19 block skill program $65.00.

★ 1723 ★
BUSINESS MANAGEMENT
University of Kentucky
Independent Study Program
Freeze Hall, Room 1
Lexington, Kentucky 40506
Correspondence course.

★ 1724 ★
BUSINESS MANAGEMENT
La Salle Extension University
417 South Dearborn Street
Chicago, Illinois 60605
Correspondence course.

★ 1725 ★
FUNDAMENTALS OF MANAGEMENT
University of Missouri
Center for Independent Study
514 South Fifth Street
Columbia, Missouri 65211
Correspondence course. $80.00.

★ 1726 ★
PRINCIPLES OF MANAGEMENT
University of Florida
Division of Continuing Education
2012 West University Avenue
Gainesville, Florida 32603
Correspondence course.

★ 1727 ★
PRINCIPLES OF MANAGEMENT
University of Nebraska
511 Nebraska Hall
Lincoln, Nebraska 68588
Correspondence course.

★ 1728 ★
PRINCIPLES OF MANAGEMENT
University of South Carolina
Department of Correspondence Study
Division of Continuing Education
Columbia, South Carolina 29208
Correspondence course. $69.00.

★ 1729 ★
PRINCIPLES OF MANAGEMENT
University of Southern Mississippi
Department of Independent Study
Southern Station, Box 56
Hattiesburg, Mississippi 39401
Correspondence course.

Films/Video/Filmstrips

★ 1730 ★
HOW TO FAIL IN MANAGEMENT WITHOUT REALLY
TRYING
Salenger Educational Media
1635 12th Street
Santa Monica, California 90404
Film, guide and studybook. $410.00 (rental available).

★ 1731 ★
THE PETER PRINCIPLE: WHY THINGS ALWAYS GO WRONG
>   Salenger Educational Media
>   1635 12th Street
>   Santa Monica, California 90404
Film, guide and tests. $495.00 (rental available).

Games/Simulations

★ 1732 ★
THE CONTINUING MANAGE GAME SERVICE
>   Society of Manufacturing Engineers
>   20501 Ford Road
>   Post Office Box 930
>   Dearborn, Michigan 48128
Simulation with correspondent feedback. $117.00.

★ 1733 ★
THE IMAGINIT MANAGEMENT GAME
Richard Barton
>   Active Learning Incorporated
>   Post Office Box 16382
>   Lubbock, Texas 79490
Game, book. 1974. $8.95.

★ 1734 ★
MANAGEMENT GAMES SEMINAR
>   Society of Manufacturing Engineers
>   20501 Ford Road
>   Post Office Box 930
>   Dearborn, Michigan 48128
Simulation with correspondent feedback. $85.00.

Multimedia Kits

★ 1735 ★
CONTROLLING
>   Resources for Education and Management
>   Incorporated
>   544 Medlock Road, Suite 210
>   Decatur, Georgia 30030
Filmstrip with cassette. $60.00.

★ 1736 ★
JOE BATTEN'S MANAGEMENT COURSE
>   Creative Media Films
>   820 Keo Way
>   Des Moines, Iowa 50309
Multimedia course – books, films, cassettes with training guides.

★ 1737 ★
MANAGEMENT BUSINESS GAMES
>   Addison Wesley Publishing Company
>   Incorporated
>   Jacob Way
>   Reading, Massachusetts 01867
Color filmstrip with cassette tape and leader guide. $30.00.

★ 1738 ★
MANAGEMENT EFFECTIVENESS
>   Lansford Publishing Company
>   Post Office Box 8711
>   San Jose, California 95155
Multimedia kit. $95.95.

★ 1739 ★
MANAGING BY DECISION-MAKING
>   Resources for Education and Management
>   Incorporated
>   544 Medlock Road, Suite 210
>   Decatur, Georgia 30030
Filmstrip with cassette. $60.00.

★ 1740 ★
MANAGING THE JOB
>   Resources for Education and Management
>   Incorporated
>   544 Medlock Road, Suite 210
>   Decatur, Georgia 30030
Filmstrip with cassette. $60.00.

★ 1741 ★
A PERSPECTIVE: MANAGER IN THE MIDDLE
>   Ergonco Performance Source
>   Northwest O'Hare Office Park, Suite 119
>   2474 Dempster Street
>   Des Plains, Illinois 60016
Multimedia self-study program.

★ 1742 ★
PRINCIPLES AND CONCEPTS OF MANAGEMENT.
>   Lansford Publishing Company
>   Post Office Box 8711
>   San Jose, California 95155
Multimedia kit. $189.95.

★ 1743 ★
WHAT IS MANAGING?
>   Resources for Education and Management
>   Incorporated
>   544 Medlock Road, Suite 210
>   Decatur, Georgia 30030
Filmstrip with cassette. $60.00.

Printed Materials

★ 1744 ★
EXPLORATIONS IN MANAGING
Addison Wesley Publishing Company Incorporated
Jacob Way
Reading, Massachusetts   01867
Book. $13.95.

★ 1745 ★
WHAT MANAGERS DO
American Management Associations
135 West 50th Street
New York, New York   10020
Self-study text. $55.00.

Programmed Learning Materials

★ 1746 ★
PRINCIPLES OF MANAGEMENT
George R. Terry
Learning Systems Company
1818 Ridge Road
Homewood, Illinois   60430
Programmed learning aid. $4.50.

MANAGEMENT, SAFETY
See: SAFETY, MANAGEMENT

MANAGERIAL ACCOUNTING

See also: Accounting; Financial
Management

Audio Cassettes/Tapes

★ 1747 ★
MANAGEMENT ACCOUNTING FOR BUSINESS
DECISIONS
National Association of Accountants
919 Third Avenue
New York, New York   10022
Text and cassettes.

Correspondence Courses

★ 1748 ★
INTRODUCTION TO MANAGEMENT ACCOUNTING
University of North Carolina
Independent Study by Extension
121 Abernethy Hall 002A
Chapel Hill, North Carolina   27514

Correspondence course. $12.95.

★ 1749 ★
MANAGERIAL ACCOUNTING
University of Nebraska
511 Nebraska Hall
Lincoln, Nebraska   68588
Correspondence course.

Printed Materials

★ 1750 ★
ACCOUNTING PRINCIPLES FOR MANAGEMENT
Robert E. Seiler
Charles E. Merrill Publishing Company
1300 Alum Creek Drive
Box 508
Columbus, Ohio   43216
Text and exercises.   1975. $15.50.

★ 1751 ★
MANAGERIAL ACCOUNTING
James Rossell,   William Frasure
Charles E. Merrill Publishing Company
1300 Alum Creek Drive
Box 508
Columbus, Ohio   43216
Text.   1972. $15.50.

Programmed Learning Materials

★ 1752 ★
MANAGEMENT ACCOUNTING
Robert Anthony
Learning Systems Company
1818 Ridge Road
Homewood, Illinois   60430
Programmed learning aid. $4.50.

★ 1753 ★
MANAGERIAL ACCOUNTING
Richard D. Irwin Incorporated
1818 Ridge Road
Homewood, Illinois   60430
Programmed text.

MANAGERIAL COMMUNICATION

Audio Cassettes/Tapes

★ 1754 ★
MANAGERIAL COMMUNICATION: HOW TO
MASTER IT
    AMACOM
    American Management Associations
    135 West 50th Street
    New York, New York 10020
6 cassettes with manual. $110.00.

★ 1755 ★
MANAGERIAL COMMUNICATIONS
    Van De Water Associates
    7914 Jason Avenue
    Canoga Park, California 91304
Cassette and workbook. $23.50.

Correspondence Courses

★ 1756 ★
MANAGERIAL COMMUNICATION
    Texas Tech University
    Division of Continuing Education
    Post Office Box 4110
    Lubbock, Texas 79409
Correspondence course.

★ 1757 ★
MANAGERIAL COMMUNICATIONS
    University of Southern Mississippi
    Department of Independent Study
    Southern Station Box 56
    Hattiesburg, Mississippi 39401
Correspondence course.

Films/Video/Filmstrips

★ 1758 ★
THE OTHER SIDE OF THE DESK (Effective
communication with subordinates)
    Thompson-Mitchell and Associates
    3384 Peachtree Road Northeast
    Atlanta, Georgia 30326
Filmstrip (16 mm). $250.00.

Multimedia Kits

★ 1759 ★
THE SUPERVISOR AS A COMMUNICATOR

    Resources for Education and Management
        Incorporated
    544 Medlock Road, Suite 210
    Decatur, Georgia 30030
Filmstrip with cassette. $60.00.

Printed Materials

★ 1760 ★
COMMUNICATION SKILLS FOR MANAGERS
    American Management Associates
    135 West 50th Street
    New York, New York 10020
Self-study text. $55.00.

MANDARIN
See: CHINESE

MANUFACTURING OPERATIONS

Printed Materials

★ 1761 ★
OPERATIONS (Manufacturing)
    Scientific Methods Incorporated
    Box 195
    Austin, Texas 78767
Workbook. $6.00.

MAORI

Printed Materials

★ 1762 ★
TEACH YOURSELF MAORI
K. T. Harawira
    A. H. Reed and A. W. Books
    Rutland, Vermont 05701
Book. 1975. $3.50.

MARKETING

See also: International Marketing; Sales
                Techniques

Audio Cassettes/Tapes

★ 1763 ★
DIRECT MARKETING IN THE 70's
    Tape Rental Library Incorporated
    Post Office Box 2107, 2507 Edna Drive
    South Vineland, New Jersey 08360
Cassette. $12.00.

★ 1764 ★
INDUSTRIAL SURVIVAL IN THE 70'S
American Management Associations
135 West 50th Street
New York, New York 10020
Cassette. $12.00.

★ 1765 ★
THE MULTIMEDIA CONCEPT IN MODERN
MARKETING
Tape Rental Library Incorporated
Post Office Box 2107
2507 Edna Drive
South Vineland, New Jersey 08360
Cassette. $12.00.

★ 1766 ★
RESEARCH THAT HELPS YOU SELL CONSUMERS IN
THE 70'S
American Management Associations
135 West 50th Street
New York, New York 10020
2 cassettes. $24.00.

★ 1767 ★
"RESULTS ORIENTED" SALES-MANAGEMENT
Fred Herman
Tape Rental Library Incorporated
Post Office Box 2107
2507 Edna Drive
South Vineland, New Jersey 08360
12 cassettes with workbook. $165.00.

★ 1768 ★
THE TOTAL MEDIA CONCEPT
Tape Rental Library Incorporated
Post Office Box 2107
2507 Edna Drive
South Vineland, New Jersey 08360
Cassette. $12.00.

★ 1769 ★
WHAT WORKS IN MARKETING MANAGEMENT
American Management Associates
135 West 50th Street
New York, New York 10020
3 cassettes. $36.00.

Correspondence Courses •

★ 1770 ★
BASIC MARKETING CONCEPTS
Virgil L. Almond

Western Kentucky University
Office of Special Programs
Bowling Green, Kentucky 42101
Independent study course.

★ 1771 ★
MARKETING
University of South Carolina
Department of Correspondence Study
Division of Continuing Education
Columbia, South Carolina 29208
Correspondence course.

★ 1772 ★
MARKETING
University of Washington
Office of Independent Study
222 Lewis Hall DW-30
Seattle, Washington 98195
Correspondence course.

★ 1773 ★
MARKETING MANAGEMENT
University of Kentucky
Independent Study Program
Freeze Hall, Room 1
Lexington, Kentucky 40506
Correspondence course.

★ 1774 ★
PRINCIPLES OF MARKETING
University of Missouri
514 South Fifth Street
Center for Independent Study
Columbia, Missouri 65211
Correspondence course. $80.00.

Films/Video/Filmstrips

★ 1775 ★
PROMOTION
United Transparencies
Box 688
Binghamton, New York 13902
11 transparencies. $20.00.

★ 1776 ★
WHAT IS MARKETING?
Roundtable Films
113 North San Vincente Boulevard
Beverly Hills, California 90211
Film and guide book.

Games/Simulations

★ 1777 ★
MARKETING STRATEGY
Louis Boone, Edwin Hackman
        Charles E. Merrill Publishing Company
        1300 Alum Creek Drive
        Box 508
        Columbus, Ohio 43216
Game text. $7.95.

Printed Materials

★ 1778 ★
MARKETING AND SALES
        Scientific Methods Incorporated
        Box 195
        Austin, Texas 78767
Workbook. $6.00.

Programmed Learning Materials

★ 1779 ★
PRINCIPLES OF MARKETING
William T. Ryan
        Learning Systems Company
        1818 Ridge Road
        Homewood, Illinois 60430
Programmed learning aid. $4.50.

MASONRY

Correspondence Courses

★ 1780 ★
MASONRY
        International Correspondence School
        Scranton, Pennsylvania 18515
Multi-module correspondence course.

Films/Video/Filmstrips

★ 1781 ★
ARCH CONSTRUCTION
        The Kenalex Corporation
        2960 South Fox Street
        Englewood, Colorado 80110
Filmstrip and study book. $89.50.

★ 1782 ★
BASIC BLOCKLAYING
        The Kenalex Corporation
        2960 South Fox Street
        Englewood, Colorado 80110
Filmstrip and study guide.

★ 1783 ★
BASIC BRICKLAYING
        The Kenalex Corporation
        2960 South Fox Street
        Englewood, Colorado 80110
Filmstrip and study book. $89.50.

★ 1784 ★
LAYING OF HEADERS, ROWLOCKS AND SOLDIERS
        The Kenalex Corporation
        2960 South Fox Street
        Englewood, Colorado 80110
Filmstrip and study book. $89.50.

Printed Materials

★ 1785 ★
BRICKLAYING SIMPLIFIED
Donald Brann
        Directions Simplified Incorporated
        529 North State Road
        Briarcliff Manor, New York 10510
Book.   1975. $2.50.

★ 1786 ★
BRICKWORK FOR APPRENTICES
J. C. Hodge
        Herman Publishing Company
        45 Newbury Street
        Boston, Massachusetts 02116
Book.   1971. $6.50.

★ 1787 ★
CALCULATIONS FOR BRICKLAYERS
N. A. Sedwell
        Herman Publishing Company
        45 Newbury Street
        Boston, Massachusetts 02116
Book.   1966. $2.95.

MASS COMMUNICATION

See also: Communication

Printed Materials

★ 1788 ★
INTRODUCTION TO MASS COMMUNICATION
Warren Agee
Harper and Row Publishers Incorporated
Scranton, Pennsylvania 18512
Book. 1976. $7.95.

MATERIAL HANDLING

Programmed Learning Materials

★ 1789 ★
MATERIAL HANDLING
E. I. du Pont de Nemours and Company
Applied Technology Division
Room B 4204
Wilmington, Delaware 19898
5 unit programmed course. Approximately $5.00
each.

MATHEMATICS

See also: Biomathematics; Business
Mathematics

Audio Cassettes/Tapes

★ 1790 ★
INSTANT MATH
Thompson-Mitchell and Associates
3384 Peachtree Road Northeast
Atlanta, Georgia 30326
Cassette. $9.98.

★ 1791 ★
PLANE GEOMETRY
Thompson-Mitchell and Associates
3384 Peachtree Road Northeast
Atlanta, Georgia 30326
Cassette. $9.98.

Films/Video/Filmstrips

★ 1792 ★
BASIC MATH SKILLS
Telstar Productions Incorporated
366 North Prior Avenue
Saint Paul, Minnesota 55104

34 video tapes, 34 audio tapes, pre tests, post tests
and work packets. $3,980.00.

Printed Materials

★ 1793 ★
COMPLETE COURSE IN SHORT-CUT
MATHEMATICS
B. A. Slade
Nelson-Hall Publishers
325 West Jackson Boulevard
Chicago, Illinois 60606
Self instruction text. $7.95.

★ 1794 ★
MODERN GEOMETRY: COMPLETE COURSE
John Ashley, E. R. Harvey
Glencoe Press
Distributed by MacMillan Company
Riverside, New Jersey 08075
Self instruction book. 1970. $9.95.

★ 1795 ★
PRACTICAL MATHEMATICS FOR EVERYONE
Jan Kobbernagel
Theodore Audel Company
Distributed by Bobbs Merrill Company
Incorporated
4300 West 62nd Street
Indianapolis, Indiana 46268
2 volumes. $5.50 each.

Programmed Learning Materials

★ 1796 ★
AREA AND VOLUME OF COMMON FIGURES
E. I. du Pont de Nemours and Company
Applied Technology Division
Room B 4204
Wilmington, Delaware 19898
Programmed course of approximately 5 hours.
$10.90.

★ 1797 ★
BACKGROUND MATH FOR A COMPUTER WORLD
Ruth Ashley
John Wiley and Sons
605 Third Avenue
New York, New York 10016
Programmed text. 286 pages. $4.95.

★ 1798 ★
CONSUMER MATH
McGraw-Hill Book Company
1221 Avenue of the Americas
New York, New York 10019
Programmed text. $2.04.

★ 1799 ★
DECIMALS AND PERCENTS
E. I. du Pont de Nemours and Company
Applied Technology Division
Room B 4204
Wilmington, Delaware 19898
Programmed course of approximately 25 hours.
$32.40.

★ 1800 ★
FRACTIONS
E. I. du Pont de Nemours and Company
Applied Technology Division
Room B 4204
Wilmington, Delaware 19898
Programmed course of approximately 19 hours.
$32.60.

★ 1801 ★
FRACTIONS, DECIMALS AND PROPORTION
Resources Development Corporation
240 North Loop West, Suite 204
Houston, Texas 77018
Programmed text. $9.00.

★ 1802 ★
POSITIVE AND NEGATIVE NUMBERS
E. I. du Pont de Nemours and Company
Applied Technology Division
Room B 4204
Wilmington, Delaware 19898
Programmed course of approximately 4 hours. $9.15.

★ 1803 ★
RATIO AND PROPORTION
E. I. du Pont de Nemours and Company
Applied Technology Division
Room B 4204
Wilmington, Delaware 19898
Programmed course of approximately 10 hours. $18.85.

★ 1804 ★
RIGHT ANGLE TRIGONOMETRY
E. I. du Pont de Nemours and Company
Applied Technology Division
Room B 4204
Wilmington, Delaware 19898

Programmed course of approximately 8 hours. $15.60.

★ 1805 ★
SQUARES AND SQUARE ROOT TABLES
E. I. du Pont de Nemours and Company
Applied Technology Division
Room B 4204
Wilmington, Delaware 19898
Programmed course of approximately 4 hours. $8.60.

★ 1806 ★
WHOLE NUMBERS
E. I. du Pont de Nemours and Company
Applied Technology Division
Room B 4204
Wilmington, Delaware 19898
Programmed course of approximately 14 hours. $25.30.

MEASUREMENT

See also: Metric System

Programmed Learning Materials

★ 1807 ★
BASIC PRINCIPLES
E. I. du Pont de Nemours and Company
Applied Technology Division
Room B 4204
Wilmington, Delaware 19898
Programmed course of approximately 15 hours. $26.50.

★ 1808 ★
BOURDON TUBE AND OTHER GAGES
E. I. du Pont de Nemours and Company
Applied Technology Division
Room B 4204
Wilmington, Delaware 19898
Programmed course of approximately 8 hours. $15.60.

★ 1809 ★
CALIPERS
E. I. du Pont de Nemours and Company
Applied Technology Division
Room B 4204
Wilmington, Delaware 19898
Programmed course of approximately 3 hours. $7.40.

★ 1810 ★
LEVEL MEASUREMENT
    E. I. du Pont de Nemours and Company
    Applied Technology Division
    Room B 4204
    Wilmington, Delaware 19898
5 unit programmed course.   Approximately $10.00
each.

★ 1811 ★
MEASUREMENT
TPC Training Systems
    Technical Publishing Company
    1301 South Grove Avenue
    Barrington, Illinois 60010
Programmed text of 10 lessons. $20.50.

★ 1812 ★
MEASUREMENTS FOR INSTALLATION AND
CONSTRUCTION
    E. I. du Pont de Nemours and Company
    Applied Technology Division
    Room B 4204
Wilmington, Delaware 19898
Programmed course of approximately 10 hours.
$18.85.

★ 1813 ★
PRESSURE AND ITS MEASUREMENT
    Xerox Learning Systems
    30 Buxton Farms Road
    Stanford, Connecticut 06904
Programmed text. $19.00.

★ 1814 ★
VERNIERS
    E. I. du Pont de Nemours and Company
    Applied Technology Division
    Room B 4204
    Wilmington, Delaware 19898
Programmed course of approximately 1 1/2 hour.
$4.10.

MECHANICAL MAINTENANCE

Programmed Learning Materials

★ 1815 ★
DEVELOPING TROUBLESHOOTING SKILLS
TPC Training Systems
    Technical Publishing Company
    1301 South Grove Avenue
    Barrington, Illinois 60010
Programmed text of 10 lessons. $22.50.

★ 1816 ★
PLATE AND FRAME FILTER PRESSES
    E. I. du Pont de Nemours and Company
    Applied Technology Division
    Room B 4204
    Wilmington, Delaware 19898
Programmed course of approximately 14 hours. $23.90.

MECHANICS

See also: Automobile Mechanics

Programmed Learning Materials

★ 1817 ★
BASIC HYDRAULICS
TPC Training Systems
    Technical Publishing Company
    1301 South Grove Avenue
    Barrington, Illinois 60010
Programmed text of 10 lessons. $22.50.

★ 1818 ★
BASIC PNEUMATICS
TPC Training Systems
    Technical Publishing Company
    1301 South Grove Avenue
    Barrington, Illinois 60010
Programmed text of 10 lessons. $22.50.

★ 1819 ★
BEARINGS
TPC Training Systems
    Technical Publishing Company
    1301 South Grove Avenue
    Barrington, Illinois 60010
Programmed text of 10 lessons. $22.50.

★ 1820 ★
DRIVE COMPONENTS
TPC Training Systems
    Technical Publishing Company
    1301 South Grove Avenue
    Barrington, Illinois 60010
Programmed text of 10 lessons. $22.50.

★ 1821 ★
ELEMENTS OF MECHANICS
TPC Training Systems
    Technical Publishing Company
    1301 South Grove Avenue
    Barrington, Illinois 60010
Programmed text of 10 lessons. $22.50.

★ 1822 ★
HYDRAULIC TROUBLESHOOTING
TPC Training Systems
 Technical Publishing Company
 1301 South Grove Avenue
 Barrington, Illinois 60010
Programmed text of 10 lessons. $22.50.

★ 1823 ★
LUBRICATION
TPC Training Systems
 Technical Publishing Company
 1301 South Grove Avenue
 Barrington, Illinois 60010
Programmed text of 10 lessons. $22.50.

★ 1824 ★
PIPING SYSTEMS
TPC Training Systems
 Technical Publishing Company
 1301 South Grove Avenue
 Barrington, Illinois 60010
Programmed text of 10 lessons. $22.50.

★ 1825 ★
PNEUMATIC TROUBLESHOOTING
TPC Training Systems
 Technical Publishing Company
 1301 South Grove Avenue
 Barrington, Illinois 60010
Programmed text of 10 lessons. $22.50.

★ 1826 ★
PUMPS
TPC Training Systems
 Technical Publishing Company
 1301 South Grove Avenue
 Barrington, Illinois 60010
Programmed text of 10 lessons. $22.50.

MEDICAL CARE
See: headings under HEALTH

MEETINGS

See also: Conferences

Audio Cassettes/Tapes

★ 1827 ★
CONDUCTING MEETINGS

Educational Century Programming
1201 East Johnson Street
Jonesboro, Arkansas 72401
Cassette. $6.00.

★ 1828 ★
HOW TO RUN PRODUCTIVE MEETINGS
AMACOM
 American Management Associations
 135 West 50th Street
 New York, New York 10020
6 cassettes with workbook. $100.00.

★ 1829 ★
MAKING MEETINGS PAY OFF
 Thompson-Mitchell and Associates
 3384 Peachtree Road Northeast
 Atlanta, Georgia 30326
Cassette. $15.00.

★ 1830 ★
PRODUCTIVE MEETINGS
 Tape Rental Library Incorporated
 Post Office Box 2107
 2507 Edna Drive
 South Vineland, New Jersey 08360
Cassette.

Correspondence Courses

★ 1831 ★
HOW TO EFFECTIVELY CONTRIBUTE TO BUSINESS
MEETINGS
 Society of Manufacturing Engineers
 20501 Ford Road
 Post Office Box 930
 Dearborn, Michigan 48128
4 hour self instruction course. $10.00.

Films/Video/Filmstrips

★ 1832 ★
HOW TO HOLD A MEETING
 Creative Media Films
 820 Keo Way
 Des Moines, Iowa 50309
Film or video cassette. $450.00 (rental available).

★ 1833 ★
MEETING IN PROGRESS
 Roundtable Films
 113 North San Vincente Boulevard
 Beverly Hills, California 90211
Film and guidebook.

Multimedia Kits

★ 1834 ★
PLANNING AND RUNNING EFFECTIVE
MEETINGS
     Lansford Publishing Company
     Post Office Box 8711
     San Jose, California 95155
Multimedia kit. $159.95.

★ 1835 ★
RUNNING EFFECTIVE MEETINGS AND
CONFERENCES
     Ergonco Performance Source
     Northwest O'Hare Office Park, Suite 119
     2474 Dempster Street
     Des Plains, Illinois 60016
Multimedia self-study program.

★ 1836 ★
SUCCESSFUL PRESENTATION TECHNIQUES
     Ergonco Performance Source
     Northwest O'Hare Office Park, Suite 119
     2474 Dempster Street
     Des Plains, Illinois 60016
Multimedia self-study program.

Printed Materials

★ 1837 ★
HOW TO CONDUCT A MEETING
Dun and Bradstreet Business Library
     Apollo Editions
     Conklin Book Center
     Post Office Box 5555
     Binghamton, New York 13902
Book. 1970. $2.65.

Programmed Learning Materials

★ 1838 ★
HOW TO CONTRIBUTE TO BUSINESS MEETINGS
     Preston Publishing Company
     151 East 50th Street
     New York, New York 10022
Programmed text. $12.00.

MEMORY
See also: Personal Development

Audio Cassettes/Tapes

★ 1839 ★
MEMORY

     Success Tapes
     6954 Hanover Parkway #300
     Greenbelt, Maryland 20770
Cassette. $9.95.

★ 1840 ★
MEMORY
     Tape Rental Library Incorporated
     Post Office Box 2107
     2507 Edna Drive
     South Vineland, New Jersey 08360
Cassette. $9.00.

★ 1841 ★
MEMORY MADE EASY
Robert L. Montgomery
     American Management Associations
     135 West 50th Street
     New York, New York 10020
3 cassettes and guide.

★ 1842 ★
MEMORY MAGIC
William Hayes
     Cassette House
     530 West Northwest Highway
     Mount Prospect, Illinois 60056
Cassette. $9.95.

★ 1843 ★
MEMORY RECALL TRAINING
     Realtors National Marketing Institute
     430 North Michigan Avenue
     Chicago, Illinois 60611
Cassette. $12.00.

★ 1844 ★
REMEMBERING FACES AND NAMES
     Educational Century Programming
     1201 East Johnson Street
     Jonesboro, Arkansas 72401
Cassette. $6.00.

★ 1845 ★
REMEMBERING FACTS AND FIGURES
     Educational Century Programming
     1201 East Johnson Street
     Jonesboro, Arkansas 72401
Cassette. $6.00.

Correspondence Courses

★ 1846 ★
MEMORY COURSE
    Career Institute
    1500 Cardinal Drive
    Little Falls, New Jersey   07424
Correspondence course.

Programmed Learning Materials

★ 1847 ★
HUMAN MEMORY AND FORGETTING
N. Cofer
    Learning Systems Company
    1818 Ridge Road
    Homewood, Illinois   60430
Programmed learning aid. $1.75.

METALLURGY

See also: Instrumentation

Correspondence Courses

★ 1848 ★
TOOLING DESIGN FOR POWDER METALLURGY PARTS
    Society of Manufacturing Engineers
    20501 Ford Road
    Post Office Box 930
    Dearborn, Michigan 48128
9 lessons, self instruction course. $7.00.

Films/Video/Filmstrips

★ 1849 ★
ADJUSTMENTS, THREADS AND CARE OF A
MICROMETER
    Thompson-Mitchell and Associates
    3384 Peachtree Road Northeast
    Atlanta, Georgia   30326
Filmstrip. $24.00.

★ 1850 ★
THE BEVEL PROTRACTOR
    Thompson-Mitchell and Associates
    3384 Peachtree Road Northeast
    Atlanta, Georgia   30326
Filmstrip. $150.00.

★ 1851 ★
BLADE OF A COMBINATION SET
    Thompson-Mitchell and Associates
    3384 Peachtree Road Northeast
    Atlanta, Georgia   30326
Filmstrip. $24.00.

★ 1852 ★
CENTER HEAD OF A COMBINATION SET
    Thompson-Mitchell and Associates
    3384 Peachtree Road Northeast
    Atlanta, Georgia   30326
Filmstrip. $24.00.

★ 1853 ★
CHECKING WORK WITH THE BEVEL PROTRACTOR
    Thompson-Mitchell and Associates
    3384 Peachtree Road Northeast
    Atlanta, Georgia   30326
Filmstrip.

★ 1854 ★
CHECKING WORK WITH THE COMBINATION
SQUARE
    Thompson-Mitchell and Associates
    3384 Peachtree Road Northeast
    Atlanta, Georgia   30326
Filmstrip. $24.00..

★ 1855 ★
THE COMBINATION SET
    Thompson-Mitchell and Associates
    3384 Peachtree Road Northeast
    Atlanta, Georgia   30326
Filmstrip. $150.00.

★ 1856 ★
COMMON TOOLS
    Thompson-Mitchell and Associates
    3384 Peachtree Road Northeast
    Atlanta, Georgia   30326
Filmstrip. $24.00.

★ 1857 ★
DECIMAL EQUIVALENTS
    Thompson-Mitchell and Associates
    3384 Peachtree Road Northeast
    Atlanta, Georgia   30326
Filmstrip. $24.00.

★ 1858 ★
GRINDING THEORY
National Tool, Die and Precision Machining
Association
9300 Livingston Road
Washington, D.C. 20022
Sound film, test and review.

★ 1859 ★
HOW TO HANDLE A MICROMETER
Thompson-Mitchell and Associates
3384 Peachtree Road Northeast
Atlanta, Georgia 30326
Filmstrip. $24.00.

★ 1860 ★
LAYING OUT THE BEVEL PROTRACTOR
Thompson-Mitchell and Associates
3384 Peachtree Road Northeast
Atlanta, Georgia 30326
Filmstrip. $24.00.

★ 1861 ★
LAYING OUT THE COMBINATION SQUARE
Thompson-Mitchell and Associates
3384 Peachtree Road Northeast
Atlanta, Georgia 30326
Filmstrip. $24.00.

★ 1862 ★
MAIN PARTS OF A MICROMETER
Thompson-Mitchell and Associates
3384 Peachtree Road Northeast
Atlanta, Georgia 30326
Filmstrip. $24.00.

★ 1863 ★
METAL FORMING
Society of Manufacturing Engineers
20501 Ford Road
Post Office Box 930
Dearborn, Michigan 48128
Video tape.

★ 1864 ★
METAL REMOVAL
Society of Manufacturing Engineers
20501 Ford Road
Post Office Box 930
Dearborn, Michigan 48128
Video tape.

★ 1865 ★
THE OUTSIDE MICROMETER
Thompson-Mitchell and Associates
3384 Peachtree Road Northeast
Atlanta, Georgia 30326
Filmstrip. $150.00.

★ 1866 ★
PARTS OF A COMBINATION SET
Thompson-Mitchell and Associates
3384 Peachtree Road Northeast
Atlanta, Georgia 30326
Filmstrip. $24.00.

★ 1857 ★
PARTS OF A MICROMETER
Thompson-Mitchell and Associates
3384 Peachtree Road Northeast
Atlanta, Georgia 30326
Filmstrip. $24.00.

★ 1868 ★
PROPER CARE OF A MICROMETER
Thompson-Mitchell and Associates
3384 Peachtree Road Northeast
Atlanta, Georgia 30326
Filmstrip. $24.00.

★ 1869 ★
PROTRACTOR
Thompson-Mitchell and Associates
3384 Peachtree Road Northeast
Atlanta, Georgia 30326
Filmstrip. $24.00.

★ 1870 ★
READING IN TEN-THOUSANDTHS
Thompson-Mitchell and Associates
3384 Peachtree Road Northeast
Atlanta, Georgia 30326
Filmstrip. $24.00.

★ 1871 ★
READING IN THOUSANDTHS
Thompson-Mitchell and Associates
3384 Peachtree Road Northeast
Atlanta, Georgia 30326
Filmstrip. $24.00.

★ 1872 ★
READING IN THREE STEPS
     Thompson-Mitchell and Associates
     3384 Peachtree Road Northeast
     Atlanta, Georgia 30326
Filmstrip. $24.00.

★ 1873 ★
SCALE AND THE BEVAL PROTRACTOR
     Thompson-Mitchell and Associates
     3384 Peachtree Road Northeast
     Atlanta, Georgia 30326
Filmstrip. $24.00.

★ 1874 ★
SCREW THREAD MEASURING PRINCIPLES
     Thompson-Mitchell and Associates
     3384 Peachtree Road Northeast
     Atlanta, Georgia 30326
Filmstrip. $24.00.

★ 1875 ★
SETTING UP THE BEVAL PROTRACTOR
     Thompson-Mitchell and Associates
     3384 Peachtree Road Northeast
     Atlanta, Georgia 30326
Filmstrip. $24.00.

★ 1876 ★
SETTING UP THE COMBINATION SQUARE
     Thompson-Mitchell and Associates
     3384 Peachtree Road Northeast
     Atlanta, Georgia 30326
Filmstrip. $24.00.

★ 1877 ★
SHEET METAL
     Robert J. Brady Company
     Charles Press Publishers
     Prentice-Hall Companies
     Bowie, Maryland 20715
Filmstrip $19.95.   Slide $29.95.

★ 1878 ★
SINGLE POINT CUTTING TOOLS
     National Tool, Die and Precision Machining
       Association
     9300 Livingston Road
     Washington, D.C. 20022
Sound film with test and review.

★ 1879 ★
THE TWIST DRILL
     National Tool, Die and Precision Machining
       Association
     9300 Livingston Road
     Washington, D.C. 20022
Sound film, test and review.

★ 1880 ★
TYPES OF MICROMETERS
     Thompson-Mitchell and Associates
     3384 Peachtree Road Northeast
     Atlanta, Georgia 30326
Filmstrip. $24.00.

★ 1881 ★
USES OF A COMBINATION SQUARE
     Thompson-Mitchell and Associates
     3384 Peachtree Road Northeast
     Atlanta, Georgia 30326
Filmstrip. $24.00.

★ 1882 ★
USES OF THE BEVEL PROTRACTOR
     Thompson-Mitchell and Associates
     3384 Peachtree Road Northeast
     Atlanta, Georgia 30326
Filmstrip. $24.00.

METEOROLOGY
See: CLIMATOLOGY

METER READING

Films/Video/Filmstrips

★ 1883 ★
READING DEMAND METERS (Two part program)
     Resource Incorporated
     13902 North Dale Mabry Highway
     Tampa, Florida 33624
2 video cartridges and workbook available. $200.00.
Available individually $100.00.

★ 1884 ★
WATER METER READING (Four unit series)
     Resource Incorporated
     13902 North Dale Mabry Highway
     Tampa, Florida 33624
4 video cartridges and workbook available. $400.00.
Available individually $100.00.

★ 1885 ★
WATT HOUR METER READING (Five unit series)
> Resource Incorporated
> 13902 North Dale Mabry Highway
> Tampa, Florida 33624

5 video cartridges and workbook. $500.00.
Available individually $100.00.

METRIC SYSTEM

See also: Measurement

Audio Cassettes/Tapes

★ 1886 ★
METRICATION - ITS IMPACT ON INSTRUMENTATION
Donald C. Strain
> Instrument Society of America
> 400 Stanwix Street
> Pittsburgh, Pennsylvania 15222

Workbook and cassette. $10.00.

Correspondence Courses

★ 1887 ★
METRICATION FOR ENGINEERS
Ernest Wolff
> Society of Manufacturing Engineers
> 20501 Ford Road
> Post Office Box 930
> Dearborn, Michigan 48128

Self instruction course. $10.50.

Films/Video/Filmstrips

★ 1888 ★
DECIMAL CALCULATING
> Thompson-Mitchell and Associates
> 3384 Peachtree Road Northeast
> Atlanta, Georgia 30326

Filmstrip. $24.00.

★ 1889 ★
DESIGNING FOR METRIC MANUFACTURING
> Society of Manufacturing Engineers
> 20501 Ford Road
> Post Office Box 930
> Dearborn, Michigan 48128

Video tape.

★ 1890 ★
ENGLISH AND METRIC LENGTHS
> Thompson-Mitchell and Associates
> 3384 Peachtree Road Northeast
> Atlanta, Georgia 30326

Filmstrip. $24.00.

★ 1891 ★
ENGLISH AND METRIC WEIGHT AND VOLUME
> Thompson-Mitchell and Associates
> 3384 Peachtree Road Northeast
> Atlanta, Georgia 30326

Filmstrip. $24.00.

★ 1892 ★
HISTORY OF MEASUREMENT
> Thompson-Mitchell and Associates
> 3384 Peachtree Road Northeast
> Atlanta, Georgia 30326

Filmstrip. $24.00.

★ 1893 ★
ITS ADVANTAGES - METRIC SYSTEM
> Thompson-Mitchell and Associates
> 3384 Peachtree Road Northeast
> Atlanta, Georgia 30326

Filmstrip. $24.00.

★ 1894 ★
LONG LENGTHS
> Thompson-Mitchell and Associates
> 3384 Peachtree Road Northeast
> Atlanta, Georgia 30326

Filmstrip. $24.00.

★ 1895 ★
METER, LITER AND GRAM
> Salenger Educational Media
> 1635 12th Street
> Santa Monica, California 90404

Film and worksheets. $195.00 (rental available).

★ 1896 ★
METRIC CONVERSION
> Society of Manufacturing Engineers
> 20501 Ford Road
> Post Office Box 930
> Dearborn, Michigan 48128

Video tape.

★ 1897 ★
METRIC ORIENTATION
     Society of Manufacturing Engineers
     20501 Ford Road
     Post Office Box 930
     Dearborn, Michigan 48128
Video tape.

★ 1898 ★
THE METRIC SYSTEM
     Thompson-Mitchell and Associates
     3384 Peachtree Road Northeast
     Atlanta, Georgia 30326
Filmstrip or cassette. $300.00.

★ 1899 ★
METRIC UNITS AND READING
     Thompson-Mitchell and Associates
     3384 Peachtree Road Northeast
     Atlanta, Georgia 30326
Filmstrip. $24.00.

★ 1900 ★
PLANNING AND IMPLEMENTATION (Explains metric
conversion procedures
     Society of Manufacturing Engineers
     20501 Ford Road
     Post Office Box 930
     Dearborn, Michigan 48128
Video tape.

★ 1901 ★
SHORT LENGTHS (Metric system)
     Thompson-Mitchell and Associates
     3384 Peachtree Road Northeast
     Atlanta, Georgia 30326
Filmstrip. $24.00.

★ 1902 ★
UNDERSTANDING S I UNITS (Explains the
international system of metrics)
     Society of Manufacturing Engineers
     20501 Ford Road
     Post Office Box 930
     Dearborn, Michigan 48128
Video tape.

★ 1903 ★
VOLUME
     Thompson-Mitchell and Associates
     3384 Peachtree Road Northeast
     Atlanta, Georgia 30326
Filmstrip. $24.00.

★ 1904 ★
WEIGHT
     Thompson-Mitchell and Associates
     3384 Peachtree Road Northeast
     Atlanta, Georgia 30326
Filmstrip. $24.00.

Programmed Learning Materials

★ 1905 ★
USING THE METRIC SYSTEM
Robert Mason, Walter Lange
     Learning Systems Company
     1818 Ridge Road
     Homewood, Illinois 60430
Programmed learning aid. $3.95.

MICROBIOLOGY

Films/Video/Filmstrips

★ 1906 ★
MICROBIOLOGY
     Telstar Productions Incorporated
     366 North Prior Avenue
     Saint Paul, Minnesota 55104
48 video tape lessons. $250.00 each.

MINORITY SUPERVISION
See: SUPERVISION, MINORITIES

MOTIVATION

Audio Cassettes/Tapes

★ 1907 ★
BETTER THAN MONEY
John Tscohl
     General Cassette Corporation
     1324 North 22nd Avenue
     Post Office Box 6940
     Phoenix, Arizona 85005
Cassette and workbook. $39.50.

★ 1908 ★
BOB RICHARDS ON MOTIVATION AND
ACHIEVEMENT
     Tape Rental Library Incorporated
     2507 Edna Drive, Post Office Box 2107
     South Vineland, New Jersey 08360
2 cassettes.

★ 1909 ★
EMPLOYEE MOTIVATION - EMPLOYEE
ORIENTATION
  Thompson-Mitchell and Associates
  3384 Peachtree Road Northeast
  Atlanta, Georgia 30326
Cassette. $6.00.

★ 1910 ★
FACE TO FACE MOTIVATION
  Creative Media Films
  820 Keo Way
  Des Moines, Iowa 50309
4 cassettes. $45.00.

★ 1911 ★
GELLERMAN ON MOTIVATION
  American Management Associations
  135 West 50th Street
  New York, New York 10020
Cassette and manual. $24.00.

★ 1912 ★
HOW TO USE THE JOB DESCRIPTION AS A
MOTIVATOR
  Thompson-Mitchell and Associates
  3384 Peachtree Road Northeast
  Atlanta, Georgia 30326
Cassette. $15.00.

★ 1913 ★
THE KEY TO MOTIVATION
Bob Conklin
  E. F. Wonderlic and Associates Incorporated
  820 Frontage Road
  Northfield, Illinois 60093
Cassette. $10.00.

★ 1914 ★
MOTIVATING FOR PROFIT
  Management Resources Incorporated
  757 Third Avenue
  New York, New York 10017
2 cassettes and workbooks. $49.95.

★ 1915 ★
MOTIVATING YOUR EMPLOYEES: WHY PEOPLE
WORK
  Training House Incorporated
  Box 688
  Binghamton, New York 13902
Cassette with workbook. $36.00.

★ 1916 ★
MOTIVATION
George Odiorne
  MBO Incorporated
  157 Pontoosic Road
  Westfield, Massachusetts 01085
Cassette and manual. $15.00.

★ 1917 ★
MOTIVATION THROUGH THE WORK ITSELF
  Development Digest Incorporated
  3347 Motor Avenue
  Los Angeles, California 90034
Cassette. $13.75.

★ 1918 ★
MOTIVATIONAL FACTORS IN MANAGEMENT
  Van De Water Associates
  7914 Jason Avenue
  Canoga Park, California 91304
Cassette and workbook. $23.50.

★ 1919 ★
NEW DIMENSIONS FOR TODAY
Chris Hegarty
  General Cassette Corporation
  1324 North 22nd Avenue
  Phoenix, Arizona 85009
4 cassettes. $59.00.

★ 1920 ★
PERSONAL MOTIVATION AND GOAL
ADJUSTMENT
  Learning Dynamics Institute
  1401 Wilson Boulevard #101
  Arlington, Virginia 22209
6 cassettes. $129.00.

★ 1921 ★
SALES "HUMAN ENGINEERING" MOTIVATION
Cavett Robert
  Tape Rental Library Incorporated
  Post Office Box 2107
  2507 Edna Drive
  South Vineland, New Jersey 08360
6 cassettes. $44.95.

★ 1922 ★
SELF-MOTIVATION
Orison Swett Marden, M.D.
  Tape Rental Library Incorporated
  2507 Edna Drive, Post Office Box 2107
  South Vineland, New Jersey 08360
Cassette.

★ 1923 ★
THE THREE-FACTOR THEORY OF MOTIVATION
George Odiorne
    MBO Incorporated
    157 Pontoosic Road
    Westfield, Massachusetts 01085
Cassette and manual. $15.00.

★ 1924 ★
THREE WAYS OF ACTIVATING OTHERS
George Odiorne
    MBO Incorporated
    157 Pontoosic Road
    Westfield, Massachusetts 01085
Cassette and manual. $15.00.

★ 1925 ★
YOU CAN'T HEAT AN OVEN WITH SNOWBALLS
(Human motivation)
Cavett Robert
    Tape Rental Library Incorporated
    Post Office Box 2107
    2507 Edna Drive
    South Vineland, New Jersey 08360
Cassette. $10.00.

★ 1926 ★
YOUR HIDDEN POWER - ENTHUSIASM - DO IT
NOW
    Thompson-Mitchell and Associates
    3384 Peachtree Road Northeast
    Atlanta, Georgia 30326
Cassette. $9.95.

Correspondence Courses

★ 1927 ★
HOW TO MOTIVATE EMPLOYEES
    Society of Manufacturing Engineers
    20501 Ford Road
    Post Office Box 930
    Dearborn, Michigan 48128
4 hours self instruction course. $10.00.

Films/Video/Filmstrips

★ 1928 ★
FUNDAMENTALS OF COMMERCIAL AND
INDUSTRIAL LIGHTING
    The Electrification Council
    90 Park Avenue
    New York, New York 10016
Text and slides. $180.00.

★ 1929 ★
HIERARCHY OF NEEDS
Dr. Abraham Maslow
    Salenger Educational Media
    1635 12th Street
    Santa Monica, California 90404
Film, guide worksheets and chart. $360.00 (rental
available).

★ 1930 ★
IT'S A MATTER OF PRIDE
    Salenger Educational Media
    1635 12th Street
    Santa Monica, California 90404
Film and worksheets. $275.00 (rental available).

★ 1931 ★
JOB ENRICHMENT: MANAGERIAL MILESTONE
OR MYTH
    Salenger Educational Media
    1635 12th Street
    Santa Monica, California 90404
Film and worksheets. $350.00 (rental available).

★ 1932 ★
MASLOW'S HIERARCHY OF NEEDS
    Salenger Educational Media
    1635 12th Street
    Santa Monica, California 90404
Film.

★ 1933 ★
MOTIVATION THROUGH JOB ENRICHMENT
    BNA Communications Incorporated
    9401 Decoverly Hall Road
    Rockville, Maryland 20850
Film.

★ 1934 ★
A POSITIVE APPROACH TO MOTIVATION
    Thompson-Mitchell and Associates
    3384 Peachtree Road Northeast
    Atlanta, Georgia 30326
Filmstrip. 16 minutes. $24.95.

★ 1935 ★
THE SUPERVISOR - MOTIVATING THROUGH
INSIGHT
    National Restaurant Association
    One IBM Plaza, Suite 2600
    Chicago, Illinois 60611
Video cartridge or 8 mm, 16 mm, and study guide.
$190.00.

Multimedia Kits

★ 1936 ★
COMMUNICATION AND MOTIVATION
    Lansford Publishing Company
    Post Office Box 8711
    San Jose, California 95155
Multimedia kit. $189.95.

★ 1937 ★
HOW TO MOTIVATE YOUR PEOPLE
    Resources for Education and Management
        Incorporated
    544 Medlock Road, Suite 210
    Decatur, Georgia 30030
Filmstrip with cassette. $55.00.

★ 1938 ★
MANAGEMENT BY MOTIVATION
    Resources for Education and Management
        Incorporated
    544 Medlock Road, Suite 210
    Decatur, Georgia 30030
Filmstrip with cassette. $60.00.

★ 1939 ★
MEASURING MOTIVATION
    Lansford Publishing Company
    Post Office Box 8711
    San Jose, California 95155
Multimedia kit. $155.00.

★ 1940 ★
MOTIVATING EMPLOYEES: WHY PEOPLE WORK
    Ergonco Performance Source
    Northwest O'Hare Office Park, Suite 119
    2474 Dempster Street
    Des Plains, Illinois 60016
Multimedia self-study program.

★ 1941 ★
TRAINING AND COACHING THE WORK TEAM:
STEPS TO IMPROVE PERFORMANCE
    Ergonco Performance Source
    Northwest O'Hare Office Park, Suite 119
    2474 Dempster Street
    Des Plains, Illinois 60016
Multimedia self-study program.

★ 1942 ★
WHAT MOTIVATES MAN TO WORK
    Resources for Education and Management
        Incorporated
    544 Medlock Road, Suite 210
    Decatur, Georgia 30030
Filmstrip with cassette. $65.00.

Printed Materials

★ 1943 ★
MOTIVATION AND JOB ENRICHMENT
    C. L. Carter Jr. and Associates Incorporated
    434 First Bank and Trust Building
    811 South Central Expressway
    Richardson, Texas 75080
Text. $13.50.

★ 1944 ★
STRATEGIES FOR MOTIVATION
    Didactic Systems Incorporated
    Box 457
    Cranford, New Jersey 07016
Self-study text. $9.00.

Programmed Learning Materials

★ 1945 ★
HOW TO MOTIVATE EMPLOYEES
    Preston Publishing Company
    151 East 50th Street
    New York, New York 10022
Programmed text. $10.00.

★ 1946 ★
MOTIVATION AND MODERN MANAGEMENT
Joan Guilford, David Gray
    Addison Wesley Publishing Company Incorporated
    Jacob Way
    Reading, Massachusetts 01867
Programmed text. $5.95.

MOTORCYCLING

Correspondence Courses

★ 1947 ★
MOTORCYCLE MECHANICS
    Commercial Trades Institute
    6201 West Howard Street
    Chicago, Illinois 60648
Correspondence course.

★ 1948 ★
MOTORCYCLE MECHANICS
    North American Correspondence School
    4401 Birch Street
    Newport Beach, California   92663
Correspondence course.

Films/Video/Filmstrips

★ 1949 ★
MOTORCYCLE RIDER COURSE
    Motorcycle Safety Foundation
    6755 Elkridge Landing Road
    Linthicum, Maryland   21090
Films and textbook. $385.00.

MOTORS

Films/Video/Filmstrips

★ 1950 ★
MOTORS AND MOTOR CONTROLS
    The Electrification Council
    90 Park Avenue
    New York, New York   10016
Slides and text. $225.00.

MOVIE MAKING
See: CINEMATOGRAPHY

NEGOTIATION

See also: Conflict Resolution

Audio Cassettes/Tapes

★ 1951 ★
THE ART OF NEGOTIATING
    Realtors National Marketing Institute
    430 North Michigan Avenue
    Chicago, Illinois   60611
Cassette. $37.50.

★ 1952 ★
THE ART OF NEGOTIATING
    Tape Rental Library Incorporated
    Post Office Box 2107
    2507 Edna Drive
    South Vineland, New Jersey   08360
8 cassettes and guide. $295.00.

★ 1953 ★
COMMUNICATING BOTH WAYS (Techniques of Negotiation)
    AMACOM
    American Management Associations
    135 West 50th Street
    New York, New York   10020
Cassette. $18.00.

★ 1954 ★
EFFECTIVE NEGOTIATING: TACTICS AND COUNTERMEASURES THAT WORK FOR TRAINING DIRECTORS
    Development Digest Incorporated
    3347 Motor Avenue
    Los Angeles, California   90034
Cassette. $13.75.

★ 1955 ★
HOW TO BE A SUCCESSFUL NEGOTIATOR
    AMACOM
    American Management Associations
    135 West 50th Street
    New York, New York   10020
6 cassettes with workbook. $100.00.

Printed Materials

★ 1956 ★
ROLE NEGOTIATION FOR TEAM PRODUCTIVITY
    Development Publications
    5605 Lamar Road
    Washington, D.C.   20016
2 workbooks. $18.00.

NEPALI

Printed Materials

★ 1957 ★
CONVERSATIONAL NEPALI
Anna Hari
    Summer Institute of Linguistics
    Huntington Beach, California   92648
Book.   1971. $8.00.

★ 1958 ★
NEPALI SELF TAUGHT
B. Dasgupta
    S F Book Imports
    Post Office Box 526
    San Francisco, California   94101
Self-study book. $3.00.

NEW GUINEA PIDGIN

Programmed Learning Materials

★ 1959 ★
PROGRAMMED COURSE IN NEW GUINEA PIDGIN
R. Litteral
        Jacaranda Press Incorporated
        872 Massachusetts Avenue
        Cambridge, Massachusetts 02139
Programmed course. $5.95.

NOISE POLLUTION

Films/Video/Filmstrips

★ 1960 ★
NOISE ABATEMENT
        Society of Manufacturing Engineers
        20501 Ford Road
        Post Office Box 930
        Dearborn, Michigan 48128
Video tape.

NON-METAL MATERIALS

Programmed Learning Materials

★ 1961 ★
NON-METAL MATERIALS
TPC Training Systems
        Technical Publishing Company
        1301 South Grove Avenue
        Barrington, Illinois 60016
Programmed text of 10 lessons. $22.50.

NON-PROFIT ORGANIZATION

Audio Cassettes/Tapes

★ 1962 ★
MARKETING FOR NON-PROFIT ORGANIZATIONS
        Lansford Publishing Company
        Post Office Box 8711
        San Jose, California 95155
3 cassettes. $70.00.

Multimedia Kits

★ 1963 ★
MBO FOR THE NOT-FOR-PROFIT ENTERPRISE
        Lansford Publishing Company
        Post Office Box 8711
        San Jose, California 95155
Multimedia kit. $185.00.

NON-VERBAL COMMUNICATION

Audio Cassettes/Tapes

★ 1964 ★
NON-VERBAL COMMUNICATION
Dorothy Shaffer
        General Cassette Corporation
        1324 North 22nd Avenue
        Post Office Box 6940
        Phoenix, Arizona 85005
4 cassettes. $39.00.

★ 1965 ★
NON-VERBAL COMMUNICATION IN THE
EXECUTIVE SUITE - SALES AND MARKETING
        General Cassette Corporation
        1324 North 22nd Avenue
        Phoenix, Arizona 85009
Cassette. $18.00.

Films/Video/Filmstrips

★ 1966 ★
COMMUNICATION: THE NON-VERBAL AGENDA
        CRM McGraw Hill Films
        110 15th Street
        Del Mar, California 92014
Film or video cassette.

★ 1967 ★
NON-VERBAL COMMUNICATION
        Salenger Educational Media
        1635 12th Street
        Santa Monica, California 90404
Film.

Multimedia Kits

★ 1968 ★
NON-VERBAL COMMUNICATION
        Lansford Publishing Company
        Post Office Box 8711
        San Jose, California 95155
Multimedia kit. $160.00.

★ 1969 ★
NON-VERBAL COMMUNICATION AND INTER-
ACTION
    Lansford Publishing Company
    Post Office Box 8711
    San Jose, California 95155
Multimedia kit. $160.00.

NORWEGIAN

Audio Cassettes/Tapes

★ 1970 ★
BERLITZ COURSE IN NORWEGIAN
    Berlitz Language Program
    Post Office Box 5109
    FDR Station
    New York, New York 10022
Cassette $5.95. Also available on LP record.

★ 1971 ★
SPOKEN NORWEGIAN
    Spoken Language Services Incorporated
    Post Office Box 783
    Ithaca, New York 14850
Cassettes with course book. 1976.

Correspondence Courses

★ 1972 ★
NORWEGIAN
    University of Wisconsin – Extension
    Independent Study
    432 North Lake Street
    Madison, Wisconsin 53706
Various level courses available.

★ 1973 ★
NORWEGIAN LANGUAGE STUDIES
    University of Washington
    Office of Independent Study
    222 Lewis Hall DW-30
    Seattle, Washington 98195
Correspondence course.

Printed Materials

★ 1974 ★
BEGINNING NORWEGIAN: A GRAMMAR AND
READER
Einar Haugen
    Prentice-Hall Incorporated
    Englewood Cliffs, New Jersey 07632
Book.

★ 1975 ★
LEARN NORWEGIAN FOR ENGLISH SPEAKERS
    Saphrograph Company
    194 Elizabeth Street
    New York, New York 10012
Book. $5.00.

★ 1976 ★
TEACH YOURSELF NORWEGIAN
A. Sommerfelt, I. Marm
    David McKay Company Incorporated
    750 Third Avenue
    New York, New York 10017
Self-study book. $2.95.

NUMBER THEORY

Programmed Learning Materials

★ 1977 ★
NUMERICAL CONTROL: ITS APPLICATION IN
MANUFACTURING
    Society of Manufacturing Engineers
    20501 Ford Road
    Post Office Box 930
    Dearborn, Michigan 48128
Programmed learning course. $80.50.

★ 1978 ★
NUMERICAL PREFIX AND POWERS OF TEN
    E. I. du Pont de Nemours and Company
    Applied Technology Division
    Room B 4204
    Wilmington, Delaware 19898
Programmed course of approximately 5 hours. $10.90.

★ 1979 ★
PROGRAMMED INTRODUCTION TO NUMBER
SYSTEMS
Irving Drooyan
    John Wiley and Sons Incorporated
    605 Third Avenue
    New York, New York 10016
Programmed. 1973. $7.95.

NURSING MANAGEMENT
See: HEALTH, NURSING

OFFICE DESIGN

Audio Cassettes/Tapes

★ 1980 ★
SELECT AN OFFICE/SELECT OFFICE EQUIPMENT
Educational Century Programming
1201 East Johnson Street
Jonesboro, Arkansas 72401
Cassette. $6.00.

OFFICE MANAGEMENT

Correspondence Courses

★ 1981 ★
OFFICE ADMINISTRATION AND SERVICES
University of Kentucky
Independent Study Program
Freeze Hall, Room 1
Lexington, Kentucky 40506
Correspondence course.

★ 1982 ★
OFFICE MANAGEMENT
University of South Carolina
Department of Correspondence Study
Division of Continuing Education
Columbia, South Carolina 29208
Correspondence course.

★ 1983 ★
PRINCIPLES OF OFFICE MANAGEMENT
University of Colorado
Center for Lifelong Learning
170 Aurora Avenue
Boulder, Colorado 80302
Correspondence course.

Multimedia Kits

★ 1984 ★
MANAGING A SECRETARIAL SUPPORT SYSTEM
Ergonco Performance Source
Northwest O'Hare Office Park, Suite 119
2474 Dempster Street
Des Plains, Illinois 60016
Multimedia self-study program.

★ 1985 ★
OFFICE MANAGEMENT
Lansford Publishing Company
Post Office Box 8711
San Jose, California 95155
Multimedia kit. $150.00.

★ 1986 ★
OFFICE RECORDS MANAGEMENT
Lansford Publishing Company
Post Office Box 8711
San Jose, California 95155
Multimedia kit. $190.00.

OFFICE PRACTICES

See also: Dictation; Secretarial Skills

Audio Cassettes/Tapes

★ 1987 ★
BUSINESS SPELLING AND VOCABULARY
SYSTEMATIC INDEXING
Educational Century Programming
1201 East Johnson Street
Jonesboro, Arkansas 72401
Cassette. $6.00.

★ 1988 ★
FILING BY ALPHABET AND SUBJECT/RECORDS
MANAGEMENT
Educational Century Programming
1201 East Johnson Street
Jonesboro, Arkansas 72401
Cassette. $6.00.

★ 1989 ★
LEGAL DICTATION/MEDICAL DICTATION
Educational Century Programming
1201 East Johnson Street
Jonesboro, Arkansas 72401
Cassette. $6.00.

★ 1990 ★
MACHINES-CALCULATING/MACHINES-
DUPLICATING
Educational Century Programming
1201 East Johnson Street
Jonesboro, Arkansas 72401
Cassette. $6.00.

★ 1991 ★
MEDICAL OFFICE PRACTICES/LEGAL OFFICE
PRACTICES
Educational Century Programming
1201 East Johnson Street
Jonesboro, Arkansas 72401
Cassette. $6.00.

★ 1992 ★
TECHNICAL DICTATION/WORD SIMULATION
Educational Century Programming
1201 East Johnson Street
Jonesboro, Arkansas 72401
Cassette. $6.00.

Multimedia Kits

★ 1993 ★
THE ROLE OF THE OFFICE WORKER
Resources for Education and Management
Incorporated
544 Medlock Road, Suite 210
Decatur, Georgia 30030
Filmstrip with cassette. $60.00.

Printed Materials

★ 1994 ★
GENERAL OFFICE PRACTICE
F. C. Archer
McGraw-Hill Book Company
1221 Avenue of the Americas
New York, New York 10019
Book and workbook. $13.00.

OPERATIONS RESEARCH

Correspondence Courses

★ 1995 ★
INTRODUCTION TO OPERATIONS RESEARCH
The Thomas Institute
Box 22
New Canaan, Connecticut 06840
Self-study course. $150.00.

ORAL COMMUNICATION
See: COMMUNICATION, ORAL

ORGANIZATIONAL DEVELOPMENT

See also: Management Development

Audio Cassettes/Tapes

★ 1996 ★
DIMENSION IN ORGANIZATION DEVELOPMENT
Development Digest Incorporated
3347 Motor Avenue
Los Angeles, California 90034
Cassette. $13.75.

★ 1997 ★
INNOVATION - THE KEY TO EXCELLENCE
George Odiorne
MBO Incorporated
157 Pontoosic Road
Westfield, Massachusetts 01085
Cassette and manual. $15.00.

★ 1998 ★
ORGANIZATION DEVELOPMENT AND SENSITIVITY
TRAINING
George Odiorne
MBO Incorporated
157 Pontoosic Road
Westfield, Massachusetts 01085
Cassette and manual. $15.00.

★ 1999 ★
ORGANIZATION DEVELOPMENT OVERVIEW
Jack N. Fordyce
Addison Wesley Publishing Company Incorporated
Jacob Way
Reading, Massachusetts 01867
Cassette. $15.00.

★ 2000 ★
ORGANIZATIONAL DEVELOPMENT
Addison Wesley Publishing Company Incorporated
Jacob Way
Reading, Massachusetts 01867
Cassette with workbook. $15.00.

★ 2001 ★
RELATING INDIVIDUAL DEVELOPMENT AND
ORGANIZATION DEVELOPMENT
Development Digest Incorporated
3347 Motor Avenue
Los Angeles, California 90034
Cassette. $13.75.

Correspondence Courses

★ 2002 ★
ANALYSES OF ORGANIZATIONAL BEHAVIOR
  University of Kentucky
  Independent Study Program
  Freeze Hall, Room 1
  Lexington, Kentucky 40506
Correspondence course.

Films/Video/Filmstrips

★ 2003 ★
COPING WITH CHANGE
  BNA Communications Incorporated
  9401 Decoverly Hall Road
  Rockville, Maryland 20850
Film.

★ 2004 ★
OVERCOMING RESISTANCE TO CHANGE
  Roundtable Films
  113 North San Vincente Boulevard
  Beverly Hills, California 90211
Film and guidebook.

Multimedia Kits

★ 2005 ★
COPING WITH CHANGE AND CONFLICT
Gordon Lippitt
  Development Publications
  5605 Lamar Road
  Washington, D.C. 20016
Film (rental), cassette and notebook. $165.00.

★ 2006 ★
GETTING STARTED IN ORGANIZATION
DEVELOPMENT
  Resources for Education and Management
   Incorporated
  544 Medlock Road, Suite 210
  Decatur, Georgia 30030
Filmstrip with cassette. $65.00.

★ 2007 ★
INTRODUCING CHANGE
  Resources for Education and Management
   Incorporated
  544 Medlock Road, Suite 210
  Decatur, Georgia 30030
Filmstrip with cassette. $70.00.

★ 2008 ★
IS CHANGE A PROBLEM?
  Resources for Education and Management
   Incorporated
  544 Medlock Road, Suite 210
  Decatur, Georgia 30030
Filmstrip with cassette. $70.00.

★ 2009 ★
MAKING A CHANGE WORK
  Resources for Education and Management
   Incorporated
  544 Medlock Road, Suite 210
  Decatur, Georgia 30030
Filmstrip with cassette. $70.00.

★ 2010 ★
ORGANIZATION DEVELOPMENT
  Lansford Publishing Company
  Post Office Box 8711
  San Jose, California 95155
Multimedia kit. $189.95.

★ 2011 ★
WHAT IS ORGANIZATION DEVELOPMENT?
  Resources for Education and Management
   Incorporated
  544 Medlock Road, Suite 210
  Decatur, Georgia 30030
Filmstrip with cassette. $65.00.

Printed Materials

★ 2012 ★
ORGANIZATION DEVELOPMENT FOR MANAGERS
Glenn H. Varney
  Addison Wesley Publishing Company Incorporated
  Jacob Way
  Reading, Massachusetts 01867
Workbook. $8.95.

ORGANIZATIONAL STRUCTURE

Audio Cassettes/Tapes

★ 2013 ★
METHODICAL REORGANIZATION – SYSTEMIC
DECISIONS
  Thompson-Mitchell and Associates
  3384 Peachtree Road Northeast
  Atlanta, Georgia 30326
Cassette. $6.00.

Correspondence Courses

★ 2014 ★
ORGANIZATION AND MANAGEMENT
Eugene E. Evans
    Western Kentucky University
    Office of Special Programs
    Bowling Green, Kentucky   42101
Independent study course.

Films/Video/Filmstrips

★ 2015 ★
GROWTH STAGES OF ORGANIZATION
    BNA Communications Incorporated
    9401 Decoverly Hall Road
    Rockville, Maryland 20850
Film.

Multimedia Kits

★ 2016 ★
COMPANY ORGANIZATION
    Gamco-Siboney
    Box 1911
    Big Spring, Texas 79720
2 filmstrips with cassette. $34.00.

Printed Materials

★ 2017 ★
BUSINESS PRINCIPLES ORGANIZATION AND
MANAGEMENT
Herbert Tonne
    McGraw-Hill Book Company
    1221 Avenue of the Americas
    New York, New York 10019
Text and guides. $14.00.

★ 2018 ★
ORGANIZATIONAL BEHAVIOR: CONCEPTS AND
APPLICATIONS
Jerry L. Gray, Frederick Starke
    Charles E. Merrill Publishing Company
    1300 Alum Creek Drive
    Box 508
    Columbus, Ohio 43216
Text with exercises.   1977. $13.95.

ORGANIZATIONAL VALUES

Audio Cassettes/Tapes

★ 2019 ★
HUMAN VALUES IN MANAGEMENT
Dr. John R. Van De Water
    Van De Water Associates
    7914 Jason Avenue
    Canoga Park, California 91304
Cassette with workbook. $23.50.

Films/Video/Filmstrips

★ 2020 ★
VALUES AND DECISIONS
    Salenger Educational Media
    1635 12th Street
    Santa Monica, California 90404
Film.

Games/Simulations

★ 2021 ★
OFFICE MANAGEMENT
    Didactic Systems Incorporated
    Box 457
    Cranford, New Jersey 07016
Simulation game. $24.00.

Multimedia Kits

★ 2022 ★
APPROACHES TO ORGANIZATION IMPROVEMENTS
    Resources for Education and Management
        Incorporated
    544 Medlock Road, Suite 210
    Decatur, Georgia 30030
Filmstrip with cassette. $65.00.

★ 2023 ★
DEVELOPING GOAL ATTITUDES
    Gamco-Siboney
    Box 1911
    Big Spring, Texas 79720
2 filmstrips with cassettes. $34.00.

★ 2024 ★
THE IMPORTANCE OF ATTITUDES
    Gamco-Siboney
    Box 1911
    Big Spring, Texas 79720
3 filmstrips with cassette. $51.00.

★ 2025 ★
JOB ATTITUDES - THE COMPANY AND THE
COMMUNITY
    Gamco-Siboney
    Box 1911
    Big Spring, Texas 79720
2 filmstrips with cassette. $34.00.

★ 2026 ★
THE WELL-BEING OF AN ORGANIZATION
    Resources for Education and Management
       Incorporated
    544 Medlock Road, Suite 210
    Decatur, Georgia 30030
Filmstrip with cassette. $65.00.

ORGANIZING SKILLS

    See also: headings under Management;
      Personal Development; Planning

Multimedia Kits

★ 2027 ★
ORGANIZING
    Resources for Education and Management
       Incorporated
    544 Medlock Road, Suite 210
    Decatur, Georgia 30030
Filmstrip with cassette. $60.00.

★ 2028 ★
ORGANIZING AND PLANNING SKILLS
    Resources for Education and Management
       Incorporated
    544 Medlock Road, Suite 210
    Decatur, Georgia 30030
Filmstrip with cassette. $60.00.

★ 2029 ★
ORGANIZING FOR RESULTS
    Resources for Education and Management
       Incorporated
    544 Medlock Road, Suite 210
    Decatur, Georgia 30030
Filmstrip with cassette. $60.00.

OSHA
See: SAFETY, OSHA

PACKAGING

Films/Video/Filmstrips

★ 2030 ★
PACKAGING DESIGN
    Scope Productions Incorporated
    Post Office Box 5515
    Fresno, California 93755
3 films (8 mm) and student guides. $63.00.

Programmed learning Materials

★ 2031 ★
CASING MACHINERY
TPC Training Systems
    Technical Publishing Company
    1301 South Grove Avenue
    Barrington, Illinois 60016
Programmed text of 10 lessons. $22.75.

★ 2032 ★
INTRODUCTION TO PACKAGING
TPC Training Systems
    Technical Publishing Company
    1301 South Grove Avenue
    Barrington, Illinois 60010
Programmed text of 10 lessons. $22.50.

★ 2033 ★
PACKAGING MACHINERY
TPC Training Systems
    Technical Publishing Company
    1301 South Grove Avenue
    Barrington, Illinois 60010
Programmed text of 10 lessons. $22.50.

PAINTING CONTRACTING

Correspondence Courses

★ 2034 ★
PAINTING CONTRACTING COURSE
    International Correspondence School
    Scranton, Pennsylvania 18515
Multi-module correspondence course.

PAPER MAKING

Correspondence Courses

★ 2035 ★
PAPER MAKING
 International Correspondence School
 Scranton, Pennsylvania 18515
Multi-module correspondence course.

★ 2036 ★
PULP AND PAPER TECHNOLOGY
 International Correspondence School
 Scranton, Pennsylvania 18515
Multi-module correspondence course.

★ 2037 ★
PULP MAKING
 International Correspondence School
 Scranton, Pennsylvania 18515
Multi-module correspondence course.

PARLIAMENTARY PROCEDURE

Programmed Learning Materials

★ 2038 ★
PARLIAMENTARY PROCEDURE
J. Gray, R. Rea
 Scott, Foresman and Company
 1900 East Lake Avenue
 Glenview, Illinois 60025
Programmed text. $3.00.

PASTORAL MINISTRIES

See also: Preaching

Audio Cassettes/Tapes

★ 2039 ★
THE PASTOR AS A PERSON
 Southern Baptist Convention
 Seminary Extension Department
 460 James Robertson Parkway
 Nashville, Tennessee 37219
Cassette, home study course. $26.90.

★ 2040 ★
THE PASTOR AS COUNSELOR
 Southern Baptist Convention
 Seminary Extension Department
 460 James Robertson Parkway
 Nashville, Tennessee 37219
Cassette, home study program. $15.00.

★ 2041 ★
THE PASTOR AS LEADER
 Southern Baptist Convention
 Seminary Extension Department
 460 James Robertson Parkway
 Nashville, Tennessee 37219
Cassette, home study program. $15.00.

★ 2042 ★
THE PASTOR IN SECULAR EMPLOYMENT
 Southern Baptist Convention
 Seminary Extension Department
 460 James Robertson Parkway
 Nashville, Tennessee 37219
Cassette, home study program. $15.00.

★ 2043 ★
THE WORK OF A PASTOR
 Southern Baptist Convention
 Seminary Extension Department
 460 James Robertson Parkway
 Nashville, Tennessee 37219
Cassette, home study program. $15.00.

PATENTS

Correspondence Courses

★ 2044 ★
PATENT PREPARATION AND PROSECUTION
PRACTICE
 Patent Resources Institute Incorporated
 2011 Eye Street, Northwest
 Washington, D.C. 20006
7 volume self-study program. $450.00.

PERFORMANCE APPRAISAL

See also: Accountability;
Assessment

Audio Cassettes/Tapes

★ 2045 ★
THE APPRAISAL INTERVIEW
American Management Associations
135 West 50th Street
New York, New York 10020
Cassette. $18.00.

★ 2046 ★
CAPITALIZING ON EMPLOYEE IDEAS -
MEASURING EMPLOYEE PERFORMANCE
Thompson-Mitchell and Associates
3384 Peachtree Road Northeast
Atlanta, Georgia 30326
Cassette. $6.00.

★ 2047 ★
EVALUATING HUMAN PERFORMANCE
Training House Incorporated
Box 688
Binghamton, New York 13902
Cassette with workbook. $36.00.

★ 2048 ★
HOW TO INSTALL A TOUGH-MINDED
PERFORMANCE APPRAISAL SYSTEM
Thompson-Mitchell and Associates
3384 Peachtree Road Northeast
Atlanta, Georgia 30326
Cassette. $19.95.

★ 2049 ★
MEASURING PEOPLE
Educational Century Programming
1201 East Johnson Street
Jonesboro, Arkansas 72401
Cassette. $6.00.

★ 2050 ★
PERFORMANCE STANDARDS AND SPECIFIC
OBJECTIVES
Development Digest Incorporated
3347 Motor Avenue
Los Angeles, California 90034
Cassette. $13.75.

Correspondence Courses

★ 2051 ★
APPRAISING EMPLOYEE PERFORMANCE
Didactic System Incorporated
Box 457
Cranford, New Jersey 07016
Self-study text. $9.00.

Films/Video/Filmstrips

★ 2052 ★
EVALUATION AND FOLLOW-UP
Addison Wesley Publishing Company Incorporated
Jacob Way
Reading, Massachusetts 01867
Filmstrip. $55.00.

★ 2053 ★
PERFORMANCE APPRAISAL
Van De Water Associates
7914 Jason Avenue
Canoga Park, California 91304
Video tape. $495.00 (rental available).

Games/Simulations

★ 2054 ★
LOU BOXELL'S PERFORMANCE REVIEW
Training House Incorporated
Box 688
Binghamton, New York 13902
Simulation game. $60.00.

Multimedia Kits

★ 2055 ★
ACHIEVING MORE EFFECTIVE PERFORMANCE:
OVERCOMING FEAR OF REJECTION
Ergonco Performance Source
Northwest O'Hare Office Park, Suite 119
2474 Dempster Street
Des Plains, Illinois 60016
Multimedia self-study program.

★ 2056 ★
EVALUATING HUMAN PERFORMANCE: GUIDE-
LINES FOR DEVELOPING EMPLOYEES
Ergonco Performance Source
Northwest O'Hare Office Park, Suite 119
2474 Dempster Street
Des Plains, Illinois 60016
Multimedia self-study program.

★ 2057 ★
EVALUATION AND FOLLOW-UP
Resources for Education and Management
Incorporated
544 Medlock Road, Suite 210
Decatur, Georgia 30030
Filmstrip with cassette. $55.00.

★ 2058 ★
HOW TO APPRAISE YOUR PEOPLE
Resources for Education and Management
Incorporated
544 Medlock Road, Suite 210
Decatur, Georgia 30030
Filmstrip with cassette. $60.00.

★ 2059 ★
THE NUTS AND BOLTS OF PERFORMANCE
APPRAISAL
Joe Batten
Creative Media Films
820 Keo Way
Des Moines, Iowa 50309
Film or video cassette and guide. $450.00 (rental available).

★ 2060 ★
PERFORMANCE APPRAISAL: THE HUMAN
DYNAMICS
CRM McGraw Hill Films
110 15th Street
Del Mar, California 92014
Film or video cassette.

Printed Materials

★ 2061 ★
AN ASSESSMENT CENTER PROGRAM FOR
SUPERVISORS
Addison Wesley Publishing Company Incorporated
Jacob Way
Reading, Massachusetts 01867
Printed material. $325.00.

★ 2062 ★
EFFECTIVE MOTIVATION THROUGH PERFORMANCE
APPRAISAL
Robert Lefton, et al.
John Wiley and Sons
605 Third Avenue
New York, New York 10016
Book. $17.95.

★ 2063 ★
THE PERFORMANCE APPRAISAL KIT
Addison Wesley Publishing Company Incorporated
Jacob Way
Reading, Massachusetts 01867
Printed material. $75.00.

PERFORMING ARTS

Correspondence Courses

★ 2064 ★
COMPOSE MUSIC
King Palmer - Teach Yourself Series
David McKay Company Incorporated
750 Third Avenue
New York, New York 10017
Self-study text. 1974.

Films/Video/Filmstrips

★ 2065 ★
CONTEMPORARY DANCE FORMS
Scope Productions Incorporated
Post Office Box 5515
Fresno, California 93755
8 films (8 mm), and student guides. $168.00.

★ 2066 ★
PERFORMING ARTS
Scope Productions Incorporated
Post Office Box 5515
3 films (8 mm), and student guides. $63.00.

PERSIAN

Audio Cassettes/Tapes

★ 2067 ★
SPOKEN PERSIAN
Serge Obolinsky
Spoken Language Services Incorporated
Post Office Box 783
Ithaca, New York 14850
Cassette and workbooks.

Printed Materials

★ 2068 ★
LEARN THE PERSIAN LANGUAGE
Saphrograph Company
194 Elizabeth Street
New York, New York 10012
Book.

★ 2069 ★
LEARN THE PERSIAN LANGUAGE
C. Elwell-Sutton
    P. Shalom Publications
    5409 18th Avenue
    Brooklyn, New York 11204
Book. $7.50.

★ 2070 ★
TEACH YOURSELF PERSIAN
John Mace
    David McKay Company Incorporated
    750 Third Avenue
    New York, New York 10017
Self-study text. $3.95.

PERSONAL DEVELOPMENT

See also: Creativity; Memory; Motivation;
                Success

Audio Cassettes/Tapes

★ 2071 ★
AS A MAN THINKETH
James Allen
    Tape Rental Library Incorporated
    Post Office, Box 2107
    2507 Edna Drive
    South Vineland, New Jersey 08360
2 cassettes. $18.00.

★ 2072 ★
AS OTHERS SEE US
Frank G. Maher
    Tape Rental Library Incorporated
    Post Office Box 2107
    2507 Edna Drive
    South Vineland, New Jersey 08360
Cassette.

★ 2073 ★
BE A LEADER/BE A FOLLOWER
    Educational Century Programming
    1201 East Johnson Street
    Jonesboro, Arkansas 72401
Cassette. $6.00.

★ 2074 ★
CONQUERING NUMBERS
    Educational Century Programming
    1201 East Johnson Street
    Jonesboro, Arkansas 72401
Cassette. $6.00.

★ 2075 ★
CORPORATE BIGAMY: HOW TO LIVE WITH JOB
AND FAMILY
    AMACOM
    American Management Associations
    135 West 50th Street
    New York, New York 10020
3 cassettes. $65.00.

★ 2076 ★
CRITICAL THINKING
    Educational Century Programming
    1201 East Johnson Street
    Jonesboro, Arkansas 72401
Cassette. $6.00.

★ 2077 ★
CYBERNETICS FOR GREATER SUCCESS
    General Cassette Corporation
    1324 North 22nd Avenue
    Phoenix, Arizona 85009
4 cassettes. $39.50.

★ 2078 ★
CYBERNETICS FOR GREATER SUCCESS
Thom Norman
    Tape Rental Library Incorporated
    Post Office Box 2107
    2507 Edna Drive
    South Vineland, New Jersey 08360
4 cassettes. $39.50.

★ 2079 ★
DEVELOPING ENTHUSIASM
Paul W. Schuette
    Tape Rental Library Incorporated
    Post Office Box 2107
    2507 Edna Drive
    South Vineland, New Jersey 08360
Cassette. $7.95.

★ 2080 ★
DYNAMICS FOR MOOD CONTROL
    Learning Dynamics
    167 Corey Road
    Boston, Massachusetts 02146
6 cassettes. $129.00.

★ 2081 ★
THE DYNAMICS OF MOOD CONTROL
    Tape Rental Library Incorporated
    Post Office Box 2107, 2507 Edna Drive
    South Vineland, New Jersey 08360
6 cassettes with workbook.

★ 2082 ★
EVALUATING HUMAN DRIVES/THE CHAIN-LINKS
OF HABIT
　　　Educational Century Programming
　　　1201 East Johnson Street
　　　Jonesboro, Arkansas 72401
Cassette. $6.00.

★ 2083 ★
EVERYTHING YOU'VE ALWAYS WANTED TO
KNOW ABOUT ENERGY BUT WERE TO WEAK
TO ASK
Naura Hayden
　　　Success Motivation Institute
　　　5000 Lakewood Drive
　　　Waco, Texas 76710
Cassette. $9.95.

★ 2084 ★
EXERTING WILL POWER
　　　Educational Century Programming
　　　1201 East Johnson Street
　　　Jonesboro, Arkansas 72401
Cassette. $6.00.

★ 2085 ★
FRIENDSHIP
Orison S. Marden, M.D.
　　　Tape Rental Library Incorporated
　　　Post Office Box 2107
　　　2507 Edna Drive
　　　South Vineland, New Jersey 08360
Cassette. $4.95.

★ 2086 ★
THE GREATEST SECRET
　　　Thompson-Mitchell and Associates
　　　3384 Peachtree Road Northeast
　　　Atlanta, Georgia 30326
Cassette. $14.50.

★ 2087 ★
HANDLING PRESSURES
　　　Educational Century Programming
　　　1201 East Johnson Street
　　　Jonesboro, Arkansas 72401
Cassette. $6.00.

★ 2088 ★
HAPPINESS ON TAPE
Paul W. Schuette

　　　Tape Rental Library Incorporated
　　　Post Office Box 2107
　　　2507 Edna Drive
　　　South Vineland, New Jersey 08360
Cassette. $7.95.

★ 2089 ★
HOW TO DEVELOP THE POWER OF ENTHUSIASM
Paul J. Meyer
　　　Cassette House
　　　530 West Northwest Highway
　　　Mount Prospect, Illinois 60056
Cassette. $9.95.

★ 2090 ★
HOW TO GET PEOPLE TO THINK AND ACT
FAVORABLY WITH YOU
　　　Cassette House
　　　530 West Northwest Highway
　　　Mount Prospect, Illinois 60056
Cassette. $9.95.

★ 2091 ★
HOW TO LIVE 365 DAYS A YEAR
Dr. John A. Schindler
　　　Tape Rental Library Incorporated
　　　Post Office Box 2107
　　　2507 Edna Drive
　　　South Vineland, New Jersey 08360
Cassette.

★ 2092 ★
HOW TO LOSE WEIGHT
　　　Tape Rental Library Incorporated
　　　Post Office Box 2107
　　　2507 Edna Drive
　　　South Vineland, New Jersey 08360
Cassette. $9.98.

★ 2093 ★
HOW TO REALLY QUIT SMOKING
　　　Tape Rental Library Incorporated
　　　Post Office Box 2107
　　　2507 Edna Drive
　　　South Vineland, New Jersey 08360
Cassette. $9.95.

★ 2094 ★
I ENJOY SWIMMING
Paul W. Schuette
　　　Tape Rental Library Incorporated
　　　Post Office Box 2107, 2507 Edna Drive
　　　South Vineland, New Jersey 08360
Cassette. $7.95.

★ 2095 ★
I WANT TO QUIT SMOKING
Paul W. Schuette
    Tape Rental Library Incorporated
    Post Office Box 2107
    2507 Edna Drive
    South Vineland, New Jersey 08360
Cassette. $7.95.

★ 2096 ★
IMPROVE YOUR ENVIRONMENT/DEFINING SELF-
DRIVE
    Educational Century Programming
    1201 East Johnson Street
    Jonesboro, Arkansas 72401
Cassette. $6.00.

★ 2097 ★
IMPROVING ENGLISH AND SPEECH
    Educational Century Programming
    1201 East Johnson Street
    Jonesboro, Arkansas 72401
Cassette. $6.00.

★ 2098 ★
KEEPING INFORMED
    Educational Century Programming
    1201 East Johnson Street
    Jonesboro, Arkansas 72401
Cassette. $6.00.

★ 2099 ★
THE KINGSHIP OF SELF-CONTROL
William George Jordan
    Tape Rental Library Incorporated
    Post Office Box 2107
    2507 Edna Drive
    South Vineland, New Jersey 08360
Cassette. $8.95.

★ 2100 ★
LEARN TO LEARN
    Educational Century Programming
    1201 East Johnson Street
    Jonesboro, Arkansas 72401
Cassette. $6.00.

★ 2101 ★
LIFE'S HIGHER GOALS
Bob Richards
    Cassette House
    530 West Northwest Highway
    Mount Prospect, Illinois 60056
Cassette. $12.00.

★ 2102 ★
LISTEN TO LIFE
Norman Vincent Peale
    Cassette House
    530 West Northwest Highway
    Mount Prospect, Illinois 60056
6 cassettes. $44.95.

★ 2103 ★
LISTEN TO LIFE
Dr. Norman Vincent Peale
    Tape Rental Library Incorporated
    Post Office Box 2107
    2507 Edna Drive
    South Vineland, New Jersey 08360
6 cassettes. $44.95.

★ 2104 ★
LIVING PSYCHO-CYBERNETICS
Maxwell Maltz
    Tape Rental Library Incorporated
    Post Office Box 2107
    2507 Edna Drive
    South Vineland, New Jersey 08360
6 cassettes.

★ 2105 ★
MAKE YOUR OWN OPPORTUNITIES/PRODUCTIVE
WORK IS THERAPEUTIC
    Educational Century Programming
    1201 East Johnson Street
    Jonesboro, Arkansas 72401
Cassette. $6.00.

★ 2106 ★
MAKING YOUR IDEAS WORK IN YOUR
ORGANIZATION
    Thompson-Mitchell and Associates
    3384 Peachtree Road Northeast
    Atlanta, Georgia 30326
Cassette. $15.00.

★ 2107 ★
OVERCOMING LONELINESS
Paul W. Schuette
    Tape Rental Library Incorporated
    Post Office Box 2107
    2507 Edna Drive
    South Vineland, New Jersey 08360
Cassette. $7.95.

★ 2108 ★
OVERCOMING PROCRASTINATION
Paul W. Schuette
Tape Rental Library Incorporated
Post Office Box 2107
2507 Edna Drive
South Vineland, New Jersey 08360
Cassette. $7.95.

★ 2109 ★
PACE-SETTER HIGH PERFORMANCE PROGRAM
The J. W. Newman Corporation
4311 Wilshire Boulevard
Los Angeles, California 90010
Cassettes and workbooks. $240.00.

★ 2110 ★
PEACE OF MIND
Paul W. Schuette
Tape Rental Library Incorporated
Post Office Box 2107
2507 Edna Drive
South Vineland, New Jersey 08360
Cassette. $7.95.

★ 2111 ★
PERSONAL DEVELOPMENT PORTFOLIO
Thompson-Mitchell and Associates
3384 Peachtree Road Northeast
Atlanta, Georgia 30326
6 cassettes. $95.00.

★ 2112 ★
POSITIVE SELF-CONCEPT
Lansford Publishing Company
Post Office Box 8711
San Jose, California 95155
4 cassettes. $80.00.

★ 2113 ★
POWER! HOW TO GET IT, HOW TO USE IT
Michael Korda
Success Motivation Institute
5000 Lakewood Drive
Waco, Texas 76710
Cassette. $9.95.

★ 2114 ★
THE POWER OF CONCENTRATION
Educational Century Programming
1201 East Johnson Street
Jonesboro, Arkansas 72401
Cassette. $6.00.

★ 2115 ★
POWER OF GOAL SETTING
Paul J. Meyer
Cassette House
530 West Northwest Highway
Mount Prospect, Illinois 60056
Cassette. $9.95.

★ 2116 ★
THE POWER OF RIGHT THOUGHT
Ella Wheeler Wilcox
Tape Rental Library Incorporated
Post Office Box 2107
2507 Edna Drive
South Vineland, New Jersey 08360
Cassette. $8.95.

★ 2117 ★
PREVENTION OF TROUBLE
Educational Century Programming
1201 East Johnson Street
Jonesboro, Arkansas 72401
Cassette. $6.00.

★ 2118 ★
"THE PRO ON THE GO" THE CHALLENGE
OF A PRO
Art Holst
Tape Rental Library Incorporated
Post Office Box 2107
2507 Edna Drive
South Vineland, New Jersey 08360
2 cassettes. $5.95.

★ 2119 ★
PURSUIT OF HAPPINESS
Winston K. Pendleton
Tape Rental Library Incorporated
Post Office Box 2107
2507 Edna Drive
South Vineland, New Jersey 08360
2 cassettes. $34.95.

★ 2120 ★
REVIEW YOUR SOCIAL HABITS/BECOME
INVOLVED WITH LIFE
Educational Century Programming
1201 East Johnson Street
Jonesboro, Arkansas 72401
Cassette. $6.00.

★ 2121 ★
SELF-CONTROL
Educational Century Programming
1201 East Johnson Street
Jonesboro, Arkansas 72401
Cassette. $6.00.

★ 2122 ★
SELF ORGANIZATION
Educational Century Programming
1201 East Johnson Street
Jonesboro, Arkansas 72401
Cassette. $6.00.

★ 2123 ★
SUCCESS THROUGH A POSITIVE MENTAL
ATTITUDE
Napoleon Hill, W. Clement Stone
Tape Rental Library Incorporated
Post Office Box 2107
2507 Edna Drive
South Vineland, New Jersey 08360
Cassette.

★ 2124 ★
SUCCESSFUL JOB THINKING - YOUR PERSONAL
LIFE
Thompson-Mitchell and Associates
3384 Peachtree Road Northeast
Atlanta, Georgia 30326
Cassette. $6.00.

★ 2125 ★
THINKING AS A SCIENCE
Henry Hazlett
Tape Rental Library Incorporated
Post Office Box 2107
2507 Edna Drive
South Vineland, New Jersey 08360
Cassette.

★ 2126 ★
THINKING MYSELF THIN
Paul W. Schuette
Tape Rental Library Incorporated
Post Office Box 2107
2507 Edna Drive
South Vineland, New Jersey 08360
Cassette. $7.95.

★ 2127 ★
USE YOUR MENTAL COMPUTER/TECHNIQUES OF
CREATIVE CONCEPTION
Educational Century Programming
1201 East Johnson Street
Jonesboro, Arkansas 72401
Cassette. $6.00.

★ 2128 ★
USING NATURAL TALENTS
Educational Century Programming
1201 East Johnson Street
Jonesboro, Arkansas 72401
Cassette. $6.00.

★ 2129 ★
THE VITAL FORCE (Personal goal setting)
Fred Herman
Tape Rental Library Incorporated
Post Office Box 2107
2507 Edna Drive
South Vineland, New Jersey 08360
Cassette. $12.00.

★ 2130 ★
WHO CARES ABOUT ME?
Bill Sands
Tape Rental Library Incorporated
Post Office Box 2107
2507 Edna Drive
South Vineland, New Jersey 08360
Cassette. $9.95.

★ 2131 ★
WHY I LOVE MY JOB
Art Fettig
Tape Rental Library Incorporated
Post Office Box 2107
2507 Edna Drive
South Vineland, New Jersey 08360
Cassette. $7.95.

Films/Video/Filmstrips

★ 2132 ★
DEALING WITH PEOPLE
Salenger Educational Media
1635 12th Street
Santa Monica, California 90404
Film.

★ 2133 ★
HOW DO YOU LOOK WHEN IT COUNTS?
National Restaurant Association
One IBM Plaza, Suite 2600
Chicago, Illinois 60611
Video cartridge or 8 mm, 16 mm, and study guide.
$190.00.

★ 2134 ★
UNDERSTANDING YOURSELF
Thompson-Mitchell and Associates
3384 Peachtree Road Northeast
Atlanta, Georgia 30326
Filmstrip. $125.00.

★ 2135 ★
"WHO AM I?" (How moods effect work)
Resource Incorporated
13902 North Dale Mabry Highway
Tampa, Florida 33624
Video cartridge and workbook available. $100.00.

★ 2136 ★
"WHO ARE YOU?" (Explanation of various
personality patterns)
Resource Incorporated
13902 North Dale Mabry Highway
Tampa, Florida 33624
Video cartridge and workbook available. $100.00.

Multimedia Kits

★ 2137 ★
AWARENESS
Thompson-Mitchell and Associates
3384 Peachtree Road Northeast
Atlanta, Georgia 30326
Filmstrip with cassette. $65.00.

★ 2138 ★
DEVELOPING GOOD ATTITUDES
Gamco-Siboney
Box 1911
Big Spring, Texas 79720
2 filmstrips with cassette. $34.00.

★ 2139 ★
ENTHUSIASM
Thompson-Mitchell and Associates
3384 Peachtree Road Northeast
Atlanta, Georgia 30326
Filmstrip with cassette. $65.00.

★ 2140 ★
EXAMINING THE WILL TO WORK
H. S. Strauss Productions
619 West 54th Street
New York, New York 10019
Filmstrip with record. $80.00.

★ 2141 ★
THE IMPORTANCE OF ATTITUDES
Gamco-Siboney
Box 1911
Big Spring, Texas 79720
3 filmstrips with cassette. $51.00.

★ 2142 ★
INTEGRITY
Thompson-Mitchell and Associates
3384 Peachtree Road Northeast
Atlanta, Georgia 30326
Filmstrip with cassette. $65.00.

★ 2143 ★
SELF DEVELOPMENT: KEY TO THE FUTURE
Resources for Education and Management
Incorporated
544 Medlock Road, Suite 210
Decatur, Georgia 30030
Filmstrip with cassette. $60.00.

PERSONAL FINANCE
See: FINANCIAL PLANNING

PERSONAL HEALTH
See: HEALTH, PERSONAL

PERSONNEL MANAGEMENT

See also: headings under Management;
headings under Supervision

Audio Cassettes/Tapes

★ 2144 ★
DELEGATING RESPONSIBILITY - MEASURING
EMPLOYEE INITIATIVE
Thompson-Mitchell and Associates
3384 Peachtree Road Northeast
Atlanta, Georgia 30326
Cassette. $6.00.

★ 2145 ★
DRUG ABUSE AS A MANAGEMENT PROBLEM
American Management Associations
135 West 50th Street
New York, New York 10020
4 cassettes with workbook. $89.00.

★ 2146 ★
EXECUTAPE'S ALBUM ON PERSONNEL
MANAGEMENT
Thompson-Mitchell and Associates
3384 Peachtree Road Northeast
Atlanta, Georgia 30326
6 cassettes. $95.00.

★ 2147 ★
FACE TO FACE MANAGEMENT
Thompson-Mitchell and Associates
3384 Peachtree Road Northeast
Atlanta, Georgia 30326
4 cassettes. $39.00.

★ 2148 ★
FITTING THE EMPLOYEE TO THE JOB –
HANDLING OFFICE CONFLICTS
Thompson-Mitchell and Associates
3384 Peachtree Road Northeast
Atlanta, Georgia 30326
Cassette. $6.00.

★ 2149 ★
HANDLING COMPLAINTS AND GRIEVANCES
AMACOM
American Management Associations
135 West 50th Street
New York, New York 10020
Cassette. $18.00.

★ 2150 ★
HANDLING EMPLOYEE QUESTIONS ABOUT PAY
AMACOM
American Management Associations
135 West 50th Street
New York, New York 10020
Cassette with manual. $25.00.

★ 2151 ★
HANDLING THE GIFTED EMPLOYEE – HANDLING
PROBLEM EXECUTIVES
Thompson-Mitchell and Associates
3384 Peachtree Road Northeast
Atlanta, Georgia 30326
Cassette. $6.00.

★ 2152 ★
HANDLING THE PROBLEM EMPLOYEE
George Odiorne
MBO Incorporated
157 Pontoosic Road
Westfield, Massachusetts 01085
Cassette and manual. $15.00.

★ 2153 ★
THE HUMAN RESOURCES REVOLUTION
George Odiorne
MBO Incorporated
157 Pontoosic Road
Westfield, Massachusetts 01085
Cassette and workbook. $15.00.

★ 2154 ★
THE INDISPENSABLE EMPLOYEE – HIRING KEY
EMPLOYEE
Thompson-Mitchell and Associates
3384 Peachtree Road Northeast
Atlanta, Georgia 30326
Cassette. $6.00.

★ 2155 ★
MANAGEMENT OF PEOPLE
Educational Century Programming
1201 East Johnson Street
Jonesboro, Arkansas 72401
Cassette. $6.00.

★ 2156 ★
MANAGING COMPENSATION BY OBJECTIVES
George Odiorne
MBO Incorporated
157 Pontoosic Road
Westfield, Massachusetts 01085
Cassette and workbook. $15.00.

★ 2157 ★
MANAGING EMPLOYMENT BY OBJECTIVES
George Odiorne
MBO Incorporated
157 Pontoosic Road
Westfield, Massachusetts 01085
Cassette and workbook. $15.00.

★ 2158 ★
MANAGING HUMAN RESOURCES
George Odiorne
MBO Incorporated
157 Pontoosic Road
Westfield, Massachusetts 01085
Cassette and manual. $15.00.

★ 2159 ★

THE OBJECTIVES - CENTERED PERSONNEL
DEPARTMENT
George Odiorne
     MBO Incorporated
     157 Pontoosic Road
     Westfield, Massachusetts 01085
Cassette and workbook. $15.00.

★ 2160 ★

PEOPLE MANAGEMENT
     Tape Rental Library Incorporated
     Post Office Box 2107
     2507 Edna Drive
     South Vineland, New Jersey 08360
Cassette.

★ 2161 ★

PERSONNEL ADMINISTRATION BY OBJECTIVES
George Odiorne
     MBO Incorporated
     157 Pontoosic Road
     Westfield, Massachusetts 01085
6 cassettes and workbook. $100.00.

★ 2162 ★

PROBLEM EMPLOYEES - CAUSES AND CURES
     Thompson-Mitchell and Associates
     3384 Peachtree Road Northeast
     Atlanta, Georgia 30326
Cassette. $20.00.

★ 2163 ★

THE PROBLEMS OF JOB PROMOTION, JOB
APPRECIATION
     Thompson-Mitchell and Associates
     3384 Peachtree Road Northeast
     Atlanta, Georgia 30326
Cassette. $6.00.

★ 2164 ★

STAFF DEVELOPMENT
     Thompson-Mitchell and Associates
     3384 Peachtree Road Northeast
     Atlanta, Georgia 30326
18 cassettes and manuals. $168.75.

★ 2165 ★

YARDSTICKS FOR PERSONNEL MANAGEMENT
George Odiorne
     MBO Incorporated
     157 Pontoosic Road
     Westfield, Massachusetts 01085
Cassette and workbook. $15.00.

Correspondence Courses

★ 2166 ★

ADVANCED PERSONNEL ADMINISTRATION
     University of Nebraska
     511 Nebraska Hall
     Lincoln, Nebraska 68588
Correspondence course.

★ 2167 ★

PERSONNEL MANAGEMENT
     University of Florida
     Division of Continuing Education
     2012 West University Avenue
     Gainesville, Florida 32603
Correspondence course.

★ 2168 ★

PERSONNEL MANAGEMENT
     La Salle Extension University
     417 South Dearborn Street
     Chicago, Illinois 60605
Correspondence course.

★ 2169 ★

PERSONNEL MANAGEMENT
     University of Missouri
     Center for Independent Study
     514 South Fifth Street
     Columbia, Missouri 65211
Correspondence course. $80.00.

★ 2170 ★

POSITIVE DISCIPLINE
     Didactic Systems Incorporated
     Box 457
     Cranford, New Jersey 07016
Self-study text. $9.00.

Films/Video/Filmstrips

★ 2171 ★

ALTERNATIVES TO DISCHARGE: A CASE STUDY
     Salenger Educational Media
     1635 12th Street
     Santa Monica, California 90404
Film and worksheets. $325.00 (rental available).

★ 2172 ★

THE PEOPLE FACTOR: THE HAWTHORNE STUDIES
FOR TODAY'S MANAGERS
     Salenger Educational Media
     1635 12th Street
     Santa Monica, California 90404

Film guide and tests. $335.00 (rental available).

Games/Simulations

★ 2173 ★
GRIEVANCE HANDLING (Industrial)
      Didactic Systems Incorporated
      Box 457
      Cranford, New Jersey   07016
Simulation game. $24.00.

★ 2174 ★
GRIEVANCE HANDLING (Non-industrial)
      Didactic Systems Incorporated
      Box 457
      Cranford, New Jersey   07016
Simulation game. $24.00.

★ 2175 ★
PEOPLE MANAGEMENT GAME SEMINAR
      Society of Manufacturing Engineers
      20501 Ford Road
      Post Office Box 930
      Dearborn, Michigan   48128
Simulation with correspondent feedback. $110.00.

Multimedia Kits

★ 2176 ★
COMPANY ORGANIZATION
      Gamco-Siboney
      Box 1911
      Big Spring, Texas   79720
2 filmstrips with cassettes. $34.00.

★ 2177 ★
GETTING THE JOB DONE THROUGH OTHERS
      Resources for Education and Management
         Incorporated
      544 Medlock Road, Suite 210
      Decatur, Georgia   30030
Filmstrip with cassette. $60.00.

★ 2178 ★
MATCHING PEOPLE AND POSITIONS
      Resources for Education and Management
         Incorporated
      544 Medlock Road, Suite 210
      Decatur, Georgia   30030
Filmstrip with cassette. $60.00.

Printed Materials

★ 2179 ★
MANAGEMENT AND SUPERVISION OF PEOPLE
      C. L. Carter Jr. and Associates Incorporated
      434 First Bank and Trust Building
      811 South Central Expressway
      Richardson, Texas   75080
Text. $26.50.

★ 2180 ★
PERSONNEL MANAGEMENT
      Scientific Methods Incorporated
      Box 195
      Austin, Texas   78767
Workbook. $6.00.

Programmed Learning Materials

★ 2181 ★
PERSONNEL ADMINISTRATION
George S. Odiorne
      Learning Systems Company
      1818 Ridge Road
      Homewood, Illinois   60430
Programmed learning aid. $4.50.

PERSONNEL SELECTION

See also: Interviewing

Audio Cassettes/Tapes

★ 2182 ★
SELECTION OF MEN (Hiring and appraising new
personnel)
      Tape Rental Library Incorporated
      Post Office Box 2107
      2507 Edna Drive
      South Vineland, New Jersey   08360
6 cassettes. $90.00.

Correspondence Courses

★ 2183 ★
SELECTION AND TRAINING IN BUSINESS AND
INDUSTRY
      Western Washington State College
      Center for Continuing Education
      Edens Hall South
      Bellingham, Washington   98225
Correspondence course.

PERT (PROGRAM EVALUATION AND REVIEW TECHNIQUE)
See: PROGRAM EVALUATION AND REVIEW TECHNIQUE (PERT)

PHARMACOLOGY
See: headings under HEALTH

PHOTOGRAPHY

Correspondence Courses

★ 2184 ★
PHOTOGRAPHY
    American School of Photography
    25 Andrews Drive
    West Paterson, New Jersey 07424
Correspondence course.

★ 2185 ★
PHOTOGRAPHY
    Famous Schools
    Westport, Connecticut 06880
Correspondence course.

★ 2186 ★
PHOTOGRAPHY
    School of Modern Photography
    1500 Cardinal Drive
    Little Falls, New Jersey 07424
Correspondence course.

Films/Video/Filmstrips

★ 2187 ★
PHOTOGRAPHY
    Scope Productions Incorporated
    Post Office Box 5515
    Fresno, California 93755
10 films (8 mm) and student guides. $210.00.

PHYSICAL SCIENCE

Correspondence Courses

★ 2188 ★
GENERAL PHYSICS FOR THE LIFE SCIENCES

University of Nebraska
511 Nebraska Hall
Lincoln, Nebraska 68588
Correspondence course.

PHYSIOLOGY
See: headings under HEALTH

PIANO TUNING

Correspondence Courses

★ 2189 ★
PIANO TUNING
    Aubrey Willis School
    Post Office Drawer 15190
    Orlando, Florida 32858
Home study program. $450.00.

★ 2190 ★
PIANO TUNING
    Empire School of Piano Tuning
    1753 Southwest 23rd Terrace
    Miami, Florida 33145
Multi unit course with tests. $540.00.

Printed Materials

★ 2191 ★
PIANO TUNING, REPAIR AND REBUILDING
Floyd Stevens
    Nelson-Hall Publishers
    325 West Jackson Boulevard
    Chicago, Illinois 60606
Text. $29.95.

PIPEFITTING

Correspondence Courses

★ 2192 ★
PIPEFITTING
    International Correspondence School
    Scranton, Pennsylvania 18515
Multi-module correspondence course.

Programmed Learning Materials

★ 2193 ★
LAYOUT PRACTICES
    E. I. du Pont de Nemours and Company
    Applied Technology Division
    Room B 4204
    Wilmington, Delaware 19898
Programmed course of approximately 7 1/2 hours.
$15.60.

★ 2194 ★
MANUALLY CUTTING AND REAMING PIPE
    E. I. du Pont de Nemours and Company
    Applied Technology Division
    Room B 4204
    Wilmington, Delaware 19898
Programmed course of approximately 4 1/2 hours.
$10.90.

★ 2195 ★
MEASUREMENT AND LAYOUT
    E. I. du Pont de Nemours and Company
    Applied Technology Division
    Room B 4204
    Wilmington, Delaware 19898
Programmed course of approximately 36 hours.
$32.60.

★ 2196 ★
PIPE AND FITTING IDENTIFICATION
    E. I. du Pont de Nemours and Company
    Applied Technology Division
    Room B 4204
    Wilmington, Delaware 19898
Programmed course of approximately 14 hours.
$25.30.

★ 2197 ★
SIMPLE AND ROLLING OFFSETS
    E. I. du Pont de Nemours and Company
    Applied Technology Division
    Room B 4204
    Wilmington, Delaware 19898
Programmed course of approximately 20 hours.
$32.60.

PLANNING

See also: Program Evaluation and Review
            Technique (PERT)

Audio Cassettes/Tapes

★ 2198 ★
IMPROVING PROFITS AND PERFORMANCE
THROUGH MORE EFFECTIVE CORPORATE PLANNING
    Tape Rental Library Incorporated
    Post Office Box 2107
    2507 Edna Drive
    South Vineland, New Jersey 08360
12 cassettes. $295.00.

Correspondence Courses

★ 2199 ★
OPERATIONS PLANNING AND CONTROL SYSTEMS
    University of Nebraska
    511 Nebraska Hall
    Lincoln, Nebraska 68588
Correspondence course.

Games/Simulations

★ 2200 ★
LONG RANGE PLANNING
    Didactic Systems Incorporated
    Box 457
    Cranford, New Jersey 07016
Simulation game. $24.00.

Printed Materials

★ 2201 ★
PLANNING AND CONTROL FOR MANAGERS
    American Management Associations
    135 West 50th Street
    New York, New York 10020
Self-study text. $65.00.

Programmed Learning Materials

★ 2202 ★
HOW TO SET OBJECTIVES
    Preston Publishing Company
    151 East 50th Street
    New York, New York 10022
Programmed text. $10.00.

★ 2203 ★
MACROECONOMICS AND COMPANY PLANNING
    American Management Associations
    135 West 50th Street
    New York, New York 10020
Programmed text. $50.00.

★ 2204 ★
PLANNING-SCHEDULING-CONTROLLING
  Preston Publishing Company
  151 East 50th Street
  New York, New York 10022
Programmed text. $10.00.

PLASTICS

Films/Video/Filmstrips

★ 2205 ★
PLASTICS
  Society of Manufacturing Engineers
  20501 Ford Road
  Post Office Box 930
  Dearborn, Michigan 48128
Video tape.

Programmed Learning Materials

★ 2206 ★
FUNDAMENTALS OF PLASTICS
  Penton/IPC Education Division
  614 Superior Avenue West
  Cleveland, Ohio 44113
Programmed text. $15.00.

★ 2207 ★
PLASTICS, THEIR USE IN MANUFACTURING
Laurence Pursglove
  Entelek Incorporated
  42 Pleasant Street
  Newburyport, Massachusetts 01950
Programmed text. $58.00.

★ 2208 ★
PLASTICS: THEIR USE IN MANUFACTURING
  Society of Manufacturing Engineers
  20501 Ford Road
  Post Office Box 930
  Dearborn, Michigan 48128
Programmed learning course. $57.50.

PLUMBING

See also: Custodial Maintenance

Correspondence Courses

★ 2209 ★
PLUMBING

  International Correspondence School
  Scranton, Pennsylvania 18515
Multi-module correspondence course.

★ 2210 ★
PLUMBING AND HEATING
  International Correspondence School
  Scranton, Pennsylvania 18515
Multi-module correspondence course.

★ 2211 ★
PRACTICAL PLUMBING
  International Correspondence School
  Scranton, Pennsylvania 18515
Multi-module correspondence course.

Printed Materials

★ 2212 ★
PLUMBING
J. H. Innes
  David McKay Company Incorporated
  750 Third Avenue
  New York, New York 10017
Self-study book. 1975. $3.95.

POLICE SCIENCE

Correspondence Courses

★ 2213 ★
CORRECTIONAL INSTITUTIONS
  Indiana State University
  Independent Study Office
  Terre Haute, Indiana 47809
Independent study course.

★ 2214 ★
CRIMINAL INVESTIGATION
  Indiana State University
  Independent Study Office
  Terre Haute, Indiana 47809
Independent study course.

★ 2215 ★
CRIMINOLOGY
  Indiana State University
  Independent Study Office
  Terre Haute, Indiana 47809
Independent study course.

★ 2216 ★

INTRODUCTION TO LAW ENFORCEMENT
 Bringham Young University
 Department of Independent Study
 210 Herald R. Clark Building
 Provo, Utah 84602
Correspondence course. $81.50.

★ 2217 ★

INTRODUCTION TO LAW ENFORCEMENT
 University of Nebraska
 511 Nebraska Hall
 Lincoln, Nebraska 68588
Correspondence course.

★ 2218 ★

AN ORIENTATION OF LAW ENFORCEMENT
 University of Nebraska
 511 Nebraska Hall
 Lincoln, Nebraska 68588
Correspondence course.

★ 2219 ★

PATROL ADMINISTRATION
 Bringham Young University
 Department of Independent Study
 210 Herald R. Clark Building
 Provo, Utah 84602
Correspondence course. $81.50.

★ 2220 ★

POLICE SCIENCE
 North American Correspondence School
 4401 Birch Street
 Newport Beach, California 92663
Correspondence course.

★ 2221 ★

POLICE SCIENCE AND LAW ENFORCEMENT
 Police Sciences Institute
 4401 Birch Street
 Newport Beach, California 92663
Correspondence course with field kits.

★ 2222 ★

SURVEY OF CRIMINAL JUSTICE
 University of Nebraska
 511 Nebraska Hall
 Lincoln, Nebraska 68588
Correspondence course.

Films/Video/Filmstrips

★ 2223 ★

EVALUATING THE PERFORMANCE OF LAW
ENFORCEMENT PERSONNEL
 Creative Media Films
 820 Keo Way
 Des Moines, Iowa 50309
Film. $375.00 (rental available).

★ 2224 ★

TOUGH-MINDED INTERPERSONAL COMMUNICATION
FOR LAW ENFORCEMENT
 Creative Media Films
 820 Keo Way
 Des Moines, Iowa 50309
Film. $375.00 (rental available).

★ 2225 ★

TOUGH-MINDED SUPERVISION FOR LAW
ENFORCEMENT
 Creative Media Films
 820 Keo Way
 Des Moines, Iowa 50309
Film. $375.00 (rental available).

Multimedia Kits

★ 2226 ★

INTRODUCTION TO CRIMINAL JUSTICE
 Lansford Publishing Company
 Post Office Box 8711
 San Jose, California 95155
Multimedia kit. $140.00.

Printed Materials

★ 2227 ★

BALLISTIC SCIENCE FOR THE LAW ENFORCEMENT
OFFICER
Charles Wilber
 Charles C. Thomas, Publishers
 301-327 East Lawrence Avenue
 Springfield, Illinois 62717
Book. 1976.

★ 2228 ★

FUNDAMENTALS OF PROTECTIVE SYSTEMS
Albert Mandelbaum
 Charles C. Thomas, Publishers
 301-327 East Lawrence Avenue
 Springfield, Illinois 62717
Book. 1973. $11.50.

★ 2229 ★
INTRODUCTION TO CRIMINAL INVESTIGATION
Richard Ward
     Addison Wesley Publishing Company Incorporated
     Jacob Way
     Reading, Massachusetts   01867
Book. $9.95.

POLISH

Correspondence Courses

★ 2230 ★
LET'S LEARN POLISH
Zofia Bastgen
     Arthur Vanous Company
     616 Kinderkamack Road
     River Edge, New Jersey   07661
Self instruction book.   1974. $4.50.

★ 2231 ★
MOWIMY PO POLSKU: A BEGINNERS COURSE
W. Bisko
     Arthur Vanous Company
     616 Kinderkamack Road
     River Edge, New Jersey   07661
Self-study book.   1973. $5.00.

Multimedia Kits

★ 2232 ★
COMMUNICATING IN POLISH
     General Services Administration
     Foreign Service Institute Language Course
     National Audiovisual Center
     Order Section RR
     Washington, D.C.   20409
Audio tapes, cassettes and text also available.

Printed Materials

★ 2233 ★
LEARN POLISH: FOR ENGLISH SPEAKERS
     Saphrograph Company
     194 Elizabeth Street
     New York, New York   10012
Book. $6.00.

★ 2234 ★
POLISH
M. Corbridge,   Pat Kaniowska
     David McKay Company Incorporated
     750 Third Avenue
     New York, New York   10017
Self-study book.   1974. $3.95.

POLLUTION CONTROL

Programmed Learning Materials

★ 2235 ★
UNDERSTANDING INDUSTRIAL POLLUTION
CONTROL
TPC Training Systems
     Technical Publishing Company
     1301 South Grove Avenue
     Barrington, Illinois   60010
Programmed text of 5 lessons. $16.75.

PORTUGUESE

Audio Cassettes/Tapes

★ 2236 ★
BERLITZ COURSE IN PORTUGUESE
     Berlitz Language Program
     Post Office Box 5109
     FDR Station
     New York, New York   10022
Cassette $5.95.   Also available on LP record.

★ 2237 ★
LIVING PORTUGUESE
Oscar Fernandez
     Crown Publishers Incorporated
     419 Park Avenue South
     New York, New York   10016
Records and manual. $11.95.

Correspondence Courses

★ 2238 ★
PORTUGUESE
     Bringham Young University
     Department of Independent Study
     210 Herald R. Clark Building
     Provo, Utah   84602
Correspondence course. $108.00.

★ 2239 ★
PORTUGUESE
     University of Wisconsin – Extension
     Independent Study
     432 North Lake Street
     Madison, Wisconsin   53706
Various level courses available.

Multimedia Kits

★ 2240 ★
PORTUGUESE PROGRAMMATIC COURSE
    General Services Administration
    Foreign Service Institute Language Course
    National Audiovisual Center
    Order Section RR
    Washington, D.C.   20409
Audio tapes, cassettes and text also available.
Approximately $150.00.

Printed Materials

★ 2241 ★
CONVERSATIONAL BRAZILIAN-PORTUGUESE
    Doubleday and Company Incorporated
    501 Franklin Avenue
    Garden City, New York   11530
Self instruction book. $4.95.

★ 2242 ★
LEARN PORTUGUESE FOR ENGLISH SPEAKERS
    Saphrograph Company
    194 Elizabeth Street
    New York, New York   10012
Book.   1974. $5.00.

★ 2243 ★
TEACH YOURSELF PORTUGUESE
J. W. Barker
    David McKay Company Incorporated
    750 Third Avenue
    New York, New York   10017
Self-study book. $2.95.

POWER HOUSE OPERATIONS

Films/Video/Filmstrips

★ 2244 ★
INDUSTRIAL AND COMMERCIAL POWER
DISTRIBUTION
    The Electrification Council
    90 Park Avenue
    New York, New York   10016
Text and slides. $200.00.

Programmed Learning Materials

★ 2245 ★
PRINCIPLES OF COMBUSTION

    E. I. du Pont de Nemours and Company
    Applied Technology Division
    Room B 4204
    Wilmington, Delaware   19898
Programmed course of approximately 14 hours.

POWER PLANT, ELECTRICAL

See also: Electrical Maintenance;   Electronics

Films/Video/Filmstrips

★ 2246 ★
AC AND DC MOTORS
    Resource Incorporated
    13902 North Dale Mabry Highway
    Tampa, Florida   33624
Video cartridge with workbook. $100.00.

★ 2247 ★
AC GENERATORS
    Resource Incorporated
    13902 North Dale Mabry Highway
    Tampa, Florida   33624
Video cartridge with workbook. $100.00.

★ 2248 ★
AUXILIARY POWER SUPPLIES
    Resource Incorporated
    13902 North Dale Mabry Highway
    Tampa, Florida   33624
Video cartridge with workbook. $100.00.

★ 2249 ★
BUSES, BUS DUCTS AND DISCONNECTS
    Resource Incorporated
    13902 North Dale Mabry Highway
    Tampa, Florida   33624
Video cartridge with workbook. $100.00.

★ 2250 ★
EXCITATION SYSTEMS
    Resource Incorporated
    13902 North Dale Mabry Highway
    Tampa, Florida   33624
Video cartridge with workbook. $100.00.

★ 2251 ★
GENERATION AND SYSTEM STABILITY
    Resource Incorporated
    13902 North Dale Mabry Highway
    Tampa, Florida   33624
Video cartridge with workbook. $100.00.

★ 2252 ★
INSIDE A LARGE AC GENERATOR
    Resource Incorporated
    13902 North Dale Mabry Highway
    Tampa, Florida 33624
Video cartridge with workbook. $100.00.

★ 2253 ★
INSIDE A POWER TRANSFORMER
    Resource Incorporated
    13902 North Dale Mabry Highway
    Tampa, Florida 33624
Video cartridge with workbook. $100.00.

★ 2254 ★
METERING THE POWER SYSTEMS
    Resource Incorporated
    13902 North Dale Mabry Highway
    Tampa, Florida 33624
Video cartridge with workbook. $100.00.

★ 2255 ★
MOTORS AND CONTROLS
    Resource Incorporated
    13902 North Dale Mabry Highway
    Tampa, Florida 33624
Video cartridge with workbook. $100.00.

★ 2256 ★
OPERATING EXCITER SYSTEMS
    Resource Incorporated
    13902 North Dale Mabry Highway
    Tampa, Florida 33624
Video cartridge with workbook. $100.00.

★ 2257 ★
POWER CIRCUIT BREAKERS
    Resource Incorporated
    13902 North Dale Mabry Highway
    Tampa, Florida 33624
Video cartridge with workbook. $100.00.

★ 2258 ★
POWER PLANT MOTORS
    Resource Incorporated
    13902 North Dale Mabry Highway
    Tampa, Florida 33624
Video cartridge with workbook. $100.00.

★ 2259 ★
POWER SUPPLIES, BATTERIES AND RECTIFIERS
    Resource Incorporated
    13902 North Dale Mabry Highway
    Tampa, Florida 33624
Video cartridge with workbook. $100.00.

★ 2260 ★
POWER SYSTEM PROTECTION
    Resource Incorporated
    13902 North Dale Mabry Highway
    Tampa, Florida 33624
Video cartridge with workbook. $100.00.

★ 2261 ★
POWER TRANSFORMERS
    Resource Incorporated
    13902 North Dale Mabry Highway
    Tampa, Florida 33624
Video cartridge with workbook. $100.00.

★ 2262 ★
RELAY SYSTEMS
    Resource Incorporated
    13902 North Dale Mabry Highway
    Tampa, Florida 33624
Video cartridge with workbook. $100.00.

★ 2263 ★
THREE-PHASE TRANSFORMER
    Resource Incorporated
    13902 North Dale Mabry Highway
    Tampa, Florida 33624
Video cartridge with workbook. $100.00.

★ 2264 ★
TRANSFORMER PRINCIPLES
    Resource Incorporated
    13902 North Dale Mabry Highway
    Tampa, Florida 33624
Video cartridge with workbook. $100.00.

POWER PLANT, MECHANICAL

See also: Mechanics; Pumps

Films/Video/Filmstrips

★ 2265 ★
ASH REMOVAL
    Resource Incorporated
    13902 North Dale Mabry Highway
    Tampa, Florida 33624
Video cartridge with workbook. $100.00.

★ 2266 ★
BASIC COMBUSTION
    Resource Incorporated
    13902 North Dale Mabry Highway
    Tampa, Florida   33624
Video cartridge with workbook. $100.00.

★ 2267 ★
COMBUSTION AIR AND GASES
    Resource Incorporated
    13902 North Dale Mabry Highway
    Tampa, Florida   33624
Video cartridge with workbook. $100.00.

★ 2268 ★
COMBUSTION HEAT FLOW
    Resource Incorporated
    13902 North Dale Mabry Highway
    Tampa, Florida   33624
Video cartridge with workbook. $100.00.

★ 2269 ★
COMPRESSORS
    Resource Incorporated
    13902 North Dale Mabry Highway
    Tampa, Florida   33624
Video cartridge with workbook. $100.00.

★ 2270 ★
CONDENSATE AND BOILER FEED PUMPS
    Resource Incorporated
    13902 North Dale Mabry Highway
    Tampa, Florida   33624
Video cartridge with workbook. $100.00.

★ 2271 ★
CONDENSER OPERATION
    Resource Incorporated
    13902 North Dale Mabry Highway
    Tampa, Florida   33624
Video cartridge with workbook. $100.00.

★ 2272 ★
FUEL PREPARATION AND HANDLING
    Resource Incorporated
    13902 North Dale Mabry Highway
    Tampa, Florida   33624
Video cartridge with workbook. $100.00.

★ 2273 ★
FURNACE EXPLOSION
    Resource Incorporated
    13902 North Dale Mabry Highway
    Tampa, Florida   33624
Video cartridge with workbook. $100.00.

★ 2274 ★
INSTRUMENTATION
    Resource Incorporated
    13902 North Dale Mabry Highway
    Tampa, Florida   33624
2 video cartridges with workbook. $200.00.

★ 2275 ★
INTERLOCKS
    Resource Incorporated
    13902 North Dale Mabry Highway
    Tampa, Florida   33624
Video cartridge with workbook. $100.00.

★ 2276 ★
INTRODUCTION TO STEAM/WATER CYCLE
    Resource Incorporated
    13902 North Dale Mabry Highway
    Tampa, Florida   33624
Video cartridge with workbook. $100.00.

★ 2277 ★
MAIN CONTROL SYSTEMS
    Resource Incorporated
    13902 North Dale Mabry Highway
    Tampa, Florida   33624
Video cartridge with workbook. $100.00.

★ 2278 ★
OIL AND LUBRICATION
    Resource Incorporated
    13902 North Dale Mabry Highway
    Tampa, Florida   33624
Video cartridge with workbook. $100.00.

★ 2279 ★
OPERATING THE PLANT - STATION
PERFORMANCE
    Resource Incorporated
    13902 North Dale Mabry Highway
    Tampa, Florida   33624
Video cartridge with workbook. $100.00.

★ 2280 ★
PRESSURE AND FLOWS
 Resource Incorporated
 13902 North Dale Mabry Highway
 Tampa, Florida 33624
Video cartridge with workbook. $100.00.

★ 2281 ★
PROPERTIES OF WATER
 Resource Incorporated
 13902 North Dale Mabry Highway
 Tampa, Florida 33624
Video cartridge with workbook. $100.00.

★ 2282 ★
STEAM/WATER CYCLE - THE BOILER
 Resource Incorporated
 13902 North Dale Mabry Highway
 Tampa, Florida 33624
Video cartridge with workbook. $100.00.

★ 2283 ★
SUPER-CRITICAL BOILERS - INTRODUCTION
 Resource Incorporated
 13902 North Dale Mabry Highway
 Tampa, Florida 33624
Video cartridge with workbook. $100.00.

★ 2284 ★
SUPER-CRITICAL BOILERS - OPERATION
 Resource Incorporated
 13902 North Dale Mabry Highway
 Tampa, Florida 33624
Video cartridge with workbook. $100.00.

★ 2285 ★
TURBINE OPERATION
 Resource Incorporated
 13902 North Dale Mabry Highway
 Tampa, Florida 33624
2 video cartridges with workbook. $200.00.

★ 2286 ★
VALVES, TRAPS AND PIPING
 Resource Incorporated
 13902 North Dale Mabry Highway
 Tampa, Florida 33624
2 video cartridges with workbook. $200.00.

★ 2287 ★
WATER AND AIR
 Resource Incorporated
 13902 North Dale Mabry Highway
 Tampa, Florida 33624
Video cartridge with workbook. $100.00.

★ 2288 ★
WATER TREATMENT
 Resource Incorporated
 13902 North Dale Mabry Highway
 Tampa, Florida 33624
Video cartridge with workbook. $100.00.

Printed Materials

★ 2289 ★
COMPRESSORS
 Howell Training
 2040 North Loop West, Suite 204
 Houston, Texas 77018
Workbooks and tests. $33.25.

Programmed Learning Materials

★ 2290 ★
GENERATING STEAM IN THE POWER PLANT
TPC Training Systems
 Technical Publishing Company
 1301 South Grove Avenue
 Barrington, Illinois 60010
Programmed text of 5 lessons. $16.75.

★ 2291 ★
HOW POWER PLANTS WORK
TPC Training Systems
 Technical Publishing Company
 1301 South Grove Avenue
 Barrington, Illinois 60010
Programmed text of 5 lessons. $16.75.

★ 2292 ★
USING STEAM IN THE POWER PLANT
TPC Training Systems
 Technical Publishing Company
 1301 South Grove Avenue
 Barrington, Illinois 60010
Programmed text of 5 lessons. $16.75.

PREACHING

See also: Pastoral Ministries; Public
Speaking

Audio Cassettes/Tapes

★ 2293 ★
HOW TO PREPARE AND DELIVER A SERMON
Southern Baptist Convention
Seminary Extension Department
460 James Robertson Parkway
Nashville, Tennessee 37219
Cassette home study program. $15.00.

Correspondence Courses

★ 2294 ★
PRINCIPLES OF PREACHING
Southern Baptist Convention
Seminary Extension Department
460 James Robertson Parkway
Nashville, Tennessee 37219
Home study course.

PREGNANCY
See: headings under HEALTH

PROBLEM SOLVING

See also: Decision Making

Audio Cassettes/Tapes

★ 2295 ★
PROBLEM SOLVING IN DIRECT RESPONSE
ADVERTISING
Tape Rental Library Incorporated
Post Office Box 2107
2507 Edna Drive
South Vineland, New Jersey 08360
Cassette. $12.00.

Films/Video/Filmstrips

★ 2296 ★
PROBLEM SOLVING: SOME BASIC PRINCIPLES
Roundtable Films
113 North San Vincente Boulevard
Beverly Hills, California 90211
Film.

Multimedia Kits

★ 2297 ★
DEFINE GOALS - DETERMINE OPTIONS
Resources for Education and Management
Incorporated
544 Medlock Road, Suite 210
Decatur, Georgia 30030
Filmstrip with cassette. $60.00.

★ 2298 ★
DETERMINING CAUSES AND GENERATING OPTIONS
Resources for Education and Management
Incorporated
544 Medlock Road
Decatur, Georgia 30030
Filmstrip with cassette. $55.00.

★ 2299 ★
GATHERING NECESSARY INFORMATION
Resources for Education and Management
Incorporated
544 Medlock Road, Suite 210
Decatur, Georgia 30030
Filmstrip with cassette. $55.00.

★ 2300 ★
PROBLEM SOLVING
Lansford Publishing Company
Post Office Box 8711
San Jose, California 95155
Multimedia kit. $120.00.

★ 2301 ★
PROBLEM SOLVING: AN INTRODUCTION
Lansford Publishing Company
Post Office Box 8711
San Jose, California 95155
Multimedia kit. $195.00.

★ 2302 ★
PROBLEM SOLVING AND DECISION MAKING
Ergonco Performance Source
Northwest O'Hare Office Park, Suite 119
2474 Dempster Street
Des Plains, Illinois 60016
Multimedia self-study program.

★ 2303 ★
PUTTING THE SOLUTION INTO ACTION
Resources for Education and Management
Incorporated
544 Medlock Road, Suite 210
Decatur, Georgia 30030
Filmstrip with cassette. $55.00.

★ 2304 ★
RECOGNIZING AND IDENTIFYING THE PROBLEM
 Resources for Education and Management
  Incorporated
 544 Medlock Road, Suite 210
 Decatur, Georgia 30030
Filmstrip with cassette. $55.00.

★ 2305 ★
SELECT, OPTION AND IMPLEMENT
 Resources for Education and Management
  Incorporated
 544 Medlock Road, Suite 210
 Decatur, Georgia 30030
Filmstrip with cassette. $60.00.

★ 2306 ★
SELECTING THE BEST SOLUTION
 Resources for Education and Management
  Incorporated
 544 Medlock Road, Suite 210
 Decatur, Georgia 30030
Filmstrip with cassette. $55.00.

★ 2307 ★
WRITE DECISION STATEMENT – ESTABLISH GOALS
 Resources for Education and Management
  Incorporated
 544 Medlock Road, Suite 210
 Decatur, Georgia 30030
Filmstrip with cassette. $60.00.

PROCESS CONTROL

See also: Mechanics

Audio Cassettes/Tapes

★ 2308 ★
FUNDAMENTALS OF FLOW MEASUREMENT
Carmen Sprague
 Instrument Society of America
 400 Stanwix Street
 Pittsburgh, Pennsylvania 15222
Workbook and cassette. $10.00.

★ 2309 ★
PRINCIPLES OF FREQUENCY RESPONSE
 Instrument Society of America
 400 Stanwix Street
 Pittsburgh, Pennsylvania 15222
Workbook and cassette.

★ 2310 ★
THEORY OF AUTOMATIC CONTROL IN SIMPLE
LANGUAGE
 Instrument Society of America
 400 Stanwix Street
 Pittsburgh, Pennsylvania 15222
Workbook and cassette. $10.00.

Films/Video/Filmstrips

★ 2311 ★
AUTOMATIC PROCESS CONTROL
 Instrument Society of America
 400 Stanwix Street
 Pittsburgh, Pennsylvania 15222
Film with study guide. $455.00.

★ 2312 ★
BOILERS AND THEIR CONTROL
 Instrument Society of America
 400 Stanwix Street
 Pittsburgh, Pennsylvania 15222
Video tape $475.00.   Film $500.00.

Printed Materials

★ 2313 ★
SIGNIFICANCE OF PROCESS CONTROL
 Howell Training
 2040 North Loop West, Suite 204
 Houston, Texas 77018
Workbook and tests. $11.80.

Programmed Learning Materials

★ 2314 ★
APPLICATION OF RELIABILITY TECHNIQUES
 Society of Manufacturing Engineers
 20501 Ford Road
 Post Office Box 930
 Dearborn, Michigan 48128
Programmed learning course. $12.00.

★ 2315 ★
MACHINE CONTROL AND CONTROL SYSTEMS
 Society of Manufacturing Engineers
 20501 Ford Road
 Post Office Box 930
 Dearborn, Michigan 48128
Programmed learning course. $77.00.

PRODUCT DEVELOPMENT

See also: Marketing

Correspondence Courses

★ 2316 ★
NEW PRODUCTS: DESIGN TO COMPLETION
    Society of Manufacturing Engineers
    20501 Ford Road
    Post Office Box 930
    Dearborn, Michigan 48128
6 two hour lessons, self instruction course. $6.50.

PRODUCTION CONTROL

See also: Process Control

Correspondence Courses

★ 2317 ★
PRODUCTION CONTROL
    The Thomas Institute
    Box 22
    New Canaan, Connecticut 06840
Self study course. $150.00.

Printed Materials

★ 2318 ★
CASES IN PRODUCTION AND OPERATIONS
Joe C. Iverstine, Jerry Kinard
    Charles E. Merrill Publishing Company
    1300 Alum Creek Drive
    Box 508
    Columbus, Ohio 43216
Case study text. $6.95.

Programmed Learning Materials

★ 2319 ★
PRODUCTION AND OPERATIONS MANAGEMENT
Elwood Buffa
    Learning Systems Company
    1818 Ridge Road
    Homewood, Illinois 60430
Programmed learning aid. $4.95.

PRODUCTIVITY

Audio Cassettes/Tapes

★ 2320 ★
GELLERMAN ON PRODUCTIVITY
    American Management Associations
    135 West 50th Street
    New York, New York 10020
Cassette. $24.00.

★ 2321 ★
KEEPING THE COMPANY CURRENT - RAISING
PRODUCTIVITY
    Thompson-Mitchell and Associates
    3384 Peachtree Road Northeast
    Atlanta, Georgia 30326
Cassette. $6.00.

Films/Video/Filmstrips

★ 2322 ★
INCREASING PRODUCTIVITY
    National Restaurant Association
    One IBM Plaza, Suite 2600
    Chicago, Illinois 60611
Video cartridge or 8 mm, 16 mm, and study guide.
$190.00.

Multimedia Kits

★ 2323 ★
ATTITUDES TOWARD PRODUCTION
    Resources for Education and Management
        Incorporated
    544 Medlock Road, Suite 210
    Decatur, Georgia 30030
Filmstrip with cassette. $65.00.

★ 2324 ★
HOW TO IMPROVE PRODUCTION
    Resources for Education and Management
        Incorporated
    544 Medlock Road, Suite 210
    Decatur, Georgia 30030
Filmstrip with cassette. $65.00.

★ 2325 ★
INFLATION AND PRODUCTIVITY
    Resources for Education and Management
        Incorporated
    544 Medlock Road, Suite 210
    Decatur, Georgia 30030
Filmstrip with cassette. $65.00.

PROFIT

Audio Cassettes/Tapes

★ 2326 ★
CONTROLLING COSTS FOR PROFIT
Management Resources Incorporated
757 Third Avenue
New York, New York 10017
2 audio cassettes and workbooks.

★ 2327 ★
COST - A CONTINUING BATTLE
Tape Rental Library Incorporated
Post Office Box 2107
2507 Edna Drive
South Vineland, New Jersey 08360
Cassette.

★ 2328 ★
DETERMINING PROFIT STRUCTURE HANDLING
CONTROVERSY
Thompson-Mitchell and Associates
3384 Peachtree Road Northeast
Atlanta, Georgia 30326
Cassette. $6.00.

★ 2329 ★
HOW TO STOP THE CORPORATION FROM
STIFLING PEOPLE AND STRANGLING PROFITS
Tape Rental Library Incorporated
Post Office Box 2107
2507 Edna Drive
South Vineland, New Jersey 08360
12 cassettes. $295.00.

Multimedia Kits

★ 2330 ★
BUSINESS FAILURE
Lansford Publishing Company
Post Office Box 8711
San Jose, California 95155
Multimedia kit. $110.00.

★ 2331 ★
THE COMPANY AND PROFIT
Gamco-Siboney
Box 1911
Big Spring, Texas
3 filmstrips with cassette. $51.00.

★ 2332 ★
COST AND REVENUE
Lansford Publishing Company
Post Office Box 8711
San Jose, California 95155
Multimedia kit. $70.00.

Printed Materials

★ 2333 ★
HOW TO USE TOP SECRETS OF INNOVATION
TO EXPAND COMPANY PROFITS AND THE
EXECUTIVE'S PERSONAL SUCCESS
H. Koch
Prentice-Hall Incorporated
Englewood Cliffs, New Jersey 07632
Book. 1972. $34.95.

PROFIT SHARING

See also: Employee Benefits

Audio Cassettes/Tapes

★ 2334 ★
INCREASING PRODUCTIVITY THROUGH PROFIT
SHARING
Thompson-Mitchell and Associates
3384 Peachtree Road Northeast
Atlanta, Georgia 30326
3 cassettes. $45.00.

★ 2335 ★
PROFIT SHARING
David B. Newstadt
Tape Rental Library Incorporated
Post Office Box 2107
2507 Edna Drive
South Vineland, New Jersey 08360
Cassette.

PROGRAM EVALUATION AND
REVIEW TECHNIQUE (PERT)

See also: Planning

Multimedia Kits

★ 2336 ★
PRINCIPLES AND APPLICATIONS OF PERT/CPM
Lansford Publishing Company
Post Office Box 8711
San Jose, California 95155
Multimedia kit. $215.95.

Printed Materials

★ 2337 ★
PERT, BUSINESS APPLICATION KIT
    Halcomb Associates Incorporated
    Project Management Center
    510 East Maude Avenue
    Sunnyvale, California 94086
Workbook and exercises. $69.50.

★ 2338 ★
PERT, CONSTRUCTION APPLICATION KIT
    Halcomb Associates Incorporated
    Project Management Center
    510 East Maude Avenue
    Sunnyvale, California 94086
Workbook and exercises. $69.50.

★ 2339 ★
PERT, INDUSTRIAL APPLICATION KIT
    Halcomb Associates Incorporated
    Project Management Center
    510 East Maude Avenue
    Sunnyvale, California 94086
Workbook and exercises. $69.50.

★ 2340 ★
PERT, MARKETING APPLICATION KIT
    Halcomb Associates Incorporated
    Project Management Center
    510 East Maude Avenue
    Sunnyvale, California 94086
Workbook and exercises. $69.50.

★ 2341 ★
PERT-O-GRAPH COMPUTER KIT
    Halcomb Associates Incorporated
    Project Management Center
    510 East Maude Avenue
    Sunnyvale, California 94086
Handbook with exercises. $39.50.

Programmed Learning Materials

★ 2342 ★
FUNDAMENTALS OF PERT
    Penton/IPC Education Division
    614 Superior Avenue West
    Cleveland, Ohio 44113
Programmed learning course. $15.00.

PROJECT MANAGEMENT

See also: headings under Supervision

Correspondence Courses

★ 2343 ★
EFFECTIVE PROJECT MANAGEMENT
    Society of Manufacturing Engineers
    20501 Ford Road
    Post Office Box 930
    Dearborn, Michigan 48128
26 hour self instruction course. $33.80.

★ 2344 ★
PROJECT PLANNING AND SCHEDULING
    The Thomas Institute
    Box 22
    New Canaan, Connecticut 06840
Self-study course. $110.00.

PUBLIC RELATIONS

Multimedia Kits

★ 2345 ★
THE COMPANY AND THE COMMUNITY
    Gamco-Siboney
    Box 1911
    Big Spring, Texas 79720
2 filmstrips with cassette. $34.00.

PUBLIC SERVICE UTILITIES

Films/Video/Filmstrips

★ 2346 ★
HISTORY OF ELECTRIC POWER AND LIGHT
    Resource Incorporated
    13902 North Dale Mabry Highway
    Tampa, Florida 33624
Video cartridge. $100.00.

★ 2347 ★
THE HISTORY OF ELECTRIC COOPERATIVES
    Resource Incorporated
    13902 North Dale Mabry Highway
    Tampa, Florida 33624
Video cartridge. $100.00.

★ 2348 ★
COUNTDOWN TO THE MILLENNIUM (History of
Electrical Energy Technology)
        Resource Incorporated
        13902 North Dale Mabry Highway
        Tampa, Florida 33624
Video cartridge. $100.00.

★ 2349 ★
WHAT'S BEHIND THE SWITCH? (How electrical
energy is generated, transmitted and distributed to
the   user)
        Resource Incorporated
        13902 North Dale Mabry Highway
        Tampa, Florida 33624
Video cartridge. $100.00.

★ 2350 ★
WISE ENERGY MANAGEMENT
        Resource Incorporated
        13902 North Dale Mabry Highway
        Tampa, Florida 33624
Video cartridge. $100.00.

PUBLIC SPEAKING

See also: Communication, Oral

Audio Cassettes/Tapes

★ 2351 ★
ART OF PUBLIC SPEAKING
Millard Bennett
        Cassette House
        530 West Northwest Highway
        Mount Prospect, Illinois 60056
Cassette. $9.95.

★ 2352 ★
ART OF PUBLIC SPEAKING
Millard Bennett
        Success Motivation Institute
        5000 Lakewood Drive
        Waco, Texas 76710
Cassette. $9.95.

★ 2353 ★
ART OF PUBLIC SPEAKING
        Thompson-Mitchell and Associates
        3384 Peachtree Road Northeast
        Atlanta, Georgia 30326
Cassette. $9.95.

★ 2354 ★
EFFECTIVE SPEAKING FOR MANAGERS
        American Management Associations
        135 West 50th Street
        New York, New York 10020
4 cassettes and guide. $80.00.

★ 2355 ★
EFFECTIVE SPEAKING FOR MANAGERS
        Lansford Publishing Company
        Post Office Box 8711
        San Jose, California 95155
4 cassettes. $115.00.

★ 2356 ★
THE MASTER SPEAKING COURSE
        Tape Rental Library Incorporated
        Post Office Box 2107
        2507 Edna Drive
        South Vineland, New Jersey 08360
Cassette. $9.98.

★ 2357 ★
PUBLIC SPEAKING
        Educational Century Programming
        1201 East Johnson Street
        Jonesboro, Arkansas 72401
10 cassette tapes. $72.00.

★ 2358 ★
PUBLIC SPEAKING
        General Cassette Corporation
        1324 North 22nd Avenue
        Phoenix, Arizona 85009
Cassette. $9.95.

★ 2359 ★
SPEAK
Bill Gove,   Cavett Robert
        Tape Rental Library Incorporated
        Post Office Box 2107
        2507 Edna Drive
        South Vineland, New Jersey 08360
6 cassettes. $49.00.

★ 2360 ★
SPEAK (Effective Public Speaking)
        General Cassette Corporation
        1324 North 22nd Avenue
        Phoenix, Arizona 85009
6 cassettes. $49.00.

★ 2361 ★
SPEAKING EFFECTIVELY
Educational Century Programming
1201 East Johnson Street
Jonesboro, Arkansas 72401
Cassette. $6.00.

★ 2362 ★
SPEAKING TO AN AUDIENCE
Educational Century Programming
1201 East Johnson Street
Jonesboro, Arkansas 72401
Cassette. $6.00.

★ 2363 ★
VOICE, VOCABULARY, AND DELIVERY
Tape Rental Library Incorporated
Post Office Box 2107
2507 Edna Drive
South Vineland, New Jersey 08360
Cassette. $9.00.

★ 2364 ★
YOUR GUIDE TO MAKING EFFECTIVE
PRESENTATIONS
John Wiley and Sons Incorporated
605 Third Avenue
New York, New York 10016
Cassette. $59.95.

Films/Video/Filmstrips

★ 2365 ★
EFFECTIVE SPEECHMAKING
Ronald M. Brown
Telstar Productions Incorporated
366 North Prior Avenue
Saint Paul, Minnesota 55104
10 video tape lessons.

Multimedia Kits

★ 2366 ★
DELIVERING YOUR SPEECH
Resources for Education and Management
Incorporated
544 Medlock Road, Suite 210
Decatur, Georgia 30030
Filmstrip with cassette. $55.00.

★ 2367 ★
DEVELOPING YOUR SPEECH
Resources for Education and Management
Incorporated
544 Medlock Road, Suite 210
Decatur, Georgia 30030
Filmstrip with cassette. $55.00.

★ 2368 ★
EFFECTING AIDS TO SPEAKING
Resources for Education and Management
Incorporated
544 Medlock Road, Suite 210
Decatur, Georgia 30030
Filmstrip with cassette. $55.00.

★ 2369 ★
GETTING IT DONE RIGHT WITH BETTER TALK
TECHNIQUES
Thompson-Mitchell and Associates
3384 Peachtree Road Northeast
Atlanta, Georgia 30326
Filmstrip with cassette. $55.00.

★ 2370 ★
PREPARING TO SPEAK
Resources for Education and Management
Incorporated
544 Medlock Road, Suite 210
Decatur, Georgia 30030
Filmstrip with cassette. $55.00.

★ 2371 ★
PUBLIC SPEAKING
Lansford Publishing Company
Post Office Box 8711
San Jose, California 95155
Multimedia kit. $100.00.

★ 2372 ★
YOU CAN SPEAK WELL
Resources for Education and Management
Incorporated
544 Medlock Road, Suite 210
Decatur, Georgia 30030
Filmstrip with cassette. $55.00.

PUMPS

Films/Video/Filmstrips

★ 2373 ★
PUMPS
Resource Incorporated
13902 North Dale Mabry Highway
Tampa, Florida 33624
Video cartridge with workbook. $100.00.

Printed Materials

★ 2374 ★
PUMPS
Howell Training
2040 North Loop West, Suite 204
Houston, Texas 77018
Workbooks and tests. $42.05.

PURCHASING

Correspondence Courses

★ 2375 ★
FUNDAMENTALS OF EFFECTIVE PURCHASING
Society of Manufacturing Engineers
20501 Ford Road
Post Office Box 930
Dearborn, Michigan 48128
5 hour self instruction course. $10.00.

Printed Materials

★ 2376 ★
PURCHASING MANAGEMENT
American Management Associations
135 West 50th Street
New York, New York 10020
Self-study text.

Programmed Learning Materials

★ 2377 ★
FUNDAMENTALS OF EFFECTIVE PURCHASING
Preston Publishing Company
151 East 50th Street
New York, New York 10022
Programmed text. $10.00.

PSYCHOLOGY

Audio Cassettes/Tapes

★ 2378 ★
BASIC PSYCHOLOGY
Thompson-Mitchell and Associates
3384 Peachtree Road Northeast
Atlanta, Georgia 30326
Cassette. $9.98.

Films/Video/Filmstrips

★ 2379 ★
PSYCHOLOGY (A program designed for health
professionals)
Telstar Productions Incorporated
366 North Prior Avenue
Saint Paul, Minnesota 55104
48 video tape lessons. $250.00 each.

QUALITY CONTROL

Correspondence Courses

★ 2380 ★
QUALITY CONTROL
International Correspondence School
Scranton, Pennsylvania 18515
Multi-module correspondence course.

★ 2381 ★
QUALITY CONTROL PRINCIPLES
The Thomas Institute
Box 22
New Canaan, Connecticut 06840
Self-study course. $125.00.

★ 2382 ★
QUALITY CONTROL SYSTEMS
The Thomas Institute
Box 22
New Canaan, Connecticut 06840
Self-study course. $110.00.

★ 2383 ★
STATISTICAL QUALITY CONTROL
The Thomas Institute
Box 22
New Canaan, Connecticut 06840
Self-study course. $110.00.

Games/Simulations

★ 2384 ★
MANAGING THE QUALITY CONTROL FUNCTION
    Didactic Systems Incorporated
    Box 457
    Cranford, New Jersey 07016
Simulation game. $24.00.

Multimedia Kits

★ 2385 ★
FUNDAMENTALS OF QUALITY CONTROL
    Lansford Publishing Company
    Post Office Box 8711
    San Jose, California 95155
Multimedia kit. $119.95.

RADIO
See: TELEVISION AND RADIO

READING SKILLS
See: STUDY AND READING SKILLS

REAL ESTATE

See also: Investment; Urban Planning

Audio Cassettes/Tapes

★ 2386 ★
APPRAISAL REPORT WRITING
Edward L. White
    Tape Rental Library Incorporated
    Post Office Box 2107
    2507 Edna Drive
    South Vineland, New Jersey 08360
Cassette.

★ 2387 ★
BABCOCK REVISITED, A RETURN TO
FUNDAMENTALS
McCloud B. Hodges
    Tape Rental Library Incorporated
    Post Office Box 2107
    2507 Edna Drive
    South Vineland, New Jersey 08360
Cassette.

★ 2388 ★
BUY A BUSINESS/SELL A BUSINESS
    Educational Century Programming
    1201 East Johnson Street
    Jonesboro, Arkansas 72401
Cassette. $6.00.

★ 2389 ★
BUYING A HOME
    Tape Rental Library Incorporated
    Post Office Box 2107
    2507 Edna Drive
    South Vineland, New Jersey 08360
Cassette.

★ 2390 ★
CAPITALIZATION TECHNIQUE
Dr. James A. Graaskamp
    Tape Rental Library Incorporated
    Post Office Box 2107
    2507 Edna Drive
    South Vineland, New Jersey 08360
Cassette.

★ 2391 ★
CLOSING
John Lumbleau
    Tape Rental Library Incorporated
    Post Office Box 2107
    2507 Edna Drive
    South Vineland, New Jersey 08360
8 cassettes. $60.00.

★ 2392 ★
COMPARISONS IN REAL ESTATE
Frederick M. Babcock
    Tape Rental Library Incorporated
    Post Office Box 2107
    2507 Edna Drive
    South Vineland, New Jersey 08360
Cassette.

★ 2393 ★
COMPUTER VALUATION (Real estate)
Dr. William M. Shenkel
    Tape Rental Library Incorporated
    Post Office Box 2107
    2507 Edna Drive
    South Vineland, New Jersey 08360
Cassette.

★ 2394 ★
THE ECONOMICS OF REAL ESTATE INVESTMENTS
Philip L. David PhD.
>   Tape Rental Library Incorporated
>   Post Office Box 2107
>   2507 Edna Drive
>   South Vineland, New Jersey   08360

Cassette.

★ 2395 ★
FINANCING ALTERNATIVES
>   Tape Rental Library Incorporated
>   Post Office Box 2107
>   2507 Edna Drive
>   South Vineland, New Jersey   08360

Cassette.

★ 2396 ★
GOVERNMENT HOUSING PROGRAMS
Richard W. O'Neill
>   Tape Rental Library Incorporated
>   Post Office Box 2107
>   2507 Edna Drive
>   South Vineland, New Jersey   08360

Cassette.

★ 2397 ★
HOW I TURNED $1,000 INTO REAL ESTATE
>   Tape Rental Library Incorporated
>   Post Office Box 2107
>   2507 Edna Drive
>   South Vineland, New Jersey   08360

Cassette.

★ 2398 ★
HOW TO GET THE CORPORATION INTO REAL
ESTATE   (Acquisition of the real estate concern)
Thomas L. Karsten
>   Tape Rental Library Incorporated
>   Post Office Box 2107
>   2507 Edna Drive
>   South Vineland, New Jersey   08360

Cassette.

★ 2399 ★
INDUSTRIAL LOCATION DECISION MAKING
Robert P. Boblett
>   Tape Rental Library Incorporated
>   Post Office Box 2107
>   2507 Edna Drive
>   South Vineland, New Jersey   08360

Cassette.

★ 2400 ★
LISTING
John Lumbleau
>   Tape Rental Library Incorporated
>   Post Office Box 2107
>   2507 Edna Drive
>   South Vineland, New Jersey   08360

8 cassettes. $60.00.

★ 2401 ★
MANAGING THE INVESTMENT PROPERTY
Earle S. Altman
>   Tape Rental Library Incorporated
>   Post Office Box 2107
>   2507 Edna Drive
>   South Vineland, New Jersey   08360

Cassette.

★ 2402 ★
MORTGAGE EQUITY FOR BEGINNERS
James E. Gibbons
>   Tape Rental Library Incorporated
>   Post Office Box 2107
>   2507 Edna Drive
>   South Vineland, New Jersey   08360

Cassette.

★ 2403 ★
MORTGAGE PARTICIPATIONS: EQUITY KICKERS
Dr. Halbert C. Smith
>   Tape Rental Library Incorporated
>   Post Office Box 2107
>   2507 Edna Drive
>   South Vineland, New Jersey   08360

Cassette.

★ 2404 ★
NEW TOWN DEVELOPMENT AND FINANCING
(The National Housing Partnership)
John G. Heimann,   Richard W. O'Neill
>   Tape Rental Library Incorporated
>   Post Office Box 2107
>   2507 Edna Drive
>   South Vineland, New Jersey   08360

Cassette.

★ 2405 ★
PRINCIPLES AND PRACTICES OF REAL ESTATE
>   Atlanta Institute of Real Estate
>   6065 Roswell Road Northeast
>   Atlanta, Georgia 30328

12 cassette tapes. $200.00.

★ 2406 ★
THE PROFESSIONAL APPROACH TO LISTING AND
SELLING APARTMENT HOUSES
    Realtors National Marketing Institute
    430 North Michigan Avenue
    Chicago, Illinois 60611
Cassette. $90.00.

★ 2407 ★
PROSPECTING
John Lumbleau
    Tape Rental Library Incorporated
    Post Office Box 2107
    2507 Edna Drive
    South Vineland, New Jersey 08360
8 cassettes with workbook. $60.00.

★ 2408 ★
THE QUESTION MARKS OF PROPERTY AND THE
STAGES OF PROPERTY
Chuck Gaines
    Tape Rental Library Incorporated
    Post Office Box 2107
    2507 Edna Drive
    South Vineland, New Jersey 08360
Cassette.

★ 2409 ★
REAL ESTATE INVESTMENT
Dr. Carl J. Tschappat
    Tape Rental Library Incorporated
    Post Office Box 2107
    2507 Edna Drive
    South Vineland, New Jersey 08360
Cassette.

★ 2410 ★
REAL ESTATE INVESTMENT TRUSTS
James L. Levi, Cornelious C. Rose Jr.
    Tape Rental Library Incorporated
    Post Office Box 2107
    2507 Edna Drive
    South Vineland, New Jersey 08360
Cassette.

★ 2411 ★
REAL ESTATE SALES SYSTEM
    Tape Rental Library Incorporated
    Post Office Box 2107
    2507 Edna Drive
    South Vineland, New Jersey 08360
6 cassettes. $85.00.

★ 2412 ★
REAL ESTATE SALES SYSTEM
    Thompson-Mitchell and Associates
    3384 Peachtree Road Northeast
    Atlanta, Georgia 30326
12 cassettes and workbook. $165.00.

★ 2413 ★
SUCCESS PATTERNS IN LISTING AND SELLING
    Realtors National Marketing Institute
    430 North Michigan Avenue
    Chicago, Illinois 60611
Cassette. $50.00.

★ 2414 ★
SUCCESS PATTERNS IN LISTING AND SELLING
    Tape Rental Library Incorporated
    Post Office Box 2107
    2507 Edna Drive
    South Vineland, New Jersey 08360
6 cassettes.

★ 2415 ★
SUCCESSFUL REAL ESTATE SELLING
John Grogan
    General Cassette Corporation
    1324 North 22nd Avenue
    Post Office Box 6940
    Phoenix, Arizona 85005
8 cassettes. $69.00.

★ 2416 ★
THE TAX REFORM ACT AND REAL ESTATE
Alan J. B. Aronsohn
    Tape Rental Library Incorporated
    Post Office Box 2107
    2507 Edna Drive
    South Vineland, New Jersey 08360
Cassette.

★ 2417 ★
TECHNIQUES
John Lumbleau
    Tape Rental Library Incorporated
    Post Office Box 2107
    2507 Edna Drive
    South Vineland, New Jersey 08360
8 cassettes. $60.00.

Correspondence Courses

★ 2418 ★
FUNDAMENTALS OF REAL ESTATE
    University of South Carolina
    Department of Correspondence Study
    Division of Continuing Education
    Columbia, South Carolina 29208
Correspondence course. $50.00.

★ 2419 ★
INTRODUCTION TO REAL ESTATE AND URBAN
DEVELOPMENT
    University of South Carolina
    Department of Correspondence Study
    Division of Continuing Education
    Columbia, South Carolina 29208
Correspondence course. $69.00.

★ 2420 ★
PRINCIPLES OF REAL ESTATE
    University of Arkansas
    Department of Independent Study
    346 West Avenue
    Fayetteville, Arkansas 72701
Correspondence course.

★ 2421 ★
REAL ESTATE
    Indiana State University
    Independent Study Office
    Terre Haute, Indiana 47809
Independent study course.

★ 2422 ★
REAL ESTATE
    University of North Carolina
    Independent Study by Extension
    121 Abernethy Hall 002A
    Chapel Hill, North Carolina 27514
Correspondence course. $13.95.

★ 2423 ★
REAL ESTATE
    Pennsylvania State University
    Department of Independent Study
    Three Sheilds Building
    University Park, Pennsylvania 16802
Correspondence course.

★ 2424 ★
REAL ESTATE BASICS
    University of Colorado
    Center for Lifelong Learning
    170 Aurora Avenue
    Boulder, Colorado 80302
Correspondence course.

★ 2425 ★
REAL ESTATE COURSE
    La Salle Extension University
    417 South Dearborn Street
    Chicago, Illinois 60605
Correspondence course.

★ 2426 ★
REAL ESTATE FINANCE
    University of Nebraska
    511 Nebraska Hall
    Lincoln, Nebraska 68588
Correspondence course.

★ 2427 ★
REAL ESTATE INVESTMENTS
    University of Nebraska
    511 Nebraska Hall
    Lincoln, Nebraska 68588
Correspondence course.

★ 2428 ★
REAL ESTATE LAW
    University of Colorado
    Center for Lifelong Learning
    170 Aurora Avenue
    Boulder, Colorado 80302
Correspondence course.

★ 2429 ★
REAL ESTATE PRINCIPLES AND PRACTICE
    University of Nebraska
    511 Nebraska Hall
    Lincoln, Nebraska 68588
Correspondence course.

Multimedia Kits

★ 2430 ★
HOW TO CREATE A SALEABLE RESIDENTIAL
LISTING
    Better Selling Bureau
    1150 West Olive Avenue
    Burbank, California 91506
6 filmstrips with cassettes. $495.00.

★ 2431 ★
HOW TO LIST REAL ESTATE
        Realtors National Marketing Institute
        430 North Michigan Avenue
        Chicago, Illinois 60611
Multimedia training program. $425.00.

★ 2432 ★
HOW TO SELL REAL ESTATE
        Realtors National Marketing Institute
        430 North Michigan Avenue
        Chicago, Illinois 60611
Multimedia training program. $425.00.

★ 2433 ★
HOW TO SELL RESIDENTIAL PROPERTY
SUCCESSFULLY
        Better Selling Bureau
        1150 West Olive Avenue
        Burbank, California 91506
6 filmstrips with cassette. $495.00.

★ 2434 ★
REAL ESTATE SELLING SKILLS
        Realtors National Marketing Institute
        430 North Michigan Avenue
        Chicago, Illinois 60611
Multimedia training program. $99.00.

★ 2435 ★
WHAT THE SELLER DOESN'T KNOW CAN HURT
YOU
        Realtors National Marketing Institute
        430 North Michigan Avenue
        Chicago, Illinois 60611
Multimedia training program. $100.00.

Printed Materials

★ 2436 ★
REAL ESTATE EXAMINATIONS GUIDE
Thomas P. Henderson, Ross H. Johnson, Dennis
Kruse,   Edmund F. Ficek
        Charles E. Merrill Publishing Company
        1300 Alum Creek Drive
        Box 508
        Columbus, Ohio 43216
Text. $13.95.

RECORD KEEPING

See also: Accounting; Bookkeeping;
Organizing Skills; Secretarial Skills

Audio Cassettes/Tapes

★ 2437 ★
TRAINING THE RECEPTIONIST/KEEPING RECORDS
        Educational Century Programming
        1201 East Johnson Street
        Jonesboro, Arkansas 72401
Cassette. $6.00.

Printed Materials

★ 2438 ★
PRACTICAL RECORD KEEPING COURSE
Baron and Steineld
        South-Western Publishing Company
        5101 Madison Road
        Cincinnati, Ohio 45227
Book.   1975. $8.64.

REFRIGERATION
See: AIR CONDITIONING
AND REFRIGERATION

RELAXATION

See also: Personal Development

Audio Cassettes/Tapes

★ 2439 ★
MEDITATION/RELAXATION: THE SECRET OF
INNER PEACE
        Cassette House
        530 West Northwest Highway
        Mount Prospect, Illinois 60056
Cassette. $5.95.

★ 2440 ★
RELAX YOUR WAY TO SUCCESS
Hendon R. Crane
        Cassette House
        530 West Northwest Highway
        Mount Prospect, Illinois 60056
Cassette. $9.98.

RESEARCH AND DEVELOPMENT

<u>Printed Materials</u>

★ 2441 ★
RESEARCH AND DEVELOPMENT
Scientific Methods Incorporated
Box 195
Austin, Texas 78767
Workbook. $6.00.

RESTAURANT MANAGEMENT
See: HOTEL AND
RESTAURANT MANAGEMENT

RETAILING

See also: Loss Prevention;   Salesmanship

<u>Audio Cassettes/Tapes</u>

★ 2442 ★
HOW TO SERVE THE CUSTOMER IN A QUICK
SERVICE STORE
Thompson-Mitchell and Associates
3384 Peachtree Road Northeast
Atlanta, Georgia 30326
Cassette. $15.00.

★ 2443 ★
THE POWER OF STORE MORALE
Thompson-Mitchell and Associates
3384 Peachtree Road Northeast
Atlanta, Georgia 30326
Cassette. $15.00.

★ 2444 ★
RETAIL SELLING SYSTEM
Fred Herman
Tape Rental Library Incorporated
Post Office Box 2107
2507 Edna Drive
South Vineland, New Jersey 08360
8 cassettes. $125.00.

★ 2445 ★
STORE RULES MAKE GOOD SENSE
Thompson-Mitchell and Associates
3384 Peachtree Road Northeast
Atlanta, Georgia 30326
6 cassettes. $15.00.

<u>Correspondence Courses</u>

★ 2446 ★
RETAILING
University of Washington
Office of Independent Study
222 Lewis Hall DW-30
Seattle, Washington 98195
Correspondence course.

★ 2447 ★
STORE: SELF TRAINING OF RETAIL EXECUTIVES
National Retail Merchants Association
100 West 31st Street
New York, New York 10001
Correspondence course.

<u>Films/Video/Filmstrips</u>

★ 2448 ★
ESSENTIAL RETAIL SKILLS
United Transparencies
Box 688
Binghamton, New York 13902
15 transparencies. $27.23.

<u>Printed Materials</u>

★ 2449 ★
FOOD RETAILING MATHEMATICS: A PRACTICAL
APPROACH
Daniel McLaughlin
Chain Store Publishing Company
425 Park Avenue
New York, New York 10022
Book.   1975. $8.95.

★ 2450 ★
RETAIL MANAGEMENT
Didactic Systems Incorporated
Box 457
Cranford, New Jersey 07016
Self-study text. $9.00.

<u>Programmed Learning Materials</u>

★ 2451 ★
RETAILING: MODERN CONCEPTS AND
PRACTICES
Delbert J. Duncan
Learning Systems Company
1818 Ridge Road
Homewood, Illinois 60430
Programmed learning aid. $4.95.

RETIREMENT
See: CAREER PLANNING

REWEAVING

Correspondence Courses

★ 2452 ★
FABRICON REWEAVING COURSE
    Fabricon Company
    2021 Montrose Avenue
    Chicago, Illinois 60618
Correspondence course. $112.00.

ROBOTS

Films/Video/Filmstrips

★ 2453 ★
THE INDUSTRIAL ROBOT – AN INTRODUCTION
    Society of Manufacturing Engineers
    20501 Ford Road
    Post Office Box 930
    Dearborn, Michigan 48128
Video tape.

ROCK BLASTING

Printed Materials

★ 2454 ★
BORING PRACTICE
V. Smirnov
    Beekman Publishers Incorporated
    38 Hicks Street
    Brooklyn Heights, New York 11201
Book. 1975. $12.50.

★ 2455 ★
MODERN TECHNIQUE OF ROCK BLASTING
U. Langefors, Bjorn Kihlstrom
    Halsted Press
    Division of John Wiley and Sons Incorporated
    605 Third Avenue
    New York, New York 10016
Book. $20.00.

RUSSIAN

Correspondence Courses

★ 2456 ★
BEGINNING RUSSIAN
    University of Nebraska
    511 Nebraska Hall
    Lincoln, Nebraska 68588
Correspondence course.

★ 2457 ★
RUSSIAN
    University of Wisconsin – Extension
    Independent Study
    432 North Lake Street
    Madison, Wisconsin 53706
Various level courses available.

Multimedia Kits

★ 2458 ★
SPOKEN RUSSIAN
I. Lesnin, Luba Petrova
    Spoken Language Services Incorporated
    Post Office Box 783
    Ithaca, New York 14850
Multimedia course.

Printed Materials

★ 2459 ★
TEACH YOURSELF RUSSIAN
M. Fourman
    David McKay Company Incorporated
    750 Third Avenue
    New York, New York 10017
Self instruction book. $3.95.

SAFETY, AUTOMOBILE

See also: Driving

Films/Video/Filmstrips

★ 2460 ★
FIVE TO DRIVE BY (Five basic driving rules for the professional truck driver)
    Resource Incorporated
    13902 North Dale Mabry Highway
    Tampa, Florida 33624
Video cartridge. $75.00.

★ 2461 ★
A FOLLOWING DISTANCE YOU CAN COUNT ON
Resource Incorporated
13902 North Dale Mabry Highway
Tampa, Florida   33624
Video cartridge. $75.00.

★ 2462 ★
KEEP YOUR DISTANCE (How the front and rear
end collision is related to speed, reaction time,
and stopping distance)
Resource Incorporated
13902 North Dale Mabry Highway
Tampa, Florida   33624
Video cartridge. $75.00.

★ 2463 ★
REHEARSAL FOR AN ACCIDENT (How ignoring safe
driving rules set you up for an accident)
Resource Incorporated
13902 North Dale Mabry Highway
Tampa, Florida   33624
Video cartridge. $75.00.

★ 2464 ★
SCHOOL BUS SAFETY FOR DRIVERS
Resource Incorporated
13902 North Dale Mabry Highway
Tampa, Florida   33624
Video cartridge. $75.00.

★ 2465 ★
SCHOOL BUS SAFETY - LOADING AND UNLOADING
Resource Incorporated
13902 North Dale Mabry Highway
Tampa, Florida   33624
Video cartridge. $75.00.

SAFETY, FIRE

See also: Fire Fighting

Films/Video/Filmstrips

★ 2466 ★
THE FACTS OF FIRE (Potential fire hazards in the
home and fire emergency procedures)
Resource Incorporated
13902 North Dale Mabry Highway
Tampa, Florida   33624
Video cartridge. $75.00.

★ 2467 ★
FIRE SAFETY IN THE HOME
Resource Incorporated
13902 North Dale Mabry Highway
Tampa, Florida   33624
Video cartridge. $100.00.

★ 2468 ★
FIRE SAFETY SYSTEMS
Resource Incorporated
13902 North Dale Mabry Highway
Tampa, Florida   33624
Video cartridge. $100.00.

★ 2469 ★
FIRE SAFETY SYSTEMS FOR POWER PLANTS
Resource Incorporated
13902 North Dale Mabry Highway
Tampa, Florida   33624
Video cartridge with workbook. $100.00.

SAFETY, FOOD SERVICE

See also: Safety, Personal

Films/Video/Filmstrips

★ 2470 ★
THE ANGRY FLAME (Food service safety)
National Restaurant Association
One IBM Plaza, Suite 2600
Chicago, Illinois   60611
Sound filmstrip. $12.50.

★ 2471 ★
DINING ROOM SAFETY
National Restaurant Association
One IBM Plaza, Suite 2600
Chicago, Illinois   60611
Video cartridge or 8 mm, 16 mm, and study guide.
$190.00.

★ 2472 ★
FIRST AID FOR CHOKING
National Restaurant Association
One IBM Plaza, Suite 2600
Chicago, Illinois   60611
Sound filmstrip. $15.95.

★ 2473 ★
THE FREELOADERS (Food service safety)
       National Restaurant Association
       One IBM Plaza, Suite 2600
       Chicago, Illinois 60611
Sound filmstrip. $14.95.

★ 2474 ★
KITCHEN SAFETY: PREVENTING BURNS
       National Restaurant Association
       One IBM Plaza, Suite 2600
       Chicago, Illinois 60611
Video cartridge or 8 mm, 16 mm, and study guide.
$190.00.

★ 2475 ★
KITCHEN SAFETY: PREVENTING CUTS AND
STRAINS
       National Restaurant Association
       One IBM Plaza, Suite 2600
       Chicago, Illinois 60611
Video cartridge or 8 mm, 16 mm, and study guide.
$190.00.

★ 2476 ★
KITCHEN SAFETY: PREVENTING FALLS
       National Restaurant Association
       One IBM Plaza, Suite 2600
       Chicago, Illinois 60611
Video cartridge or 8 mm, 16 mm, and study guide.
$190.00.

★ 2477 ★
KITCHEN SAFETY: PREVENTING FIRES
       National Restaurant Association
       One IBM Plaza, Suite 2600
       Chicago, Illinois 60611
Video cartridge or 8 mm, 16 mm, and study guide.
$190.00.

★ 2478 ★
KITCHEN SAFETY: PREVENTING MACHINE
INJURIES
       National Restaurant Association
       One IBM Plaza, Suite 2600
       Chicago, Illinois 60611
Video cartridge or 8 mm, 16 mm, and study guide.
$190.00.

★ 2479 ★
PROTECTING THE PUBLIC (Food service safety)
       National Restaurant Association
       One IBM Plaza, Suite 2600
       Chicago, Illinois 60611
3 sound filmstrips. $35.95.

★ 2480 ★
SAFETY: IT'S NO ACCIDENT
       National Restaurant Association
       One IBM Plaza, Suite 2600
       Chicago, Illinois 60611
Sound filmstrip. $25.00.

★ 2481 ★
WORK SMART - STAY SAFE
       National Restaurant Association
       One IBM Plaza, Suite 2600
       Chicago, Illinois 60611
Sound filmstrip. $14.95.

Multimedia Kits

★ 2482 ★
PROTECTING THE PUBLIC HEALTH
       National Restaurant Association
       One IBM Plaza, Suite 2600
       Chicago, Illinois 60611
Slides and tape cassette. $125.00.

SAFETY, INDUSTRIAL

Films/Video/Filmstrips

★ 2483 ★
AIR TOOL SAFETY
       Resource Incorporated
       13902 North Dale Mabry Highway
       Tampa, Florida 33624
Video cartridge. $75.00.

★ 2484 ★
ANATOMY OF THE ELECTRIC SHOCK
       Resource Incorporated
       13902 North Dale Mabry Highway
       Tampa, Florida 33624
Video cartridge. $60.00.

★ 2485 ★
ANY PLACE A CAT CAN GO (Electrical safety
for firemen)
    Resource Incorporated
    13902 North Dale Mabry Highway
    Tampa, Florida 33624
Video cartridge. $100.00.

★ 2486 ★
CRANE CONTACTS WITH OVERHEAD POWER LINES
    Resource Incorporated
    13902 North Dale Mabry Highway
    Tampa, Florida 33624
Video cartridge. $75.00.

★ 2487 ★
DON'T PUSH YOUR LUCK
    C. L. Carter Jr. and Associates Incorporated
    434 First Bank and Trust Building
    811 South Central Expressway
    Richardson, Texas 75080
Film. $55.00.

★ 2488 ★
ELECTRICAL EMERGENCIES AND ACCIDENTS
(Law enforcement officers)
    Resource Incorporated
    13902 North Dale Mabry Highway
    Tampa, Florida 33624
Video cartridge. $100.00.

★ 2489 ★
EXCAVATING NEAR UNDERGROUND UTILITIES
    Resource Incorporated
    13902 North Dale Mabry Highway
    Tampa, Florida 33624
Video cartridge. $75.00.

★ 2490 ★
HAND TOOLS (Proper use and storage of hand tools)
    Resource Incorporated
    13902 North Dale Mabry Highway
    Tampa, Florida 33624
Video cartridge. $75.00.

★ 2491 ★
HERE TODAY - HERE TOMORROW (Choice for line-
men concerning checking of equipment, use and care
of protective clothing and using line hose and
platforms)
    Resource Incorporated
    13902 North Dale Mabry Highway
    Tampa, Florida 33624
Video cartridge. $60.00.

★ 2492 ★
HOW TO STOP SHOCK
    Resource Incorporated
    13902 North Dale Mabry Highway
    Tampa, Florida 33624
Video cartridge. $75.00.

★ 2493 ★
KEEP IT CLEAN FOR SAFETY'S SAKE
    Resource Incorporated
    13902 North Dale Mabry Highway
    Tampa, Florida 33624
Video cartridge. $75.00.

★ 2494 ★
METER MAN SAFETY
    Resource Incorporated
    13902 North Dale Mabry Highway
    Tampa, Florida 33624
Video cartridge. $100.00.

★ 2495 ★
METER READER SAFETY
    Resource Incorporated
    13902 North Dale Mabry Highway
    Tampa, Florida 33624
Video cartridge. $100.00.

★ 2496 ★
SAFETY ATTITUDES
    Resource Incorporated
    13902 North Dale Mabry Highway
    Tampa, Florida 33624
Video cartridge. $75.00.

★ 2497 ★
SAFETY IS CONTAGIOUS
    Resource Incorporated
    13902 North Dale Mabry Highway
    Tampa, Florida 33624
Video cartridge. $100.00.

★ 2498 ★
SAFETY PRECAUTIONS FOR THE TRENCHING
CREW
    Resource Incorporated
    13902 North Dale Mabry Highway
    Tampa, Florida 33624
Video cartridge and worksheets available. $120.00.

Programmed Learning Materials

★ 2499 ★
CONSTRUCTION SAFETY HANDBOOK
      E. I. du Pont de Nemours and Company
      Applied Technology Division
      Room B 4204
      Wilmington, Delaware 19898
Programmed course. $50.00.

★ 2500 ★
PLANT SAFETY
TPC Training Systems
      Technical Publishing Company
      1301 South Grove Avenue
      Barrington, Illinois 60010
Programmed text of 10 lessons. $22.50.

SAFETY, MANAGEMENT

Audio Cassettes/Tapes

★ 2501 ★
ACCIDENT PREVENTION
      Tape Rental Library Incorporated
      Post Office Box 2107
      2507 Edna Drive
      South Vineland, New Jersey 08360
Cassette.

★ 2502 ★
SUPERVISOR'S RESPONSIBILITY FOR SAFETY
      AMACOM
      American Management Associations
      135 West 50th Street
      New York, New York 10020
2 cassettes and workbook. $60.00.

Films/Video/Filmstrips

★ 2503 ★
THE INVISIBLE CURTAIN (Development of mental
alertness in sub-station activities)
      Resource Incorporated
      13902 North Dale Mabry Highway
      Tampa, Florida 33624
Video cartridge. $60.00.

★ 2504 ★
A MEETING OF THE MINDS (Gaining employee
confidence)

      Resource Incorporated
      13902 North Dale Mabry Highway
      Tampa, Florida 33624
Video cartridge. $100.00.

★ 2505 ★
PREVENTING OFFICE ACCIDENTS
      Resource Incorporated
      13902 North Dale Mabry Highway
      Tampa, Florida 33624
Video cartridge. $75.00.

★ 2506 ★
SAFETY AND THE SUPERVISOR
      Resource Incorporated
      13902 North Dale Mabry Highway
      Tampa, Florida 33624
Video cartridge. $75.00.

★ 2507 ★
SAFETY DETECTION
      Resource Incorporated
      13902 North Dale Mabry Highway
      Tampa, Florida 33624
Video cartridge. $100.00.

★ 2508 ★
TIPS FOR NEW EMPLOYEES (Basic safety rules at
work)
      Resource Incorporated
      13902 North Dale Mabry Highway
      Tampa, Florida 33624
Video cartridge. $75.00.

★ 2509 ★
WALK A MILE IN MY MOCASSINS (Handling
employee complaints)
      Resource Incorporated
      13902 North Dale Mabry Highway
      Tampa, Florida 33624
Video cartridge. $100.00.

Multimedia Kits

★ 2510 ★
GETTING IT DONE RIGHT WITH SAFETY TIPPING
      Thompson-Mitchell and Associates
      3384 Peachtree Road Northeast
      Atlanta, Georgia 30326
Filmstrip with cassette. $55.00.

★ 2511 ★
THE SUPERVISOR'S RESPONSIBILITY FOR SAFETY
　　AMACOM
　　　American Management Associations
　　　135 West 50th Street
　　　New York, New York　10020
Cassette with programmed text.　$60.00.

Printed Materials

★ 2512 ★
ACCIDENT CONTROL TECHNIQUES
　　　Howell Training
　　　2040 North Loop West, Suite 204
　　　Houston, Texas　77018
Workbooks and tests.　$7.80.

Programmed Learning Materials

★ 2513 ★
ACCIDENT CONTROL TECHNIQUES
　　　Resources Development Corporation
　　　2040 North Loop West, Suite 204
　　　Houston, Texas　77018
Programmed text.　$6.00.

SAFETY, OSHA

Correspondence　Courses

★ 2514 ★
OCCUPATIONAL SAFETY MANAGEMENT
　　　University of Colorado
　　　Center for Lifelong Learning
　　　170 Aurora Avenue
　　　Boulder, Colorado　80302
Correspondence course.

Films/Video/Filmstrips

★ 2515 ★
AFTER HE'S GONE (Stresses positive, prompt action
to correct violations reported by the OSHA compliance
officer)
　　　Resource Incorporated
　　　13902 North Dale Mabry Highway
　　　Tampa, Florida　33624
Video cartridge and worksheets available.　$100.00.

★ 2516 ★
ARE YOU READY FOR THE OCCUPATIONAL SAFETY
AND HEALTH ACT - MAN?
　　　Resource Incorporated
　　　13902 North Dale Mabry Highway
　　　Tampa, Florida　33624
Video cartridge and worksheets available.　$100.00.

★ 2517 ★
HUNTING FOR HAZARDS - FIELD
　　　Resource Incorporated
　　　13902 North Dale Mabry Highway
　　　Tampa, Florida　33624
Video cartridge and worksheets available.　$100.00.

★ 2518 ★
HUNTING FOR HAZARDS - OFFICE
　　　Resource Incorporated
　　　13902 North Dale Mabry Highway
　　　Tampa, Florida　33624
Video cartridge and worksheets available.　$100.00.

★ 2519 ★
HUNTING FOR HAZARDS - SHOP
　　　Resource Incorporated
　　　13902 North Dale Mabry Highway
　　　Tampa, Florida　33624
Video cartridge and worksheets available.　$100.00.

★ 2520 ★
OCCUPATIONAL SAFETY AND HEALTH ACT - AN
INTRODUCTION FOR EMPLOYEES
　　　Resource Incorporated
　　　13902 North Dale Mabry Highway
　　　Tampa, Florida　33624
Video cartridge and worksheets available.　$100.00.

★ 2521 ★
OCCUPATIONAL SAFETY AND HEALTH ACT- AN
INTRODUCTION FOR SUPERVISORS
　　　Resource Incorporated
　　　13902 North Dale Mabry Highway
　　　Tampa, Florida　33624
Video cartridge and worksheets available.　$100.00.

★ 2522 ★
OCCUPATIONAL SAFETY AND HEALTH ACT - MAN
COMETH
　　　Resource Incorporated
　　　13902 North Dale Mabry Highway
　　　Tampa, Florida　33624
Video cartridge and worksheets available.　$100.00.

★ 2523 ★
PERSONAL PROTECTIVE EQUIPMENT
        Resource Incorporated
        13902 North Dale Mabry Highway
        Tampa, Florida 33624
Video cartridge and worksheets available. $100.00.

SAFETY, PERSONAL

Films/Video/Filmstrips

★ 2524 ★
ANATOMY OF A BACK INJURY
        Resource Incorporated
        13902 North Dale Mabry Highway
        Tampa, Florida 33624
Video cartridge. $60.00.

★ 2525 ★
ELECTRICAL HAZARDS IN THE HOME
        Resource Incorporated
        13902 North Dale Mabry Highway
        Tampa, Florida 33624
Video cartridge. $75.00.

★ 2526 ★
FALLS AREN'T FUNNY (Falls and how to avoid
them)
        Resource Incorporated
        13902 North Dale Mabry Highway
        Tampa, Florida 33624
Video cartridge. $75.00.

★ 2527 ★
GUARD YOUR HANDS (Protection of hands in shop
work)
        Resource Incorporated
        13902 North Dale Mabry Highway
        Tampa, Florida 33624
Video cartridge.

★ 2528 ★
GUARD YOUR SIGHT (How to prevent eye injuries)
        Resource Incorporated
        13902 North Dale Mabry Highway
        Tampa, Florida 33624
Video cartridge. $75.00.

★ 2529 ★
IT'S YOUR HEARING (excessive noise and ear
protection)
        Resource Incorporated
        13902 North Dale Mabry
        Tampa, Florida 33624
Video cartridge. $75.00.

★ 2530 ★
MANUAL LIFTING AND HANDLING
        Resource Incorporated
        13902 North Dale Mabry Highway
        Tampa, Florida 33624
Video cartridge. $75.00.

★ 2531 ★
OH, MY ACHING BACK (Backaches: How to
avoid them and their relationship to age)
        Resource Incorporated
        13902 North Dale Mabry Highway
        Tampa, Florida 33624
Video cartridge. $75.00.

★ 2532 ★
POISON PERILS (How to prevent accidental
poisoning)
        Tape Rental Library Incorporated
        Post Office Box 2107
        2507 Edna Drive
        South Vineland, New Jersey 08360
Video cartridge. $75.00.

★ 2533 ★
SAFETY OFF THE JOB (Family safety)
        Resource Incorporated
        13902 North Dale Mabry Highway
        Tampa, Florida 33624
Video cartridge. $75.00.

★ 2534 ★
WHAT'S YOUR HOME SAFETY IQ?
        Resource Incorporated
        13902 North Dale Mabry Highway
        Tampa, Florida 33624
Video cartridge. $75.00.

★ 2535 ★
YOUR FEET ARE YOUR FORTUNE (A guide to proper
foot care)
        Resource Incorporated
        13902 North Dale Mabry Highway
        Tampa, Florida 33624
Video cartridge. $75.00.

SALES GRID

See also: Sales Management;
Sales Techniques

Films/Video/Filmstrips

★ 2536 ★
THE SALES GRID: 9,9 - SOLUTION SELLING
    BNA Communications Incorporated
    9401 Decoverly Hall Road
    Rockville, Maryland 20850
Film with participant booklets.

★ 2537 ★
THE SALES GRID: WHAT IT IS AND HOW IT
WORKS
    BNA Communications Incorporated
    9401 Decoverly Hall Road
    Rockville, Maryland 20850
Film with participant booklets.

Printed Materials

★ 2538 ★
BILL HOLMES (A grid case study)
    Scientific Methods Incorporated
    Box 195
    Austin, Texas 78767
Workbook. $7.50.

SALES MANAGEMENT

See also: headings under Management;
Salesmanship

Audio Cassettes/Tapes

★ 2539 ★
THE ART OF SALES MANAGEMENT
Don Hutson
    General Cassette Corporation
    1324 North 22nd Avenue
    Post Office Box 6940
    Phoenix, Arizona 85005
6 cassettes and workbook. $59.50.

★ 2540 ★
DEVELOPING EFFECTIVE SALES FORECASTS
    Tape Rental Library Incorporated
    Post Office Box 2107
    2507 Edna Drive
    South Vineland, New Jersey 08360
10 cassettes. $295.00.

★ 2541 ★
DR. JOHN R. VAN DE WATER ON MANAGEMENT
    Tape Rental Library Incorporated
    Post Office Box 2107
    2507 Edna Drive
    South Vineland, New Jersey 08360
6 cassettes. $59.50.

★ 2542 ★
DR. KENNETH MCFARLAND FOR SALESMEN
Dr. McFarland
    Tape Rental Library Incorporated
    Post Office Box 2107
    2507 Edna Drive
    South Vineland, New Jersey 08360
6 cassettes. $49.50.

★ 2543 ★
J. DOUGLAS EDWARDS ON SELLING
J. Douglas Edwards
    Tape Rental Library Incorporated
    Post Office Box 2107
    2507 Edna Drive
    South Vineland, New Jersey 08360
4 cassettes. $40.00.

★ 2544 ★
MANAGEMENT BY SUBJECTIVES FOR SALES
MANAGERS
Thom Norman
    General Cassette Corporation
    1324 North 22nd Avenue
    Post Office Box 6940
    Phoenix, Arizona 85005
6 cassettes. $55.00.

★ 2545 ★
MANAGEMENT DEVELOPMENT
    Tape Rental Library Incorporated
    Post Office Box 2107
    2507 Edna Drive
    South Vineland, New Jersey 08360
5 cassettes. $75.00.

★ 2546 ★
MANAGEMENT OF FIELD SALES
    Tape Rental Library Incorporated
    Post Office Box 2107
    2507 Edna Drive
    South Vineland, New Jersey 08360
6 cassettes and workbook. $95.00.

★ 2547 ★
RESULTS ORIENTED SALES MANAGEMENT
General Cassette Corporation
1324 North 22nd Avenue
Post Office Box 6940
Phoenix, Arizona 85005
12 cassettes and workbook. $165.00.

★ 2548 ★
RESULTS ORIENTED SALES MANAGEMENT
Thompson-Mitchell and Associates
3384 Peachtree Road Northeast
Atlanta, Georgia 30326
12 cassettes and workbook. $165.00.

★ 2549 ★
SALES MANAGEMENT
Thompson-Mitchell and Associates
3384 Peachtree Road Northeast
Atlanta, Georgia 30326
2 cassettes. $30.00.

★ 2550 ★
SALES MANAGEMENT MINI COURSE
Fred Herman
General Cassette Corporation
1324 North 22nd Avenue
Post Office Box 6940
Phoenix, Arizona 85005
4 cassettes. $49.00.

★ 2551 ★
SALES MANAGERS MINI COURSE
Fred Herman
General Cassette Corporation
1324 North 22nd Avenue
Post Office Box 6940
Phoenix, Arizona 85005
2 volumes, 4 cassettes. $49.00 each.

★ 2552 ★
SUPERVISORY SKILLS
George Odiorne
Tape Rental Library Incorporated
Post Office Box 2107
2507 Edna Drive
South Vineland, New Jersey 08360
12 cassettes. $150.00.

Correspondence Courses

★ 2553 ★
SALES MANAGEMENT
International Correspondence School
Scranton, Pennsylvania 18515
Multi-module correspondence course.

★ 2554 ★
SALES MANAGEMENT
University of Washington
Office of Independent Study
222 Lewis Hall DW-30
Seattle, Washington 98195
Correspondence course.

Multimedia Kits

★ 2555 ★
SELF-MANAGEMENT SKILLS FOR THE SALES
PROFESSIONAL
Lansford Publishing Company
Post Office Box 8711
San Jose, California 95155
Multimedia kit. $170.00.

Printed Materials

★ 2556 ★
SALES MANAGEMENT: OPERATIONS,
ADMINISTRATION, MARKETING
H. Webster Johnson
Charles E. Merrill Publishing Company
1300 Alum Creek Drive
Box 508
Columbus, Ohio 43216
Text with exercises. $15.95.

SALES TECHNIQUES

See also: Marketing; Salesmanship

Audio Cassettes/Tapes

★ 2557 ★
CASHING OBJECTIONS
Thompson-Mitchell and Associates
3384 Peachtree Road Northeast
Atlanta, Georgia 30326
Cassette. $12.50.

★ 2558 ★
CLOSING THE SALE
Dr. James Hofford
  The Center for Cassette Studies
  8110 Webb Avenue
  North Hollywood, California 91605
Cassette. $15.95.

★ 2559 ★
CLOSING THE SALE
  Thompson-Mitchell and Associates
  3384 Peachtree Road Northeast
  Atlanta, Georgia 30326
Cassette. $12.50.

★ 2560 ★
CREATIVE SELLING MINI COURSE
Fred Herman
  General Cassette Corporation
  1324 North 22nd Avenue
  Post Office Box 6940
  Phoenix, Arizona 85005
4 cassettes. $49.00.

★ 2561 ★
CREATIVE SELLING MINI COURSE
Fred Herman
  General Cassette Corporation
  1324 North 22nd Avenue
  Post Office Box 6940
  Phoenix, Arizona 85005
2 volumes, 4 cassettes. $49.00 each.

★ 2562 ★
DYNAMICS OF A SALES PRESENTATION
PSYCHOLOGY OF A SALES INTERVIEW
  Thompson-Mitchell and Associates
  3384 Peachtree Road Northeast
  Atlanta, Georgia 30326
Cassette. $9.95.

★ 2563 ★
THE GENTLE ART OF HIGH PRESSURE SALESMAN-
SHIP
  Tape Rental Library Incorporated
  Post Office Box 2107
  2507 Edna Drive
  South Vineland, New Jersey 08360
Cassette. $9.98.

★ 2564 ★
HOW SALES PEOPLE MAKE THINGS HAPPEN
George Odiorne
  MBO Incorporated
  157 Pontoosic Road
  Westfield, Massachusetts 01085
Cassette and workbook. $15.00.

★ 2565 ★
HOW TO CLOSE SALES AND WHEN
Paul J. Meyer
  Success Motivation Institute
  5000 Lakewood Drive
  Waco, Texas 76710
Cassette. $9.95.

★ 2566 ★
HOW TO GIVE YOUR SALES TALK MORE
IMPACT
Fred Herman
  Tape Rental Library Incorporated
  Post Office Box 2107
  2507 Edna Drive
  South Vineland, New Jersey 08360
Cassette. $12.00.

★ 2567 ★
HOW TO MULTIPLY YOUR SALES POWER
  Thompson-Mitchell and Associates
  3384 Peachtree Road Northeast
  Atlanta, Georgia 30326
Cassette. $9.95.

★ 2568 ★
HOW TO OVERCOME PRICE RESISTANCE
  Thompson-Mitchell and Associates
  3384 Peachtree Road Northeast
  Atlanta, Georgia 30326
Cassette. $9.95.

★ 2569 ★
HOW TO SCORE THROUGH STROKING (Sales
techniques)
  Tape Rental Library Incorporated
  Post Office Box 2107
  2507 Edna Drive
  South Vineland, New Jersey 08360
Cassette. $39.50.

★ 2570 ★
MODERN SECTION CARE BUILDS SALES
    Thompson-Mitchell and Associates
    3384 Peachtree Road Northeast
    Atlanta, Georgia 30326
Cassette. $15.00.

★ 2571 ★
MORE CLOSES
    Thompson-Mitchell and Associates
    3384 Peachtree Road Northeast
    Atlanta, Georgia 30326
Cassette. $12.50.

★ 2572 ★
A NEW WAY OF LOOKING AT SALES LEADS
    Tape Rental Library Incorporated
    Post Office Box 2107
    2507 Edna Drive
    South Vineland, New Jersey 08360
Cassette. $12.00.

★ 2573 ★
PLAN FOR PROGRESS (Selling skills)
    Tape Rental Library Incorporated
    Post Office Box 2107
    2507 Edna Drive
    South Vineland, New Jersey 08360
12 cassettes. $180.00.

★ 2574 ★
PLANNED CREATIVE SELLING
Fred Herman
    General Cassette Corporation
    1324 North 22nd Avenue
    Post Office Box 6940
    Phoenix, Arizona 85005
12 cassettes and workbook. $165.00.

★ 2575 ★
PLANNING - THE FOUNDATION OF SUCCESSFUL
SELLING
    Thompson-Mitchell and Associates
    3384 Peachtree Road Northeast
    Atlanta, Georgia 30326
Cassette. $9.95.

★ 2576 ★
THE PRINCIPLES OF PERSUASION
    Thompson-Mitchell and Associates
    3384 Peachtree Road Northeast
    Atlanta, Georgia 30326
12 cassettes with workbook. $150.00.

★ 2577 ★
P'S and Q'S (PROSPECTING AND QUALIFICATION)
    Thompson-Mitchell and Associates
    3384 Peachtree Road Northeast
    Atlanta, Georgia 30326
Cassette. $12.50.

★ 2578 ★
SELL THE CUSTOMER BY LISTENING
George Odiorne
    MBO Incorporated
    157 Pontoosic Road
    Westfield, Massachusetts 01085
Cassette and workbook. $15.00.

★ 2579 ★
SELLING SYSTEMS FOR MEN
    Jaine Carter Personnel Development
        Incorporated
    112 West Garden Avenue
    Palatine, Illinois 60067
Cassette workbook program.

★ 2580 ★
SELLING THE SIZZLE
Elmer Wheeler
    Cassette House
    530 West Northwest Highway
    Mount Prospect, Illinois 60056
Cassette. $9.95.

★ 2581 ★
SELLING THE SIZZLE
    Thompson-Mitchell and Associates
    3384 Peachtree Road Northeast
    Atlanta, Georgia 30326
Cassette. $9.95.

★ 2582 ★
SERVING AND SELLING THE PROBLEM CUSTOMER
    Thompson-Mitchell and Associates
    3384 Peachtree Road Northeast
    Atlanta, Georgia 30326
Cassette. $20.00.

★ 2583 ★
THE SEVEN SECRETS OF SELLING TO WOMEN
    Thompson-Mitchell and Associates
    3384 Peachtree Road Northeast
    Atlanta, Georgia 30326
Cassette. $9.95.

★ 2584 ★
SUCCESSFUL PERSONAL SELLING THROUGH
MANAGEMENT BY OBJECTIVE
George Odiorne
MBO Incorporated
157 Pontoosic Road
Westfield, Massachusetts 01085
4 cassettes and workbook. $65.00.

★ 2585 ★
TEAMWORK: KEY TO SALES AND SUCCESS
Thompson-Mitchell and Associates
3384 Peachtree Road Northeast
Atlanta, Georgia 30326
Cassette. $35.00.

★ 2586 ★
TOMORROW'S TECHNIQUES FOR TODAY'S
SALESMEN
John J. Tarrnat
Tape Rental Library Incorporated
Post Office Box 2107
2507 Edna Drive
South Vineland, New Jersey 08360
Cassette.

★ 2587 ★
TRAINING SALESMEN IN PERSUASION SKILLS
Tape Rental Library Incorporated
Post Office Box 2107
2507 Edna Drive
South Vineland, New Jersey 08360
Cassette.

★ 2588 ★
TRAINING SALESMEN TO HANDLE RESISTANCE
Tape Rental Library Incorporated
Post Office Box 2107
2507 Edna Drive
South Vineland, New Jersey 08360
Cassette.

★ 2589 ★
TRAINING SALESMEN TO SELL BENEFITS
Tape Rental Library Incorporated
Post Office Box 2107
2507 Edna Drive
South Vineland, New Jersey 08360
Cassette.

★ 2590 ★
TRANSACTIONAL ANALYSIS: A NEW TOOL FOR
PERSONAL SELLING
George Odiorne
MBO Incorporated
157 Pontoosic Road
Westfield, Massachusetts 01085
Cassette and workbook. $15.00.

★ 2591 ★
YOUR SELF IMAGE - HOW TO WIN AND KEEP
WINNING
Thompson-Mitchell and Associates
3384 Peachtree Road Northeast
Atlanta, Georgia 30326
Cassette. $9.95.

Films/Video/Filmstrips

★ 2592 ★
CLOSE THAT SALE
Roundtable Films
113 North San Vincente Boulevard
Beverly Hills, California 90211
Film and guide book.

★ 2593 ★
HANDLING COMPLAINTS
National Restaurant Association
One IBM Plaza, Suite 2600
Chicago, Illinois 60611
Video cartridge or 8 mm, 16 mm, and study guide.
$190.00.

★ 2594 ★
SELL BENEFITS
Salenger Educational Media
1635 12th Street
Santa Monica, California 90404
Film.

★ 2595 ★
SELL BENEFITS: THE KEY TO CREATIVE SELLING
Salenger Educational Media
1635 12th Street
Santa Monica, California 90404
Film guide and worksheets. $325.00 (rental
available).

★ 2596 ★
SELLING WINE AND LIQUOR
National Restaurant Association
One IBM Plaza, Suite 2600
Chicago, Illinois 60611
Video cartridge or 8 mm, 16 mm, and study guide.
$190.00.

★ 2597 ★
YOUR PERSONAL APPEARANCE
National Restaurant Association
One IBM Plaza, Suite 2600
Chicago, Illinois 60611
Video cartridge or 8 mm, 16 mm, and study guide.
$190.00.

Multimedia Kits

★ 2598 ★
THE PRINCIPLES OF PERSUASION
Bert Munk Productions
56 East Walton Place
Chicago, Illinois 60611
12 unit multimedia course.

★ 2599 ★
TOP DOG
Close Productions
2020 San Carlos Boulevard
Fort Myers Beach, Florida 33931
Filmstrip with cassette. $18.75.

Printed Materials

★ 2600 ★
ANALYZING AND ORGANIZING TIME
Addison Wesley Publishing Company Incorporated
Jacob Way
Reading, Massachusetts 01867
Printed material. $50.00.

★ 2601 ★
CONSULTATIVE SELLING
Mack Hanan
American Management Associations
135 West 50th Street
New York, New York 10020
Book. 1973. $12.95.

SALESMANSHIP

See also: Telephone Sales

Audio Cassettes/Tapes

★ 2602 ★
ACRES OF DIAMONDS (Salesmanship)
Thompson-Mitchell and Associates
3384 Peachtree Road Northeast
Atlanta, Georgia 30326
Cassette. $9.95.

★ 2603 ★
ARE YOU AN AMATEUR OR PRO IN SELLING
Dr. Herb True
Success Motivation Institute
5000 Lakewood Drive
Waco, Texas 76710
Cassette. $9.95.

★ 2604 ★
ARE YOU AN AMATEUR OR PRO IN SELLING?
Thompson-Mitchell and Associates
3384 Peachtree Road Northeast
Atlanta, Georgia 30326
Cassette. $9.95.

★ 2605 ★
ARE YOU THE CAUSE OR THE RESULT?
Thompson-Mitchell and Associates
3384 Peachtree Road Northeast
Atlanta, Georgia 30326
Cassette. $9.95.

★ 2606 ★
ARE YOU WORTH THE INVESTMENT
Thompson-Mitchell and Associates
3384 Peachtree Road Northeast
Atlanta, Georgia 30326
Cassette. $9.95.

★ 2607 ★
BASIC SELLING PRINCIPLES THAT WORK
Dick Gardner
Tape Rental Library Incorporated
2507 Edna Drive, Post Office Box 2107
South Vineland, New Jersey 08360
6 cassettes. $80.00.

★ 2608 ★
THE BEST OF BILL GOVE (Sales consulting)
General Cassette Corporation
1324 North 22nd Avenue
Phoenix, Arizona 85009
Cassette. $35.00.

★ 2609 ★
BETTER THAN MONEY
Tape Rental Library Incorporated
Post Office Box 2107
2507 Edna Drive
South Vineland, New Jersey 08360
Cassette. $39.50.

★ 2610 ★
BILL GOVE ON SELLING
Tape Rental Library Incorporated
Post Office Box 2107
2507 Edna Drive
South Vineland, New Jersey 08360
4 cassettes. $31.80.

★ 2611 ★
CREATIVE RETAIL SELLING
Fred Herman
General Cassette Corporation
1324 North 22nd Avenue
Post Office Box 6940
Phoenix, Arizona 85005
6 cassettes and workbook. $59.50.

★ 2612 ★
THE DARTNELL/ANDERSON 20-POINT SYSTEM
FOR GUARANTEED SALES SUCCESS
Thompson-Mitchell and Associates
3384 Peachtree Road Northeast
Atlanta, Georgia 30326
7 cassettes. $179.50.

★ 2613 ★
DEVELOPING YOUR OWN SALES IDEA TECHNIQUE
BOOK
Ted Kibble
Tape Rental Library Incorporated
Post Office Box 2107
2507 Edna Drive
South Vineland, New Jersey 08360
Cassette.

★ 2614 ★
DICK GARDNER (Problem areas salesmen face)
Tape Rental Library Incorporated
Post Office Box 2107
2507 Edna Drive
South Vineland, New Jersey 08360
2 cassettes.

★ 2615 ★
FIVE STEPS TO SALES SUCCESS
Realtors National Marketing Institute
430 North Michigan Avenue
Chicago, Illinois 60611
Cassette. $50.00.

★ 2616 ★
FOUR KEYS TO SALES SUCCESS
Murray McBride
General Cassette Corporation
1324 North 22nd Avenue
Post Office Box 6940
Phoenix, Arizona 85005
2 cassettes. $19.50.

★ 2617 ★
GREAT IDEAS IN SELLING
Earl Nightingale
Tape Rental Library Incorporated
Post Office Box 2107
2507 Edna Drive
South Vineland, New Jersey 08360
6 cassettes with workbook. $80.00.

★ 2618 ★
THE GREATEST SALESMAN IN THE WORLD
Thompson-Mitchell and Associates
3384 Peachtree Road Northeast
Atlanta, Georgia 30326
Cassette. $9.95.

★ 2619 ★
HAMMER HOME THE DIFFERENCE (Sales training)
Thompson-Mitchell and Associates
3384 Peachtree Road Northeast
Atlanta, Georgia 30326
Cassette. $9.95.

★ 2620 ★
HOW I RAISED MYSELF FROM FAILURE TO SUCCESS
IN SELLING
Frank Bettger
      E. F. Wonderlic and Associates Incorporated
      820 Frontage Road
      Northfield, Illinois 60093
Cassette. $10.00.

★ 2621 ★
HOW I RAISED MYSELF FROM FAILURE TO SUCCESS
IN SELLING
      Thompson-Mitchell and Associates
      3384 Peachtree Road Northeast
      Atlanta, Georgia 30326
Cassette. $9.95.

★ 2622 ★
HOW I SOLD $9,000,000 IN 146 DAYS
Tom J. Wolff
      Tape Rental Library Incorporated
      Post Office Box 2107
      2507 Edna Drive
      South Vineland, New Jersey 08360
Cassette.

★ 2623 ★
HOW TO EARN $100,000 A YEAR AS A SALES-
MAN...IDEAS AND TECHNIQUES YOU CAN USE
TO EARN A LARGE INCOME
Joe Gandolfo
      Tape Rental Library Incorporated
      Post Office Box 2107
      2507 Edna Drive
      South Vineland, New Jersey 08360
Cassette. $11.95.

★ 2624 ★
HOW TO LET YOUR WIFE HELP YOU SUCCEED IN
SELLING
      Thompson-Mitchell and Associates
      3384 Peachtree Road Northeast
      Atlanta, Georgia 30326
Cassette. $9.95.

★ 2625 ★
HOW TO SELL
      Educational Century Programming
      1201 East Johnson Street
      Jonesboro, Arkansas 72401
Cassette. $6.00.

★ 2626 ★
I AM A SALESMAN - DON'T TELL MY MOTHER
(Sales techniques)
Dave Yoho
      Tape Rental Library Incorporated
      Post Office Box 2107
      2507 Edna Drive
      South Vineland, New Jersey 08360
Cassette. $9.95.

★ 2627 ★
KISS (KEEP IT SIMPLE, SALESMAN!)
Fred Herman
      Tape Rental Library Incorporated
      Post Office Box 2107
      2507 Edna Drive
      South Vineland, New Jersey 08360
6 cassettes with workbook. $80.00.

★ 2628 ★
LEAD THE FIELD - RULES FOR SUCCESS
Earl Nightingale
      Tape Rental Library Incorporated
      Post Office Box 2107
      2507 Edna Drive
      South Vineland, New Jersey 08360
6 cassettes with book. $80.00.

★ 2629 ★
MANAGEMENT BY SUBJECTIVES
Thom Norman
      Tape Rental Library Incorporated
      Post Office Box 2107
      2507 Edna Drive
      South Vineland, New Jersey 08360
4 cassettes. $39.50.

★ 2630 ★
MULTI-MILLION DOLLAR SALES IDEAS
John A. Athanson
      Tape Rental Library Incorporated
      Post Office Box 2107
      2507 Edna Drive
      South Vineland, New Jersey 08360
Cassette.

★ 2631 ★
A NEW LOOK AT YOUR JOB
      Thompson-Mitchell and Associates
      3384 Peachtree Road Northeast
      Atlanta, Georgia 30326
Cassette. $15.00.

★ 2632 ★
OFFICE FURNISHINGS SALES COURSE
National Office Products Association
301 North Fairfax Street
Alexandria, Virginia   22314
Workbook and cassettes. $75.00.

★ 2633 ★
101 NEW SECRETS FOR CLOSING MORE SALES
Thompson-Mitchell and Associates
3384 Peachtree Road Northeast
Atlanta, Georgia 30326
Cassette. $9.98.

★ 2634 ★
THE PEOPLE BUSINESS
Thompson-Mitchell and Associates
3384 Peachtree Road Northeast
Atlanta, Georgia   30326
Cassette. $12.50.

★ 2635 ★
PERSONAL SELLING SKILLS
American Management Associations
135 West 50th Street
New York, New York   10020
6 cassettes with workbook. $100.00.

★ 2636 ★
PLANNED CREATIVE SELLING
Thompson-Mitchell and Associates
3384 Peachtree Road Northeast
Atlanta, Georgia   30326
10 cassettes. $165.00.

★ 2637 ★
PROFESSIONAL SELLING SKILLS COURSE
National Office Products Association
301 North Fairfax Street
Alexandria, Virginia   22314
Workbooks and cassettes. $150.00.

★ 2638 ★
QUALITIES OF A SUCCESSFUL SALESMAN
Paul J. Meyer
Success Motivation Institute
5000 Lakewood Drive
Waco, Texas 76710
Cassette. $9.95.

★ 2639 ★
QUESTIONS ARE THE ANSWER (Salesmanship)
Thompson-Mitchell and Associates
3384 Peachtree Road Northeast
Atlanta, Georgia 30326
Cassette. $12.50.

★ 2640 ★
SALES CONCEPTS THAT WORK
Murray McBride
Tape Rental Library Incorporated
Post Office Box 2107
2507 Edna Drive
South Vineland, New Jersey   08360
2 cassettes. $7.95.

★ 2641 ★
SALES, HUMAN ENGINEERING AND MOTIVATION
Cavette Robert
General Cassette Corporation
1324 North 22nd Avenue
Post Office Box 6940
Phoenix, Arizona   85005
6 cassettes. $49.50.

★ 2642 ★
SALESMANSHIP
National Book Company
1019 Southwest Tenth Avenue
Portland, Oregon 97206
15 cassettes. $206.40.

★ 2643 ★
SALESMANSHIP
Tape Rental Library Incorporated
Post Office Box 2107
2507 Edna Drive
South Vineland, New Jersey 08360
7 cassettes. $87.50.

★ 2644 ★
THE SCIENCE OF SELLING
Learning Dynamics Institute
1401 Wilson Boulevard #101
Arlington, Virginia 22209
18 cassettes. $180.00.

★ 2645 ★
SELF-DISCOVERY FOR THE MANAGER
American Management Associations
135 West 50th Street
New York, New York   10020
3 cassettes. $59.95.

★ 2646 ★
SELL LIKE AN ACE, LIVE LIKE A KING
 Thompson-Mitchell and Associates
 3384 Peachtree Road Northeast
 Atlanta, Georgia 30326
Cassette. $9.95.

★ 2647 ★
SELLING SUCCESS PROGRAM
 Tape Rental Library Incorporated
 Post Office Box 2107
 2507 Edna Drive
 South Vineland, New Jersey 08360
22 cassettes. $196.90.

★ 2648 ★
THE SEVEN SECRETS OF SELLING TO WOMEN
Dottie Walters
 Success Motivation Institute
 5000 Lakewood Drive
 Waco, Texas 76710
Cassette. $9.95.

★ 2649 ★
SIX SALES WINNERS
J. Douglas Edwards
 General Cassette Corporation
 1324 North 22nd Avenue
 Post Office Box 6940
 Phoenix, Arizona 85005
6 cassettes. $59.50.

★ 2650 ★
SO YOU'RE A SALESMAN
Bob Grinde
 Cassette House
 530 West Northwest Highway
 Mount Prospect, Illinois 60056
5 cassettes. $39.95.

★ 2651 ★
SO YOU'RE A SALESMAN (Sales techniques)
Bob Grinde
 Tape Rental Library Incorporated
 Post Office Box 2107
 2507 Edna Drive
 South Vineland, New Jersey 08360
5 cassettes. $44.95.

★ 2652 ★
SUBCONSCIOUS SALESPOWER
Paul W. Schuette

 Tape Rental Library Incorporated
 Post Office Box 2107
 2507 Edna Drive
 South Vineland, New Jersey 08360
Cassette. $7.95.

★ 2653 ★
THE SUCCESS SYSTEM THAT NEVER FAILS
W. Clement Stone
 Tape Rental Library Incorporated
 Post Office Box 2107
 2507 Edna Drive
 South Vineland, New Jersey 08360
2 cassettes. $16.95.

★ 2654 ★
SUCCESSFUL LOW-PRESSURE SALESMANSHIP
 Close Productions
 2020 San Carlos Boulevard
 Fort Myers Beach, Florida 33931
8 cassettes. $45.00.

★ 2655 ★
SUCCESSFUL PERSONAL SELLING
George Odiorne
 Tape Rental Library Incorporated
 Post Office Box 2107
 2507 Edna Drive
 South Vineland, New Jersey 08360
4 cassettes. $65.00.

★ 2656 ★
SUCCESSFUL SELLING
John Grogan
 General Cassette Corporation
 1324 North 22nd Avenue
 Post Office Box 6940
 Phoenix, Arizona 85005
4 cassettes. $39.00.

★ 2657 ★
SUCCESSFUL SELLING
Dr. Sidney Bremer
 Tape Rental Library Incorporated
 Post Office Box 2107
 2507 Edna Drive
 South Vineland, New Jersey 08360
6 cassettes. $24.95.

★ 2658 ★

THE SYSTEM THAT NEVER FAILS
    Thompson-Mitchell and Associates
    3384 Peachtree Road Northeast
    Atlanta, Georgia 30326
Cassette. $9.95.

★ 2659 ★

THE TECHNIQUES AND TACTICS OF PROFESSIONAL
SELLING
    Thompson-Mitchell and Associates
    3384 Peachtree Road Northeast
    Atlanta, Georgia 30326
6 cassettes. $75.00.

★ 2660 ★

TIME TABLE TO SUCCESS AND PRAISE AND
APPRECIATION
    Thompson-Mitchell and Associates
    3384 Peachtree Road Northeast
    Atlanta, Georgia 30326
Cassette. $9.95.

★ 2661 ★

UNLIMITED PROSPECTS
Mark Victor Hansen
    Tape Rental Library Incorporated
    Post Office Box 2107
    2507 Edna Drive
    South Vineland, New Jersey 08360
6 cassettes. $59.95.

★ 2662 ★

VIVE LA DIFFERENCE (Salesmanship)
    Thompson-Mitchell and Associates
    3384 Peachtree Road Northeast
    Atlanta, Georgia 30326
Cassette. $12.50.

★ 2663 ★

WANTED ALIVE - A REAL SALESPERSON -
TASKS FOR THE TOUGH-MINDED
    Development Digest Incorporated
    3347 Motor Avenue
    Los Angeles, California 90034
Cassette. $13.75.

★ 2664 ★

WINNING THROUGH INTIMIDATION
Robert Ringer
    Success Motivation Institute
    5000 Lakewood Drive
    Waco, Texas 76710
Cassette. $9.95.

★ 2665 ★

YOU'RE GOING TO SELL
Art Fettig
    Tape Rental Library Incorporated
    Post Office Box 2107
    2507 Edna Drive
    South Vineland, New Jersey 08360
Cassette. $8.35.

Correspondence Courses

★ 2666 ★

MODERN SALESMAN
    International Correspondence School
    Scranton, Pennsylvania 18515
Multi-module correspondence course.

★ 2667 ★

PRECISION TRUCK SELLING
    Truck Marketing Institute
    Post Office Box 188
    Carpinteria, California 93013
Correspondence test with tests.

★ 2668 ★

SALES ACHIEVEMENT
    International Correspondence School
    Scranton, Pennsylvania 18515
Multi-module correspondence course.

Films/Video/Filmstrips

★ 2669 ★

COURTESY IS THE ANSWER
    National Restaurant Association
    One IBM Plaza, Suite 2600
    Chicago, Illinois 60611
Video cartridge or 8 mm, 16 mm, and study guide.
$190.00.

★ 2670 ★

THE FINE ART OF KEEPING YOUR COOL
    National Restaurant Association
    One IBM Plaza, Suite 2600
    Chicago, Illinois 60611
Video cartridge or 8 mm, 16 mm, and study guide.
$190.00.

★ 2671 ★

PEOPLE MUST BUY FIRST
    United Transparencies
    Box 688
    Binghamton, New York 13902
6 transparencies. $11.88.

★ 2672 ★
POWER-PACKED SELLING - PUTTING YOUR
CUSTOMER FIRST
  Creative Media Films
  820 Keo Way
  Des Moines, Iowa 50309
Film or video cassette, guide and manual. $475.00
(rental available).

★ 2673 ★
SALES AND MARKETING
  United Transparencies
  Box 688
  Binghamton, New York 13902
70 transparencies. $130.99.

★ 2674 ★
SELLING
  National Restaurant Association
  One IBM Plaza, Suite 2600
  Chicago, Illinois 60611
Video cartridge or 8 mm, 16 mm, and study guide.
$190.00.

★ 2675 ★
STRATEGY FOR WINNING
  National Restaurant Association
  One IBM Plaza, Suite 2600
  Chicago, Illinois 60611
Video cartridge or 8 mm, 16 mm, and study guide.
$190.00.

★ 2676 ★
SUCCESSFUL PERSUASION
  National Restaurant Association
  One IBM Plaza, Suite 2600
  Chicago, Illinois 60611
Video cartridge or 8 mm, 16 mm, and study guide.
$190.00.

Multimedia Kits

★ 2677 ★
THE BASIC SALES SERIES
  Resources for Education and Management
   Incorporated
  544 Medlock Road, Suite 210
  Decatur, Georgia 30030
6 filmstrips with cassette. $275.00.

★ 2678 ★
CREATIVE SELLING
  Better Selling Bureau
  1150 West Olive Avenue
  Burbank, California 91506
7 filmstrips with cassettes. $695.00.

★ 2679 ★
DEVELOPING A WINNING SALES PERSONALITY
  Thompson-Mitchell and Associates
  3384 Peachtree Road Northeast
  Atlanta, Georgia 30326
Filmstrip with cassette. $42.00.

★ 2680 ★
ERGONIC SELLING PROGRAM
  Ergonco Performance Source
  Northwest O'Hare Office Park, Suite 119
  2474 Dempster Street
  Des Plains, Illinois 60016
Multimedia self-study program.

★ 2681 ★
HOW TO WIN
  Ergonco Performance Source
  Northwest O'Hare Office Park, Suite 119
  2474 Dempster Street
  Des Plains, Illinois 60016
Multimedia self-study program.

★ 2682 ★
NOTHING HAPPENS UNTIL SOMEBODY SELLS
SOMETHING
  Thompson-Mitchell and Associates
  3384 Peachtree Road Northeast
  Atlanta, Georgia 30326
Filmstrip with cassette. $65.00.

★ 2683 ★
THE SALE THAT TURNED THE TIDE
  Close Productions
  2020 San Carlos Boulevard
  Fort Myers Beach, Florida 33931
Filmstrip with cassette. $37.50.

★ 2684 ★
THE SALESMAKERS
  Ergonco Performance Source
  Northwest O'Hare Office Park, Suite 119
  2474 Dempster Street
  Des Plains, Illinois 60016
Multimedia self-study program.

★ 2685 ★
SUCCESSFUL SELLING
 Thompson-Mitchell and Associates
 3384 Peachtree Road Northeast
 Atlanta, Georgia 30326
7 filmstrips with cassettes. $350.00.

★ 2686 ★
200 ON ALFRED (Basic sales training)
 Close Productions
 2020 San Carlos Boulevard
 Fort Myers Beach, Florida 33931
6 filmstrips with cassettes. $256.50.

Programmed Learning Materials

★ 2687 ★
PRINCIPLES OF SALESMANSHIP
Richard Howland
 Learning Systems Company
 1818 Ridge Road
 Homewood, Illinois 60430
Programmed learning aid. $1.51.

SALES TRAINING

Audio Cassettes/Tapes

★ 2688 ★
HOW COMPETENT SALES MANAGERS DEVELOP
SELF DIRECTED AND MOTIVATED SALESMEN
 Development Digest Incorporated
 3347 Motor Avenue
 Los Angeles, California 90034
Cassette. $13.75.

★ 2689 ★
HOW TO TRAIN SALESMEN IN PRODUCT
KNOWLEDGE
 Tape Rental Library Incorporated
 Post Office Box 2107
 2507 Edna Drive
 South Vineland, New Jersey 08360
Cassette.

★ 2690 ★
HOW TO TRAIN SALESMEN IN SELLING SKILLS
 Tape Rental Library Incorporated
 Post Office Box 2107
 2507 Edna Drive
 South Vineland, New Jersey 08360
Cassette.

★ 2691 ★
NEW SALES TRAINER
 Development Digest Incorporated
 3347 Motor Avenue
 Los Angeles, California 90034
2 cassettes. $13.75.

★ 2692 ★
PROFILE OF A MEMBER
Max Notowitz
 Tape Rental Library Incorporated
 Post Office Box 2107
 2507 Edna Drive
 South Vineland, New Jersey 08360
Cassette.

★ 2693 ★
REFRESHER TRAINING FOR EXPERIENCED
SALESMEN
 Tape Rental Library Incorporated
 Post Office Box 2107
 2507 Edna Drive
 South Vineland, New Jersey 08360
Cassette.

★ 2694 ★
SALES EXECUTIVES ROUNDTABLE (Sales
management problems)
 Listner Corporation
 6777 Hollywood Boulevard
 Hollywood, California 90028
12 cassettes. $180.00.

★ 2695 ★
SELF-TRAINING PROGRAMS FOR SALESMEN
 Tape Rental Library Incorporated
 Post Office Box 2107
 2507 Edna Drive
 South Vineland, New Jersey 08360
Cassette.

★ 2696 ★
THE STATEMENT OF POLICY
 Tape Rental Library Incorporated
 Post Office Box 2107
 2507 Edna Drive
 South Vineland, New Jersey 08360
Cassette with manual.

★ 2697 ★
TRAINING SALESMEN THROUGH ON-THE-JOB
COACHING
Tape Rental Library Incorporated
Post Office Box 2107
2507 Edna Drive
South Vineland, New Jersey   08360
Cassette.

★ 2698 ★
TRAINING SALESMEN THROUGH SALES MEETINGS
Tape Rental Library Incorporated
Post Office Box 2107
2507 Edna Drive
South Vineland, New Jersey   08360
Cassette.

★ 2699 ★
TRAINING SALESMEN TO CLOSE MORE SALES
Tape Rental Library Incorporated
Post Office Box 2107
2507 Edna Drive
South Vineland, New Jersey   08360
Cassette.

★ 2700 ★
WORKSHOP FOR SALES PROFESSIONALS
General Cassette Corporation
1324 North 22nd Avenue
Phoenix, Arizona   85009
6 cassettes. $59.00.

Correspondence Courses

★ 2701 ★
SALES TRAINING
Dun and Bradstreet Incorporated
Business Education Division
Box 803
Church Street Station
New York, New York   10008
Instruction through self-study text and correspondence
with instructor. $125.00.

Multimedia Kits

★ 2702 ★
RECRUITING AND SELECTING SALES WINNERS
Ergonco Performance Source
Northwest O'Hare Office Park, Suite 119
2474 Dempster Street
Des Plains, Illinois   60016
Multimedia self-study program.

SAMOAN

Printed Materials

★ 2703 ★
TEACH YOURSELF SAMOAN
C. G. Marsack
David McKay Company Incorporated
750 Third Avenue
New York, New York   10017
Self instruction book. $2.95.

SANITATION

See also: Health, Employee

Films/Video/Filmstrips

★ 2704 ★
DINING ROOM SANITATION
National Restaurant Association
One IBM Plaza, Suite 2600
Chicago, Illinois   60611
Video cartridge or 8mm, 16 mm, and study guide.
$190.00.

★ 2705 ★
SANITATION: "MORE THAN MEETS THE EYE"
National Restaurant Association
One IBM Plaza, Suite 2600
Chicago, Illinois   60611
Sound filmstrip. $25.00.

★ 2706 ★
SANITATION: RODENT AND INSECT CONTROL
National Restaurant Association
One IBM Plaza, Suite 2600
Chicago, Illinois   60611
Video cartridge or 8 mm, 16 mm, and study guide.
$190.00.

★ 2707 ★
SANITATION: RULES MAKE SENSE
National Restaurant Association
One IBM Plaza, Suite 2600
Chicago, Illinois   60611
Video cartridge or 8 mm, 16 mm, and study guide.
$190.00.

★ 2708 ★
SANITATION: WHY ALL THE FUSS?
　　　National Restaurant Association
　　　One IBM Plaza, Suite 2600
　　　Chicago, Illinois 60611
Video cartridge or 8 mm, 16 mm, and study guide.
$190.00.

SCHEDULING

See also: Planning

Multimedia Kits

★ 2709 ★
OUR TIME IS OVERTIME
　　　Resources for Education and Management
　　　　Incorporated
　　　544 Medlock Road, Suite 210
　　　Decatur, Georgia 30030
Filmstrip with cassette. $65.00.

SCHEMATICS

See also: Blueprint Reading

Printed Materials

★ 2710 ★
HOW TO READ SCHEMATIC DIAGRAMS
Donald Herrington
　　　Howard W. Sams and Company
　　　4300 West 62nd Street
　　　Indianapolis, Indiana   46268
Book.   1975. $4.95.

Programmed Learning Materials

★ 2711 ★
READING SCHEMATICS AND SYMBOLS
TPC Training Systems
　　　Technical Publishing Company
　　　1301 South Grove Avenue
　　　Barrington, Illinois   60010
Programmed text of 10 lessons. $20.50.

SECRETARIAL SKILLS

See also: Dictation; Office Practices;
　　　　Shorthand; Typewriting

Audio Cassettes/Tapes

★ 2712 ★
BECOME A SECRETARY/BECOME A RECEPTIONIST
　　　Educational Century Programming
　　　1201 East Johnson Street
　　　Jonesboro, Arkansas   72401
Cassette. $6.00.

★ 2713 ★
CLASSROOM INSTRUCTION PROGRAM
　　　National Book Company
　　　1019 Southwest Tenth Avenue
　　　Portland, Oregon   97206
Cassette. $203.05.

★ 2714 ★
CLERICAL TRAINING/OFFICE PROCEDURE
　　　Educational Century Programming
　　　1201 East Johnson Street
　　　Jonesboro, Arkansas   72401
Cassette. $6.00.

★ 2715 ★
DICTATION AND TRANSCRIPTION
　　　National Book Company
　　　1019 Southwest Tenth Avenue
　　　Portland, Oregon   97206
6 cassettes. $79.85.

★ 2716 ★
EXECUTIVE SECRETARY PROGRAM
　　　National Book Company
　　　1019 Southwest Tenth Avenue
　　　Portland, Oregon   97206
Cassette. $206.65.

★ 2717 ★
FILING
　　　National Book Company
　　　1019 Southwest Tenth Avenue
　　　Portland, Oregon   97206
6 cassettes. $89.45.

★ 2718 ★
GUIDE FOR EXECUTIVE SECRETARIES AND
ADMINISTRATIVE ASSISTANTS
　　　AMACOM
　　　American Management Associations
　　　135 West 50th Street
　　　New York, New York   10020
6 cassettes with workbook. $100.00.

★ 2719 ★
INDIVIDUALIZED INSTRUCTION PROGRAM
National Book Company
1019 Southwest Tenth Avenue
Portland, Oregon 97206
15 cassettes. $203.05.

★ 2720 ★
LEGAL SECRETARIAL (Typewriting and dictation)
National Book Company
1019 Southwest Tenth Avenue
Portland, Oregon 97206
6 cassettes. $88.90.

★ 2721 ★
THE MASTER SUCCESSFUL SECRETARY'S COURSE
Tape Rental Library Incorporated
Post Office Box 2107
2507 Edna Drive
South Vineland, New Jersey 08360
Cassette. $9.98.

★ 2722 ★
PHONETIC TRANSCRIPTION
Donald Dew, Paul Jensen
Charles E. Merrill Publishing Company
1300 Alum Creek Drive
Box 508
Columbus, Ohio 43216
Workbook and cassette. $19.00.

★ 2723 ★
REINFORCEMENT OF GREGG SYMBOLS AND
THEORY
Reinforcement Learning Incorporated
87 Dimmig Road
Post Office Box 562
Upper Saddle River, New Jersey 07458
Cassettes and workbook. $158.00.

★ 2724 ★
SECRETARIAL PRACTICE
National Book Company
1019 Southwest Tenth Avenue
Portland, Oregon 97206
6 cassettes with workbook. $86.15.

★ 2725 ★
SECRETARIAL PRACTICES/ADMINISTRATIVE
SECRETARIAL PRACTICES
Educational Century Programming
1201 East Johnson Street
Jonesboro, Arkansas 72401
Cassette. $6.00.

★ 2726 ★
SHORT LETTER DICTATION
National Book Company
1019 Southwest Tenth Avenue
Portland, Oregon 97206
27 cassettes. $354.30.

★ 2727 ★
SHORTHAND - PRINCIPLES/SHORTHAND -
BEGINNING
Educational Century Programming
1201 East Johnson Street
Jonesboro, Arkansas 72401
Cassette. $6.00.

★ 2728 ★
SHORTHAND - TRANSCRIPTION/SHORTHAND
SPEED AND TRANSCRIPTION
Educational Century Programming
1201 East Johnson Street
Jonesboro, Arkansas 72401
Cassette. $6.00.

★ 2729 ★
WORD PROCESSING: SECRETARIAL TRAINING
Educational Century Programming
1201 East Johnson Street
Jonesboro, Arkansas 72401
12 cassettes. $99.00.

Correspondence Courses

★ 2730 ★
ACCOUNTING FOR SECRETARIES
Western Washington State College
Center for Continuing Education
Edens Hall South
Bellingham, Washington 98225
Correspondence course.

★ 2731 ★
EXECUTIVE SECRETARIAL SKILLS COURSE
La Salle Extension University
417 South Dearborn Street
Chicago, Illinois 60605
Correspondence course.

★ 2732 ★
EXECUTIVE SECRETARY HOME STUDY COURSE
Technical Information Center
64 Society Street
Charleston, South Carolina 29401
14 lesson multimedia correspondence course.

★ 2733 ★
THEORY AND PRACTICE OF SHORTHAND
         University of Kentucky
         Independent Study Program
         Freeze Hall, Room 1
         Lexington, Kentucky 40506
Correspondence course.

Printed Materials

★ 2734 ★
ACCOUNTING ESSENTIALS FOR CAREER
SECRETARIES
Alexander Carson
         South Western Publishing Company
         5101 Madison Road
         Cincinnati, Ohio 45227
Book.   1972. $6.68.

Programmed Learning Materials

★ 2735 ★
ENGLISH STYLE SKILL BUILDERS - FOR
TRANSCRIBERS AND TYPISTS
         McGraw-Hill Book Company
         1221 Avenue of the Americas
         New York, New York 10019
Programmed text. $3.50.

★ 2736 ★
PROGRAMMED GREGG SHORTHAND
         McGraw-Hill Book Company
         1221 Avenue of the Americas
         New York, New York 10019
Programmed text. $6.60.

★ 2737 ★
SPEEDWRITING
         ITT Educational Services Incorporated
         55 West 42nd Street
         New York, New York 10036
Programmed text. $200.00.

SECURITIES INVESTMENT

         See also: Financial Planning;
                  Investment

Correspondence Courses

★ 2738 ★
FUNDAMENTALS OF THE SECURITY INDUSTRY

         New York Institute of Finance
         70 Pine Street
         New York, New York 10005
Correspondence course. $155.00.

★ 2739 ★
THE SECURITIES INDUSTRY
         New York Institute of Finance
         70 Pine Street
         New York, New York 10005
Correspondence course. $330.00.

★ 2740 ★
SECURITY ANALYSIS
         New York Institute of Finance
         70 Pine Street
         New York, New York 10005
20 lesson correspondence course. $140.00.

Multimedia Kits

★ 2741 ★
THE SECURITIES INDUSTRY
         Thompson-Mitchell and Associates
         3384 Peachtree Road Northeast
         Atlanta, Georgia 30326
6 filmstrips with cassette. $98.50.

Printed Materials

★ 2742 ★
SECURITIES PROGRAM - BONDS
         American Bankers Association
         1120 Connecticut Avenue Northwest
         Washington, D.C. 20036
Self instruction text of 6 lessons.   1976. $10.00.

★ 2743 ★
SELLING SECURITIES SUCCESSFULLY
Leo Fleur
         Prentice-Hall Incorporated
         Englewood Cliffs, New Jersey 07632
Book. $7.95.

SECURITY

Correspondence Courses

★ 2744 ★
PRACTICAL BURGLAR AND FIRE ALARM SALES
         Security Systems Management School
         1500 Cardinal Drive
         Little Falls, New Jersey 07424
Correspondence course. $375.00.

SELF CONFIDENCE

See also: Personal Development

Audio Cassettes/Tapes

★ 2745 ★
DISCOVER YOUR HIDDEN ABILITIES
Tape Rental Library Incorporated
Post Office Box 2107
2507 Edna Drive
South Vineland, New Jersey 03360
Cassette. $9.00.

★ 2746 ★
HOW TO CONQUER DISCOURAGEMENT
Tape Rental Library Incorporated
Post Office Box 2107
2507 Edna Drive
South Vineland, New Jersey 03360
Cassette. $9.98.

★ 2747 ★
HOW TO OVERCOME DISCOURAGEMENT
J. Martin Kohe
Cassette House
530 West Northwest Highway
Mount Prospect, Illinois 60056
Cassette. $9.95.

★ 2748 ★
I'M OK - YOU'RE OK
Thomas A. Harris M.D.
Cassette House
530 West Northwest Highway
Mount Prospect, Illinois 60056
Cassette. $9.95.

★ 2749 ★
THE NEGATIVE POWER OF POSITIVE THINKING
Edward L. Kramer
Tape Rental Library Incorporated
Post Office Box 2107
2507 Edna Drive
South Vineland, New Jersey 08360
Cassette. $4.98.

★ 2750 ★
OVERCOMING STAGEFRIGHT
Paul W. Schuette
Tape Rental Library Incorporated
Post Office Box 2107
2507 Edna Drive
South Vineland, New Jersey 03360
Cassette. $7.95.

★ 2751 ★
THE PROPER IMAGE
Educational Century Programming
1201 East Johnson Street
Jonesboro, Arkansas 72401
Cassette. $6.00.

★ 2752 ★
REALIZE YOUR POTENTIAL
Robert J. McKain Jr.
Cassette House
530 West Northwest Highway
Mount Prospect, Illinois 60056
Cassette. $9.95.

★ 2753 ★
SELF CONFIDENCE
Educational Century Programming
1201 East Johnson Street
Jonesboro, Arkansas 72401
Cassette. $6.00.

★ 2754 ★
SELF CONFIDENCE
Paul W. Schuette
Tape Rental Library Incorporated
Post Office Box 2107
2507 Edna Drive
South Vineland, New Jersey 08360
Cassette. $7.95.

★ 2755 ★
SELF CONFIDENCE THROUGH VISUALIZATION
SELF CONFIDENCE THROUGH AFFIRMATION
Thompson-Mitchell and Associates
3384 Peachtree Road Northeast
Atlanta, Georgia 30326
Cassette. $9.95.

Multimedia Kits

★ 2756 ★
SELF ESTEEM
Thompson-Mitchell and Associates
3384 Peachtree Road Northeast
Atlanta, Georgia 30326
Filmstrip with cassette. $65.00.

SELF EMPLOYMENT

See also: Free Lancing; Small Business
Management

Printed Materials

★ 2757 ★
BUYING AND RUNNING YOUR OWN BUSINESS
Ian Ford
Cahners Publishing Company Incorporated
221 Columbus Avenue
Boston, Massachusetts 02166
Book. 1970. $16.50.

★ 2758 ★
HOW TO EARN A FORTUNE AND BECOME
INDEPENDENT IN YOUR OWN BUSINESS
Merle Dowd
Prentice-Hall Incorporated
Englewood Cliffs, New Jersey 07632
Book. 1971. $8.95.

★ 2759 ★
PRIVATE BUSINESS ENTERPRISE
Hale Newcomer
Charles E. Merrill Company
1300 Alum Creek Drive
Columbus, Ohio 43216
Book. 1974. $13.95.

SERBO-CROATIAN

Multimedia Kits

★ 2760 ★
SERBO-CROATIAN - BASIC COURSE
General Services Administration
Foreign Service Institute Language Course
National Audiovisual Center
Order Section RR
Washington, D.C. 20409
Audio tapes, cassettes and text available.
Approximately $300.00.

Printed Materials

★ 2761 ★
LEARN SERBO-CROATIAN FOR ENGLISH SPEAKERS
Saphrograph Company
194 Elizabeth Street
New York, New York 10012
Book. $5.00.

★ 2762 ★
TEACH YOURSELF SERBO-CROATIAN
Viola Ellis
David McKay Company Incorporated
750 Third Avenue
New York, New York 10017
Self instruction book. $2.95.

SERVICE STATION OPERATION
See: AUTOMOBILE MECHANICS

SHEET METAL

Correspondence Courses

★ 2763 ★
SHEET METAL LAYOUT
International Correspondence School
Scranton, Pennsylvania 18515
Multi-module correspondence course.

Films/Video/Filmstrips

★ 2764 ★
SHEET METAL FABRICATION
DCA Educational Products
424 Valley Road
Warrington, Pennsylvania 18976
Sound filmstrips of 7 units. $45.00 each.

SHOE REPAIR

Printed Materials

★ 2765 ★
PRACTICAL COURSE IN MODERN SHOE REPAIRING
Ralph E. Sarlette
Nelson-Hall Publishers
325 West Jackson Boulevard
Chicago, Illinois 60606
Text. $10.95.

SHONA

Multimedia Kits

★ 2766 ★
SHONA - BASIC COURSE
General Services Administration
Foreign Service Institute Language Course
National Audiovisual Center
Order Section RR
Washington, D.C. 20409
Audio tapes, cassettes and text available.
Approximately $50.00.

SHORTHAND
See: SECRETARIAL SKILLS

SIGN LANGUAGE

Printed Materials

★ 2767 ★
SIGN LANGUAGE MADE SIMPLE
Edgar Lawrence
Gospel Publishing House
1445 Booneville Avenue
Springfield, Missouri 65802
Book. 1975. $8.95.

SINHALESE

Multimedia Kits

★ 2768 ★
COLLOQUIAL SINHALESE
General Services Administration
Foreign Service Institute Language Course
National Audiovisual Center
Order Section RR
Washington, D.C. 20409
Audio tapes, cassettes and text available.
Approximately $200.00.

SMALL BUSINESS MANAGEMENT

See also: Self Employment

Audio Cassettes/Tapes

★ 2769 ★
BIRTH OF A BUSINESS (Starting a business of your own)

Thompson-Mitchell and Associates
3384 Peachtree Road Northeast
Atlanta, Georgia 30326
12 cassettes. $72.00.

★ 2770 ★
THE FRANCHISE BOOM
Harry Kursh
Tape Rental Library Incorporated
Post Office Box 2107
2507 Edna Drive
South Vineland, New Jersey 08360
Cassette.

★ 2771 ★
HOW TO BE SUCCESSFUL IN YOUR OWN
BUSINESS
Tape Rental Library Incorporated
Post Office Box 2107
2507 Edna Drive
South Vineland, New Jersey 08360
Cassette. $9.98.

★ 2772 ★
YOU'RE IN BUSINESS
Art Fettig
Tape Rental Library Incorporated
Post Office Box 2107
2507 Edna Drive
South Vineland, New Jersey 08360
Cassette. $8.35.

Correspondence Courses

★ 2773 ★
MANAGING A SMALL BUSINESS
International Correspondence School
Scranton, Pennsylvania 18515
Multi-module correspondence course.

★ 2774 ★
SMALL BUSINESS MANAGEMENT
La Salle Extension University
417 South Dearborn Street
Chicago, Illinois 60605
Correspondence course.

Printed Materials

★ 2775 ★
BUSINESS! HOW TO START ONE
Eugene Ferkauf
Chelsea House Publishers
70 West 40th Street
New York, New York 10018

Book. 1976. $8.95.

★ 2776 ★
HOW TO FORM A PRIVATE COMPANY
Nigel Spinks
    McGraw-Hill Book Company
    1221 Avenue of the Americas
    New York, New York 10036
Book. 1972. $2.25.

★ 2777 ★
SMALL BUSINESS MANAGEMENT
William Macfarlane
    McGraw-Hill Book Company
    1221 Avenue of the Americas
    New York, New York 10036
Book. 1977. $13.95.

★ 2778 ★
SMALL BUSINESS MANAGEMENT: ESSENTIALS
FOR ENTREPRENEURSHIP
Lawrence Klatt
    Wadsworth Publishing Company Incorporated
    Ten Davis Drive
    Belmont, California 94002
Book. $9.95.

★ 2779 ★
SUCCESSFUL SMALL BUSINESS MANAGEMENT
Leon Wortman
    American Management Associations
    135 West 50th Street
    New York, New York 10020
Book. 1977. $10.95.

SMALL ENGINE REPAIR

Correspondence Courses

★ 2780 ★
BASIC SMALL ENGINE REPAIR COURSE
    NRI Schools
    3939 Wisconsin Avenue
    Washington, D.C. 20016
30 lesson home study program. $450.00.

★ 2781 ★
MASTER COURSE IN SMALL ENGINE REPAIR
    NRI Schools
    3939 Wisconsin Avenue
    Washington, D.C. 20016
45 lesson home study program. $560.00.

★ 2782 ★
SMALL ENGINE EQUIPMENT MECHANICS
    Commercial Trades Institute
    6201 West Howard Street
    Chicago, Illinois 60648
Correspondence course.

★ 2783 ★
SMALL ENGINE REPAIR
    Belsaw Institute
    315 Westport Road
    Kansas City, Missouri 64111
Home study course. $399.50.

SOCIOLOGY

Audio Cassettes/Tapes

★ 2784 ★
BASIC SOCIOLOGY
    Thompson-Mitchell and Associates
    3384 Peachtree Road Northeast
    Atlanta, Georgia 30326
Cassette. $9.98.

SOLDERING

Films/Video/Filmstrips

★ 2785 ★
RELIABLE SOLDERING
    C. L. Carter Jr. and Associates Incorporated
    434 First Bank and Trust Building
    811 South Central Expressway
    Richardson, Texas 75080
Film. $375.00 (rental available)

SPACE TECHNOLOGY

Programmed Learning Materials

★ 2786 ★
CONTROLLED GUIDANCE SYSTEMS
Hal Hellman
    Howard W. Sams and Company
    4300 West 62nd Street
    Indianapolis, Indiana 46268
Programmed text. $5.00.

★ 2787 ★
INTERTIAL GUIDANCE SYSTEMS
Robert Gates
        Howard W. Sams and Company
        4300 West 62nd Street
        Indianapolis, Indiana   46268
Programmed text. $5.00.

★ 2788 ★
LASERS AND MASERS
Charles Pike
        Howard W. Sams and Company
        4300 West 62nd Street
        Indianapolis, Indiana   46268
Programmed text. $5.00.

★ 2789 ★
MICROMINIATURE ELECTRONICS
Israel Kalish
        Howard W. Sams and Company
        4300 West 62nd Street
        Indianapolis, Indiana   46268
Programmed text. $6.00.

SPANISH

Audio Cassettes/Tapes

★ 2790 ★
BEGINNING SPANISH COURSE
Donald Barton,   Richard Tyler
        D.C. Heath and Company
        2700 North Richardt Avenue
        Indianapolis, Indiana   46219
Text, tapes and workbook.   1976.

★ 2791 ★
BERLITZ COMPREHENSIVE COURSE IN SPANISH
        Berlitz Language Program
        Post Office Box 5109
        FDR Station
        New York, New York   10022
6 cassettes with workbook. $85.00.

★ 2792 ★
BERLITZ COURSE IN SPANISH (Castilian)
        Berlitz Language Program
        Post Office Box 5109
        FDR Station
        New York, New York   10022
Cassette $5.95.   Also available on 8 track and LP
record.

★ 2793 ★
BERLITZ COURSE IN SPANISH (Latin American)
        Berlitz Language Program
        Post Office Box 5109
        FDR Station
        New York, New York   10022
Cassette $5.95.   Also available on 8 track and LP
record.

★ 2794 ★
CONVERSATIONAL SPANISH
        Educational Century Programming
        1201 East Johnson Street
        Jonesboro, Arkansas   72401
12 cassettes. $72.00.

★ 2795 ★
SPANISH
        Thompson-Mitchell and Associates
        3384 Peachtree Road Northeast
        Atlanta, Georgia   30326
Cassette. $9.98.

★ 2796 ★
SPANISH WITHOUT TOIL
Albert Cherel
        French and European Publications Incorporated
        Rockerfeller Center Promenade
        610 Fifth Avenue
        New York, New York   10020
Text and cassettes.

Correspondence Courses

★ 2797 ★
BEGINNING SPANISH
        University of Nebraska
        511 Nebraska Hall
        Lincoln, Nebraska   68588
Correspondence course.

★ 2798 ★
BEGINNING SPANISH
        University of Southern Mississippi
        Department of Independent Study
        Southern Station Box 56
        Hattisburg, Mississippi   39401
Correspondence course.

★ 2799 ★
SPANISH
University of Arkansas
Department of Independent Study
346 West Avenue
Fayetteville, Arkansas 72701
Correspondence course.

★ 2800 ★
SPANISH
Bringham Young University
Department of Independent Study
210 Herald R. Clark Building
Provo, Utah 84602
Correspondence course. $108.00.

★ 2801 ★
SPANISH LANGUAGE STUDIES
University of Washington
Office of Independent Study
222 Lewis Hall DW-30
Seattle, Washington 98195
Correspondence course.

Films/Video/Filmstrips

★ 2802 ★
CONVERSATIONAL SPANISH
Howard H. Hathway
Telstar Productions Incorporated
366 North Prior Avenue
Saint Paul, Minnesota 55104
20 video tape lessons. $4,400.00.

Multimedia Kits

★ 2803 ★
SPANISH - BASIC COURSE
General Services Administration
Foreign Service Institute Language Course
National Audiovisual Center
Order Section RR
Washington, D.C. 20409
Audio tapes, cassettes and text available.
Approximately $400.00.

★ 2804 ★
SPANISH - PROGRAMMATIC
General Services Administration
Foreign Service Institute Language Course
National Audiovisual Center
Order Section RR
Washington, D.C. 20409
Audio tapes, cassettes and text available.
Approximately $150.00.

Printed Materials

★ 2805 ★
SPANISH, EVERYDAY
L. D. Collier
David McKay Company Incorporated
750 Third Avenue
New York, New York 10017
Self instruction book. 1974. $2.95.

SPEED READING
See: STUDY AND READING SKILLS

SPEED WRITING
See: SECRETARIAL SKILLS

SPELLING

See also: Study and Reading Skills

Audio Cassettes/Tapes

★ 2806 ★
SPELLING
Thompson-Mitchell and Associates
3384 Peachtree Road Northeast
Atlanta, Georgia 30326
8 cassettes. $280.00.

STAFF DEVELOPMENT

See also: Management Development;
Personnel Management

Audio Cassettes/Tapes

★ 2807 ★
TRAINING AND COACHING YOUR WORK TEAM:
STEPS TO IMPROVED PERFORMANCE
Training House Incorporated
Box 688
Binghamton, New York 13902
Cassette and workbook. $36.00.

STATISTICS

Correspondence Courses

★ 2808 ★
BUSINESS GRAPHS AND STATISTICS
    Society of Manufacturing Engineers
    20501 Ford Road
    Post Office Box 930
    Dearborn, Michigan 48128
5 hour self instruction course. $10.00.

★ 2809 ★
INTRODUCTION TO STATISTICS
    Western Washington State College
    Center for Continuing Education
    Edens Hall South
    Bellingham, Washington 98225
Correspondence course.

★ 2810 ★
INTRODUCTION TO STATISTICS FOR ENGINEERS
    University of North Carolina
    Independent Study by Extension
    121 Abernethy Hall 002A
    Chapel Hill, North Carolina 27514
Correspondence course. $13.95.

★ 2811 ★
STATISTICAL METHOD
    University of Kentucky
    Independent Study Program
    Freeze Hall, Room 1
    Lexington, Kentucky 40506
Correspondence course.

★ 2812 ★
STATISTICS
    University of Nebraska
    511 Nebraska Hall
    Lincoln, Nebraska 68588
Correspondence course.

★ 2813 ★
STATISTICS
    The Thomas Institute
    Box 22
    New Canaan, Connecticut 06840
Self-study course. $110.00.

Multimedia Kits

★ 2814 ★
COMPLETE COURSE IN STATISTICS
    Lansford Publishing Company
    Post Office Box 8711
    San Jose, California 95155
Multimedia course. $1,900.00.

Programmed Learning Materials

★ 2815 ★
BUSINESS AND ECONOMIC STATISTICS
Robert Mason
    Learning Systems Company
    1818 Ridge Road
    Homewood, Illinois 60430
Programmed learning aid. $4.50.

STEAM TRAPS

Programmed Learning Materials

★ 2816 ★
DISC STEAM TRAPS
    E. I. du Pont de Nemours and Company
    Applied Technology Division
    Room B 4204
    Wilmington, Delaware 19898
Programmed course of approximately 2 hours. $5.90.

★ 2817 ★
FLOAT-THERMOSTATIC STEAM TRAPS
    E. I. du Pont de Nemours and Company
    Applied Technology Division
    Room B 4204
    Wilmington, Delaware 19898
Programmed course of approximately 1 hour. $4.10.

★ 2818 ★
IMPULSE STEAM TRAPS
    E. I. du Pont de Nemours and Company
    Applied Technology Division
    Room B 4204
    Wilmington, Delaware 19898
Programmed course of approximately 2 1/2 hours.
$7.40.

★ 2819 ★

INSTALLATION OF STEAM TRAPS
E. I. du Pont de Nemours and Company
Applied Technology Division
Room B 4204
Wilmington, Delaware 19898
Programmed course of approximately 3 hours. $7.40.

★ 2820 ★

INTRODUCTION TO STEAM TRAPS
E. I. du Pont de Nemours and Company
Applied Technology Division
Room B 4204
Wilmington, Delaware 19898
Programmed course of approximately 2 hours. $5.90.

★ 2821 ★

INVERTED BUCKET STEAM TRAPS
E. I. du Pont de Nemours and Company
Applied Technology Division
Room B 4204
Wilmington, Delaware 19898
Programmed course of approximately 1 1/2 hours.
$5.90.

★ 2822 ★

STEAM AND THE STEAM GENERATING UNIT
E. I. du Pont de Nemours and Company
Applied Technology Division
Room B 4204
Wilmington, Delaware 19898
Programmed course of approximately 4 1/2 hours.
$10.90.

★ 2823 ★

TESTING PROCEDURES FOR STEAM TRAPS
E. I. du Pont de Nemours and Company
Applied Technology Division
Room B 4204
Wilmington, Delaware 19898
Programmed course of approximately 4 1/2 hours.
$10.90.

★ 2824 ★

THERMOSTATIC STEAM TRAPS
E. I. du Pont de Nemours and Company
Applied Technology Division
Room B 4204
Wilmington, Delaware 19898
Programmed course of approximately 2 hours. $5.90.

★ 2825 ★

TROUBLE SHOOTING IN STEAM TRAPS
E. I. du Pont de Nemours and Company
Applied Technology Division
Room B 4204
Wilmington, Delaware 19898
Programmed course of approximately 2 hours. $5.90.

STOCKS
See: INVESTMENT

STRESS

See also: Personal Development; Relaxation;
Time Management

Audio Cassettes/Tapes

★ 2826 ★

GUIDELINES TO LIVING WITH STRESS
Hans Selye M.D.
Tape Rental Library Incorporated
Post Office Box 2107
2507 Edna Drive
South Vineland, New Jersey 08360
Cassette.

★ 2827 ★

HOW TO LICK EXECUTIVE STRESS
Dr. Robert C. Page
Tape Rental Library Incorporated
Post Office Box 2107
2507 Edna Drive
South Vineland, New Jersey 08360
Cassette.

★ 2828 ★

LIVING WITH STRESS SUCCESSFULLY
Dr. Ken Olson
General Cassette Corporation
1324 North 22nd Avenue
Post Office Box 6940
Phoenix, Arizona 85005
4 cassettes. $39.00.

★ 2829 ★

LIVING WITH STRESS SUCCESSFULLY
Lansford Publishing Company
Post Office Box 8711
San Jose, California 95155
4 cassettes. $59.95.

★ 2830 ★
STRESS/GOALS
Fraser Deacon
    Tape Rental Library Incorporated
    Post Office Box 2107
    2507 Edna Drive
    South Vineland, New Jersey 08360
Cassette.

★ 2831 ★
SUCCESS WITHOUT STRESS
    AMACOM
    American Management Associations
    135 West 50th Street
    New York, New York 10020
2 cassettes. $35.00.

STUDY AND READING SKILLS

See also: Spelling; Vocabulary
                Skills

Audio Cassettes/Tapes

★ 2832 ★
ADULT READING PROGRAM
    Educational Century Programming
    1201 East Johnson Street
    Jonesboro, Arkansas 72401
24 cassette. $144.00.

★ 2833 ★
ASSOCIATIVE LEARNING TECHNIQUES
    Westinghouse Learning Press
    College Publications
    Post Office Box 10680
    Palo Alto, California 94303
6 cassettes. $97.50.

★ 2834 ★
FASTER, EFFICIENT READING
    Educational Century Programming
    1201 East Johnson Street
    Jonesboro, Arkansas 72401
Cassette. $6.00.

★ 2835 ★
GOOD STUDY HABITS
    Success Tapes
    6954 Hanover Parkway #300
    Greenbelt, Maryland 20770
Cassette. $9.95.

★ 2836 ★
HOW TO INCREASE YOUR READING SPEED IN SEVEN DAYS
    Tape Rental Library Incorporated
    Post Office Box 2107
    2507 Edna Drive
    South Vineland, New Jersey 08360
Cassette. $9.98.

★ 2837 ★
HOW TO SCORE HIGH ON EXAMINATIONS
    Tape Rental Library Incorporated
    Post Office Box 2107
    2507 Edna Drive
    South Vineland, New Jersey 08360
Cassette.

★ 2838 ★
PROBE 2: A SHORT COURSE IN COLLEGE READING
Marvin D. Glock, David Bender, Karen Tosi, Valerie Faith
    Charles E. Merrill Publishing Company
    1300 Alum Creek Drive
    Box 508
    Columbus, Ohio 43216
Work text and cassettes. $275.00.

★ 2839 ★
READING (Help Yourself to Better Reading)
    National Book Company
    1019 Southwest Tenth Avenue
    Portland, Oregon 97206
15 cassettes. $201.95.

★ 2840 ★
A READING PROGRAM THAT BOOSTS UNDERSTANDING AND PROFIT
    Thompson-Mitchell and Associates
    3384 Peachtree Road Northeast
    Atlanta, Georgia 30326
Cassette. $15.00.

★ 2841 ★
THE SECRET OF SUCCESS
James Allen
    Tape Rental Library Incorporated
    Post Office Box 2107
    2507 Edna Drive
    South Vineland, New Jersey 08360
Cassette. $8.95.

★ 2842 ★
SEVEN DAYS TO FASTER READING
William S. Schaill
    Tape Rental Library Incorporated
    Post Office Box 2107
    2507 Edna Drive
    South Vineland, New Jersey   08360
Cassette.

★ 2843 ★
SPEED LEARNING
    Learn Incorporated
    Mount Laurel Plaza
    113 Gaither Drive
    Mount Laurel, New Jersey   08054
Workbook and cassettes. $79.95.

★ 2844 ★
SPEED LEARNING COURSE
    National Association of Accountants
    919 Third Avenue
    New York, New York   10022
Text and cassettes. $99.00.

★ 2845 ★
SPEED READING
    Educational Century Programming
    1201 East Johnson Street
    Jonesboro, Arkansas   72401
12 cassettes. $72.00.

★ 2846 ★
SPEEDWAY READING SYSTEM
Dr. Wayne Otto
    Hy Cite Corporation
    340 Coyier Lane
    Madison, Wisconsin   53713
16 unit cassette and workbook. $129.90.

★ 2847 ★
STUDENT SPECIAL – "SUCCESSFUL STUDY HABITS"
Paul W. Schuette
    Tape Rental Library Incorporated
    Post Office Box 2107
    2507 Edna Drive
    South Vineland, New Jersey   08360
Cassette. $7.95.

★ 2848 ★
SUCCESS IN THE CLASSROOM
Dr. J. Clifton Williams

    E. F. Wonderlic and Associates Incorporated
    820 Frontage Road
    Northfield, Illinois   60093
Cassette. $10.00.

★ 2849 ★
SUCCESSFUL STUDY HABITS
    Success Tapes
    6954 Hanover Parkway #300
    Greenbelt, Maryland   20770
Cassette. $9.95.

★ 2850 ★
TECHNIQUES FOR ACADEMIC SUCCESS
Dr. Clifton Williams
    E. F. Wonderlic and Associates Incorporated
    820 Frontage Road
    Northfield, Illinois   60093
Cassette. $10.00.

Films/Video/Filmstrips

★ 2851 ★
BETTER LEARNING HABITS
David M. Wark
    Telstar Productions Incorporated
    366 North Prior Avenue
    Saint Paul, Minnesota   55104
5 video tape lessons. $220.00 each.

★ 2852 ★
EFFICIENT READING
James I. Brown
    Telstar Productions Incorporated
    366 North Prior Avenue
    Saint Paul, Minnesota   55104
12 video tape lessons. $3,600.00.

★ 2853 ★
PERCEPTION EXERCISES FOR EFFICIENT READING
    Telstar Productions Incorporated
    366 North Prior Avenue
    Saint Paul, Minnesota   55104
4 video tapes. $600.00.

Multimedia Kits

★ 2854 ★
SPEED LEARNING
    United Media International Incorporated
    306 Dartmouth Street
    Boston, Massachusetts   02116
Multimedia self instruction program. $80.00.

Printed Materials

★ 2855 ★
HOW TO MANAGE YOUR READING
Thomas Anastasi
     General Electric Company Training and
       Education Publications
     One River Road
     Post Office Box BP
     Schenectady, New York 12345
Book. 1974. $5.00.

★ 2856 ★
READING IMPROVEMENT
Barbara Macknick Klaeser
     Nelson-Hall Publishers
     325 West Jackson Boulevard
     Chicago, Illinois 60606
Self instruction text. $7.95.

Programmed Learning Materials

★ 2857 ★
LISTENING AND NOTETAKING
     McGraw-Hill Book Company
     1221 Avenue of the Americas
     New York, New York 10019
Programmed text. $3.95.

SUCCESS

See also: Personal Development

Audio Cassettes/Tapes

★ 2858 ★
ACHIEVEMENT DYNAMICS
     Thompson-Mitchell and Associates
     3384 Peachtree Road Northeast
     Atlanta, Georgia 30326
Cassette. $150.00.

★ 2859 ★
BORN TO WIN
Muriel James, Dorothy Jongeward
     E. F. Wonderlic and Associates Incorporated
     820 Frontage Road
     Northfield, Illinois 60093
Cassette. $10.00.

★ 2860 ★
BUSINESS SUCCESS
Charles M. Schwab
     Tape Rental Library Incorporated
     Post Office Box 2107
     2507 Edna Drive
     South Vineland, New Jersey 08360
Cassette. $8.95.

★ 2861 ★
CATCH A SUCCESS SYNDROME - HOMING-IN
ON SUCCESS
     Educational Century Programming
     1201 East Johnson Street
     Jonesboro, Arkansas 72401
Cassette. $6.00.

★ 2862 ★
THE COMMON DENOMINATOR OF SUCCESS
Earl Nightingale
     Tape Rental Library Incorporated
     Post Office Box 2107
     2507 Edna Drive
     South Vineland, New Jersey 08360
Cassette. $16.95.

★ 2863 ★
DOORWAY TO SUCCESS
Paul W. Schuette
     Tape Rental Library Incorporated
     Post Office Box 2107
     2507 Edna Drive
     South Vineland, New Jersey 08360
Cassette. $9.95.

★ 2864 ★
GOLDEN GOAL POWER
Paul W. Schuette
     Tape Rental Library Incorporated
     Post Office Box 2107
     2507 Edna Drive
     South Vineland, New Jersey 08360
Cassette. $7.95.

★ 2865 ★
HANDLING SUCCESS
     Educational Century Programming
     1201 East Johnson Street
     Jonesboro, Arkansas 72401
Cassette. $6.00.

★ 2866 ★
I AM RICH
Paul W. Schuette
    Tape Rental Library Incorporated
    Post Office Box 2107
    2507 Edna Drive
    South Vineland, New Jersey   03360
Cassette. $7.95.

★ 2867 ★
I AM SUCCESSFUL
Paul W. Schuette
    Tape Rental Library Incorporated
    Post Office Box 2107
    2507 Edna Drive
    South Vineland, New Jersey   08360
Cassette. $7.95.

★ 2868 ★
THE MILLION DOLLAR PERSONAL SUCCESS PLAN
Paul J. Meyer
    Success Motivation Institute
    5000 Lakewood Drive
    Waco, Texas   76710
Cassette. $9.95.

★ 2869 ★
MORE AND BETTER LUCK
    Educational Century Programming
    1201 East Johnson Street
    Jonesboro, Arkansas   72401
Cassette. $6.00.

★ 2870 ★
PERSONAL DEVELOPMENT (Success seminar)
    Tape Rental Library Incorporated
    Post Office Box 2107
    2507 Edna Drive
    South Vineland, New Jersey   08360
8 cassettes. $55.00.

★ 2871 ★
THE POWER OF THOUGHT/FIRST STEPS TO
SUCCESS
    Educational Century Programming
    1201 East Johnson Street
    Jonesboro, Arkansas   72401
Cassette. $6.00.

★ 2872 ★
SCIENCE OF PERSONAL SUCCESS
    Learning Dynamics
    167 Corey Road
    Boston, Massachusetts   02146

6 cassettes. $129.00.

★ 2873 ★
SELL YOURSELF ON SUCCESS/WHY COMPROMISE
ETHICS?
    Educational Century Programming
    1201 East Johnson Street
    Jonesboro, Arkansas   72401
Cassette. $6.00.

★ 2874 ★
THE SMILE OF SUCCESS (Service with a smile)
    Thompson-Mitchell and Associates
    3384 Peachtree Road Northeast
    Atlanta, Georgia   30326
Cassette. $6.00.

★ 2875 ★
THE STRANGEST SECRET (Method for achievement)
Earl Nightingale
    Tape Rental Library Incorporated
    Post Office Box 2107
    2507 Edna Drive
    South Vineland, New Jersey   08360
Cassette. $9.00.

★ 2876 ★
SUCCESS SYSTEM THAT NEVER FAILS
W. Clement Stone
    Cassette House
    530 West Northwest Highway
    Mount Prospect, Illinois   60056
2 cassettes. $16.95.

★ 2877 ★
SUCCESS THROUGH GOAL SETTING
    Tape Rental Library Incorporated
    Post Office Box 2107
    2507 Edna Drive
    South Vineland, New Jersey   08360
Cassette. $9.98.

★ 2878 ★
THINK AND GROW RICH
Napolean Hill
    Cassette House
    530 West Northwest Highway
    Mount Prospect, Illinois   60056
Cassette. $9.95.

★ 2879 ★
THINK AND GROW RICH
Napoleon Hill
        Tape Rental Library Incorporated
        Post Office Box 2107
        2507 Edna Drive
        South Vineland, New Jersey   08360
Cassette. $9.00.

Films/Video/Filmstrips

★ 2880 ★
STRATEGY FOR WINNING
        National Restaurant Association
        One IBM Plaza, Suite 2600
        Chicago, Illinois   60611
Video cartridge or 8 mm, 16 mm, and study guide.
$190.00.

★ 2881 ★
YOU CAN SURPASS YOURSELF
        Ramic Productions
        4910 Birch Street
        Newport Beach, California   92660
Film and manual. $550.00.

SUPERVISION (GENERAL)

        See also: headings under Management;
Organizational Development; Staff Development

Audio Cassettes/Tapes

★ 2882 ★
AND IT WORKS (Supervision)
        Thompson-Mitchell and Associates
        3384 Peachtree Road Northeast
        Atlanta, Georgia   30326
Cassette. $13.75.

★ 2883 ★
BUILDING TEAMWORK
George Odiorne
        MBO Incorporated
        157 Pontoosic Road
        Westfield, Massachusetts   01085
Cassette and manual. $15.00.

★ 2884 ★
THE EFFECTIVE SUPERVISOR: DEALING WITH
CONFLICTING VALUE SYSTEMS

        Westinghouse Learning Press
        College Publications
        Post Office Box 10580
        Palo Alto, California   94303
Cassette with workbook. $60.00.

★ 2885 ★
FUNDAMENTALS OF SUPERVISION
        Practical Management Associates
          Incorporated
        Post Office Box 751
        Woodland Hills, California   91365
Cassette and workbook kit.

★ 2886 ★
MEADOWS SUPERVISOR DEVELOPMENT PROGRAM
        Meadow Communications
        Post Office Box 447
        Flushing, New York   11365
2 cassettes and workbook. $55.00.

★ 2887 ★
THE NEW SUPERVISOR PROGRAM
        Addison Wesley Publishing Company
          Incorporated
        Jacob Way
        Reading, Massachusetts   01867
14 cassettes and assignment sheets. $200.00.

★ 2888 ★
THE SITUATIONAL MANAGER
George Odiorne
        MBO Incorporated
        157 Pontoosic Road
        Westfield, Massachusetts   01085
Cassette and manual. $15.00.

Correspondence Courses

★ 2889 ★
EFFECTIVE SUPERVISION OF PEOPLE
        Dun and Bradstreet Incorporated
        Business Education Division
        Box 803
        Church Street Station
        New York, New York   10008
Instruction through self-study text and correspondence
with instructor. $125.00.

★ 2890 ★
HOW TO IMPROVE YOUR SUPERVISORY COST
REDUCTION SKILLS
        Society of Manufacturing Engineers
        20501 Ford Road
        Post Office Box 930
        Dearborn, Michigan   48128
8 hours self instruction course. $14.00.

★ 2891 ★
INSPECTION SUPERVISION
        The Thomas Institute
        Box 22
        New Canaan, Connecticut   06840
Self-study course. $110.00.

★ 2892 ★
PRINCIPLES OF SUPERVISION
        The Thomas Institute
        Box 22
        New Canaan, Connecticut   06840
Self-study course. $110.00.

Films/Video/Filmstrips

★ 2893 ★
EYE OF THE SUPERVISOR
        National Restaurant Association
        One IBM Plaza, Suite 2600
        Chicago, Illinois   60611
Video cartridge or 8 mm, 16 mm, and study guide.
$190.00.

Games/Simulations

★ 2894 ★
EFFECTIVE SUPERVISION
        Didactic Systems Incorporated
        Box 457
        Cranford, New Jersey   07016
Simulation game. $24.00.

Multimedia Kits

★ 2895 ★
MAN ON THE LINE (A foreman's job performance)
        Westinghouse Learning Press
        College Publications
        Post Office Box 10680
        Palo Alto, California   94303
5 filmstrips with cassettes. $395.00.

★ 2896 ★
THE NEED FOR PRE-SUPERVISORY TRAINING
        Resources for Education and Management
            Incorporated
        544 Medlock Road, Suite 210
        Decatur, Georgia   30030
Filmstrip with cassette. $70.00.

★ 2897 ★
THE ROLE OF A SUPERVISOR
        Gamco-Siboney
        Box 1911
        Big Spring, Texas   79720
3 filmstrips with cassettes. $51.00.

Programmed Learning Materials

★ 2898 ★
ESSENTIALS OF SUPERVISION
George R. Terry
        Learning Systems Company
        1818 Ridge Road
        Homewood, Illinois   60430
Programmed learning aid. $4.95.

SUPERVISION, MINORITIES

        See also: Equal Employment Opportunity

Multimedia Kits

★ 2899 ★
GENERAL PROBLEMS IN SUPERVISING THE
DISADVANTAGED
        Resources for Education and Management
            Incorporated
        544 Medlock Road, Suite 210
        Decatur, Georgia   30030
Filmstrip with cassette. $60.00.

★ 2900 ★
INTERVIEWING THE DISADVANTAGED
        Resources for Education and Management
            Incorporated
        544 Medlock Road, Suite 210
        Decatur, Georgia   30030
Filmstrip with cassette. $60.00.

★ 2901 ★
MOTIVATING THE DISADVANTAGED
  Resources for Education and Management
   Incorporated
  544 Medlock Road, Suite 210
  Decatur, Georgia 30030
Filmstrip with cassette. $60.00.

SUPERVISION SKILLS

Audio Cassettes/Tapes

★ 2902 ★
FIVE MINUTES A DAY
  Tape Rental Library Incorporated
  Post Office Box 2107
  2507 Edna Drive
  South Vineland, New Jersey 08360
Cassette.

★ 2903 ★
GETTING THINGS DONE IN SUPERVISION
George Odiorne
  MBO Incorporated
  157 Pontoosic Road
  Westfield, Massachusetts 01085
Cassette and manual. $15.00.

★ 2904 ★
HOW TO BE AN EFFECTIVE SUPERVISOR
  American Management Associations
  135 West 50th Street
  New York, New York 10020
Cassettes and workbooks. $100.00.

★ 2905 ★
SUPERVISORY EFFECTIVENESS
  American Management Associations
  135 West 50th Street
  New York, New York 10020
Cassette. $100.00.

★ 2906 ★
SUPERVISORY SKILLS
George Odiorne
  MBO Incorporated
  157 Pontoosic Road
  Westfield, Massachusetts 01085
12 cassettes and manual. $150.00.

★ 2907 ★
YOU AS A SUPERVISOR
George Odiorne
  MBO Incorporated
  157 Pontoosic Road
  Westfield, Massachusetts 01085
Cassette and manual. $15.00.

Multimedia Kits

★ 2908 ★
HOW TO GET WORK DONE
  Resources for Education and Management
   Incorporated
  544 Medlock Road, Suite 210
  Decatur, Georgia 30030
Filmstrip with cassette. $55.00.

Printed Materials

★ 2909 ★
NEW SUPERVISOR
Martin M. Broadwell
  Addison Wesley Publishing Company Incorporated
  Jacob Way
  Reading, Massachusetts 01867
Training guide. $6.95.

★ 2910 ★
PRACTICE OF SUPERVISING: MAKING EXPERIENCE
PAY
Martin M. Broadwell
  Addison Wesley Publishing Company Incorporated
  Jacob Way
  Reading, Massachusetts 01867
Training guide. $6.95.

SUPERVISION, TRAINING

  See also: Management Development;
   Training Techniques

Correspondence Courses

★ 2911 ★
HOW TO IMPROVE YOUR SUPERVISORY TRAINING
SKILLS
  Society of Manufacturing Engineers
  20501 Ford Road
  Post Office Box 930
  Dearborn, Michigan 48128
4 hours self instruction course. $10.00.

Printed Materials

★ 2912 ★
THE SUPERVISOR AND ON-THE-JOB TRAINING
Martin M. Broadwell
      Addison Wesley Publishing Company Incorporated
      Jacob Way
      Reading, Massachusetts   01867
Training guide. $6.95.

SWAHILI

Multimedia Kits

★ 2913 ★
SWAHILI - ACTIVE INTRODUCTION, GENERAL
CONVERSATION
      General Services Administration
      Foreign Service Institute Language Course
      National Audiovisual Center
      Order Section RR
      Washington, D.C.   20409
Audio tapes, cassettes and text also available.
Approximately $15.00.

★ 2914 ★
SWAHILI - BASIC COURSE
      General Services Administration
      Foreign Service Institute Language Course
      National Audiovisual Center
      Order Section RR
      Washington, D.C.   20409
Audio tapes, cassettes and text also available.
Approximately $100.00.

Printed Materials

★ 2915 ★
LEARN SWAHILI FOR ENGLISH SPEAKERS
Ernest Haddon
      Saphrograph Company
      194 Elizabeth Street
      New York, New York   10012
Book. $7.50.

★ 2916 ★
LIVING SWAHILI
Ahmed Salim
      Crown Publishers Incorporated
      419 Park Avenue South
      New York, New York   10016
Book. $11.95.

★ 2917 ★
SIMPLIFIED SWAHILI
P. M. Wilson
      International Publications Service
      114 East 32nd Street
      New York, New York   10016
Book.   1970. $10.00.

★ 2918 ★
TEACH YOURSELF SWAHILI
D. V. Perrott
      David McKay Company Incorporated
      750 Third Avenue
      New York, New York   10017
Self instruction book.   1974. $2.95.

SWEDISH

Correspondence Courses

★ 2919 ★
SWEDISH LANGUAGE STUDIES
      University of Washington
      Office of Independent Study
      222 Lewis Hall DW-30
      Seattle, Washington   98195
Correspondence course.

Multimedia Kits

★ 2920 ★
SWEDISH - BASIC COURSE
      General Services Administration
      Foreign Service Institute Language Course
      National Audiovisual Center
      Order Section RR
      Washington, D.C.   20409
Audio tapes, cassettes and text also available.
Approximately $150.00.

Printed Materials

★ 2921 ★
LEARN SWEDISH FOR ENGLISH SPEAKERS
      Saphrograph Company
      194 Elizabeth Street
      New York, New York   10012
Book. $5.00.

★ 2922 ★
SWEDISH FOR FOREIGNERS
A. Rosen
    Arthur Vanous Company
    616 Kinderkamack Road
    River Edge, New Jersey 07661
Book. $6.00.

★ 2923 ★
TEACH YOURSELF SWEDISH
R. J. McClean
    David McKay Company Incorporated
    750 Third Avenue
    New York, New York 10017
Self instruction. $3.95.

SYSTEMS ANALYSIS

See also: Data Processing; Planning

Audio Cassettes/Tapes

★ 2924 ★
EFFECTIVE METHODS FOR SYSTEMS ANALYSIS
    QED Incorporated
    Box 1608
    Burbank, California 91507
10 cassettes and workbook. $275.00.

★ 2925 ★
TECHNIQUES FOR SYSTEMS, DESIGN, AND
IMPLEMENTATION
    QED Incorporated
    Box 1608
    Burbank, California 91507
10 cassettes with workbook. $275.00.

TAXES

Audio Cassettes/Tapes

★ 2926 ★
DEDUCTIONS
    Tape Rental Library Incorporated
    Post Office Box 2107
    2507 Edna Drive
    South Vineland, New Jersey 08360
Cassette.

★ 2927 ★
INTRODUCTION TO TAXES TODAY
    Tape Rental Library Incorporated
    Post Office Box 2107
    2507 Edna Drive
    South Vineland, New Jersey 08360
Cassette.

★ 2928 ★
MARRIAGE AND TAXES
    Tape Rental Library Incorporated
    Post Office Box 2107
    2507 Edna Drive
    South Vineland, New Jersey 08360
Cassette.

★ 2929 ★
MORE DEDUCTIONS
    Tape Rental Library Incorporated
    Post Office Box 2107
    2507 Edna Drive
    South Vineland, New Jersey 08360
Cassette.

★ 2930 ★
PROTECTION FOR INCOME
    Tape Rental Library Incorporated
    Post Offixe Box 2107
    2507 Edna Drive
    South Vineland, New Jersey 08360
Cassette.

★ 2931 ★
SYNDICATION TAX RAMIFICATIONS -
STRUCTURING YOUR DEAL
William A. Kelley Jr.
    Tape Rental Library Incorporated
    Post Office Box 2107
    2507 Edna Drive
    South Vineland, New Jersey 08360
Cassette.

★ 2932 ★
TAXES ON INSURANCE
Bernard Corak
    Tape Rental Library Incorporated
    Post Office Box 2107
    2507 Edna Drive
    South Vineland, New Jersey 08360
Cassette. $8.50.

★ 2933 ★
TAXPAYER'S RIGHTS
    Tape Rental Library Incorporated
    Post Office Box 2107
    2507 Edna Drive
    South Vineland, New Jersey 08360
Cassette.

Correspondence Courses

★ 2934 ★
FEDERAL INCOME TAX COURSE
    National Tax Training School
    Monsey, New York 10952
Correspondence course.

★ 2935 ★
FEDERAL INCOME TAX PROCEDURE
    University of South Carolina
    Department of Correspondence Study
    Division of Continuing Education
    Columbia, South Carolina 29208
Correspondence course.

★ 2936 ★
FEDERAL TAXATION
    Pennsylvania State University
    Department of Independent Study by
        Correspondence
    Three Sheilds Building
    University Park, Pennsylvania 16802
Correspondence course.

★ 2937 ★
INCOME TAX ACCOUNTING
    Texas Tech University
    Division of Continuing Education
    Post Office Box 4110
    Lubbock, Texas 79409
Correspondence course.

★ 2938 ★
INDIVIDUAL TAX PLANNING
    University of South Carolina
    Department of Correspondence Study
    Division of Continuing Education
    Columbia, South Carolina 29208
Correspondence course. $69.00.

Printed Materials

★ 2939 ★
THE INCOME TAX AND BUSINESS DECISIONS
William Raby
    Prentice-Hall Incorporated
    Englewood Cliffs, New Jersey 07632
Book. 1975. $14.95.

Programmed Learning Materials

★ 2940 ★
FEDERAL INCOME TAX
James L. Wittenbach, Ken Milani
    Learning Systems Company
    1818 Ridge Road
    Homewood, Illinois 60430
Programmed learning aid. $4.95.

TAXIDERMY

Correspondence Courses

★ 2941 ★
TAXIDERMY
    The Northwestern School of Taxidermy
    1202 Howard Street
    Omaha, Nebraska 68103
Correspondence course.

TEACHING

    See also: Classroom Instruction;
        Training Techniques

Audio Cassettes/Tapes

★ 2942 ★
ARE YOU A TEACHER
    Tape Rental Library Incorporated
    Post Office Box 2107
    2507 Edna Drive
    South Vineland, New Jersey 08360
Cassette.

★ 2943 ★
SUCCESSFUL TEACHING
    Educational Century Programming
    1201 East Johnson Street
    Jonesboro, Arkansas 72401
Cassette. $6.00.

Film/Video/Filmstrips

★ 2944 ★
THE TEACHING ROLE (A program designed for health professionals)
        Telstar Productions Incorporated
        366 North Prior Avenue
        Saint Paul, Minnesota 55104
12 video tape lessons. $250.00 each.

Multimedia Kits

★ 2945 ★
THE TEACHING-LEARNING PROCESS
        Resources for Education and Management
            Incorporated
        544 Medlock Road, Suite 210
        Decatur, Georgia 30030
Filmstrip with cassette. $55.00.

Printed Materials

★ 2946 ★
TEACH YOURSELF (Initial teaching alphabet)
        Fearon-Pitman Publishers Incorporated
        Six Davis Drive
        Belmont, California 94002
Self instruction text. $3.25.

TEAM BUILDING
See: GROUP DEVELOPMENT

TELEPHONE SALES

Audio Cassettes/Tapes

★ 2947 ★
COLLECTING PAST DUE ACCOUNTS BY PHONE
        American Media Incorporated
        5907 Meredith Drive
        Des Moines, Iowa 50324
Cassette. $94.50.

★ 2948 ★
GAINING NEW CUSTOMERS BY PHONE
        American Media Incorporated
        5907 Meredith Drive
        Des Moines, Iowa 50324
Cassette. $94.50.

★ 2949 ★
HANDLING COMPLAINTS BY PHONE
        American Media Incorporated
        5907 Meredith Drive
        Des Moines, Iowa 50324
Cassette. $94.50.

★ 2950 ★
HOW TO GET DAYTIME LIFE INSURANCE APPOINTMENTS BY TELEPHONE AND WHERE TO FIND THE PROSPECTS
F. C. Pfister
        Tape Rental Library Incorporated
        Post Office Box 2107
        2507 Edna Drive
        South Vineland, New Jersey 08360
Cassette. $11.95.

★ 2951 ★
INTRODUCING SOMETHING NEW BY PHONE
        American Media Incorporated
        5907 Meredith Drive
        Des Moines, Iowa 50324
Cassette. $94.50.

★ 2952 ★
MAKING TELEPHONE SALES APPOINTMENTS
        American Media Incorporated
        5907 Meredith Drive
        Des Moines, Iowa 50324
Cassette. $94.50.

★ 2953 ★
OVERCOMING SALES RESISTANCE ON THE TELEPHONE
        American Media Incorporated
        5907 Meredith Drive
        Des Moines, Iowa 50324
Cassette. $94.50.

★ 2954 ★
PAY PHONE PAY (Using telephone to supplement face-to-face selling)
        Tape Rental Library Incorporated
        Post Office Box 2107
        2507 Edna Drive
        South Vineland, New Jersey 08360
2 cassettes. $26.95.

★ 2955 ★
RESELLING YOUR OLD ACCOUNTS BY PHONE
American Media Incorporated
5907 Meredith Drive
Des Moines, Iowa 50324
Cassette. $94.50.

★ 2956 ★
SELLING BY TELEPHONE
National Office Products Association
301 North Fairfax Street
Alexandria, Virginia 22314
Cassette and handbook. $50.00.

★ 2957 ★
TELEPHONE PROSPECTING FOR GREATER SUCCESS
General Cassette Corporation
1324 North 22nd Avenue
Phoenix, Arizona 85009
Cassette. $49.50.

★ 2958 ★
TELEPHONE PROSPECTING FOR GREATER SUCCESS
Thom Norman
Tape Rental Library Incorporated
Post Office Box 2107
2507 Edna Drive
South Vineland, New Jersey 08360
4 cassettes. $49.50.

Film/Video/Filmstrips

★ 2959 ★
THE ABC OF TELEPHONE SALES
Salenger Educational Media
1635 12th Street
Santa Monica, California 90404
Film, guides and text. $400.00 (rental available).

TELEPHONE TECHNIQUES

Audio Cassettes/Tapes

★ 2960 ★
EFFECTIVE TELEPHONE TECHNIQUES FOR
DOCTOR/DENTAL RECEPTIONISTS
General Cassette Corporation
1324 North 22nd Avenue
Phoenix, Arizona 85009
3 cassettes. $35.00.

★ 2961 ★
EFFECTIVE TELEPHONE TECHNIQUES FOR
SECRETARIES AND RECEPTIONISTS
General Cassette Corporation
1324 North 22nd Avenue
Phoenix, Arizona 85009
2 cassettes. $19.50.

★ 2962 ★
GOOD PUBLIC RELATIONS ON THE TELEPHONE
American Media Incorporated
5907 Meredith Drive
Des Moines, Iowa 50324
Cassette. $94.50.

★ 2963 ★
HOW TO GET APPOINTMENTS BY TELEPHONE
Mona Ling
E. F. Wonderlic and Associates Incorporated
820 Frontage Road
Northfield, Illinois 60093
Cassette. $10.00.

★ 2964 ★
PRINCIPLES OF TELEPHONE COMMUNICATION
Thompson-Mitchell and Associates
3384 Peachtree Road Northeast
Atlanta, Georgia 30326
Cassette. $9.95.

★ 2965 ★
RECEPTION TO A BUSINESS TELEPHONE CALL
American Media Incorporated
5907 Meredith Drive
Des Moines, Iowa 50324
Cassette. $94.50.

★ 2966 ★
TAKING TELEPHONE ORDERS
American Media Incorporated
5907 Meredith Drive
Des Moines, Iowa 50324
Cassette. $94.50.

★ 2967 ★
TELEPHONE DYNAMICS
Dartnell Incorporated
4660 Ravenswood Avenue
Chicago, Illinois 60640
5 cassettes. $139.50.

★ 2968 ★
TELEPHONE MANNERS
        Educational Century Programming
        1201 East Johnson Street
        Jonesboro, Arkansas 72401
Cassette. $6.00.

★ 2969 ★
TELEPHONE TECHNIQUES
        Thompson-Mitchell and Associates
        3384 Peachtree Road Northeast
        Atlanta, Georgia 30326
Cassette. $14.95.

Film/Video/Filmstrips

★ 2970 ★
CUSTOMER ON LINE THREE
        Roundtable Films
        113 North San Vincente Boulevard
        Beverly Hills, California 90211
Film and guide book.

★ 2971 ★
THE IMPORTANCE TO YOU...TO BETTER
TELEPHONE COMMUNICATIONS
        Close Productions
        2020 San Carlos Boulevard
        Fort Myers Beach, Florida 33931
Filmstrip. $60.00.

★ 2972 ★
TELEPHONE ETIQUETTE
        Resource Incorporated
        13902 North Dale Mabry Highway
        Tampa, Florida 33624
Video cartridge and worksheets available.

★ 2973 ★
TELEPHONE MANNERS
        National Restaurant Association
        One IBM Plaza, Suite 2600
        Chicago, Illinois 60611
Video cartridge or 8 mm, 16 mm, and study guide.
$190.00.

TELEVISION AND RADIO

Correspondence Courses

★ 2974 ★
CABLE TELEVISION INSTALLER
        International Correspondence School
        Scranton, Pennsylvania 18515

Multi-module correspondence course.

★ 2975 ★
COLOR TELEVISION ELECTRONICS
        Commercial Trades Institute
        6201 West Howard Street
        Chicago, Illinois 60648
Correspondence course. $1,595.00.

★ 2976 ★
COLOR TELEVISION SERVICING
        Electronics Technical Institute
        1500 Cardinal Drive
        Little Falls, New Jersey 07424
Correspondence course.

★ 2977 ★
TELEVISION AND RADIO SERVICING
        International Correspondence School
        Scranton, Pennsylvania 18515
Multi-module correspondence course.

★ 2978 ★
TELEVISION SERVICING TECHNICIAN
        International Correspondence School
        Scranton, Pennsylvania 18515
Multi-module correspondence course.

Films/Video/Filmstrips

★ 2979 ★
TELEVISION SYMPTON DIAGNOSIS
        Bobbs-Merrill Educational Publishing
        4300 West 62nd Street
        Indianapolis, Indiana 46206
Film loop kit. $1,815.00.

Printed Materials

★ 2980 ★
BASIC COLOR TELEVISION COURSE
Stan Prentiss
        TAB Books
        Blue Ridge Summit, Pennsylvania 17214
Book. 1972. $7.95.

★ 2981 ★
COLOR TELEVISION TROUBLESHOOTING
Edward Bannon
        Reston Publishing Company
        Distributed by Prentice Hall
        Englewood Cliffs, New Jersey 07632
Book. 1976. $14.95.

★ 2982 ★
RADIO SERVICING
L. Butterworth
David McKay Company Incorporated
750 Third Avenue
New York, New York 10017
Self instruction book. $2.95.

TEMPERATURE MEASUREMENT

Audio Cassettes/Tapes

★ 2983 ★
RESISTANCE THERMOMETRY
Donald Curtis, Robert Rose
Instrument Society of America
400 Stanwix Street
Pittsburgh, Pennsylvania 15222
Cassette and workbook. $10.00.

Programmed Learning Materials

★ 2984 ★
BASIC PHYSICS AND TERMS
E. I. du Pont de Nemours and Company
Applied Technology Division
Room B 4204
Wilmington, Delaware 19898
Programmed course of approximately 6 hours.
$12.70.

★ 2985 ★
FILLED THERMAL SYSTEMS
E. I. du Pont de Nemours and Company
Applied Technology Division
Room B 4204
Wilmington, Delaware 19898
Programmed course of approximately 4 hours. $9.15.

★ 2986 ★
SCALES AND CONVERSION
E. I. du Pont de Nemours and Company
Applied Technology Division
Room B 4204
Wilmington, Delaware 19898
Programmed course of approximately 4 hours. $9.15.

★ 2987 ★
STANDARDS AND CALIBRATION
E. I. du Pont de Nemours and Company
Applied Technology Division
Room B 4204
Wilmington, Delaware 19898.
Programmed course of approximately 4 hours. $8.60.

★ 2988 ★
THERMOCOUPLE THEORY
E. I. du Pont de Nemours and Company
Applied Technology Division
Room B 4204
Wilmington, Delaware 19898
Programmed course of approximately 14 hours.
$25.30.

★ 2989 ★
THERMOMETERS
E. I. du Pont de Nemours and Company
Applied Technology Division
Room B 4204
Wilmington, Delaware 19898
Programmed course of approximately 3 hours. $7.40.

THAI

Multimedia Kits

★ 2990 ★
THAI - BASIC COURSE
General Services Administration
Foreign Service Institute Language Course
National Audiovisual Center
Order Section RR
Washington, D.C. 20409
Audio tapes, cassettes and text also available.
Approximately $150.00.

TIME MANAGEMENT

Audio Cassettes/Tapes

★ 2991 ★
EFFECTIVE TIME MANAGEMENT
Training House Incorporated
Box 688
Binghamton, New York 13902
Cassette and workbook. $36.00.

★ 2992 ★
THE EFFECTIVE USE OF MANAGEMENT TIME
Van De Water Associates
7914 Jason Avenue
Canoga Park, California 91304
Cassette and workbook. $23.50.

★ 2993 ★
HOW TO GET CONTROL OF YOUR TIME AND
YOUR LIFE
Alan Lakein
        Tape Rental Library Incorporated
        Post Office Box 2107
        2507 Edna Drive
        South Vineland, New Jersey 08360
Cassette. $9.95.

★ 2994 ★
HOW TO GET MORE WORK COMPLETED IN LESS
TIME
        Thompson-Mitchell and Associates
        3384 Peachtree Road Northeast
        Atlanta, Georgia 30326
Cassette. $15.00.

★ 2995 ★
HOW TO MASTER TIME MANAGEMENT
        Tape Rental Library Incorporated
        Post Office Box 2107
        2507 Edna Drive
        South Vineland, New Jersey 08360
Cassette. $9.98.

★ 2996 ★
HOW TO MASTER TIME ORGANIZATION
Paul J. Meyer
        Cassette House
        530 West Northwest Highway
        Mount Prospect, Illinois 60056
Cassette. $9.95.

★ 2997 ★
HOW TO MASTER TIME ORGANIZATION
Paul J. Meyer
        Success Motivation Institute
        5000 Lakewood Drive
        Waco, Texas 76710
Cassette and booklet. $9.95.

★ 2998 ★
MAKE TIME WORK FOR YOU
        Thompson-Mitchell and Associates
        3384 Peachtree Road Northeast
        Atlanta, Georgia 30326
3 cassettes. $24.95.

★ 2999 ★
THE MANAGEMENT OF TIME - SELLING YOUR
IDEAS

        Thompson-Mitchell and Associates
        3384 Peachtree Road Northeast
        Atlanta, Georgia 30326
Cassette. $6.00.

★ 3000 ★
MANAGING TIME
        Tape Rental Library Incorporated
        Post Office Box 2107
        2507 Edna Drive
        South Vineland, New Jersey 08360
9 cassettes and workbook. $295.00.

★ 3001 ★
PERSONAL TIME MANAGEMENT
        Lansford Publishing Company
        Post Office Box 8711
        San Jose, California 95155
4 cassettes. $80.00.

★ 3002 ★
SPARE TIME
        Educational Century Programming
        1201 East Johnson Street
        Jonesboro, Arkansas 72401
Cassette. $6.00.

★ 3003 ★
STUDY/PLAN YOUR TIME
        Educational Century Programming
        1201 East Johnson Street
        Jonesboro, Arkansas 72401
Cassette. $6.00.

★ 3004 ★
THE SUPERVISORY TIME STRETCHER
George Odiorne
        MBO Incorporated
        157 Pontoosic Road
        Westfield, Massachusetts 01085
Cassette and manual. $15.00.

★ 3005 ★
TIME: IT'S NEW DIMENSIONS
        Thompson-Mitchell and Associates
        3384 Peachtree Road Northeast
        Atlanta, Georgia 30326
Cassette. $9.95.

★ 3006 ★
TIME MANAGEMENT - James R. Maddux
BETTER YOUR BOTTOM LINE, BETTER YOUR LIFE -
D. J. Kerr
  Tape Rental Library Incorporated
  Post Office Box 2107
  2507 Edna Drive
  South Vineland, New Jersey 08360
Cassette.

★ 3007 ★
TOTAL TIME MANAGEMENT
  American Management Associations
  135 West 50th Street
  New York, New York 10020
6 cassettes with workbook. $100.00.

★ 3008 ★
TRAINING SALESMEN TO PROFITABLY MANAGE
TIME AND TERRITORY
  Tape Rental Library Incorporated
  Post Office Box 2107
  2507 Edna Drive
  South Vineland, New Jersey 08360
Cassette.

Films/Video/Filmstrips

★ 3009 ★
MANAGING TIME
  BNA Communications Incorporated
  9401 Decoverly Hall Road
  Rockville, Maryland 20850
Film.

★ 3010 ★
PERSONAL TIME MANAGEMENT
  Telstar Productions Incorporated
  366 North Prior Avenue
  Saint Paul, Minnesota 55104
6 video tape lessons and study guide. $2,100.00.

★ 3011 ★
THE TIME GAME
  National Restaurant Association
  One IBM Plaza, Suite 2600
  Chicago, Illinois 60611
Video cartridge or 8 mm, 16 mm, and study guide.
$190.00.

Multimedia Kits

★ 3012 ★
ANALYZING OUR TIME USAGE
  Resources for Education and Management
   Incorporated
  544 Medlock Road, Suite 210
  Decatur, Georgia 30030
Filmstrip with cassette. $65.00.

★ 3013 ★
EFFECTIVE TIME MANAGEMENT
  Ergonco Performance Source
  Northwest O'Hare Office Park, Suite 119
  2474 Dempster Street
  Des Plains, Illinois 60016
Multimedia self-study program.

★ 3014 ★
MANAGING YOUR TIME
  Resources for Education and Management
   Incorporated
  544 Medlock Road, Suite 210
  Decatur, Georgia 30030
Filmstrip with cassette. $60.00.

★ 3015 ★
THE TIME OF OUR LIVES
  Resources for Education and Management
   Incorporated
  544 Medlock Road, Suite 210
  Decatur, Georgia 30030
Filmstrip with cassette. $65.00.

★ 3016 ★
USING OTHERS TO SAVE TIME
  Resources for Education and Management
   Incorporated
  544 Medlock Road, Suite 210
  Decatur, Georgia 30030
Filmstrip with cassette. $65.00.

Printed Materials

★ 3017 ★
MANAGING TIME EFFECTIVELY
  Didactic Systems Incorporated
  Box 457
  Cranford, New Jersey 07016
Self-study text. $9.00.

★ 3018 ★
NEW TIME MANAGEMENT
R. Alec MacKenzie
     Dartnell
     4660 Ravenswood Avenue
     Chicago, Illinois 60640
314 page binder. $47.50.

TOOL AND DIEMAKING

Correspondence Courses

★ 3019 ★
TOOL AND DIE MAKER
     International Correspondence School
     Scranton, Pennsylvania 18515
Multi-module correspondence course.

TOOLS

Programmed Learning Materials

★ 3020 ★
HAND TOOLS
TPC Training Systems
     Technical Publishing Company
     1301 South Grove Avenue
     Barrington, Illinois 60010
Programmed text of 10 lessons. $22.50.

★ 3021 ★
PORTABLE POWER TOOLS
TPC Training Systems
     Technical Publishing Company
     1301 South Grove Avenue
     Barrington, Illinois 60010
Programmed text of 10 lessons. $22.50.

TRADE
See: COMMERCE

TRAINING TECHNIQUES

See also: Management Development;
     headings under Supervision

Audio Cassettes/Tapes

★ 3022 ★
ACTION TRAINING: WHY LECTURES ARE
OBSOLETE
George Odiorne
     MBO Incorporated
     157 Pontoosic Road
     Westfield, Massachusetts 01085
Cassette and workbook.

★ 3023 ★
ADAPTING TRAINING AND DEVELOPMENT TO
CHANGING VALUES
     Development Digest Incorporated
     3347 Motor Avenue
     Los Angeles, California 90034
Cassette. $13.75.

★ 3024 ★
COMMUNITY DEVELOPMENT TRAINING
     Development Digest Incorporated
     3347 Motor Avenue
     Los Angeles, California 90034
Cassette. $13.75.

★ 3025 ★
DIAGNOSTIC STUDIES - EFFECTIVE TOOLS FOR
MANAGEMENT DEVELOPMENT AND ORGANIZA-
TIONAL DEVELOPMENT
     Development Digest Incorporated
     3347 Motor Avenue
     Los Angeles, California 90034
Cassette. $13.75.

★ 3026 ★
DIMENSIONAL TRAINING
     Development Digest Incorporated
     3347 Motor Avenue
     Los Angeles, California 90034
Cassette. $13.75.

★ 3027 ★
EVALUATING TRAINING
George Odiorne
     MBO Incorporated
     157 Pontoosic Road
     Westfield, Massachusetts 01085
Cassette and workbook. $15.00.

★ 3028 ★

EVALUATION OF TRAINING
Development Digest Incorporated
3347 Motor Avenue
Los Angeles, California 90034
Cassette. $13.75.

★ 3029 ★

FEEDBACK SYSTEMS
Development Digest Incorporated
3347 Motor Avenue
Los Angeles, California 90034
Cassette. $13.75.

★ 3030 ★

GOOD TRAINING STARTS WITH DIAGNOSIS
George Odiorne
MBO Incorporated
157 Pontoosic Road
Westfield, Massachusetts 01085
Cassette and workbook. $15.00.

★ 3031 ★

HOW TO DESIGN A TRAIN-THE-TRAINER COURSE
Development Digest Incorporated
3347 Motor Avenue
Los Angeles, California 90034
Cassette. $13.75.

★ 3032 ★

HOW TO JUSTIFY THE TRAINING FUNCTION
Development Digest Incorporated
3347 Motor Avenue
Los Angeles, California 90034
2 cassettes. $27.50.

★ 3033 ★

HOW TO MANAGE TRAINING: A CYBERNETIC SYSTEM
George Odiorne
MBO Incorporated
157 Pontoosic Road
Westfield, Massachusetts 01085
Cassette and workbook. $15.00.

★ 3034 ★

HOW TO PINPOINT A TRAINING NEED
George Odiorne
MBO Incorporated
157 Pontoosic Road
Westfield, Massachusetts 01085
Cassette and workbook. $15.00.

★ 3035 ★

HOW TO TEACH GROWN-UPS
Practical Management Associates
Post Office Box 751
20929 Ventura Boulevard
Woodland Hills, California 91365
Cassettes and workbooks. $175.00.

★ 3036 ★

INDUSTRIAL APPLICATIONS OF COMPUTER-ASSISTED INSTRUCTION
Development Digest Incorporated
3347 Motor Avenue
Los Angeles, California 90034
Cassette. $13.75.

★ 3037 ★

THE INTERNAL TRAINING CONSULTANT
Development Digest Incorporated
3347 Motor Avenue
Los Angeles, California 90034
Cassette. $13.75.

★ 3038 ★

LEARNING TO LEARN
George Odiorne
MBO Incorporated
157 Pontoosic Road
Westfield, Massachusetts 01085
Cassette and manual. $15.00.

★ 3039 ★

MANAGING TRAINING BY OBJECTIVES
George Odiorne
MBO Incorporated
157 Pontoosic Road
Westfield, Massachusetts 01085
Cassette and workbook. $15.00.

★ 3040 ★

THE NEW MANAGER OF TRAINING
Development Digest Incorporated
3347 Motor Avenue
Los Angeles, California 90034
Cassette. $13.75.

★ 3041 ★

NON-TRADITIONAL APPROACHES TO HUMAN POTENTIAL DEVELOPMENT
Development Digest Incorporated
3347 Motor Avenue
Los Angeles, California 90034
Cassette. $13.75.

★ 3042 ★
TRAINER MANAGER OR ANIMAL TRAINER?
    Development Digest Incorporated
    3347 Motor Avenue
    Los Angeles, California   90034
Cassette. $13.75.

★ 3043 ★
TRAINING BY OBJECTIVES
George Odiorne
    MBO Incorporated
    157 Pontoosic Road
    Westfield, Massachusetts   01085
6 cassettes and workbook. $100.00.

★ 3044 ★
TRAINING SYSTEMS APPROACH TO PRODUCTIVITY
IMPROVEMENT
    Development Digest Incorporated
    3347 Motor Avenue
    Los Angeles, California   90034
Cassette. $13.75.

★ 3045 ★
USING A SYSTEMS APPROACH TO TRAINING
George Odiorne
    MBO Incorporated
    157 Pontoosic Road
    Westfield, Massachusetts   01085
Cassette and workbook. $15.00.

Film/Video/Filmstrips

★ 3046 ★
EFFECTIVE TEACHING TECHNIQUES
    Addison Wesley Publishing Company Incorporated
    Jacob Way
    Reading, Massachusetts   01867
Filmstrip. $55.00.

★ 3047 ★
FOLLOWING UP ON TRAINING
    Addison Wesley Publishing Company Incorporated
    Jacob Way
    Reading, Massachusetts   01867
Filmstrip. $55.00.

★ 3048 ★
HELPING THE LEARNER LEARN
    Addison Wesley Publishing Company Incorporated
    Jacob Way
    Reading, Massachusetts   01867
Filmstrip. $55.00.

★ 3049 ★
HOW TO DO ON-THE-JOB TRAINING
    Addison Wesley Publishing Company Incorporated
    Jacob Way
    Reading, Massachusetts   01867
Filmstrip. $55.00.

★ 3050 ★
PREPARING TO TRAIN
    Addison Wesley Publishing Company Incorporated
    Jacob Way
    Reading, Massachusetts   01867
Filmstrip. $55.00.

★ 3051 ★
PREPLANNING AND OBJECTIVES
    Addison Wesley Publishing Company Incorporated
    Jacob Way
    Reading, Massachusetts   01867
Filmstrip. $55.00.

★ 3052 ★
THE TEACHING-LEARNING PROCESS
    Addison Wesley Publishing Company Incorporated
    Jacob Way
    Reading, Massachusetts   01867
Filmstrip. $55.00.

★ 3053 ★
TRAINING FOR RESULTS
    Addison Wesley Publishing Company Incorporated
    Jacob Way
    Reading, Massachusetts   01867
Filmstrip. $55.00.

★ 3054 ★
THE TRAINING MEMORANDUM
    National Restaurant Association
    One IBM Plaza, Suite 2600
    Chicago, Illinois   60611
Video cartridge or 8 mm, 16 mm, and study guide.
$190.00.

Multimedia Kits

★ 3055 ★
ANALYZING FOR TRAINING
    Resources for Education and Management
      Incorporated
    544 Medlock Road, Suite 210
    Decatur, Georgia   30030
Filmstrip with cassette. $60.00.

★ 3056 ★

EFFECTIVE TRAINING TECHNIQUES
   Resources for Education and Management
      Incorporated
   544 Medlock Road, Suite 210
   Decatur, Georgia 30030
Filmstrip with cassette. $55.00.

★ 3057 ★

FOLLOWING UP ON TRAINING
   Resources for Education and Management
      Incorporated
   544 Medlock Road, Suite 210
   Decatur, Georgia 30030
Filmstrip with cassette. $60.00.

★ 3058 ★

HELPING THE LEARNER LEARN
   Resources for Education and Management
      Incorporated
   544 Medlock Road, Suite 210
   Decatur, Georgia 30030
Filmstrip with cassette. $55.00.

★ 3059 ★

HOW TO DO ON-THE-JOB TRAINING
   Resources for Education and Management
      Incorporated
   544 Medlock Road, Suite 210
   Decatur, Georgia 30030
Filmstrip with cassette. $60.00.

★ 3060 ★

PLANNING AND PRODUCING SLIDE SHOWS
   Visual Horizons
   208 Westfall Road
   Rochester, New York 14620
Multimedia kit. $79.95.

★ 3061 ★

PREPARING TRAINING OBJECTIVES
   Resources for Education and Management
      Incorporated
   544 Medlock Road, Suite 210
   Decatur, Georgia 30030
Filmstrip with cassette. $60.00.

★ 3062 ★

TRAINING: A MAJOR RESPONSIBILITY
   Resources for Education and Management
      Incorporated
   544 Medlock Road, Suite 210
   Decatur, Georgia 30030
Filmstrip with cassette. $60.00.

★ 3063 ★

THE TRAINING ACTIVITY
   Resources for Education and Management
      Incorporated
   544 Medlock Road, Suite 210
   Decatur, Georgia 30030
Filmstrip with cassette. $70.00.

★ 3064 ★

TRAINING FOR UPWARD MOBILITY
   Resources for Education and Management
      Incorporated
   544 Medlock Road, Suite 210
   Decatur, Georgia 30030
Filmstrip with cassette. $60.00.

★ 3065 ★

TRAINING THE DISADVANTAGED
   Resources for Education and Management
      Incorporated
   544 Medlock Road, Suite 210
   Decatur, Georgia 30030
Filmstrip with cassette. $60.00.

Printed Materials

★ 3066 ★

CONSTRUCTION AND USE OF WRITTEN
SIMULATIONS
   Management Resources Incorporated
   757 Third Avenue
   New York, New York 10017
Workbook. $17.95.

★ 3067 ★

THE EDUCATION, TRAINING AND DEVELOPMENT
GRID
   Scientific Methods Incorporated
   Box 195
   Austin, Texas 78767
Workbook. $15.00.

★ 3068 ★

PRACTICAL ON-THE-JOB TRAINING
   Didactic Systems Incorporated
   Box 457
   Cranford, New Jersey 07016
Self-study text. $9.00.

★ 3069 ★
THE SUPERVISOR AS AN INSTRUCTOR: A GUIDE
FOR CLASSROOM TRAINING
Martin M. Broadwell
      Addison Wesley Publishing Company Incorporated
      Jacob Way
      Reading, Massachusetts 01867
Training guide. $6.95.

★ 3070 ★
TRAINING AND DEVELOPING TODAY'S WORK
FORCE
      American Management Associations
      135 West 50th Street
      New York, New York 10020
Self-study text. $55.00.

TRANSACTIONAL ANALYSIS

<u>See also</u>: Personal Development; Stress

<u>Audio Cassettes/Tapes</u>

★ 3071 ★
APPLIED TRANSACTIONAL ANALYSIS
      Training House Incorporated
      Box 688
      Binghamton, New York 13902
Cassette and workbook. $36.00.

★ 3072 ★
PRACTICAL TRANSACTIONAL ANALYSIS FOR
MANAGERS
      AMACOM
      American Management Associations
      135 West 50th Street
      New York, New York 10020
6 cassettes with workbook. $100.00.

★ 3073 ★
SUCCESS THROUGH TRANSACTIONAL ANALYSIS
Jut Meininger
      Success Motivation Institute
      5000 Lakewood Drive
      Waco, Texas 76710
Cassette. $9.95.

★ 3074 ★
TRANSACTIONAL ANALYSIS - CUSTOMER TREAT-
MENT PROGRAM
      Development Digest Incorporated
      3347 Motor Avenue
      Los Angeles, California 90034
2 cassettes. $13.75.

★ 3075 ★
TRANSACTIONAL ANALYSIS FOR SECRETARIES
      Learning Concepts Incorporated
      2501 North Lamar Street
      Austin, Texas 78705
3 cassettes. $47.50.

★ 3076 ★
TRANSACTIONAL ANALYSIS FOR SECRETARIES
Clay Hardesty
      Tape Rental Library Incorporated
      Post Office Box 2107
      2507 Edna Drive
      South Vineland, New Jersey 08360
Cassette. $15.00.

★ 3077 ★
TRANSACTIONAL ANALYSIS OVERVIEW
Dorothy Jongeward
      Addison Wesley Publishing Company Incorporated
      Jacob Way
      Reading, Massachusetts 01867
Cassette. $15.00.

<u>Films/Video/Filmstrips</u>

★ 3078 ★
I UNDERSTAND, YOU UNDERSTAND: THE
DYNAMICS OF TRANSACTIONAL ANALYSIS
Joe Batten
      Creative Media Films
      820 Keo Way
      Des Moines, Iowa 50309
Film or video cassette and guide. $450.00 (rental
available).

★ 3079 ★
TRANSACTIONAL ANALYSIS
      CRM McGraw Hill Films
      110 15th Street
      Del Mar, California 92014
Film or video cassette.

★ 3080 ★
TRANSACTIONAL ANALYSIS ON THE JOB
      XICOM
      Sterling Forest
      Tuxedo, New York 10987
Films and workbooks.

Multimedia Kits

★ 3081 ★
APPLIED TRANSACTIONAL ANALYSIS
 Ergonco Performance Source
 Northwest O'Hare Office Park, Suite 119
 2474 Dempster Street
 Des Plains, Illinois 60016
Multimedia self-study program.

★ 3082 ★
ON BEING YOURSELF: WINNERS AND LOSERS
 Addison Wesley Publishing Company Incorporated
 Jacob Way
 Reading, Massachusetts 01867
140 slides, cassette tape and guide. $135.00.

★ 3083 ★
TRANSACTIONAL ANALYSIS IS FOR EVERYONE
 AMACOM
 American Management Associations
 135 West 50th Street
 New York, New York 10020
200 slides, 2 cassettes, 5 manuals. $189.00.

Printed Materials

★ 3084 ★
TRANSACTIONAL ANALYSIS FOR MANAGERS
 American Management Associations
 135 West 50th Street
 New York, New York 10020
Self-study text. $55.00.

TRAVEL

Audio Cassettes/Tapes

★ 3085 ★
EFFICIENT TRAVEL
 Educational Century Programming
 1201 East Johnson Street
 Jonesboro, Arkansas 72401
Cassette. $6.00.

Correspondence Courses

★ 3086 ★
AIRLINE/TRAVEL
 International Correspondence School
 Scranton, Pennsylvania 18515
Multi-module correspondence course.

★ 3087 ★
TRAVEL
 North American Correspondence School
 4401 Birch Street
 Newport Beach, California 92663
Correspondence course.

TURKISH

Audio Cassettes/Tapes

★ 3088 ★
BERLITZ COURSE IN TURKISH
 Berlitz Language Program
 Post Office Box 5109
 FDR Station
 New York, New York 10022
Cassette. $5.95.

Multimedia Kits

★ 3089 ★
TURKISH - BASIC COURSE
 General Services Administration
 Foreign Service Institute Language Course
 National Audiovisual Center
 Order Section RR
 Washington, D.C. 20409
Audio tapes, cassettes and text also available.
Approximately $150.00.

Printed Materials

★ 3090 ★
LEARN TURKISH FOR ENGLISH SPEAKERS
G. L. Lewis
 Saphrograph Company
 194 Elizabeth Street
 New York, New York 10012
Book. $5.00.

★ 3091 ★
TEACH YOURSELF TURKISH
G. L. Lewis
 David McKay Company Incorporated
 750 Third Avenue
 New York, New York 10017
Self instruction text. $2.95.

TWI

Multimedia Kits

★ 3092 ★
TWI - BASIC COURSE
General Services Administration
Foreign Service Institute Language Course
National Audiovisual Center
Order Section RR
Washington, D.C. 20409
Audio tapes, cassettes and text also available.
Approximately $70.00.

TYPEWRITING

See also: Secretarial Skills

Audio Cassettes/Tapes

★ 3093 ★
ADVANCED TYPING/EMPLOYMENT TEST TYPING
Educational Century Programming
1201 East Johnson Street
Jonesboro, Arkansas 72401
Cassette. $6.00.

★ 3094 ★
BEGINNING TYPING/INTERMEDIATE TYPING
Educational Century Programming
1201 East Johnson Street
Jonesboro, Arkansas 72401
Cassette. $6.00.

★ 3095 ★
CORRECTING MISTAKES - TYPEWRITER CARE
Thompson-Mitchell and Associates
3384 Peachtree Road Northeast
Atlanta, Georgia 30326
Cassette. $6.00.

★ 3096 ★
IMPROVING TYPING TECHNIQUE - PLAN YOUR
WORK
Thompson-Mitchell and Associates
3384 Peachtree Road Northeast
Atlanta, Georgia 30326
Cassette. $6.00.

★ 3097 ★
KEYBOARD MEMORIZATION
Reinforcement Learning Incorporated
87 Dimmig Road
Post Office Box 562
Upper Saddle River, New Jersey 07458
Cassettes and workbook. $89.50.

★ 3098 ★
KNOWING YOUR TYPEWRITER, PART'S I and II
Thompson-Mitchell and Associates
3384 Peachtree Road Northeast
Atlanta, Georgia 30326
Cassette. $6.00.

★ 3099 ★
MEDICAL TYPING - TECHNICAL TYPING
Educational Century Programming
1201 East Johnson Street
Jonesboro, Arkansas 72401
Cassette. $6.00.

★ 3100 ★
PRODUCTION TYPING
Reinforcement Learning Incorporated
87 Dimmig Road
Post Office Box 562
Upper Saddle River, New Jersey 07458
Cassettes and workbook. $128.00.

★ 3101 ★
STATISTICAL TYPING - LEGAL TYPING
Educational Century Programming
1201 East Johnson Street
Jonesboro, Arkansas 72401
Cassette. $6.00.

★ 3102 ★
TRICKS OF TYPING - STENCIL CUTTING
Thompson-Mitchell and Associates
3384 Peachtree Road Northeast
Atlanta, Georgia 30326
Cassette. $6.00.

★ 3103 ★
TYPING SPEED DEVELOPMENT
Reinforcement Learning Incorporated
87 Dimmig Road
Post Office Box 562
Upper Saddle River, New Jersey 07458
Cassettes and workbook. $73.50.

Correspondence Courses

★ 3104 ★
ELEMENTARY TYPEWRITING
University of Nebraska
511 Nebraska Hall
Lincoln, Nebraska 68588
Correspondence course.

★ 3105 ★
INTERMEDIATE TYPEWRITING
University of Nebraska
511 Nebraska Hall
Lincoln, Nebraska 68588
Correspondence course.

★ 3106 ★
TYPEWRITING
University of Kentucky
Independent Study Program
Freeze Hall, Room 1
Lexington, Kentucky 40506
Correspondence course.

Programmed Learning Materials

★ 3107 ★
GREGG TYPING
McGraw-Hill Book Company
1221 Avenue of the Americas
New York, New York 10019
Programmed text. $3.80.

UNDERGROUND DISTRIBUTION SYSTEMS

Films/Video/Filmstrips

★ 3108 ★
FUNDAMENTALS OF UNDERGROUND DISTRIBUTION
DESIGN AND CONSTRUCTION
Resource Incorporated
13902 North Dale Mabry Highway
Tampa, Florida 33624
2 video cartridges and worksheets available. $240.00.

★ 3109 ★
INTRODUCTION TO UNDERGROUND DISTRIBUTION
FAULT LOCATION
Resource Incorporated
13902 North Dale Mabry Highway
Tampa, Florida 33624
Video cartridge and worksheets available. $120.00.

★ 3110 ★
LOCATING FAULTS ON URD PRIMARIES
Resource Incorporated
13902 North Dale Mabry Highway
Tampa, Florida 33624
Video cartridge and worksheets available. $120.00.

★ 3111 ★
LOCATING FAULTS ON URD SECONDARIES
Resource Incorporated
13902 North Dale Mabry Highway
Tampa, Florida 33624
Video cartridge and worksheets available. $120.00.

★ 3112 ★
TRENCHING TECHNIQUES
Resource Incorporated
13902 North Dale Mabry Highway
Tampa, Florida 33624
Video cartridge and worksheets available. $120.00.

★ 3113 ★
UNDERGROUND DISTRIBUTION CABLE
TERMINATIONS
Resource Incorporated
13902 North Dale Mabry Highway
Tampa, Florida 33624
Video cartridge and worksheets available. $120.00.

★ 3114 ★
UNDERGROUND DISTRIBUTION FAULT LOCATION
(Radar)
Resource Incorporated
13902 North Dale Mabry Highway
Tampa, Florida 33624
Video cartridge and worksheets available. $120.00.

★ 3115 ★
UNDERGROUND DISTRIBUTION FAULT LOCATION
(Terminal Method)
Resource Incorporated
13902 North Dale Mabry Highway
Tampa, Florida 33624
Video cartrdige and worksheets available. $120.00.

★ 3116 ★
UNDERGROUND DISTRIBUTION FAULT LOCATION
(Tracer Methods)
Resource Incorporated
13902 North Dale Mabry Highway
Tampa, Florida 33624
2 video cartridges and worksheets available. $240.00.

★ 3117 ★
UNDERGROUND DISTRIBUTION INSTALLING
CABLE
> Resource Incorporated
> 13902 North Dale Mabry Highway
> Tampa, Florida 33624

Video cartridge and worksheets available. $120.00.

★ 3118 ★
UNDERGROUND DISTRIBUTION INSTALLING
PRIMARY SWITCHING EQUIPMENT
> Resource Incorporated
> 13902 North Dale Mabry Highway
> Tampa, Florida 33624

Video cartridge and worksheets available. $120.00.

★ 3119 ★
UNDERGROUND DISTRIBUTION SERVICE
RESTORATION
> Scientific Methods Incorporated
> Box 195
> Austin, Texas 78767

Video cartridge and worksheets available. $120.00.

★ 3120 ★
UNDERGROUND DISTRIBUTION SWITCHING
PROCEDURES
> Resource Incorporated
> 13902 North Dale Mabry Highway
> Tampa, Florida 33624

Video cartridge and worksheets available. $120.00.

★ 3121 ★
UNDERGROUND ELECTRICAL DISTRIBUTION
CONCEPTS
> Resource Incorporated
> 13902 North Dale Mabry Highway
> Tampa, Florida 33624

Video cartridge and worksheets available. $120.00.

UNIONS
See: LABOR RELATIONS

UPHOLSTERY

Correspondence Courses

★ 3122 ★
UPHOLSTERY
> Belsaw Institute
> 315 Westport Road
> Kansas City, Missouri 64111

Homestudy program. $299.00.

★ 3123 ★
UPHOLSTERY
> Modern Upholstery Institute
> 412 South Lyon Street
> Santa Ana, California 92701

Correspondence course.

★ 3124 ★
UPHOLSTERY AND DECORATING
> Upholstery and Decorating School
> 1500 Cardinal Drive
> Little Falls, New Jersey 07424

Correspondence course.

URBAN PLANNING

See also: Real Estate

Printed Materials

★ 3125 ★
TOWN DESIGN
Frederick Gibberd
> Praeger Publishers
> 111 Fourth Avenue
> New York, New York 10003

Book. $25.00.

URDU

Multimedia Kits

★ 3126 ★
COURSE IN URDU
> General Services Administration
> Foreign Service Institute Language Course
> National Audiovisual Center
> Order Section RR
> Washington, D.C. 20409

Audio tapes, cassettes and text also available.
Approximately $70.00.

★ 3127 ★
SPOKEN URDU, A COURSE IN URDU
Muhammad Barker
> Spoken Language Services Incorporated
> Post Office Box 783
> Ithaca, New York 14850

Multimedia program.   1976.

★ 3128 ★
URDU NEWSPAPER READER
     General Services Administration
     Foreign Service Institute Language Course
     National Audiovisual Center
     Order Section RR
     Washington, D.C. 20409
Audio tapes, cassettes and text also available.
Approximately $15.00.

Printed Materials

★ 3129 ★
TEACH YOURSELF URDU
Grahme Bailey
     David McKay Company Incorporated
     750 Third Avenue
     New York, New York 10017
Self instruction book. $3.95.

UTILITIES
See: PUBLIC SERVICE UTILITIES

VALUES
See: ORGANIZATIONAL VALUES

VALUES CLARIFICATION

Audio Cassettes/Tapes

★ 3130 ★
HUMAN VALUES IN MANAGEMENT
     Van De Water Associates
     7914 Jason Avenue
     Canoga Park, California 91304
Cassette and workbook. $23.50.

Films/Video/Filmstrips

★ 3131 ★
FOCUS ON ETHICS A STUDY OF VALUES IN
DECISION MAKING FOR TODAY'S MANAGERS
     Salenger Educational Media
     1635 12th Street
     Santa Monica, California 90404
3 films and workbooks. $990.00 (rental available).

VALVES
See: CONTROL VALVES

VIETNAMESE

Audio Cassettes/Tapes

★ 3132 ★
SPOKEN VIETNAMESE
Robert Jones, Huynhsanh Thong
     Spoken Language Services Incorporated
     Post Office Box 783
     Ithaca, New York 14850
Cassette course.

Multimedia Kits

★ 3133 ★
VIETNAMESE - BASIC COURSE
     General Services Administration
     Foreign Service Institute Language Course
     National Audiovisual Center
     Order Section RR
     Washington, D.C. 20409
Audio tapes, cassettes and text also available.
Approximately $200.00.

Printed Materials

★ 3134 ★
READ AND SPEAK VIETNAMESE
Nguyen-Dinh-Hoa
     C. E. Tuttle Company
     28 South Main Street
     Rutland, Vermont 05701
Book.

VOCABULARY SKILLS

     See also: Study and Reading Skills

Audio Cassettes/Tapes

★ 3135 ★
ADVANCED VOCABULARY BUILDING
     Bell and Howell
     Audio Visual Products Division
     7100 McCormick Road
     Chicago, Illinois 60645
Cassette and word cards. $45.00.

★ 3136 ★
AUDIO-ACTIVE VOCABULARY
    Educational Century Programming
    1201 East Johnson Street
    Jonesboro, Arkansas 72401
12 cassettes. $72.00.

★ 3137 ★
THE BERGEN EVANS VOCABULARY PROGRAM
Dr. Bergen Evans, Dr. Robert Breen
    Tape Rental Library Incorporated
    Post Office Box 2107
    2507 Edna Drive
    South Vineland, New Jersey 08360
Cassette.

★ 3138 ★
BUILDING WORD POWER
    Educational Century Programming
    1201 East Johnson Street
    Jonesboro, Arkansas 72401
Cassette. $6.00.

★ 3139 ★
LISTENING YOUR WAY TO USING ROGET'S
THESAURUS
    Thompson-Mitchell and Associates
    3384 Peachtree Road Northeast
    Atlanta, Georgia 30326
3 cassettes. $21.50.

★ 3140 ★
THE POWER OF WORDS
    Educational Century Programming
    1201 East Johnson Street
    Jonesboro, Arkansas 72401
6 cassettes. $40.00.

★ 3141 ★
SUCCESSFUL VOCABULARY
    Educational Century Programming
    1201 East Johnson Street
    Jonesboro, Arkansas 72401
6 cassettes. $6.00 each.

★ 3142 ★
VO-TECH VOCABULARY STUDY (Remedial level)
    Thompson-Mitchell and Associates
    3384 Peachtree Road Northeast
    Atlanta, Georgia 30326
2 albums of cassettes. $280.00.

★ 3143 ★
VOCABULARY DEVELOPMENT
    Educational Century Programming
    1201 East Johnson Street
    Jonesboro, Arkansas 72401
12 cassettes. $72.00.

★ 3144 ★
WORD POWER SUCCESS PROGRAM
    Tape Rental Library Incorporated
    Post Office Box 2107
    2507 Edna Drive
    South Vineland, New Jersey 08360
3 cassettes. $39.95.

Films/Video/Filmstrips

★ 3145 ★
WORD POWER VOCABULARY WORKOUT
James I. Brown
    Telstar Productions Incorporated
    366 North Prior Avenue
    Saint Paul, Minnesota 55104
4 video tapes. $600.00.

Multimedia Kits

★ 3146 ★
THE BERGEN EVANS VOCABULARY PROGRAM
(Words on a high school to college level)
    Thompson-Mitchell and Associates
    3384 Peachtree Road Northeast
    Atlanta, Georgia 30326
10 filmstrips and 5 cassettes. $104.00.

Programmed Learning Materials

★ 3147 ★
BASIC VOCABULARY
    McGraw-Hill Book Company
    1221 Avenue of the Americas
    New York, New York 10019
Programmed text. $3.95.

VOCATIONAL GUIDANCE

See also: Career Planning

Audio Cassettes/Tapes

★ 3148 ★
CAREER PLANNING
    Personnel Development Incorporated
    835 Sterling Avenue
    Palatine, Illinois 60067
Workbook and cassette. $90.00.

Programmed Learning Materials

★ 3149 ★
COUNSELING IN VOCATIONAL GUIDANCE
General Learning Corporation
250 James Street
Morristown, New Jersey 07960
Programmed text. $325.00.

VOLUNTEER MANAGEMENT

See also: headings under Management

Correspondence Courses

★ 3150 ★
EFFECTIVE MANAGEMENT OF VOLUNTEER
PROGRAMS
University of Colorado
Center for Lifelong Learning
970 Aurora Avenue
Boulder, Colorado 80302
Correspondence course.

★ 3151 ★
OVERVIEW OF VOLUNTEER ADMINISTRATION
University of Colorado
Center for Lifelong Learning
970 Aurora Avenue
Boulder, Colorado 80302
Correspondence course.

★ 3152 ★
PRINCIPLES OF TRAINING IN VOLUNTEER
MANAGEMENT
University of Colorado
Center for Lifelong Learning
970 Aurora Avenue
Boulder, Colorado 80302
Correspondence course.

WATCH REPAIR
See: CLOCK AND WATCH REPAIR

WATER TREATMENT

Programmed Learning Materials

★ 3153 ★
BOILER FEEDWATER

E. I. du Pont de Nemours and Company
Applied Technology Division
Room B 4204
Wilmington, Delaware 19898
Programmed course of approximately 6 hours. $12.70.

★ 3154 ★
WATER CHEMISTRY
E. I. du Pont de Nemours and Company
Applied Technology Division
Room B 4204
Wilmington, Delaware 19898
Programmed course of approximately 2 1/2 hours.
$7.40.

★ 3155 ★
WATER TESTING
E. I. du Pont de Nemours and Company
Applied Technology Division
Room B 4204
Wilmington, Delaware 19898
Programmed course of approximately 2 1/2 hours.
$7.40.

WEATHER
See: CLIMATOLOGY

WELDING

Correspondence Courses

★ 3156 ★
COMBINATION WELDER
International Correspondence School
Scranton, Pennsylvania 18515
Multi-module correspondence course.

Films/Video/Filmstrips

★ 3157 ★
ARC WELDING
DCA Educational Products
424 Valley Road
Warrington, Pennsylvania 18976
12 film loops (8 mm). $29.50 each.

★ 3158 ★
ARC WELDING
    DCA Educational Products
    424 Valley Road
    Warrington, Pennsylvania 18976
Film (16 mm). $225.00.

★ 3159 ★
JOINING
    Society of Manufacturing Engineers
    20501 Ford Road
    Post Office Box 930
    Dearborn, Michigan 48128
Video tape.

Programmed Learning Materials

★ 3160 ★
ARC WELDING PRACTICES (Maintenance applications)
TPC Training Systems
    Technical Publishing Company
    1301 South Grove Avenue
    Barrington, Illinois 60010
Programmed text of 5 lessons. $16.75.

★ 3161 ★
ARC WELDING PROCESSES (Setup and operation)
TPC Training Systems
    Technical Publishing Company
    1301 South Grove Avenue
    Barrington, Illinois 60010
Programmed text of 5 lessons. $16.75.

★ 3162 ★
BASIC FASTENING AND JOINING TECHNIQUES
    Society of Manufacturing Engineers
    20501 Ford Road
    Post Office Box 930
    Dearborn, Michigan 48128
Programmed learning course. $16.95.

★ 3163 ★
GAS WELDING PRACTICES
TPC Training Systems
    Technical Publishing Company
    1301 South Grove Avenue
    Barrington, Illinois 60010
Programmed text of 5 lessons. $16.75.

★ 3164 ★
OXYACETYLENE CUTTING AND TACKING
    E. I. du Pont de Nemours and Company
    Applied Technology Division
    Room B 4204
    Wilmington, Delaware 19898
Programmed course of approximately 4 hours. $9.15.

★ 3165 ★
TUNGSTEN INERT GAS (TIG)
    E. I. du Pont de Nemours and Company
    Applied Technology Division
    Room B 4204
    Wilmington, Delaware 19898
Programmed course of approximately 13 hours. $23.85.

★ 3166 ★
WELDING PRINCIPLES
TPC Training Systems
    Technical Publishing Company
    1301 South Grove Avenue
    Barrington, Illinois 60010
Programmed text of 5 lessons. $16.75.

WELSH

Correspondence Courses

★ 3167 ★
TEACH YOURSELF WELSH
John T. Bowan
    David McKay Company Incorporated
    750 Third Avenue
    New York, New York 10017
Self instruction. $2.95.

Printed Materials

★ 3168 ★
LEARN WELSH FOR ENGLISH SPEAKERS
    Saphrograph Company
    194 Elizabeth Street
    New York, New York 10012
Book. $5.00.

WOMEN IN BUSINESS

See also: Equal Employment Opportunity

Audio Cassettes/Tapes

★ 3169 ★
MANAGEMENT SKILLS FOR WOMEN
Jaine Carter Personnel Development Incorporated
112 West Garden Avenue
Palatine, Illinois 60067
Cassette workbook program.

★ 3170 ★
MANAGEMENT TECHNIQUES FOR WOMEN
Lansford Publishing Company
Post Office Box 8711
San Jose, California 95155
6 cassettes. $190.00.

★ 3171 ★
MOVING WOMEN INTO THE ORGANIZATION
MAINSTREAM FOR PROFIT
Development Digest Incorporated
3347 Motor Avenue
Los Angeles, California 90034
Cassette. $13.75.

★ 3172 ★
THE ROLE OF THE FEMALE IN THE WORLD OF
WORK
Development Digest Incorporated
3347 Motor Avenue
Los Angeles, California 90034
Cassette. $13.75.

★ 3173 ★
SELLING SYSTEMS FOR WOMEN
Jaine Carter Personnel Development Incorporated
112 West Garden Avenue
Palatine, Illinois 60067
Cassette workbook program.

★ 3174 ★
THE WOMAN AS EFFECTIVE EXECUTIVE
Clay Hardesty
Tape Rental Library Incorporated
Post Office Box 2107
2507 Edna Drive
South Vineland, New Jersey 08360
Cassette. $17.50.

★ 3175 ★
WOMEN IN MANAGEMENT
Learning Concepts Incorporated
2501 North Lamar Street
Austin, Texas 78705
3 cassettes. $47.50.

★ 3176 ★
WOMEN IN MANAGEMENT: OPPORTUNITY OR
TOKENISM?
Development Digest Incorporated
3347 Motor Avenue
Los Angeles, California 90034
Cassette. $13.75.

Correspondence Courses

★ 3177 ★
PRINCIPLES OF MANAGEMENT FOR WOMEN
University of Kansas
Division of Continuing Education
Lawrence, Kansas 66045
Homestudy program.

Games/Simulations

★ 3178 ★
WOMEN IN MANAGEMENT
Harvey Lieberman
Didactic Systems Incorporated
Box 457
Cranford, New Jersey 07016
Simulation game. $24.00.

Multimedia Kits

★ 3179 ★
WOMEN IN MANAGEMENT
Westinghouse Learning Press
College Publications
Post Office Box 10680
Palo Alto, California 94303
Filmstrips with cassettes. Leaders kit $495.00.
Participant kit $95.00.

WOOD WORKING

See also: Carpentry

Films/Video/Filmstrips

★ 3180 ★
CREATIVE SCULPTING FOR EVERYONE
Thompson-Mitchell and Associates
3384 Peachtree Road Northeast
Atlanta, Georgia 30326
Filmstrip. $150.00.

★ 3181 ★
THE DOVETAIL FIXTURE
    Thompson-Mitchell and Associates
    3384 Peachtree Road Northeast
    Atlanta, Georgia   30326
Filmstrip. $150.00.

★ 3182 ★
HOW TO HANG A DOOR
    Thompson-Mitchell and Associates
    3384 Peachtree Road Northeast
    Atlanta, Georgia   30326
Filmstrip. $150.00.

★ 3183 ★
HOW TO USE CHISELS AND GOUGES
    Thompson-Mitchell and Associates
    3384 Peachtree Road Northeast
    Atlanta, Georgia   30326
Filmstrip. $150.00.

★ 3184 ★
HOW TO USE HAMMERS
    Thompson-Mitchell and Associates
    3384 Peachtree Road Northeast
    Atlanta, Georgia   30326
Filmstrip. $150.00.

★ 3185 ★
HOW TO USE HAND BORING TOOLS
    Thompson-Mitchell and Associates
    3384 Peachtree Road Northeast
    Atlanta, Georgia   30326
Filmstrip. $150.00.

★ 3186 ★
HOW TO USE MEASURING TOOLS
    Thompson-Mitchell and Associates
    3384 Peachtree Road Northeast
    Atlanta, Georgia   30326
Filmstrip. $150.00.

★ 3187 ★
HOW TO USE PLANES
    Thompson-Mitchell and Associates
    3384 Peachtree Road Northeast
    Atlanta, Georgia   30326
Filmstrip. $150.00.

★ 3188 ★
HOW TO USE SAWS
    Thompson-Mitchell and Associates
    3384 Peachtree Road Northeast
    Atlanta, Georgia   30326
Filmstrip. $150.00.

★ 3189 ★
THE ROUTER
    Thompson-Mitchell and Associates
    3384 Peachtree Road Northeast
    Atlanta, Georgia   30326
Filmstrip. $150.00.

WORD PROCESSING

See also: Secretarial Skills; Typewriting

Multimedia Kits

★ 3190 ★
LANGUAGE SKILLS FOR WORD PROCESSING:
WORDS...WORDS...WORDS
    Ergonco Performance Source
    Northwest O'Hare Office Park, Suite 119
    2474 Dempster Street
    Des Plains, Illinois 60016
Multimedia self-study program.

Printed Materials

★ 3191 ★
WORD PROCESSING
Thomas Anderson,   W. Trotter
    American Management Associations
    135 West 50th Street
    New York, New York 10020
Book.   1974. $19.95.

WRITING, BUSINESS
See: BUSINESS WRITING

WRITING, COMEDY
Correspondence Courses

★ 3192 ★
COMEDY WRITING
    The Hollywood School of Comedy Writing
    16050 Liggett Street
    Sepulveda, California 91343
Correspondence course. $110.00.

WRITTEN COMMUNICATION
See: COMMUNICATION, WRITTEN

YORUBA

Multimedia Kits

★ 3193 ★
YORUBA - BASIC COURSE
General Services Administration
Foreign Service Institute Language Course
National Audiovisual Center
Order Section RR
Washington, D.C. 20409
Audio tapes, cassettes and text also available.
Approximately $200.00.

Printed Materials

★ 3194 ★
TEACH YOURSELF YORUBA
E. C. Rolands
David McKay Company Incorporated
750 Third Avenue
New York, New York 10017
Self instruction.

ZERO-BASE BUDGETING

See also: Budgeting; Financial Planning

Audio Cassettes/Tapes

★ 3195 ★
ZERO-BASE BUDGETING
National Association of Accountants
919 Third Avenue
New York, New York 10022
Text and cassettes.

Multimedia Kits

★ 3196 ★
ZERO-BASE BUDGETING: A SHORT COURSE
Lansford Publishing Company
Post Office Box 8711
San Jose, California 95155
Multimedia kit. $300.00.

Printed Materials

★ 3197 ★
ZERO-BASE BUDGETING: A PRACTICAL
MANAGEMENT TOOL FOR EVALUATING EXPENSES
Peter Pyhrr
John Wiley and Sons Incorporated
605 Third Avenue
New York, New York 10016
Book. 1973. $17.50.

★ 3198 ★
ZERO-BASE PLANNING AND BUDGETING
American Management Associations
135 West 50th Street
New York, New York 10020
Self-study text. $65.00.

SECTION II

INDEXES

A

B

C

D

E

F

G

H

I

J

K

L

M

O

P

Q

R

S

T

U

V

Wolper, Marshall   948
Wortman, Leon   2779

Y

Yoho, Dave   527, 2626
Young, James   78

Z

Zaks, Rodnay   601
Zar, Jerrold   275
Zelinsky, Daniel   136
Zinngrabe   290
Zwingle, John   1257

A

ABT Publications
55 Wheeler Street
Cambridge, Massachusetts 02138

Academic Press Incorporated
111 Fifth Avenue
New York, New York 10003

Active Learning Incorporated
Post Office Box 16382
Lubbock, Texas 79490

Addison Wesley Publishing Company
Incorporated
Jacob Way
Reading, Massachusetts 01867

Aero Press Incorporated
Post Office Box 209
Fall River, Massachusetts 02722

Allyn and Bacon Incorporated
Rockleigh, New Jersey 07647

American Bankers Association
1120 Connecticut Avenue,
Northwest
Washington, D.C. 20036

American Classical College Press
Post Office Box 4526
Albuquerque, New Mexico 87106

American Dental Trade Association
1140 Connecticut Avenue
Washington, D.C. 20036

American Institute of Architects
1735 New York Avenue, Northwest
Washington, D.C. 20006

American Institute of Certified
Public Accountants
1211 Avenue of the Americas
New York, New York 10003

American Jet School
Darby, Montana 59829

American Management Associations
135 West 50th Street
New York, New York 10020

American Media Incorporated
5907 Meredith Drive
Des Moines, Iowa 50324

American Personnel and Guidance
Association
1607 New Hampshire Avenue,
Northwest
Washington, D.C. 20009

American Plywood Association
1119 A Street
Tacoma, Washington 98401

American School of Photography
25 Andrews Drive
West Paterson, New Jersey 07424

Amiel, Leon Publications
225 Secaucus Road
Secaucus, New Jersey 07094

Apollo Editions
Conklin Book Center
Post Office Box 5555
Binghamton, New York 13902

Arabic Teaching Center
210 East 47th Street
New York, New York 10017

Arizona Press, University of
Post Office Box 3398
Tucson, Arizona 85722

Arkansas, University of
Department of Independent Study
346 West Avenue
Fayetteville, Arkansas 72701

Atlanta Institute of Real Estate
6065 Roswell Road Northeast
Atlanta, Georgia 30328

Audel, Theodore Company
Distributed by Bobbs Merrill
Company Incorporated
4300 West 62nd Street
Indianapolis, Indiana 46268

Avi Publishing Company Incorporated
Post Office Box 831
Westport, Connecticut 06880

Aviation Book Company
555 West Glenoaks Boulevard
Post Office Box 4187
Glendale, California 91202

B

Baker Book House
1019 Wealthy Street Southeast
Grand Rapids, Michigan 49506

Barnes and Noble Incorporated
Keystone Industrial Park
Scranton, Pennsylvania 18512

Barton School
North American Correspondence
School
4401 Birch Street
Newport Beach, California 92663

Beekman Publishers Incorporated
38 Hicks Street
Brooklyn Heights, New York 1120

Behrman House Incorporated
1261 Broadway
New York, New York 10001

Bell and Howell
Audio Visual Products Division
7100 McCormick Road
Chicago, Illinois 60645

Belmont-Tower Books Incorporated
185 Madison Avenue
New York, New York   10016

Belsaw Institute
315 Westport Road
Kansas City, Missouri   64111

Berlitz Language Program
Post Office Box 5109
FDR Station
New York, New York   10022

Better Selling Bureau
1150 West Olive Avenue
Burbank, California   91506

BFA Educational Media
2211 Michigan Avenue
Santa Monica, California   90406

Bloch Publishing Company
915 Broadway
New York, New York   10010

BNA Communications Incorporated
9401 Decoverly Hall Road
Rockville, Maryland   20850

Bobbs-Merrill Educational
   Publishing
4300 West 62nd Street
Indianapolis, Indiana   46206

Boeing Computer Services Company
Post Office Box 24346
Seattle, Washington   98124

Bond, Wheelwright Company
Porters Landing
Freeport, Maine   04032

Brady, Robert J. Company
Charles Press Publishers
Prentice-Hall Companies
Bowie, Maryland   20715

Bringham Young University
Department of Independent Study
210 Herald R. Clark Building
Provo, Utah   84602

Bruce Books
MacMillan Publishing Company
Riverside, New Jersey   08075

Bureau of National Affairs
1231 25th Street, Northwest
Washington, D.C.   20037

C

Cahners Publishing Company
   Incorporated
221 Columbus Avenue
Boston, Massachusetts   02166

Cambridge University Press
510 North Avenue
New Rochelle, New York   10801

Carter, C.L. Jr. and Associates
   Incorporated
434 First Bank and Trust Building
811 South Central Expressway
Richardson, Texas   75080

Carter, Jaine Personnel
   Development Incorporated
112 West Garden Avenue
Palatine, Illinois   60067

Cassette House
530 West Northwest Highway
Mount Prospect, Illinois   60056

Center for Cassette Studies
   Incorporated
8010 Webb Avenue
North Hollywood, California   91605

Century House Incorporated
Old Irelandville
Watkins Glen, New York   14891

Chain Store Publishing Company
425 Park Avenue
New York, New York   10022

Chelsea House Publishers
70 West 40th Street
New York, New York   10018

Citibank
399 Park Avenue
New York, New York   10022

Claitors Publishing Division
3165 South Acadian at Interstate 10
Box 239
Baton Rouge, Louisiana   70821

Classroom World Productions
Post Office Box 2090
22 Glenwood Avenue
Raleigh, North Carolina   27602

Cleveland Institute of Electronics
1776 East 17th Street
Cleveland, Ohio   44114

Close Productions
2020 San Carlos Boulevard
Fort Myers Beach, Florida   33931

Colorado, University of
Center for Lifelong Learning
970 Aurora Avenue
Boulder, Colorado   80302

Commercial Trades Institute
6201 West Howard Street
Chicago, Illinois   60648

Crain Books
740 Rush Street
Chicago, Illinois   60611

Crane, Russak and Company
   Incorporated
347 Madison Avenue
New York, New York   10017

CRM McGraw Hill Films
110 15th Street
Del Mar, California 92014

Creative Media Films
820 Keo Way
Des Moines, Iowa 50309

Crown Publishers Incorporated
419 Park Avenue South
New York, New York 10016

Curtis, Cally Company
1111 North Palmas
Hollywood, California 90038

Custom Decorating Institute
412 South Lyon Street
Santa Ana, California 92701

D

Dadant and Sons Incorporated
51 South Second Street
Hamilton, Illinois 62341

Dartnell
4660 Ravenswood Avenue
Chicago, Illinois 60640

Davis, F.A. Company
1915 Arch Street
Philadelphia, Pennsylvania 19103

DCA Educational Products
424 Valley Road
Warrington, Pennsylvania 18976

Delmar Publications
50 Wolf Road
Albany, New York 12205

Development Consultants Incorporated
2060 East 54th Street
Indianapolis, Indiana 46220

Development Digest Incorporated
3347 Motor Avenue
Los Angeles, California 90034

Development Publications
5605 Lamar Road
Washington, D.C. 20016

Didatic Systems Incorporated
Box 457
Cranford, New Jersey 07016

Directions Simplified Incorporated
529 North State Road
Briarcliff Manor, New York 10510

Doubleday and Company
Incorporated
501 Franklin Avenue
Garden City, New York 11530

Dover Publications Incorporated
180 Varick Street
New York, New York 10014

Dow Jones Books
Post Office Box 445
Chicopee, Massachusetts 01021

Drake Publishers
801 Second Avenue
New York, New York 10017

Dun and Bradstreet Incorporated
Business Education Division
Box 803
Church Street Station
New York, New York 10008

E

Eastman Kodak Company
343 State Street
Rochester, New York 14650

Education Systems for the Future
10451 Twin Rivers Road
Columbia, Maryland 21044

Educational Century Programming
1201 East Johnson Street
Jonesboro, Arkansas 72401

Educational Methods Incorporated
500 North Dearborn Street
Chicago, Illinois 60610

Educational Research
Post Office Box 4205
Warren, New Jersey 07060

Electronics Technical Institute
1500 Cardinal Drive
Little Falls, New Jersey 07424

Elsevier Scientific Publishing
Company Incorporated
52 Vanderbilt Avenue
New York, New York 10017

Emerson Books Incorporated
Reynolds Lane
Buchanan, New York 10511

Empire School of Piano Tuning
1753 Southwest 23rd Terrace
Miami, Florida 33145

Engineering Press
Post Office Box 5
San Jose, California 95103

Engineering Registration Studies
Post Office Box 24550
Los Angeles, California 90024

Entelek Incorporated
42 Pleasant Street
Newburyport, Massachusetts 01950

Ergonco Performance Source
Northwest O'Hare Office Park,
   Suite 119
2474 Dempster Street
Des Plains, Illinois 60016

Everett/Edwards Incorporated
Post Office Box 1060
De Land, Florida 32720

Exposition Press Incorporated
900 South Oyster Bay Road
Hicksville, New York 11801

F

Fabricon Company
2021 Montrose Avenue
Chicago, Illinois 60618

Fairchild Publications Incorporated
Seven East 12th Street
New York, New York 10003

Fearon-Pitman Publishers
   Incorporated
Six Davis Drive
Belmont, California 94002

Fibertex Industries
412 South Lyon Street
Santa Ana, California 92701

Financial Executives Research
   Foundation
633 Third Avenue
New York, New York 10017

Florida, University of
Division of Continuing Education
2012 West University Avenue
Gainesville, Florida 32603

French and European Publications
   Incorporated
Rockerfeller Center Promenade
610 Fifth Avenue
New York, New York 10020

Funk and Wagnalls Company
666 Fifth Avenue
New York, New York 10019

Furman University Press
Post Office Box 28638
Greenville, South Carolina 29613

G

Gamco-Siboney
Box 1911
Big Spring, Texas 79720

Ganong, W.L. Company
Post Office Box 2727
Chapel Hill, North Carolina 27514

General Cassette Corporation
1324 North 22nd Avenue
Phoenix, Arizona 85009

General Electric Company Training
   and Education Publications
One River Road, Box BP
Schenectady, New York 12345

General Learning Press
250 James Street
Morristown, New Jersey 07960

General Motors Education and
   Training Division
1700 West Third Avenue
Flint, Michigan 48502

General Programmed Teaching
Quail Hill
San Rafael, California 94903

General Services Administration
National Audiovisual Center
Order Section RR
Washington, D.C. 20409

Glencoe Press
Distributed by MacMillan Company
Riverside, New Jersey 08075

Goodheart-Wilcox Company
   Incorporated
123 West Taft Drive
South Holland, Illinois 60473

Gospel Publishing House
1445 Booneville Avenue
Springfield, Missouri 65802

Greenwood Press Incorporated
51 Riverside Avenue
Westport, Connecticut 06880

Grosset and Dunlap Incorporated
51 Madison Avenue
New York, New York 10010

Gulf Publishing Company
3301 Allen Parkway
Houston, Texas 77001

H

Halcomb Associates Incorporated
Project Management Center
510 East Maude Avenue
Sunnyvale, California 94086

Halsted Press
Division of John Wiley and Sons
   Incorporated
605 Third Avenue
New York, New York 10016

Harcourt Brace Jovanovich
   Incorporated
757 Third Avenue
New York, New York 10017

Harmony Press
419 Park Avenue South
New York, New York 10016

Harper and Row Publishers
   Incorporated
Scranton, Pennsylvania 18512

Hayden Book Company Incorporated
50 Essex Street
Rochelle Park, New Jersey 07662

Heath, D.C. and Company
2700 North Richardt Avenue
Indianapolis, Indiana 46219

Herman Publishing Company
45 Newbury Street
Boston, Massachusetts 02116

Holbrook Press Incorporated
Rockleigh, New Jersey 07647

Hollywood School of Comedy
Writing
16050 Liggett Street
Sepulveda, California 91343

Holt Rinehart and Winston
Incorporated
383 Madison Avenue
New York, New York 10017

Howell Training
2040 North Loop West, Suite 204
Houston, Texas 77018

Hy Cite Corporation
340 Coyier Lane
Madison, Wisconsin 53713

I

IBM International Business Machines
Corporation
Box 390
Poughkeepsie, New York 12602

Idaho Campus, University of
Correspondence Study Office
Moscow, Idaho 83843

Indiana State University
Independent Study Office
Terre Haute, Indiana 47809

Industrial Writing Institute
Hanna Building
Cleveland, Ohio 44115

Innovative Systems Limited
2301 Rockwell Road
Wilmington, Delaware 19810

Institute for Management
IFM Building
Old Saybrook, Connecticut 06475

Instructional Dynamics Incorporated
450 East Ohio Street
Chicago, Illinois 60611

Instrument Society of America
400 Stanwix Street
Pittsburgh, Pennsylvania 15222

Inter Culture Associates
Quaddick Road
Post Office Box 277
Thompson, Connecticut 06277

International Correspondence School
Scranton, Pennsylvania 18515

International Marine Publishing
Company
21 Elm Street
Camden, Maine 04843

International Publications Service
114 East 32nd Street
New York, New York 10016

International Scholarly Book Services
Incorporated
2130 Pacific Avenue
Forest Grove, Oregon 97116

Interstate Incorporated
1927 North Jackson Street
Danville, Illinois 61832

Iowa State University Press
South State Avenue
Ames, Iowa 50010

Irvington Publishers
551 Fifth Avenue
New York, New York 10017

Irwin, Richard D. Incorporated
1818 Ridge Road
Homewood, Illinois 60430

ITT Educational Services Incorporated
55 West 42nd Street
New York, New York 10036

J

Jacaranda Press Incorporated
872 Massachusetts Avenue
Cambridge, Massachusetts 02139

Japan Publications Trading Center
Incorporated
200 Clearbrook Road
Elmsford, New York 10523

K

Kenalex Corporation
2960 South Fox Street
Englewood, Colorado 80110

Kentucky, University of
Independent Study Program
Freeze Hall, Room 1
Lexington, Kentucky 40506

L

Lansford Publishing Company
Post Office Box 8711
San Jose, California 95155

La Salle Extension University
417 South Dearborn Street
Chicago, Illinois 60605

Learn Incorporated
Mount Laurel Plaza
113 Gaither Drive
Mount Laurel, New Jersey 08054

Learning Concepts Incorporated
2501 North Lamar Street
Austin, Texas 78705

Learning Dynamics
167 Corey Road
Boston, Massachusetts 02146

Learning Dynamics Institute
1401 Wilson Boulevard #101
Arlington, Virginia 22209

Learning Systems Company
1818 Ridge Road
Homewood, Illinois 60430

Listner Corporation
6777 Hollywood Boulevard
Hollywood, California 90028

Little, Brown and Company
200 West Street
Waltham, Massachusetts 02154

Locksmithing Institute
1500 Cardinal Drive
Little Falls, New Jersey 07424

Longman Incorporated
19 West 44th Street, Suite 7012
New York, New York 10036

Loyola University of Chicago
Correspondence Study Division
820 North Michigan Avenue
Chicago, Illinois 60611

Loyola University Press
3441 North Ashland Avenue
Chicago, Illinois 60657

M

MacMillan Publishing Company
Incorporated
Riverside, New Jersey 08075

Management Resources Incorporated
757 Third Avenue
New York, New York 10017

Mason/Charter
641 Lexington Avenue
New York, New York 10022

MBO Incorporated
157 Pontoosic Road
Westfield, Massachusetts 01085

McGraw-Hill Book Company
1221 Avenue of the Americas
New York, New York 10036

McKay, David Company Incorporated
750 Third Avenue
New York, New York 10017

Meadow Communications
Post Office Box 447
Flushing, New York 11365

Merchandiser Film Productions
Drawer J
Huntington, New York 11743

Merrill, Charles E. Publishing
Company
1300 Alum Creek Drive
Box 508
Columbus, Ohio 43216

Modern Upholstery Institute
412 South Lyon Street
Santa Ana, California 92701

Morgan and Morgan Incorporated
145 Palisades Street
Dobbs Ferry, New York 10522

Mosby, C.V. Company
11830 Westline Industrial Drive
Saint Louis, Missouri 63141

Motorcycle Safety Foundation
6755 Elkridge Landing Road
Linthicum, Maryland 21090

Mss Information Corporation
655 Madison Avenue
New York, New York 10021

Munk, Bert Productions
56 East Walton Place
Chicago, Illinois 60611

N

National Association of
Accountants
919 Third Avenue
New York, New York 10022

National Association of Credit
Management
475 Park Avenue South
New York, New York 10016

National Book Company
1019 Southwest Tenth Avenue
Portland, Oregon 97205

National Council to Eliminate
Death Taxes Incorporated
Route 1
New Concord, Ohio 43762

National Office Products
Association
301 North Fairfax Street
Alexandria, Virginia 22314

National Retail Merchants
Association
100 West 31st Street
New York, New York   10001

National Restaurant Association
One IBM Plaza, Suite 2600
Chicago, Illinois   60611

National Tax Training School
Monsey, New York   10952

National Tool, Die and
Precision Machining Association
9300 Livingston Road
Washington, D.C.   20022

Nebraska, University of
511 Nebraska Hall
Lincoln, Nebraska   68588

Nelson-Hall Publishers
325 West Jackson Boulevard
Chicago, Illinois   60606

New Mexico, University of
Division of Continuing Education
805 Yale Boulevard Northeast
Albuquerque, New Mexico   87131

New York Institute of Finance
70 Pine Street
New York, New York   10005

Newbury House Publishers
68 Middle Road
Rowley, Massachusetts   01969

Newman, J.W. Corporation
4311 Wilshire Boulevard
Los Angeles, California   90010

North Carolina, University of
Independent Study by Extension
121 Abernethy Hall 002A
Chapel Hill, North Carolina 27514

Northwestern School of Taxidermy
1202 Howard Street
Omaha, Nebraska   68103

Norton, W.W. and Company
Incorporated
500 Fifth Avenue
New York, New York   10036

NRI Schools
3939 Wisconsin Avenue
Washington, D.C.   20016

O

Oxford University Press
16-00 Pollitt Drive
Fair Lawn, New Jersey   07410

P

Panel Publications
14 Plaza Road
Greenvale, New York   11548

Panther House Limited
Post Office Box 3552
New York, New York   10017

Patent Resources Institute
Incorporated
2011 Eye Street Northwest
Washington, D.C.   20006

Pennsylvania State University
Department of Independent Study
by Correspondence
Three Sheilds Building
University Park, Pennsylvania 16802

Pentalic
132 West 22nd Street
New York, New York   10011

Penton/IPC Education Division
614 Superior Avenue West
Cleveland, Ohio   44113

Pergamon Press Incorporated
Maxwell House
Fairview Park
Elmsford, New York   10523

Personnel Development Incorporated
835 Sterling Avenue
Palatine, Illinois   60067

Petrocelli Books
384 Fifth Avenue
New York, New York   10018

Police Sciences Institute
4401 Birch Street
Newport Beach, California   92663

Practical Management Associates
Post Office Box 751
20929 Ventura Boulevard
Woodland Hills, California   91365

Praeger Publishers
111 Fourth Avenue
New York, New York   10003

Presbyterian and Reformed
Publishing Company
Box 185
Nutley, New Jersey   07110

Preston Publishing Company
151 East 50th Street
New York, New York   10022

Professional Book Distributors
Post Office Box 4892
Columbus, Ohio   43202

Putnam's, G.P. Sons
200 Madison Avenue
New York, New York   10016

R

Ramic Productions
4910 Birch Street
Newport Beach, California 92660

Random House Incorporated
457 Hahn Road
Westminister, Maryland 21157

Realtors National Marketing
Institute
430 North Michigan Avenue
Chicago, Illinois 60611

Reed, A.H. and A.W. Books
Rutland, Vermont 05701

Reinforcement Learning Incorporated
87 Dimmig Road
Post Office Box 562
Upper Saddle River, New Jersey
07458

Research Media Company
96 Mount Auburn Street
Cambridge, Massachusetts 02138

Resource Incorporated
13902 North Dale Mabry Highway
Tampa, Florida 33624

Resources for Education and
Management Incorporated
544 Medlock Road, Suite 210
Decatur, Georgia 30030

Roundtable Films
113 North San Vincente Boulevard
Beverly Hills, California 90211

S

St. Pierre Associates
1237 Seventh Street
Santa Monica, California 90410

Salenger Educational Media
1635 12th Street
Santa Monica, California 90404

Sams, Howard W. and Company
4300 West 62nd Street
Indianapolis, Indiana 46268

Saphrograph Company
194 Elizabeth Street
New York, New York 10012

School of Modern Photography
1500 Cardinal Drive
Little Falls, New Jersey 07424

Scientific Methods Incorporated
Box 195
Austin, Texas 78767

Scope Productions Incorporated
Post Office Box 5515
Fresno, California 93755

Scott, Foresman and Company
1900 East Lake Avenue
Glenview, Illinois 60025

Scribner's, Charles Sons
Vreeland Avenue
Totowa, New Jersey 07512

Security Systems Management School
1500 Cardinal Drive
Little Falls, New Jersey 07424

Seven Seas Press
Associated Booksellers
147 McKinley Avenue
Bridgeport, Connecticut 06606

SF Book Imports
Post Office Box 526
San Francisco, California 94101

Shalom, P. Publications
5409 18th Avenue
Brooklyn, New York 11204

Shenson, Howard L. Company
16400 Ventura Boulevard, Suite
215C
Encino, California 91436

Smith, Peter Publisher Incorporated
Six Lexington Avenue
Magnolia, Massachusetts 01930

Society for Technical Communication
1010 Vermont Avenue, Northwest
Washington, D.C. 20005

Society of Manufacturing Engineers
20501 Ford Road
Post Office Box 930
Dearborn, Michigan 48128

South Carolina, University of
Department of Correspondence Study
Division of Continuing Education
Columbia, South Carolina 29208

Southern Baptist Convention
Seminary Extension Department
460 James Robertson Parkway
Nashville, Tennessee 37219

Southern Mississippi, University of
Department of Independent Study
Southern Station, Box 56
Hattiesburg, Mississippi 39401

South-Western Publishing Company
5101 Madison Road
Cincinnati, Ohio 45227

Spoken Language Services
Incorporated
Post Office Box 783
Ithaca, New York 14850

Stipes Publishing Company
Ten Chester Street
Champaign, Illinois 61820

Strauss, H.S. Productions
619 West 54th Street
New York, New York 10019

Stuart, Lyle Incorporated
120 Enterprise Avenue
Secaucus, New Jersey   07094

Success Motivation Institute
5000 Lakewood Drive
Waco, Texas   76710

Success Tapes
6954 Hanover Parkway #300
Greenbelt, Maryland   20770

Summer Institute of Linguistics
Huntington Beach, California
    92648

Sybex Incorporated
2020 Milvia Street
Berkeley, California   94704

T

TAB Books
Blue Ridge Summit, Pennsylvania
17214

Tape Rental Library Incorporated
2507 Edna Drive
Post Office Box 2107
South Vineland, New Jersey 08360

Technical Home Study School
1500 Cardinal Drive
Little Falls, New Jersey   07424

Technical Impex Corporation
Five South Union Street
Lawrence, Massachusetts   01843

Technical Information Center
64 Society Street
Charleston, South Carolina   29401

Technical Publishing Company
1301 South Grove Avenue
Barrington, Illinois   60010

Telstar Productions Incorporated
366 North Prior Avenue
Saint Paul, Minnesota   55104

Texas Tech University
Division of Continuing Education
Post Office Box 4110
Lubbock, Texas   79409

Thomas, Charles C. Publishers
301-327 East Lawrence Avenue
Springfield, Illinois   62717

Thomas Institute
Box 22
New Canaan, Connecticut   06840

Thompson-Mitchell and Associates
3384 Peachtree Road Northeast
Atlanta, Georgia   30326

Total Tape
Post Office Box 372
Columbia, Maryland   21045

Training House Incorporated
Box 688
Binghamton, New York   13902

Transatlantic Arts Incorporated
North Village Green
Levittown, New York   11756

Truck Marketing Institute
Post Office Box 188
Carpinteria, California   93013

Tuttle, C.E. Company
28 South Main Street
Rutland, Vermont   05701

U

United Media International
    Incorporated
306 Dartmouth Street
Boston, Massachusetts   02116

Universal Schools
1500 Cardinal Drive
Little Falls, New Jersey   07424

Universal Training Systems Company
3201 Old Glenview Road
Wilmette, Illinois   60091

University of...
    See: main element of name

Upholstery and Decorating School
1500 Cardinal Drive
Little Falls, New Jersey   07424

Utah State University
Independent Study Division
UMC 50
Logan, Utah   84322

Utah, University of
Correspondence Study Department
Annex 1152
Salt Lake City, Utah   84112

V

Van De Water Associates
7914 Jason Avenue
Canoga Park, California   91304

Van Nos Reinhold Company
300 Pike Street
Cincinnati, Ohio   45202

Vanous, Arthur Company
616 Kinderkamack Road
River Edge, New Jersey   07661

Vantage Press Incorporated
516 West 34th Street
New York, New York   10001

Lawrence Verry Incorporated
16 Holmes Street
Mystic, Connecticut   06355

Visual Horizons
208 Westfall Road
Rochester, New York 14620

W

Wadsworth Publishing Company
 Incorporated
Ten Davis Drive
Belmont, California 94002

Walker and Company
720 Fifth Avenue
New York, New York 10019

Washington, University of
Office of Independent Study
222 Lewis Hall DW-30
Seattle, Washington 98195

Watson-Guptill Publications
 Incorporated
2160 Patterson Street
Cincinnati, Ohio 45214

Wehman Brothers Incorporated
Ridgedale Avenue
Cedar Knolls, New Jersey 07927

Western Kentucky University
Office of Special Programs
Bowling Green, Kentucky 42101

Western Washington State College
Center for Continuing Education
Edens Hall South
Bellingham, Washington 98225

Westinghouse Learning Press
College Publications
Post Office Box 10680
Palo Alto, California 94303

Wiley, John and Sons Incorporated
605 Third Avenue
New York, New York 10016

Williams, Heinman Incorporated
1966 Broadway
New York, New York 10023

Willis, Aubrey School
Post Office Drawer 15190
Orlando, Florida 32858

Wisconsin, University of, Extension
Independent Study
432 North Lake Street
Madison, Wisconsin 53706

WOFAC Company
Fellowship Road
Moorestown, New Jersey 08057

Wonderlic, E.F. and Associates
 Incorporated
820 Frontage Road
Northfield, Illinois 60093

Wyden Books
747 Third Avenue
New York, New York 10017

X

XICOM
Sterling Forest
Tuxedo, New York 10987